Becoming **Ray Bradbury**

Becoming

JONATHAN R. ELLER

Ray Bradbury

UNIVERSITY OF ILLINOIS PRESS Urbana, Chicago, and Springfield

Library of Congress Cataloging-in-Publication Data
Eller, Jonathan R., 1952–
Becoming Ray Bradbury / Jonathan R. Eller.
  p.   cm.
Includes bibliographical references and index.
ISBN 978-0-252-03629-3 (cloth : alk. paper)
1. Bradbury, Ray, 1920–
2. Authors, American—20th century—Biography.
3. Science fiction, American—History and criticism.
I. Title.
PS3503.R167Z65   2011
813'.54—dc22 [B]   2011008562

For Donn Albright

Amicus Librorum

Guardian of

the world of Ray Bradbury

There's the Ray Bradbury that writes, and

the "me" that watches him. I can't believe

that there are two of me, and I'm the

witness now, to what I did before. And I

think I am so lucky that God made me in

two halves—the creator and the witness.

— Ray Bradbury, October 26, 2007

Contents

Acknowledgments

In 2007 Ray Bradbury scrawled a cryptic note to himself on an early draft typescript of *Becoming Ray Bradbury*: "R. B., luckily, doesn't know I'm hiding in his body and peeking out of his eyes!" For the last forty years and more, Bradbury has shown a great curiosity about the young writer he once was, and I am profoundly grateful to those who helped me recover the essential tensions and triumphs of that young man's life.

I thank Indiana University for three New Frontier Arts and Humanities traveling grants that helped defray the cost of many West Coast working sessions with Mr. Bradbury and a week in New York to study his agent's archives at Columbia University's Butler Library. The late Don Congdon allowed me to examine the Congdon Associates portion of this archive and graciously provided an interview. Ben Camardi permitted me to examine the Harold Matson Agency deposit, which archives the earlier Bradbury-Congdon materials. Librarian Jennifer B. Lee and Bernard Crystal, Curator of Manuscripts, provided access to the Matson-Congdon deposits as well as Bradbury archives in the papers of Frederic Dannay; I'm also grateful to Tara C. Craig for coordinating my access permissions and Jason Marchi for conducting advance research in the Matson-Congdon deposits as my proxy.

Gene Bundy, archivist of the Jack Williamson Science Fiction Library at Eastern New Mexico University, provided extremely valuable research support. Betty Williamson, niece of the late Jack Williamson, Gene Bundy, and Eleanor Wood, literary agent for the estates of Bradbury mentors Leigh Brackett Hamilton, Edmond Hamilton, and Jack Williamson, provided access to Bradbury letters held in the Williamson library. Brackett film scholar Pepper Smith and publisher Stephen Haffner also provided archival insights on these three important authors. I thank Cristina Concepcion of Don Congdon Associates, literary agent for the estate of Henry Kuttner, for reviewing the chapters describing Kuttner's mentoring influence on Bradbury. I also thank Michael Congdon, now head of Don Congdon Associates, for reviewing chapters on the author-agent relationship that his father maintained with Bradbury for the better part of a lifetime.

The Wisconsin Historical Society provided permission for me to study the significant Bradbury materials in the papers of August Derleth. I'm most grateful to Archives Reference Assistant Alexis Ernst-Treutel for providing access to my proxy researcher, Kimberly O'Brien, during her long hours spent in Madison.

Librarian Carolyn Davis of Syracuse University's Bird Library provided access to the Mercury Press archives, which include Bradbury's letters to Anthony Boucher, Mick McComas, and subsequent editors of the *Magazine of Fantasy & Science Fiction*. She also led me to Bradbury correspondence in small but significant collections from the papers of Frederik Pohl and Forry Ackerman. Archivist Keith Call of Wheaton College provided access to letters discussing Bradbury in the papers of C. S. Lewis. Sharon Perry, special collections librarian at California State Fullerton's Pollak Library, Kathy Morris, and the late Professor Willis McNelly provided research copies of Bradbury typescripts that helped me document the transformation of "The Fireman" into *Fahrenheit 451* as I worked through several publishing projects leading up to (and including) *Becoming Ray Bradbury*. I'm grateful as well to author and collector Robert Weinberg for providing advice on attributions and permissions involving illustrations.

I could not have rounded out this study of Ray Bradbury's early life and career without access to the words and thoughts of others who knew him during those years. Christopher Bond deserves recognition for providing me with research copies of Bradbury's letters to his father, the late Nelson Bond. Dennis Bradbury, daughter of Doubleday's influential editor Walter Bradbury, is not related to my subject, but her encouragement has been important as I studied one of the most important author-editor relationships of Ray Bradbury's early years. California journalist Gene Beley kindly provided access to his 1982 interview with artist Joseph Mugnaini. I am especially grateful to Diana Mugnaini Robinson for permission to use her father's line art in several projects; her enthusiastic support has been amplified by Mugnaini archivist Ryan Leasher.

Comprehensive and insightful comments by William F. Nolan and Sid Stebel, two of Bradbury's oldest writer-friends, came by way of multiple interviews over a number of years; I could not have documented Bradbury's growing influence on postwar writers without their help, and I'll always be grateful for Bill Nolan's pioneering bibliographical publications. Interviews with the late Forry Ackerman (March and October 2002) and Ray Harryhausen (October 2006) helped pinpoint still earlier influences on Bradbury's development. A number of long-distance conversations with Bradbury biographer Sam Weller culminated in an April 2009 meeting, and I'm most grateful for the chance to discuss the early Bradbury with him on these occasions.

Many visits with Mr. Bradbury were enriched by a number of young writers and older Bradbury friends and associates, including Doug Menville, Nik Grant, Patrick Kachurka, Jason Marchi, and Greg Miller. Useful comments on the book also came from readings by longtime Bradbury collectors Bob O'Malley and Jim Welsh and by media scholar Phil Nichols of the University of Wolverhampton,

U. K. Closer to home, I profited from research and technical assistance by resident faculty, staff, and graduate students involved with my home unit, the Institute for American Thought, Indiana University School of Liberal Arts (IUPUI), including Robin Condon, Joseph D. Kaposta, Diana Dial Reynolds, Johanna Resler, Amanda Barrett, and Lisa King. Professor William F. Touponce, director of the Institute's Center for Ray Bradbury Studies, read intermediate drafts and provided a great deal of insight on Bradbury's relationship to Modernism, the dark fantastic, and the carnival tradition of literature.

Mr. Bradbury's principal bibliographer, Professor Donn Albright of the Pratt Institute, spent many hours reading and discussing various drafts of *Becoming Ray Bradbury*. This book could not have recovered Bradbury's emerging authorial identity if I had not had access to Donn's collection and his memories, and it's most appropriate that this volume is dedicated to him. During the final five years of her life, Maggie Bradbury provided insights into the life and career of her husband and encouraged me to fully explore the impact of broader literary traditions on his early development as a writer. Alexandra Bradbury, tireless coordinator of her father's public life and sole amanuensis of his late-life creativity, eased the scheduling challenges of my research trips and made it possible to accompany her father to many public and private events over the years. I also had the good fortune to have Joan Catapano as my editor at the University of Illinois Press; Joan took time away from her duties as Associate Director to help me focus and tighten the structure of *Becoming Ray Bradbury*. My wife Debi provided many hours of editorial objectivity as I found a way to tell the story at the heart of this book.

My deepest appreciation extends to Ray Bradbury himself, who has encouraged my work for more than two decades and provided countless hours of private interview time over the last dozen years. He has granted full access to his private library and his personal papers, and in recent years he has patiently reviewed many key passages of *Becoming Ray Bradbury*. He has asked for no more than fairness and objectivity, and in return he has helped me see through the eyes of that young writer he once knew.

Becoming **Ray Bradbury**

Introduction

Throughout his early career, Ray Bradbury was torn between two impulses—on one hand, a mounting obsession with perfection as he revised the stories that seemed to well up continuously from his subconscious mind, and on the other hand, an unflagging aversion to the advice of such genre colleagues as Henry Kuttner, Robert Bloch, and Theodore Sturgeon, who urged him to write without fear, to learn by writing, even if the result was not always the intended masterpiece.

Bradbury eventually came to understand that writing when the Muse is muted did not necessarily involve slanting to the genre or slick markets—a proposition that he loathed throughout his career. But his ability to generate impressive story drafts in a matter of hours would often play out against uncertainty as he moved through the more rational process of revising a story, or as he attempted to sustain longer forms of fiction. Bradbury's greatest nightmare was manifest in Cyril Connolly's *The Unquiet Grave*, a book that he purchased with his precious few book-buying dollars on the very day in 1946 that he proposed to his future wife, Marguerite McClure:

> . . . the true function of a writer is to produce a masterpiece . . . no other task is of any true consequence. Obvious though this should be, how few writers will admit it, or having made the admission, will be prepared to lay aside the piece of iridescent mediocrity on which they have embarked! Writers always hope that their next book is going to be their best, for they will not acknowledge that it is their present way of life which prevents them from ever creating anything different or better.

It would have been little consolation to know that a few years later Christopher Isherwood, one of the first Modernist intellectual writers to personally and publicly encourage Bradbury, was privately tormented by this same passage during a very difficult period in his own writing. Within this extended aphorism Connolly had captured the essential anxiety that Bradbury found himself facing every time he brought the more logical process of revision to bear on any of his unconsciously inspired story drafts. The fear of producing less than perfect fictions, equal to (and perhaps greater than) his fear of not finishing at all, was a constant companion, and it colored the way he presented himself to the public, his agents and editors, and his fellow writers.

During these years he also began to develop, at least in his speaking notes, a negative view of the intellectual authors who were intent on making strong distinctions between serious and popular literature, intent on defining and then aspiring to create the mirage known as the great American novel. During the first decade of his career, he would also find himself at odds with critics who were intent on defining the ways that he could navigate the margins between popular culture and the higher literary world.

Becoming Ray Bradbury explores the origins of his wariness of intellectual writing, and his conviction that intuitive things are the real truths. These origins reveal why his greatest contributions to American literature remain his unique style and his abiding creative focus on the basic emotions that define our humanity. As early as 1948, his private writing notes reveal a strong conviction that "the fiction writer is, first and foremost, an emotionalist." Four years later, in his introduction to *Timeless Stories for Today and Tomorrow*, he made his case publically, through a favorite metaphor: "I have had nothing but my emotions to go on . . . I am compensated by allowing myself to believe that while the scientific man can tell you the exact size, location, pulse, musculature and color of the heart, we emotionalists can find and touch it quicker."

He offered a similar viewpoint on the foundational importance of style—understood as emotional truth—during a late 1960s interview with Los Angeles television host John Stanley: "Style isn't worthwhile unless it's absolute truth. They're synonymous. If you tell the truth you automatically have a style. What you're trying to do is bring out all your truths at various levels. Your fear of the dark, your dread of violence, your hostility of one thing, your love of another." These are, of course, truths told by indirection through the mask of fiction; as Bradbury observed in "Death Warmed Over," a short but significant 1968 essay on writing, "Fact without interpretation is but a glimpse of the elephant's bone yard."

In their very brevity, all of these observations accurately reflect the fundamental underpinnings of his writing as it matured through the early 1940s: a highly emotional and metaphor-rich style, and an almost visceral resistance to the editorial pressures of the publishing world. For Bradbury, these imperatives are where truth and style intersect to generate a consistent ability to be faithful to one's own convictions as a writer. Even when revision failed to refine an emotional blaze of creativity into a fully realized work of fiction—and this has happened often throughout his career—his core convictions provided the strength to move on to new ideas.

Bradbury's very vocal distrust of intellectual authorship would always be controversial, and in the long run his intuitive bursts of creativity limited his ability to develop complex characters or to range into any sustained ironic forms of realism. Too much emphasis on the emotions may certainly mar a longer work, but in the context of a short story it could be invigorating. In the long run, his emphasis on personal style as truth marked him as a strong short-story writer. The remarkable and often dark fantasies at the heart of his creativity transcended genre barriers as he attempted to understand the ambiguities of life and death and the paradoxes of the human soul. National and international literary honors have come more frequently in his twilight years, and in spite of the variety of these honors the award juries all speak with one voice in acclaiming his significance as a modern truth seeker.

Becoming Ray Bradbury reveals Bradbury's emotional world as it matured through his explorations of cinema and art, his interactions with agents and editors, his reading discoveries, and the invaluable reading suggestions of older writers. Ever the keen observer, Bradbury devoured these lessons and tried to create some sort of order out of the stressful years of economic depression, world war, ideological polarization, dizzying technological progress, and the dangerous game of nuclear brinksmanship that paralleled his development from youthful amateur into a master storyteller. The subjective impact of these discoveries on the emerging and maturing writer gives a greater depth of experience to the more public armature of his professional achievements; the process of recovering and telling these discoveries becomes a biography of the mind—the story of the emerging sense of authorship at the heart of Bradbury's emotional and creative core.

The five major divisions of this book reflect Bradbury's emotional and intellectual world through the first thirty-three years of his life. "Awakenings" focuses on the influences and life-shaping experiences up to his twenty-first birthday, when his first professional sale reached the street-corner newsstand where he still made only ten dollars a week, accumulated one penny at a time as he sold each three-cent newspaper for a one-cent profit. "The Road to Autumn's House" illuminates the complex sequence of influences and reading discoveries behind Bradbury's quantum leap in talent during World War II. There were few witnesses to Bradbury's emerging style, for he pulled back from most of his friends and wrote full-time to make his living from the genre pulps. His remarkable transition into a mature storyteller represents the first major period of his writing life—the summer of 1941 through the summer of 1944.

"The Fear of Death Is Death" examines Bradbury's growing interest in the human mind and the human condition in the years leading up to his fateful encounter with life and death in Mexico. He soon became more than a genre writer who occasionally broke into major market magazines, but the transition was not an easy one; the spring 1947 publication of his first story collection, *Dark*

Carnival, masked his increasingly complex private relationships with other genre writers and his growing obsession with perfection. "The Tyranny of Words" documents Bradbury's private failures in his first attempts at Modernist novel-length fiction during the late 1940s, his frustrating encounters with the major trade publishing houses, and his earliest unpublished reflections on the nature of authorship and the challenges of editing the work of other writers. Even his sudden 1950–51 success with *The Martian Chronicles* and *The Illustrated Man* masked his continuing reliance on the short-story form to fashion book-length fiction, but he had managed nonetheless to find his own way around the Modernist crisis-of-values.

"The Last Night of the World" explores the sources of Bradbury's very conscious decisions to write controversial fictions and to voice controversial political statements at a time when his career was expanding very successfully into television, film, and radio adaptation. His defense of authorship extended beyond the political fears of the early 1950s; privately, his mistrust of Hollywood studio executives, his disgust with the world of New York publishers, and his anxiety over the proliferation of Cold War nuclear arsenals surfaced in his correspondence well before the summer of 1953 and the burst of creative energy that transformed his novella "The Fireman" into *Fahrenheit 451*. And here, for now, the story of a writer ends. In September 1953 Bradbury left for Europe and an extended screenwriting assignment for John Huston's production of *Moby Dick*; nine months later, a very different author would return.

Since I am mainly concerned in this volume with Bradbury's sources of personal truth, much of it previously undiscovered, I should say something of my own sources, and how they are weighed as "truth." Although his professional career began in 1941 and has extended through the first decade of the twenty-first century, Ray Bradbury has never written an autobiography; his extensive 1961 interview for the UCLA Oral History program remains his closest approach to this form, punctuated eight years later by less structured but more conversational interview sessions between Bradbury and his longtime agent, Don Congdon. Neither of these projects was published, although the UCLA interview is accessible to researchers. Only a handful of specialized author studies were published in subsequent decades, even as Bradbury's midcentury popularity as a unique and innovative prose stylist spread into many forms of media adaptation and international literary recognition. The first book-length study from a university press did not appear until 2004, and the only authorized biography reached print a year later.

Becoming Ray Bradbury synthesizes much of this scattered information and delves further into Bradbury's narrative worlds from the evidence that survives in the public record of his book introductions, interviews, and essays on writing. But by far the largest part of the story emerges from the vast body of unpublished materials—his correspondence; his elusive, cryptic, and rare attempts at writing diary-like comments on his early years; his equally rare but often insightful notes on writing; early drafts of his stories and story fragments; and more than a decade of private interviews. It's instructive to compare Bradbury's narrative world to that of Sherwood Anderson, a writer that Bradbury read and admired in his early twenties. In *A Story Teller's Story*, Anderson had presented himself as a composite American Man of Letters, self-made by the American experience and self-assured by the process of telling his own story in midlife, at the height of his popularity as a writer.

Bradbury, born nearly a half-century after Anderson, had similarly impoverished Midwestern roots, but he began writing at a much earlier age and with far less experience with life. The story that emerges through his memories, and through the fragmentary but highly revealing manuscript record of his teens and twenties, is more of an American *bildungsroman*, full of youthful anxieties, self-conscious attempts to emulate the writers he loved, rapid success in the genre pulps, and a broadening experience in life and literature that led to the development of a unique stylistic talent. Through his thirty-third year, the threads of his deeply intertwined life and career came together through determined effort, naive stubbornness, pure coincidence, great good fortune, and the oversight of friends and mentors who recognized the potential talent in this young writer.

Anyone seeking to write a literary biography of Ray Bradbury has to deal with the problem of the thousands of anecdotes relating to his life and times. His life comes to us surrounded by (or, perhaps, embedded within) a very public body of anecdote. In my view, anecdotes, which are often expressed in interviews, are problematic, because they tend to blur, not so much the dates, but sometimes the sequence of events. These anecdotes in turn become part of the established history of his career during his decades as a highly in-demand subject of interviews and presentations. The interviews are treasures, of course. But Bradbury's strong sense of suggestion often readjusts the time lines to emphasize the wonder of it. Anecdote becomes a teaching point for others interested in an author's growth to maturity, but it's also a reminder to himself of the debt he owes to fortune, hard work, and the desire to be true to his ideas even when pressured to slant his creativity.

However, as history, the anecdote is still of great value. Shorn of its embellishments, it can provide a useful way to uncover the process of Bradbury's evolution as a writer and cultural figure. The anecdote can be "recalibrated" (or in many cases, borne out) by the historical and biographical markers—the correspondence, the recovered order of his manuscripts, unpublished essays, and the few precious (and sporadic) diary notes he made at long intervals during his high school and young adult years. His writing career can also be illuminated by establishing the chronology of his encounters with the works of authors, artists, illustrators, playwrights, and filmmakers who stimulated his imagination throughout the first three decades of his life. Once again, the surviving but largely unexamined biographical markers reveal the full extent of these cultural influences, and do so with a far deeper impact than his more generalized spoken anecdotes have ever revealed. In the end, we may learn more about his writing process—a very personal and largely inaccessible aspect of his emerging creativity—and we may come to understand the "truth" of the many masks he assumes as he becomes Ray Bradbury.

Part I

Awakenings

Look in the *Blue and White* [Los Angeles
High School] annual. They asked me for three
quotes about myself, and in the last quote I said,
"Headed for literary distinction." I wasn't headed
anywhere. I couldn't do anything. But my ego
had to believe that maybe I would be headed
somewhere. And it finally happened. So it's
very mysterious, very mysterious.

— RB, 2004

1

From the Nursery to the Library

Bradbury's birth remains the point of departure for one of his most controversial autobiographical anecdotes—his claim to remember the trauma of birth, the sensation of breastfeeding, the pain of circumcision, and infant nightmares about being born. When he discovered (in his late seventies) that he had been delivered as a ten-month baby, Bradbury felt sure that his memories were the result of heightened development of his senses. He stands ready to argue the point with psychologists of any school and to proclaim his memories with conviction to any audience. These memories—whether imagined or real—surface with great impact in such stories as "The Small Assassin," one of his best-known weird tales of the 1940s: What if birth trauma can translate into hate during the first hours of life? What if a ten-month baby developed more quickly than the norm, and found the ability to turn on its parents with murderous intent? Is it merely fear projected by a mother who nearly died in childbirth? Or is there really a small movement in the dark at the top of the stairs, carefully planting a toy that sends the mother tumbling to her death?

But another autobiographical anecdote seems to have channeled the creative force behind all of his birth reveries, and it rings true in its essentials. In the mid-1930s, aged thirteen or fourteen, a chance encounter with a boardwalk exhibit at Santa Monica's Ocean Park led Bradbury to a mysterious row of unlabeled bottles: "They were fetuses, but at various stages of development. A couple of weeks, a month, two months, three months, and then eight months, almost a fully grown baby. And I suddenly realized, I was looking at the history of mankind. The whole thing chilled me . . . I knew nothing of life. I grew up in an age when we never discussed anything to do with sex or where children came from, or babies, or anything. I had never seen a picture of a fetus, I had never seen one before, so I left the exhibit chilled. It was strange, like I was on another planet, because no one had told me."[1]

When he fictionalized this experience in the early 1940s, Bradbury's characters each see something different in the title image of "The Jar"—a baby, a brain, a kitten, a jellyfish, an ancestral swamp mother, a hated spouse, a lost lover. Such early stories open out into Bradbury's lifelong ambiguity about the processes of life and death. In a broader sense, however, his vast body of anecdotes provides energizing experiences that are the very foundation for story writing, and they go a long way toward explaining his natural genius for the short-story form. The objects or encounters that trigger these anecdotes—often encapsulated in the brief word-association titles of his early stories—have to be sorted out along with the other more cultural and intellectual influences that have shaped Bradbury's mind, and it is here that the story of a writer begins.

There were challenges all along the way for this strange little boy who claimed to recall memories from earliest infancy and movie scenes from the age of three. He was very different from his father, Leo Bradbury, a rugged outdoorsman who worked for the Bureau of Power and Light in Waukegan until he was laid off in the third year of the Great Depression. Leonard Junior, known as Skip, was four years older than Ray and shared their father's love of sports and physical activities. In fact, Leo and young Skip were attending a baseball game across town on the Sunday afternoon when Ray Douglas Bradbury was born—August 22, 1920. It took years for father and brother to come to terms with the dreamy and bookish "Shorty," as Ray was known within his family. But they were a close and loving family nonetheless, and Bradbury received constant encouragement from his mother.

Skip's twin Sam had died of influenza during the great epidemic of 1918, and Swedish-born Esther Moberg Bradbury was determined that her third child would not share this fate. Over time Bradbury sensed an unspoken, and per-haps unconscious, desire within the family that he would grow to stand in for his brother's lost twin. But while Skip became an outstanding athlete with few intellectual interests, "Shorts" became a creature of books and imagination. Even before he could read, printed illustrations and the cinema provided cre-ative markers that would surface time and again in his writing: Lon Chaney's Hunchback and Phantom; King Tutankhamen's magnificent golden death mask; and a memento mori from Grandfather Bradbury—the mesmerizing Henri Lagos illustrations from the 1899 Harper's Weekly serialization of H. G. Wells's When the Sleeper Wakes. But Bradbury's rise to authorship began in earnest at the Waukegan Public Library, where he learned to make more logical and articulate connections between the larger-than-life images of his preschool days and the ever-widening realities of the world around him.

On one very basic level, the library had the advantage of providing unlimited reading for a family of very limited means. There were two independent book-stores on nearby Genesee Street, but the young boy spent little time in these shops; there was simply no money for books, and this made his library pilgrim-ages all the more important. Bradbury's reminiscent "Monday Night in Green Town," written three decades later for syndication during the very first National

Library Week, recaptures his own early childhood perspective in important ways. The metaphors are rich and extend into captivating analogies:

> The library was the great watering place where the animals, large and small, came from the night to drink and smile at each other across the green-glass-shadowed glades between the book-mountains. So here you were gamboling on spring nights like lambs, lolling like warm trout in winy springs on summer nights, racing the curled mice-leaves on autumn nights, always to the same Monday place, the same Monday building. You ran, you dawdled, you flew, but you got there. And there was always that special moment when, at the big doors, you paused before you opened them out and went in among all those lives, in among all those whispers of old voices so high and so quiet it would take a dog, trotting between the stacks, to hear them. And trot you did.[2]

His instinctive approach to the library was synesthetic: books were sensed by smell and look and touch, and only then could the reading process be contemplated. It was only natural, therefore, that the chosen book's characters would come alive for him through all of his senses: "quite suddenly, a man or a woman or a child leapt off the page and stood there with you in the immense silence. Then you sat with them for an hour and ran with them and laughed and wept with them." In this way his lifelong love of literature began. His enthusiasm for adaptation and for breaking down genre barriers has its roots in this same crossing of sensations; to "see" the book, to "read" the movie, and to "hear" the staged play have always been natural extensions of the traditional forms for Bradbury. This openness to all the possibilities of a creative idea was formed at an early age, and the gift proved to be both a blessing and a frustration as Bradbury extended his storytelling genius into other genres and media forms.

But it would be the voices of the authors themselves that would come to symbolize literature for Bradbury in a lasting way. Each time he entered the building as a young boy in Waukegan, he saw the authors personified in the masterpieces on the library shelves. Eventually, he came to see the shelves as populations of authors and began to dream of living among them, Bradbury between Mr. Baum and Mr. Burroughs, not far from Miss Dickinson, Mr. Melville, Mr. Poe, Miss Welty, Mr. Whitman, and an ever-expanding circle of reading loves. To burn the book is to burn the author, and to burn the author is to deny our own humanity. These essential truths underlie many of his stories as well as such central Bradbury texts as *Fahrenheit 451* and *Something Wicked This Way Comes*.

Bradbury maintained his library regimen for decades, and considered these excursions to be the true source of his education. By contrast, his final elementary school years were problematic at Waukegan's Central School, and in certain ways foreshadowed his high-school experience half a continent away in Los Angeles. He began to withdraw from his schoolmates at the age of eleven, shortly after increasing nearsightedness was mistakenly diagnosed as a degenerative condition leading to blindness. The terror subsided as it became apparent that his vision had stabilized as severe but correctable myopia; nevertheless, there was a distinct change in the schoolyard dynamic—bullies took advantage of his solitary ways and his unwillingness to fight back, and he would remain a Melvillean "isolato" for years to come.[3]

Although he won attention from his teachers, he knew that he wasn't a good student; in later years he would come to realize that he had never been able to learn effectively in a lecture hall or classroom because he was not a good listener in such environments.[4] He was, both by nature and by the cinema experiences of his earliest years, a visual learner who developed a lifelong love of architecture from his grandfather's slides of the great Columbian Exposition of 1892–93 and the St. Louis World's Fair of 1904, and from his own encounters with the Chicago World's Fair of 1933. In a similar way, his abiding love of graphic fiction fairly exploded out of his passion for Dick Calkins's *Buck Rogers* comic strips and Hal Foster's widely syndicated adaptations of Edgar Rice Burroughs's *Tarzan of the Apes*.

Burroughs's Tarzan and John Carter of Mars novels soon controlled his reading passions. In terms of hero adventures, the only rival to Tarzan in Bradbury's young mind was Ozar the Aztec, a Burroughs-inspired series by Walker Tompkins (writing as Valentine Wood). This six-novella arc appeared in the January to June 1933 issues of Street & Smith's *Top-Notch*, and Bradbury never relinquished his tear sheets of these adventures. The strangeness of Tarzan's castaway origins and savage upbringing had initially hooked Bradbury, and Ozar's similar circumstances (raised by modern-day "lost city" Aztecs who have murdered his geologist parents) held the same fascination for him.

The pioneering genre pulps provided a more direct line to Bradbury's early professional writing. He developed a brief passion for two Clark Ashton Smith fantasies he discovered in *Wonder Stories*: "The City of Singing Flame" (July 1931) and "The Master of the Asteroid" (October 1932). It's not surprising that Bradbury would be drawn to the sensual intensity of Smith's work, and a quarter-century later he would reflect on this quality: "One of the first things a fiction writer must learn is the business of enclosing his characters, and therefore his readers, in a scene, an atmosphere, providing a frame of reference. . . . From that point on, no matter how improbable the miracles you wish to introduce, your reader is unable to resist them, regardless of how high, wide, or grotesque they may be."[5] Although he soon found most of Smith's lost worlds too arcane, he never forgot Smith's gift for conveying sensation: "Take one step across the threshold of his stories and you plunge into color, sound, taste, smell, and texture; into language."

He found a more lasting attraction in the science fiction and fantasy stories of Edmond Hamilton and Jack Williamson, young genre pros who were both destined to mentor Bradbury a decade later. As a youth, he was especially attracted to the work of Hamilton, beginning with "Locked Worlds," an early Hamilton yarn in the Spring 1929 *Amazing Quarterly*. Here was the kind of science fantasy that Bradbury would come to love: a world of intelligent spiders living on metal islands floating in a sky laced with webbed highways. For a while the young boy forgot who wrote the story, but he drew pictures of Hamilton's spider world for years and kept them for decades.[6] Later, other Hamilton nature fantasies such as "Child of the Winds" (May 1936) and "Bride of the Lightning" (January 1939) came to him through *Weird Tales*, providing inspiration for "The Wind," one of Bradbury's first breakout stories in the pages of *Weird*.

For Bradbury, the significance of the first decade of science fiction centered on the imaginative power of a very small range of stories. During the formative years of his genre reading, three stories above all others fueled his growing passion for wonderment: David H. Keller's "The Revolt of the Pedestrians" (1928), Donald Wandrei's "Colossus" (1934), and Hamilton's "Fessenden's Worlds" (1937). When August Derleth included them in his 1950 anthology *Beyond Time and Space*, Bradbury offered Derleth his personal perspective: "These three stories, it seems to me, are the essence of the 1928 to 1938 era of s-f in America. There was a complete, and miraculous, preoccupation with wonder and oddness and distances, with hardly a backward glance, except in the Keller story perhaps, to characterization." He had literally forgotten the authorship and even the titles of these stories, but as he grew up he told them to other fans over and over again; each one was "the sort of story that lasts a lifetime in the memory because of its sheer imaginative power."[7]

A broader range of pulp fiction came to the boy through the pages of the venerable *Argosy Weekly*, which had absorbed its popular companion *All-Story* the year that Bradbury was born. His passion for cinema had come from his mother, but the model for his nascent reading passion came, most improbably, from his father. Along with his restlessness, his periodic urges to strike out for new fortunes in the West, and his natural enthusiasm for outdoors life, Leo Bradbury was also a constant and eclectic reader. This shared passion was, for many years, their only common bond beyond the family hearth itself; throughout the 1930s and well into the war years, Leo's Monday copy of *Argosy* became his son's reading prize on Friday.[8] The imaginative impact of two *Argosy* favorites stayed with him for years: the serialized adventures of Peter the Brazen, by George F. Wortz (writing as Loring Brent); and the vivid fantasies of A. Merritt, which inspired Bradbury to bind each issue's tear sheets into complete homemade novels.

The boy's own sense of authorship emerged quite suddenly at the age of twelve, when a life-changing encounter with the sideshow electrocution act of Mr. Electrico in 1932 convinced him he was destined to become a writer of enduring reputation. What many people would regard as an engaging carnival anecdote remains very real to this day for Bradbury, who has demonstrated throughout his life an unusually strong ability to feed from the power of suggestion in certain situations. His ability to recall and relate examples of the universal fears of childhood in riveting metaphorical prose is a manifestation of the power of suggestion in his life; another is his lifelong goal of writing every day, which originated with Mr. Electrico's admonition to "Live forever!"

Unsettled years interrupted much of this development, and Bradbury soon found himself exploring a succession of public libraries across America; between 1932 and 1934, the search for work and a better life led the family west to Tucson, back to Waukegan, and finally all the way out to Los Angeles. In Tucson he began to practice the craft that Mr. Electrico had so recently inspired; his parents bought him a toy dial-a-letter typewriter, and he soon attempted to type out his own version of The Warlord of Mars, the third volume of Burroughs's John Carter series. This painful letter-by-letter exercise sparked his lifelong sense of typing as the release point for his imagination, and he would privately reflect on this magic three quarters of a century later: "That's the process, that's why people like me, because my fingertips are releasing life into my stories, and that's why I'm popular. Not for my intellect—my intelligence is in the background, and stands there and watches, but it watches the fingertips, and all the stuff comes out in the typewriter."[9]

But this was an insight of far future times; Bradbury arrived in Los Angeles during the late spring of 1934, not yet fourteen years old and with no sense that the city and its environs would become his home for the rest of his life. Here was a whole new world, for in spite of limited means the Bradburys were living close to the fabulous people who produced the great entertainments of the day. As he entered his ninth grade year at Berendo Junior High, his personal life quickly centered on weekly autograph expeditions to the Hollywood studios along Gower Avenue and on to the various nighttime gathering places of the stars. These became daily excursions in the summertime and continued until 1939.

Bradbury also attended radio broadcasts whenever possible, and his airwave adventures proved to be even more exciting. The comedy and variety shows nearly snared him, and he tried to learn the craft by copying out broadcast scripts.

Eventually he wrote entire shows of his own; he learned how to structure and time routines, but his obsession with turning a joke or pun to good effect kept him from learning the finer points of radio dialog. One legacy of radio's heyday, however, had a lasting impact on his creative vision. This was Paul Rhymer's *Vic and Sade*, which captured quintessential aspects of small-town life during the Great Depression and the war years that followed. The show represented a daily link with his Waukegan childhood, and over time the series helped him imagine the Green Town stories he would first publish in book form as *Dandelion Wine*.[10]

L.A. High and the Science Fiction League

The legacy of Bradbury's early Hollywood madness survives in his snapshots of scores of Hollywood stars, taken with his father's box camera, and in more than a thousand autographs that form a cavalcade of Hollywood personalities at all levels, from character actors to A-film stars and executives. Many of his autographs also represent the golden age of radio as well as the Hollywood-based composers of that era. But few students and teachers at Los Angeles High School knew or cared about his obsession with stage, screen, and radio; he was barely noticed outside of his English classes and his occasional contributions to the school paper. As he entered the tenth grade in 1935 he began a two-year sequence in short fiction with Jennet Johnson, and in his junior year he took a poetry class with Snow Longley Housh; they found his dedication to writing exceptional, but his work was problematic and his desire for feedback often shortened the time available for other students.

His core tenth-grade English class with Mrs. Moore revealed weaknesses in his command of syntax and grammar that detracted from his creative efforts. Mrs. Moore's class focused on short essays, brief descriptive narratives, character sketches, and book review assignments, but he was occasionally able to write very short fictional pieces for her. Jennet Johnson's fiction elective provided more latitude and opportunities for revision than Mrs. Moore's core course, and Johnson also inspired him to read a bit *about* writing for the first time in his life. During his tenth-grade year he read *Trial and Error*, one of pulp novelist Jack Woodford's books on the art of writing.[1] Nevertheless, his stories were derivative; even as his reading range expanded, he was imitating an ever-widening circle of masters from various fields of writing.

Many of his narratives were inspired by the science fiction and fantasy pulps that were now opening into their full golden age, but his surviving high-school stories rarely suggest direct influences. He imitated his longtime favorite Edgar Rice Burroughs and tried his hand as well with imitations of Lovecraft, P. G. Wodehouse, and Sir Arthur Conan Doyle. It wasn't unusual for Bradbury to turn in a new Sherlock Holmes story, and his initial submission to Jennet Johnson for his tenth-grade fiction class was lifted from the opening scenes of *King Kong*.

Johnson saw talent beneath the self-conscious imitation, though, and encouraged him to keep experimenting with a wider range of literary models.[2]

The Astronomy course he took during the fall 1937 semester of his senior year provided him with a basic understanding of the solar system and the galactic islands of stars in the broader cosmos. He dutifully took notes on observational techniques for identifying planets and key points in the background star field, as well as notes on the principles of the telescope. But his most detailed class notes document the lectures he absorbed about the planets and asteroids. His three pages on Mars and its twin moons include a quotation from the writings of Percival Lowell ("supposed canals are seen on its surface") and one of the few personal observations that Bradbury would record in any of his notes: "Mars was responsible for all of [the] present attention in Astronomy—Lowell wrote about it and caught the public's interest!" Percival Lowell was not a new name to Bradbury—his first encounter with the canal theory came from Lowell's *Mars as the Abode of Life* (1910), a book that Bradbury had consumed with wide-eyed wonder at the age of ten. But the tone of his note suggests a new level of realization about Mars that was beginning to extend Bradbury's romantically juvenile concept into the broader aspects of adult interest in the Red Planet in particular, and astronomy in general. In the 1930s there was not so much of a gap between the two perspectives, and his high-school studies provided the basic background necessary to plot the simple planetary adventures that mark his earliest professional science fiction.[3]

Bradbury was fascinated by his instructor's lessons on the concept of space itself, which appear to have used Abbott's engaging short novel *Flatland* to illustrate one-, two-, and three-dimensional perspectives. Toward the end of the semester, he made a diary note about the most intriguing dimension of all: "Started to study the fourth dimension in Astronomy today. It is very interesting to study . . . though it gets rather complicated at times" [ellipsis Bradbury's]. Even at this age, he was far more interested in the implications of space travel and time travel than he ever would be in the underlying science and technology. In general, his note-taking for Astronomy appears routine, and reflects very little true engagement with the more technical aspects of the course. Daydreaming sketches are interspersed among the notes, including an interesting triptych of Groucho Marx, George Bernard Shaw, and FDR. He proved to be literate rather than numerate as a student of astronomy, and a weakness in math put him at a disadvantage for further study. The second semester Astronomy class involved designing and grinding telescope lenses, and both Bradbury and his instructor felt that he should shift to a different scientific elective for the spring. He opted for a second Physiology course instead and did very well.[4]

His extracurricular interests led him to art club, poetry club, and glee club activities, but by and large Bradbury moved in the shadows throughout his last year of high school. Early in his senior year, however, an outside opportunity for recognition suddenly opened up for him. On Thursday October 7, 1937, Bradbury attended a Los Angeles chapter meeting of the Science Fiction League (SFL); by this time the League, initially sponsored by Hugo Gernsback's *Wonder Stories* in 1934, was splintering, but remaining chapters and spin-off independents still connected much of early science fiction fandom across the United States. This meeting featured a display of the original drawings from E. E. "Doc" Smith's *Galactic Patrol*, at that moment a serial-in-progress for *Astounding*.[5]

The newest member was soon taken in tow by Forrest J. Ackerman, who edited the chapter newsletter, *Imagination!* Bradbury had the energy that Ackerman was looking for in an editorial assistant, and he soon began to contribute material as well. 'Madge, as the fan-mag was called by members, was a sharp-looking mimeograph production appearing at a time when most fan-mags (or fanzines, as they were beginning to be called) were still hectographed affairs, and most issues reflected the interests of superfan editor Ackerman. Bradbury found a second home with the casual and open-ended nature of SFL activities, and eventually joined in Ackerman's enthusiasm for forward-looking idealisms such as Esperanto and Technocracy. Bradbury's first whimsical fiction, "Hollerbochen's Dilemma," appeared in the January 1938 issue, and in some respects it seemed right at home within Ackerman's somewhat irreverent format.

Bradbury's Hollerbochen can stop time to avoid deadly events, but when all alternatives appear equally deadly, the energy overload in the stalled time stream destroys him anyway. This kind of conceit, which involves a playful, almost cartoonish tampering with the laws of nature, was an enjoyable exercise for Bradbury, but cross-country subscribers to 'Madge found the tale irritating: "Felt pretty low because no one enjoyed my story 'Hollerbochen's Dilemma' . . . I think it was terrible myself. . . now! Must clear my name. Why, one guy in Kansas said it was "unscientific, uninteresting, poorly written, and . . . ?" [ellipses Bradbury's].[6] But Forry Ackerman didn't let him brood too long; *Imagination!* was a monthly, and the editorial cycle demanded fast work for each issue. Circulation was equally challenging for amateur editors—the mimeo process was faster than hectograph production, which meant that more copies could be circulated locally and by mail throughout the national fanzine network. Bradbury made himself useful from the start, and even his simple line-art drawings were used for the covers of the March and June 1938 issues. He also contributed four short humorous poems, an autobiographical sketch, and (under various names) eight humorous short articles to 'Madge during its one-year run.

His editorial work with the LASFL triggered more successful writing activity at school during his final semester, and to some degree this was nurtured by his participation with the poetry club known as "The Ink Beasts." Bradbury was still too self-focused to learn much from his fellow student-writers, but Jennet Johnson felt that it was best, for now, to let him experiment freely. Her own area of excellence as a writer centered on narrative sketches where she could emphasize mood; by her own admission she was not gifted at plot development, and she rarely criticized his obsession with attempting variations on the old science fiction, detective, and adventure-romance ideas of the genre masters.[7] Her strategy may have delayed his development, for he never really progressed as a writer during high school or in the immediate years after; nonetheless, this free-writing opportunity at least let him write himself out of the worst tendencies left over from his juvenile love of the great romancers.

He had not yet learned to turn inward for his material, however, and only one short narrative sketch from his senior year showed the promise of what he could do by writing from lived experience. It was called "The Night," and it was built entirely on memories of the ravine that had nearly surrounded his Waukegan home. It's not surprising that the ravine was the only "character" in this long-lost sketch, for it has long been recognized as one of Bradbury's most pervasive dark places. As he matured, the ravine continued to fascinate him as a borderland where town and nature struggled to control the landscape—an ambiguous borderland between the rational and the irrational, between life and death. For a moment "The Night" put him on the right track as a writer, but he didn't yet recognize his own originality. Thirty years later, he would reflect on this with his agent Don Congdon: "I was too dumb to see that I had already done a very interesting piece of fiction. It was rough but it was emotional; it was correct; it had its own drive; it was terrifying."[8]

Jennet Johnson's gift for descriptive mood pieces may have sparked Bradbury's first experiment with this form of writing, and perhaps inspired his as-yet untapped ability to write self-contained paragraph-length prose poems. But that achievement was still a dozen years in the future; for now, he read this dark narrative to members of "The Ink Beasts" and a few other students and friends who were curious about his writing. During his senior year he wrote more derivative fiction, and a number of representative pieces survive. Jennet Johnson found his work full of potential and drive, but it was still heavily mired in formula science fiction and fantasy. Fanzine editor and historian Harry Warner maintained that Bradbury submitted twenty stories to the annual, but none were ever published. His creative confidence was further eroded when he failed his eleventh grade language proficiency exam. In spite of the creative potential he demonstrated in Johnson's and Housh's elective courses, he had to take a remedial grammar class during the fall term of his senior year.

In general, he left no official record of achievement in fiction at L.A. High, and only one of his poems won a place in the poetry annual. However, Bradbury had one last momentary ego boost as the school pageant neared production in May 1938. He had secured the role of the janitor, which allowed him to ham up his already humorous lines. His performance was well-received and earned him many compliments along with city newspaper photo ops. Saturday night, before the second and final performance, Bradbury arrived at the school early and took time to reflect on these final high-school moments. His sporadic diary entries, written weeks and sometimes months apart, include an upbeat summary of the evening, but his private thoughts were too dark to commit to paper. More than sixty-five years later, he recalled them in an unpublished interview: "That night of the second performance . . . I climbed the circular stairs up to the bell tower, and I went out on the roof. The sun was setting, and I just stood there and I wept. I cried, because I knew that the big wide world was waiting for me, and nobody would applaud me any more. Tonight was my last night of applause, of the world looking at me and saying, 'Well done!' And then a vast plateau of nothing waiting for me, that world waiting for me out there. I wept for myself. And I was the Lonely One."

The memory remained crystal clear, even after six decades. Bradbury had not yet been able to connect, either personally or professionally, with everyday people in any consistent way. He was, innately, a giving person, which made it all the more essential that he himself be accepted and loved in return. After graduation from Los Angeles High School, all he could do was to turn with redoubled effort to the things he knew best—he would continue to read and write. Every day.

3 Hannes Bok and the Lorelei

For the next four years Bradbury sold the afternoon edition of the Los Angeles *Herald and Express* out of a stand at Olympic and Norton from about 3:30 to 6:00 P.M. on weekdays. After graduation he had tried out as a delivery boy for the women who made costumes and dresses downtown at the Orpheum Building, but the unbearably hot working environment and the strong odors of muslins and silks outweighed the dollar-a-day wage. Later in the summer, he lasted only a single twelve-hour shift with a lawn-cutting crew.[1] But selling newspapers was different; he found that the required salesmanship was similar to the sense of showmanship he had developed in his final year at L.A. High. The newsstand offered a small but steady income of roughly ten dollars a week and provided open hours in the morning and early afternoon to write. His evenings and weekends were also free and his status sheet for July 1938 lists eleven unpublished stories with first drafts completed.

He wrote at least five more that summer, and this level of production may have prompted him to write to Jack Woodford, whose writing guide *Trial and Error* had, if nothing else, at least boosted his confidence as a writer. Woodford was now a New York publisher and gently declined Bradbury's premature request for representation. But this setback was countered by an informal short-story writing group organized by some of his fellow "Ink Beast" alums with the blessing of Jennet Johnson. During the summer, and on into the fall of 1938, Bradbury and others met in the evenings at the homes of various members.[2] His creativity was also enriched by his developing friendship with a unique artist from Seattle. In the middle of his senior year Bradbury had met Hans (later Hannes) Bok at one of the LASFL meetings and was particularly taken by Bok's tempura compositions.

Bradbury's love of Abe Merritt's fantasies burned even more brightly in Bok, who would eventually complete two of his idol's unfinished novels after Merritt's untimely death in 1943. This shared passion deepened Bradbury's appreciation for the "lost race" novels of Haggard, Merritt, Burroughs, and others who wrote their best work in the days before the golden age magazines were founded. Bok also strengthened Bradbury's romantic aesthetic through his mad love for the dynamic movie scores of Miklos Rozsa and Max Steiner and his slightly more measured appreciation of Rimsky-Korsakov, Sibelius, and Grieg's *Peer Gynt Suite*.

Two decades later, Lin Carter's late-life friendship with Bok found these passions still alive, along with a love of fairy tales, Russian music, the masks of W. T. Benda, and mysticism of all kinds.[3] In the late 1930s Bradbury certainly responded to Bok's love of fairy tales, and his own interest in mask-making as an art form also grew along with this friendship.

He quickly developed a high passion for the element of subtle whimsy in Bok's work, and found that his friend was one of the very few artists who had studied with Maxfield Parrish.[4] Bok's fantasy compositions led him into contact with science fiction fandom even before he met Bradbury, but he was especially glad to find someone who shared his fondness for fantasy literature and fairy tales. In January 1938 he presented Bradbury with a tempura painting of a strange Bokian creature as a New Year's gift. The painting inspired an idea for a short novel in Bradbury's last weeks of school, prompting Bok to toss off a few companion sketches based on the story line. He would not have to wait long to read a draft of what his art had inspired in Bradbury's mind.

The 10,000-word novella "Lorelei" is clearly the most interesting of the four unpublished tales he wrote during July 1938. It bears the strong imprint of Hannes Bok's creative encouragement and also offers a long-suppressed glimpse of Bradbury's creative hopes and fears just before his eighteenth birthday. "Lorelei" draws on Bradbury's earliest childhood reading, the fairy tale narrative form, but in setting and tone it echoes Poe's *Arthur Gordon Pym* and Ibsen's *Peer Gynt* as much as it does Hans Christian Andersen. The protagonist, Leif, comes from Swedish seafaring stock, and in the middle of the nineteenth century he sets out along the coast of Norway on a great voyage of discovery alone in a small sailboat.

He travels many weeks north into the Arctic and is marooned in the fabulous warm-water land of Lorelei, full of exotic creatures and home to one other human—a beautiful young girl named Neeahlah. He fights off an invasion from a floating island of death, and is just beginning to enjoy life with his new love when his interlocutor, an odd humanoid named Kuahdo, senses that Leif is beginning to fear that his paradise is all a dream. Kuahdo tells him he must leave, because this lack of faith will indeed destroy the land of Lorelei. He returns home, never to find Lorelei or Neeahlah again. At the end of his life, Leif realizes that Lorelei represented the gift of imagination, and he grieves for the permanent loss of his creative spirit.

"Lorelei" never reached print; here again the work is too self-conscious and full of minor discontinuities. Bradbury was still writing as much to impress as to express, as evidenced in the forced use of such terms as "rehabiliment," "raiment," "coloratura," "lachrymose," and "neoteric." Yet this long tale presented a meaningful theme, and it may represent his first sustained exploration of reverie as the conduit for unconscious creativity. Later in the year, he would read Dorothea Brande's *Becoming a Writer* and learn more about transforming daydreams into structured written reveries.

The novella's creative arc ran from the summer of 1938 through the summer of 1939, beginning and ending with Bok's tempura painting; this little creature was the model for the character Kuahdo in Bradbury's narrative, and a year later appeared (through a stencil transfer) on the cover of *Futuria Fantasia No. 1*, Bradbury's experiment with amateur fan magazine editing. Bok also remained fascinated with the concept and supplied more "Lorelei" art for subsequent numbers of FuFa. Over time, it became apparent that Bradbury had captured a dark corner of Bok's soul; the lonely lament for lost creative power that overruns the final pages of the unpublished "Lorelei" was doubtless a theme that always resonated with Bok, whose uneven career and unstable life reflected similar demons for decades.

At this time in his life Bradbury also feared the same demons, and the energy he put into writing "Lorelei" suggests that he was afraid of losing the Muse or even dying before he had left a mature literary legacy. The Fascist armies fighting in Spain and Ethiopia had already given him a recurring nightmare where he was pursued and devoured by a large dog. He soon realized that the dream was prompted by his fears that the coming World War would destroy him before he could become a writer.[5] The dream recurred through his high-school years, but it was, of course, vague and inarticulate. "Lorelei" presents his first articulation of these fears, especially in the epilogue he appended to Leif's narrative: "Lorelei was *my* world. Fragments of my mind pieced together in a strange pattern of peace away from war and frustration. . . . That is why Kuahdo wished me to go, before I disbelieved and saw Lorelei vanish before my eyes. The shock would have driven me insane." The superseded version of this passage reveals just how fully Bradbury equated the loss of creativity with death:

The land of Lorelei is dead.

It is dead because my imagination is dead. I was young when first I ventured out. Lorelei was the world of my dreams. Fantastic, yes. Weird indeed it was, but happily strange and full of contentment. It was my world of thoughts and happiness. And I let it fall from my mind when I began doubting. I listened to others and grew suspicious. Yes, now it is dead because, because I have doubted.

During this time his struggle with creativity was bound up in his struggle with religious faith. Evidence of this inner conflict emerges from the five unpublished single-spaced pages of an undated writer's narrative nested within a few leaves of diary notes from the summer of 1938. The last page of the narrative indicates that he had fallen away from the Baptist heritage of the Bradbury family:

> But I positively refuse to skip over the ocean of life only touching the wave-tips in my skin-canoe. I insist on diving down into the green-yellow deeps, to see the strange castles just out of sight, just out of reach, down there, down inside what God has chosen to call man. And that thing, is a God, itself, created from the whole of a universe, and named by Man as God. It is not a mighty, brimstone and cursing and awful, dreadful God, it is a surging spirit, it is electricity, the driving source of man, it is an innate intelligence. I do not believe in the Bible's God.

During his teenage years he had become an accumulator of religious experience, attending Jewish temple services on Wilshire Boulevard, astrology meetings, Buddhist observances, various Christian services, and even cults—always the keen observer, never a participant. In 1939, acting on a dare from his Midwest fanzine pal Earl Korshak, he presented himself to Aimee Semple McPherson at her Four Square Gospel Church for a moment under her evangelical hand. His early belief in the divine origins of human creativity conceded the certainty of a Creator for the mystery of existence—he would later come to call it the unseen master dream of the Eternal.[6] This dream implicitly reflected the steady state theory that dominated astronomy at that time; in years to come he would have trouble accepting the big bang's beginnings and endings, but he would never waiver from his youthful conviction that Man's electrifying imagination would eventually solve the riddle of the universe. This evolution in thinking may explain why in later decades he could write with conviction on Christian themes and at the same time delight in George Bernard Shaw's celebration of the human spirit. But in the summer of 1938 he was still reaching for a creative anchor, and his writer's narrative suggests that he already knew, at least in general terms, where he should focus his imagination:

> I am not the keen plotter of life. That will come later, too, I hope. But instead I love the small description, the things we all notice, but never notice, the things, the minute form and beauty of things that are stored in the subconscious and only conjured forth infrequently in life. These things must I write about.

The diary entries continued very infrequently for two more years, but he never added to the writer's narrative again. So far, he had managed to write effectively from observation and memory only once: his brief single-page ravine description of "The Night," written during his final year of high school. Nearly four more years would pass before he began to develop his own personal style and an ability to write effectively of the "things that are stored in the subconscious." He was still too self-conscious, too fixated on the adventure and romance formulas, and far too deeply mired in teenage modes of expression to find his own voice and style.

NYCon 1939

In January 1938, while still a senior in high school, Bradbury and his close friend Eddie Berrara volunteered to take over the editorship of 'Madge beginning with the March issue. They knew that Forry's library job at the Academy of Motion Pictures Arts and Sciences was making it more and more difficult for him to find time to edit. But Forry had managed to keep the fanzine going well enough with very few resources, so the LASFL membership decided to stay the course for now. One factor militating against Bradbury may have been his overly exuberant personality and the evangelical commentary he constantly put forth on his passions in film, radio, reading, and politics.

But it was also clear to everyone, except perhaps Bradbury himself, that he wasn't ready to front a publication, even an amateur fanzine. Early in 1938 he wrote an editor's introduction for his version of 'Madge. This document never reached print, but it provides a snapshot of his earliest serious attempt at editing and publishing. Bradbury gamely offered up two of his own unpublished stories, and his descriptions forthrightly but unintentionally previewed just how bad they were: "The first story, 'Alba of Alnitak,' has a few angles not approached in science-fiction (we hope) though the regular running of the story may not be as new as hundreds of others. We think we have created atmosphere anyway. The second tale, 'The Road to Autumn's House,' has captured some horror and weirdness and possibly a slightly new slant on werewolfs and the like."

Both of these stories were recent high-school creative writing submissions. Bradbury also wanted to eliminate 'Madge's policy of rejecting adventure stories, possibly because he had a few of these in progress as well. In spite of good intentions, his introduction rambled and his sole editorial promise revealed a student who had been forced to retake the introductory English core during his senior year: "And it will be done in first rate English. Our punctuation may be bad at times, but we guarantee the nearest thing to perfect English coming out of the LA League." He was, of course, only seventeen at the time, but he was immersed in a fanzine culture created just a few years earlier by teenagers like Julius Schwartz, Charlie Hornig, and Mort Weisinger; by 1938, in their early twenties, these New Yorkers had all become professional agents or editors back East. Clearly, Bradbury was not yet up to the mark of his predecessors in terms of the ability to control his editorial prose or even judge the quality of amateur submissions.

After high school, Bradbury let this urge to edit simmer for a year and focused on occasional contributions to various fanzines. Bradbury hadn't forgotten his disaster with "Hollerbochen's Dilemma," and by the fall of 1938 he chose to revisit a situation that would have been better left undisturbed. "Hollerbochen Comes Back" was among the unpublished materials at hand when Forry Ackerman's work schedule finally made it impossible for him to keep up production of *Imagination!* in its original format. The remaining submissions were triaged into various one-off and recurring chapter publications, including five issues of the untitled two-page mini-fanzine informally dubbed *Mikros*. Bradbury's second fanzine story appeared in the November 1938 issue of *Mikros*, but it was really more of an epilogue than a sequel to the first Hollerbochen tale.

In "Hollerbochen Comes back," the exploded title character reconstitutes at the author's request and returns to rescue Bradbury and his reputation. Hollerbochen looks for him in places where dark forces are at work in the world, including Berlin, Moscow, Japan, and finally Alcatraz. He finds his author at his typewriter, imprisoned by the fanzine readers who had ridiculed the first story. Bradbury has Hollerbochen round them up through a series of puns and word games involving many of his fellow science-fiction fans. The tone was more humorous than hostile and offered a gentle reminder to fanzine readers and editors that what is intended as a humorous story should be taken with good humor.

It was a point probably not worth making over a throwaway piece like "Hollerbochen's Dilemma," but together the two Hollerbochen pieces offer a first glimpse of Bradbury's lifelong defense mechanism against developing an overweening ego. Bradbury's instinctive desire to make fun of writers (including himself) who might otherwise take themselves too seriously first surfaces here, although it is somewhat masked by his own genuine irritation over the harsh reader response. But from this first salvo, Bradbury would develop an abiding and healthy sense that writers should never take themselves or their genre traditions too seriously, and this carnival sense of celebration rather than sanctification of literature would continue to color the way he approached dark fantasy, science fiction, and his late-in-life return to detective fiction.

Forry's backlog of material ran out by the spring of 1939, and Bradbury turned to his developing connections in the wider national fanzine network for a creative outlet. Most of these were parodies and spoof columns designed to lampoon prozine editors as well as the fanzine community itself, and once again Bradbury found himself viewed as more of an annoyance than as an entertainer. His fanzine contributions tapered off during the summer because a number of LASFL members were preparing to attend the first worldwide gathering of science fiction fans and writers in New York. The WorldCon, or NYCon I as it came to be called, was scheduled for early July, and it provided an opportunity for the West Coast fans to see the 1939 World's Fair as well.

To his everlasting credit, Forry loaned his friend the fifty dollars he needed to make the trip, although Bradbury would still have to watch every penny. He made the four-day trip by bus carrying an art portfolio for his friend Hannes Bok, who had returned to the Seattle area earlier that year. In May Bradbury asked Bok, who was now working for the WPA's Arts Division, to send him a portfolio of new work. Bok was in a creative slump, but by early June he had prepared seven "pics" and sent the drawings on down to Los Angeles. The plan was for Bradbury to shop the drawings while he solicited interest in his own stories from various pulp editors.[1] Since he was arriving several days early he planned to link up with Charlie Hornig, an occasional LASFL guest who was once again back in New York in an editor's chair.

The logistics of the trip were challenging, but the notes he typed along the way back East reveal that his excitement overcame both anxiety and fatigue.[2] He typed notes throughout his four-day journey, sometimes focusing on details and at other times marveling at the various landscapes and the origins of the roads that cut through it. Late on the first day he typed this reaction to the high desert:

> The road stretches endlessly away. I can't help thinking how much sweat must have been worked out of hot hides making these miles of concrete—oh, the headaches and creaking bones and sun-scarred faces that must have resulted. Imagine coming over all of this bumpy terrain fifty years ago in a wagon? Sounds almost impossible when you take a good look at the bushes and earth cracks and dry streams, not to mention boulders, valleys and mountains. Gad, but it is good to live in 1939 even if we do still have wars. That will go soon, also, I am sure.

These last words brought his mind back to the present, and his final thoughts of the day slipped back into a degree of the familiar self-consciousness and need to impress that would dominate his story submissions for a few more years: "And all of this was ocean at one time, maybe again in a few million years—which is a long time in the history of the puny manchild—but a negligible tick of the clock in the annals of cosmic incident." This trip, and the contacts he was soon to make in New York, would start the process of mentorship that would help Bradbury break away from cliché and find his own distinct narrative voice.

Typing trip notes and reading the latest SF magazines would help him work through the long days ahead, but he also carried one of his first "self-help" books, *Hartrampf's Vocabulary*. Bradbury would always be drawn to accelerated modes of learning foundational subjects, and he felt that *Hartrampf's* nontraditional strategy for learning vocabulary would compensate for the troubles he had had with basic grammar and usage in high school: "The reason I read it was because it was full of synonyms and antonyms and you could put them together . . . and have a short story. Hot and cold, tall and short—all the negatives and all the positives, so you can make plots just by reading one page in *Hartrampf's Vocabulary*. It gives you ways to look at characters."[3] He loved words, and the connotations that connected a word with other words spread out across each page of the book; it was easier to dip into than any taxonomic study of vocabulary and more creative than paging through the dictionary or a standard thesaurus. Words traceable to the Hartrampf grids appear as late as his 1942 composition of "The Crowd" but disappear from his April 1946 revisions of this story for *Dark Carnival*.

Bradbury spent much of his time in New York with Charlie Hornig, who had recently founded *Science Fiction* magazine. Hornig was the boy wonder of genre editors, having been discovered by Hugo Gernsback and given the editorship of *Wonder Stories* in 1933—at the age of seventeen. Before turning twenty, he founded the Science Fiction League under the magazine's sponsorship. Hornig left *Wonder Stories* in 1936 when new ownership refashioned it into *Thrilling Wonder Stories*, and met Bradbury a year later when he guest edited an issue of *Madge* out on the Coast. On Thursday June 29th Hornig introduced Bradbury to Julius Schwartz, who had been a pioneering New York area fanzine editor as a teenager in the early 1930s before setting up the first agency specializing in science fiction and fantasy authors. By 1939 Schwartz either knew or represented most of the science fiction and fantasy writers who published in the New York market.

Together with Hornig, Schwartz, and Conrad Rupert, a professional printer associated with the early New York fan magazines, Bradbury spent that Thursday at the World's Fair. In later years his reflections centered on the great sadness he felt as he contrasted the hopeful aspirations of the Fair's pavilions with the approaching prospect of global war. But at the time, his attention centered on the Perisphere's "Democracity" diorama; here he found another example of the futuristic architecture that he had come to love as a youth through Dick Calkins's *Buck Rogers* skylines and the pulp covers of Frank R. Paul. But he was impressed by the Perisphere's audiovisual interfaces as much as he was by the physical exhibits and architecture. The vast projected images were the work of

Fred Waller, who would later help develop the Hollywood Cinerama technology that Bradbury would come to love in the early 1950s.

The next day, Friday, June 30th, Bradbury met *Astounding* editor John W. Campbell and Futurians Donald Wollheim and Fred Pohl. Wollheim's Futurian criticism of the more fan-based clubs and chapters had already led to friction throughout the New York region. Sam Moskowitz and Jim Taurasi, leaders of the opposing First Fandom movement in Queens, viewed the Brooklyn-based Futurians as Communists and kept all but Isaac Asimov, already a bona fide writer, from attending the historic first NYCon. The outcasts held their own more informal meeting in Brooklyn on Monday, but the distances (and the fact that the only available space was in the local headquarters of the Communist party) discouraged most of the out-of-town fans. At least one writer did visit the Futurians—Jack Williamson, who had been in New York since May working on new fiction.[4]

As the convention got underway, Bradbury met the more unified Philadelphia fans led by Milton Rothman and fanzine editors Robert Madle (*Fantascience Digest*) and John Baltadonis (*Science Fiction Collector*). The main convention events were scheduled for Sunday and Monday (July 2, 3), and here Bradbury met Campbell again and his fellow editors Leo Margulies and Mort Weisinger as well as writers Jack Williamson, Nelson Bond, Manly Wade Wellman, Ray Cummings, Ross Rocklynne, Harl Vincent, Willy Ley, and the Otto half of Earl and Otto (Eando) Binder. Bradbury watched the first reel of *Metropolis* at the Sunday sessions, and made a few successful bids at the auction event from his meager funds. He had a headache Monday and slept late, but he still managed to attend Ruroy Sibley's afternoon lecture on astronomy. Bradbury couldn't afford the Monday night banquet (it was a dollar a plate), but Forry arranged for him to attend the guest of honor's remarks after dinner and the evening's principal address by scientist and writer Willy Ley, who had recently become a regular writer for Campbell's new nonfiction scientific feature in *Astounding*. The guest of honor was one of Bradbury's favorite pulp illustrators, Frank R. Paul. Fewer than three dozen people actually paid for a dinner seat, so Bradbury had no trouble moving in from the wings after dinner to meet Paul and talk with Willy Ley, one of the great popularizers of science from the early 1930s into the 1960s.

Bradbury stayed on at his Midtown YMCA for nine more days seeing films, relaxing at Coney Island, and visiting with various local area fans and editors. On Friday July 7th, he showed Bok's drawings to Farnsworth Wright, who had recently been obliged by new ownership to move the *Weird Tales* editorial offices from Chicago to New York. Mrs. Wright, who functioned as a second reader and was rumored to have significant influence on acceptances, even remembered

Bradbury's earliest submissions—a group of poems that the Wrights had rejected. Encouraged by the name recognition (and the fact that Forry had come along to add fan support), Bradbury made his case for the art. Mrs. Wright was immediately enthusiastic, and her husband agreed to send Bok a story to work up for *Weird Tales*.[5]

That day he also met highly regarded illustrator Virgil Finlay at the *American Weekly* magazine offices. Bradbury went up to the Standard Magazines office on 40th Street and visited *Thrilling Wonder* editor Mort Weisinger again. He also met the mild-mannered Robert O. Erisman, who had managed to persuade some veteran SF writers to publish in his somewhat lurid *Marvel Science Stories*, a relatively new Red Circle title that made a brief dash into the SF field between 1938 and 1940.[6] The next day, Saturday, he and Forry went back to the *American Weekly* magazine offices to meet Abe Merritt, a giant of the early pulp years; in his notes from the trip, Bradbury referred to him as the "jovial, hard of hearing author of Creep Shadow Creep and many other swellies."

He had no luck with his own tales, however; Julie Schwartz, who would later become his first agent, felt that his work was not yet ready for the professional pulp market. Charlie Hornig had critiqued one manuscript with Bradbury in his Manhattan office before WorldCon started; on Monday the 10th, Hornig and Ross Rocklynne sat in Central Park with the young writer and read the rest, but found nothing that was ready for sale.[7] Bradbury remained upbeat in spite of these disappointments; his two-week stay in New York was more important for the connections he made. His face was now known in prozine editorial circles, and Mort Weisinger had taken a genuine liking to him. Weisinger, editor of both *Thrilling Wonder Stories* and *Startling Stories*, invited Bradbury to visit his New Jersey home during his last weekend in New York with a large group that included Forry, Otto Binder, Hornig, Schwartz, and Ross Rocklynne. But the center of this group was really Julius Schwartz, who was best friends with Weisinger, Hornig, and Binder and had known them from the earliest days of fandom.[8] This extra time in the city allowed Bradbury to develop real friendships with Hornig and Rocklynne, and he would extend these friendships during the next year as they both moved out to live in Los Angeles.

Bradbury left New York by bus on Wednesday evening, July 12th, bound for Waukegan and a two-week visit with the friends and family members he had left behind more than five years earlier. While in town he went down to Pearce's bookshop and ordered *The Seven Who Fled*, Frederic Prokosch's latest romance of the Orient, but when it failed to come in he bought Steinbeck's *The Grapes of Wrath*. This book was not his initiation into Steinbeck's world of working-class America; earlier that year he had spent some of his precious newsboy income on

Of Mice and Men. But the broader panorama of *The Grapes of Wrath* was profoundly fascinating to him, and a decade later he would adapt Steinbeck's interchapter bridging structure to shape his own *Martian Chronicles*. He read Steinbeck's new novel all through the long bus ride west from Waukegan out to Seattle, where he returned Bok's portfolio and celebrated his friend's breakthrough with *Weird Tales*. As Bradbury headed south for Los Angeles and home, Bok made plans to travel to New York and begin his award-winning career illustrating for the pulp magazines. In a very real sense, Bradbury initiated the defining period of Bok's career; over the next fifteen years, Bok would provide cover art for 150 pulp magazines and win the 1953 Hugo Award for illustration.

5

Futuria Fantasia

Bradbury had been away from Los Angeles for more than a month, but he soon resumed his latest project for the LASFL—his new fanzine, *Futuria Fantasia*. He put together the inaugural Summer 1939 issue just before the WorldCon pilgrimage; this activity, along with his travels, spelled the end of his autograph-hunting trips to the studios. In the late spring he had, with Forry's help, convinced SFL members to sponsor *Futuria Fantasia*. In the brief year since his unpublished proposal for a new *'Madge*, Bradbury's ability to write readable editorial copy had improved significantly. *FuFa*, as it was soon nicknamed, would have covers and interior art by Hannes Bok, ensuring that it would continue the smart look that had characterized most issues of *'Madge*. Bradbury would also continue another aspect of *FuFa*'s predecessors by privileging the Technocracy movement in the pages of his new fanzine.

Ackerman had preached Technocracy in most issues of *'Madge* and continued to do so in the far thinner issues of *Mikros*. LASFL members had varying degrees of support for (or indifference to) the Technocracy angle, but during this period of his life Bradbury himself saw the Technocracy movement as a credible way to end the kind of crushing poverty that his family had known since the early years of the Depression and had flirted with, in one form or another, all of his life. On August 1st, 1939, two days after returning from his 6,000-mile NYCon bus odyssey, he officially signed up as a member of the Technocracy movement.[1] In contrast to his love of Hollywood glamour, Bradbury had developed a dislike for the idle rich and felt that the captains of industry were no longer qualified to run the means of production in America or anywhere else in the world.

As it turned out, his own coming of age coincided with the last significant phase of Technocracy as a political force. The Technocracy movement had begun to take shape in America in the years before World War I, as engineers and academics began to explore the possibility that the waste and inefficiency of the later industrial age was being caused by the system of production for profit. The 208-page *Technocracy Study Course* that Bradbury received from the Technocracy Regional Division on Sunset Boulevard provided scientific background for the premise that a price economy will collapse "in any civilization that converts energy at a high rate."[2]

After the Wall Street Crash of 1929, academics, engineers, and activists formed the Committee on Technocracy, but internal dissension soon led to a decline in the national influence of the movement. One source of controversy was the leadership of Howard Scott, who made it clear that his vision of Technocracy had little in common with democracy. Yet the movement still had influence in the western United States and Canada, and Scott's splinter group, Technocracy, Inc., had many supporters who were unwilling or unable to see the more draconian implications of Scott's proposals. In Bradbury's case, his support of the organization was based on simple common sense—if the technological infrastructure were more efficient, then everyone's life would be better. If he failed to see just how Scott was going to control this brave new world, it was also because he saw Technocracy as perhaps the only way to stay out of the impending European war. When the first issue of *Futuria Fantasia* went out in June 1939, Bradbury did Ackerman one better by placing the Technocracy, Inc., logo on the mailing flap—a monad below the motto, "America Must Decide."

The first issue presented a gently humorous representation of choices pro and con: Bruce Yerke's pro-Technocracy essay "The Revolt of the Scientists," and Ackerman's purportedly anti-Technocratic fable "The Record" (Bradbury wrote the final paragraphs himself). In between these selections, Bradbury placed his own humorous short-short story pseudonymously. "Don't Get Technatal" has a slight edge to the humor: Sam Stern no longer has material for his pulp fiction stories; life under the Technocracy has eliminated the material for detective, crime, and horror fiction, and the reading public of this crimeless society no longer has any interest in these traditional genres at all. His wife repeatedly insists that he should write about love, the only popular topic remaining for fiction. As his wife leans over the railing of their penthouse apartment, Stern picks up a weapon and contemplates writing a story about one of the less romantic consequences of love.

He received fairly good feedback from local and long-distance subscribers, but there was an obvious need for more fiction and Bradbury decided to tone down the Technocracy content in the second issue. His personal support for the movement remained strong, however. Henry Hasse, an established pulp writer in Seattle, wrote for a subscription and Bradbury asked him to critique the first issue. In his critique Hasse went on to suggest that individual voices can change very little in society, prompting Bradbury to offer his own account of his motivations. Fear, which had always stoked his imagination as a writer, was also a key motivator in his concern for the future. His four-page response to Hasse offered this summary of the threat:

The future of America, let me say, is threatened by the toppling of our economic setup through machinery. Unless a scientific government such as Technocracy is able to prevent it, the entire system of communications and transportations [sic] will break down and in the resulting chaos either a revolution or starvation will kill millions . . . And today with men being thrown out of work by machinery, unable to buy food and pay taxes the government finds itself coming to a stalemate. When they put men on relief they cannot tax them. Therefore what will the government run on?

For Bradbury, Technocracy offered a distinct alternative to either Capitalism or Communism, and appealed to his own oversimplified but heartfelt love of the common sense approach:

And yet, under our Price System, the best inventions of mankind have been suppressed because it would cause a loss of money on some big business man's part. . . . When you have an abundance there can be no value to a thing. Like the air you breathe. Like water. And therefore you can do nothing else with it but destroy it and keep the price up as we are doing today. But Technocracy deplores this waste, giving the necessities of life to half and leaving the rest with none. It isn't a communistic idea of sharing the rich[es], its [sic] a matter of common sense[,] of distributing what we have plenty of instead of throwing it away.

But most of all, the movement appealed to his creative vision as an emerging science fiction writer. He felt a special kinship to the engineers, technicians, and scientists who had advocated more efficient distribution of resources, and he saw the possibilities in much the same way that some of his older colleagues did:

We have enough electric power from Boulder and from the Columbia River project, when done, to send power all over the North American continents [sic]. We have power and by God it must be used. We can have the magnificent civilization of science-fiction dreams in twenty-five years once the Technate comes in. This is no dream, no bit of word-weaving. It's based on blueprinted facts, on charts, on long investigation of employment, machinery, power, distribution and many other factors.

His sense of the future had been visually reinforced by Things to Come, H. G. Wells's 1936 film adaptation of his novel The Shape of Things to Come; it was already a Bradbury favorite, and he had seen it once again just a few weeks earlier in New York with some of the other WorldCon attendees. Writers within the Los Angeles chapter itself were wrestling with similar ideas, including 32-year-old Robert Heinlein, who began to attend LASFL meetings that same summer of 1939. Over the previous year he had written his first novel, *For Us, the Living*, as a creative way of forwarding Upton Sinclair's "production for use" concept and other utopian ideas not too far afield from the solutions offered by the Technocracy movement. That novel never reached print in Heinlein's lifetime, but it provided a point of departure for many of his later social themes.

One trouble for Heinlein, Bradbury, and others in the group was that the solutions they endorsed looked better on paper than they ever could in practice. Bradbury closed his argument for Hasse with this final observation about Technocracy: "The whole LA SFL is behind it, believe me. Not because it's a dream, but because its fact, its provable, it has a yardstick that you can use anytime anywhere . . . Energy! Energy will be the 'price' on commodities in the new world" [ellipses Bradbury's]. It was an appealing notion, based on the original Committee on Technocracy's highly touted 1932 "Energy Survey of North America." But the survey was soon proven to be full of errors, and Howard Scott's single-minded notion that energy units should replace the dollar was not endorsed by many of the experts within the movement. However, there were still many nontechnical supporters who, like Bradbury and his colleagues, hoped for the better good and left the details to the Technate. As Californians, they were living in a state where factories and farms were idle and a quarter of the population was out of work, and the old order seemed incapable of changing anything for the better.

In *FuFa* #2, Bradbury began to show distinct development as an editor. This was not apparent in the introduction, which was hastily printed three weeks ahead of time; it had more than a few errors and referred to three articles that were actually dropped prior to publication. Nevertheless, other aspects of the second issue show that he was developing the strategic vision of an editor. The evidence of his emerging editorial insight can be found in the selection of contents, which included "I'm Through!," purportedly an ex-fan's critique of the prozines by Foo E. Onya (actually Henry Hasse), and a companion piece by Henry Kuttner. In soliciting the Hasse and Kuttner essays, Bradbury was initiating a debate on the state of writing in the science fiction field. This kind of debate rarely surfaced in the prozines, and when it did the commentary was usually marginalized in brief editorial letters. Kuttner's playful, indirect approach in his essay ("The Trouble with Goldfish") suggested that writers and fans alike had failed to define, in any meaningful way, the very nature and purpose of science fiction.

Hasse's argument assumed that the definition already existed, but that it was the wrong one: "When literature becomes obsessed by ideas as such, it is no longer literature." This was certainly a timely issue, for the battle lines were already evident in the widely divergent acquisition policies of the various SF pulps; in fact, Hasse felt that his attack on the dangers of science overshadowing imagination in genre fiction might not be well received at all. Prior to submission, Hasse offered Bradbury this caveat: "I warn you it's harsh, although sincere. Probably not many of your readers, nor you yourself, would agree with some of the statements."[3] Bradbury was certainly still an amateur editor, but he had the presence of mind to publish this piece; over the next ten years, editors of the earliest science fiction anthologies would examine this issue in even greater detail.

In spite of the opening editorial gaffes, the second issue was more substantial than the first. Two stories by Hannes Bok (one appearing under the *FuFa* house byline Anthony Corvais) and Bradbury's anonymous story, "The Pendulum," resulted in a longer issue for each subscriber's dime. There were also two poems—one was Hasse's, but the other was a Bradbury poem published under the pseudonym Doug Rogers. "Satan's Mistress" shows the influence of his weird genre reading, and in fact this poem is the only known piece from the group of poems that Bradbury had unsuccessfully submitted to Farnsworth Wright at *Weird Tales* a year or so earlier.[4] Bradbury's "The Pendulum" was a last-minute replacement for Hasse's "Martian Oddity," which (notwithstanding its title parody of Stanley Weinbaum's famous "Martian Odyssey") was more of a prozine quality story anyway. It was a significant substitution, for "The Pendulum" represents Bradbury's first serious metaphor-based tale and became the basis for his first professional sale.

Hannes Bok continued his unbroken run of *Futuria Fantasia* cover illustrations for the third (Winter 1940) issue, and Hasse supplied "Aw, G'Wan!!" a rebuttal to his own pseudonymous critique of the SF prozines published in the second issue. Ross Rocklynne wrote "The Best Ways to Get Around," a long and historically significant survey article on modes of space propulsion created by various masters of science fiction. Yet Bradbury's editorial judgment remained inconsistent; SFL chapter director Russ Hodgkins persuaded him not to run his 10,000-word "Lorelei" because it had no place in the slim fanzine. Bradbury's only story in this number, "The Fight of the Good Ship Clarissa," was little more than a comic radio sketch of a shootout between Earthmen and Venusians.

But the real story of *FuFa* #3 rests between the lines; Bradbury was beginning to have problems with production. Publication slipped from the advertised December date to early February 1940. At a dime a copy, each issue of 100 could defray only ten dollars of the twenty-five-dollar production cost. As the third issue was mailed out, Bradbury confided to Hasse that he was losing even more money, since the Eastern fans now preferred to exchange 'zines while writers and editors wanted free copies. The real problem came out of the Los Angeles chapter itself. Russ Hodgkins cut off *Futuria Fantasia*'s funding, and Bradbury was considering a new arrangement that would share editorial control with the chapter director. The chapter was divided, and Bradbury summarized the situation in his January 30th letter to Hasse: "Russ Hodgkins claims my mag stinks and wants to cut it out entirely and revive Imagination, but Ackerman refuses, so we are stale-mated. . . . Now what?"

The stalemate was never really broken, but after nine months Bradbury was able to pull together a fourth and final issue that surpassed the previous three in layout as well as in content quality. Bok's detailed cover painting was carefully reproduced by Forry on the Academy's multilith machine. Two of Bok's interior drawings for this final issue were based on Bradbury's unpublished 1938 novella "Lorelei," and other Bok line art was featured throughout. The issue included a table of contents, and the editor's page had a new Bok masthead. Two very short anecdotal tales by Henry Kuttner and Damon Knight were balanced by "Heil!," a longer tale of subtle vengeance taken against Hitler by a Jewish surgeon. Although "Heil!" carried a Lyle Monroe byline, it was actually contributed by Robert A. Heinlein and remains one of the hardest Heinlein titles to locate in the original printing. But the issue is equally notable for Bradbury's story "The Piper," published under his Ron Reynolds byline with a primitive sketch of the piper cut into the stencil by Bradbury himself. In rewritten form, "The Piper" would become Bradbury's first solo sale to the genre prozines.

This impressive number marked the end of *Futuria Fantasia*. Even if LASFL support had continued, Bradbury was beginning to focus more and more of his time on submissions to the professional pulps. But the end of his fanzine editorship also coincided with a major shift in the political passions that had fueled the early issues of *FuFa*. In the two years that he had championed the Technocracy movement, he had not seen Howard Scott's Technocracy, Inc., in any large-scale venue. He had not seen the gray cars of the Technate with the corporate monad printed like a police shield on the doors, or the gray double-breasted suits and gray shirts of the active membership. This all changed in a single evening: "I went to hear Howard Scott, who was head of Technocracy, at the Shriner Auditorium, and when I saw all those men I knew, in gray suits, saluting him, it reminded me of Russia, Germany, Italy—it's always the same."

His new pen pal Damon Knight suggested that the Technate would have no place for the unemployed—or for artists.[5] Technocracy would eliminate the right of the people to govern themselves, and once Bradbury discovered this consequence, he could no longer support the movement. By this time, the movement was beginning to be overtaken by events; Roosevelt's New Deal had implemented many public work programs, and the war in Europe was beginning to stimulate industrial production. It was more or less a natural progression for Bradbury to drift warily into the democratic fold as America moved steadily toward involvement with a world at war.

6

From the Fanzines to the Prozines

Bradbury's close encounters with the performing arts reached a high point during 1940, and for a time these activities restricted his writing schedule. He briefly enrolled in drama classes at City College during the spring term but dropped out after a few days; the real world always seemed to be a better teaching environment to Bradbury than a classroom, and he turned instead to production work for the spring and fall amateur comedy revues staged by Laraine Day's Wilshire Player's Guild. In 1941 a few weeks of rehearsing as the romantic lead in a canceled amateur production of *Money for Candy* confirmed his total inability to memorize lines. But this was symptomatic of a more fundamental problem in his approach to acting: "I never learned the secret of acting, which is—other people's faces. What they say comes *at* you, and *there* is your acting. The other person does it to you, so you don't have to memorize your lines; you react to what they say and you say something—which happens to be a line."[1]

He closed the door on acting, but other opportunities had already opened up; he spent the summers of 1940 and 1941 ushering on concert nights at the Hollywood Bowl, where he reinforced his passion for the great Romantic composers and such contemporary symphonic masters as Shostakovich. He saw these artists, as well as such classical Hollywood composers as Sigmund Romberg, Bernard Herrmann, Miklos Rozsa and Max Steiner, as preservers of Romantic hallmarks in an age of unproven experimental musical forms. He also developed a great and abiding love of ballet, and ushered at the Philharmonic Auditorium when touring ballet troupes performed. Touring opera found a place in his heart as well, but he also found magic in lesser spectacles; the mixed cabaret and marionette format of Turnabout Theater, as well as the parlor stage of the tiny Circle Theater, ignited an equally strong passion for intimate performance venues.[2]

But most of his attention remained focused on writing and the literary marketplace. Thanks to his work as a fanzine editor, he had learned some painful but potentially useful lessons about magazine design, marketing, and editorial acquisition. His own editorial prose was still amateurish, but with the help of Forry Ackerman and the artistic contributions of Hannes Bok, he had put together one of the better-designed fanzines of the day. Bradbury even went so far as to outline a two-volume anthology of professional stories selected from *Weird Tales*;

the thirty-eight stories in these outlines reveal his favorites from the 1935–39 issues, and include multiple story selections for Seabury Quinn (5), Robert Bloch (7), Henry Kuttner (3), and C. L. Moore (3). He proposed interlocking volume titles (*Any Time after Midnight* and *All through the Night*), a professional illustrator (Virgil Finlay, no less), and even included one of his own stories—"The Lonely One," probably an expansion of his high-school mood-piece, "The Night."

These unfulfilled outlines ended up with Forry Ackerman, and his impact on Bradbury's early editorial ventures should not be underestimated; he certainly provided a direct conduit to the historical artifacts of film and various genre literatures, and he also facilitated Bradbury's entry into the world of editorial writing. But Bradbury discovered his most important editorial lesson on his own: he learned how to invite professional writers to discuss the status and future of science fiction. Contributions solicited by Bradbury from such established writers as Hasse, Kuttner, and Rocklynne were in many ways better than the fiction that made its way into the pages of *Futuria Fantasia*, and show that Bradbury was aware of the implications of events in the genre before he himself was really able to contribute any significant fiction of his own.

In June 1941, Bradbury's last period fanzine anecdote, "Tale of the Mangledomvritch," appeared in *Snide*, published "at odd intervals" from Salem, Oregon, by Damon Knight and Bill Evans. It was essentially a prose cartoon about a four-dimensional department store, but it appealed to Knight's own cartooning passions. Some of Bradbury's humorous shorts had a social point to make, but his medium remained the kind of elementary and pun-filled humor that he had learned working around the radio comedy shows. East Coast fandom, already splintering into factions, had a field day with Bradbury's humor; many fellow fans never accepted his way of critiquing and celebrating science fiction and fantasy in the fan-based amateur magazines. He had put a lot of time and energy into this work, and his eighteen fanzine "shorts" document only part of his amateur contributions. From the fall of 1937 to the fall of 1941, more than fifty Bradbury articles, reviews, letters, illustrations, and miscellaneous items appeared in various fan publications. He honestly felt that his approach was appropriate for the amateur fanbase, but by the fall of 1940 he began to write more serious (if not more sophisticated) editorial letters for submission to the professional science fiction and fantasy magazines.

He had been sending stories out to professional magazines since high school, first to major market slicks such as the *Atlantic Monthly*, *Harpers*, *New Yorker*, and the *Saturday Evening Post*, but more of his submissions went to the science fiction pulps after his WorldCon experiences in New York. Immediately after returning home from the convention in August 1939, he wrote his new friend Frederik Pohl asking him to represent his work.[3] Besides Julius Schwartz, who had deferred representing him at this level of experience, Pohl was the only author's agent he felt comfortable with on the East Coast. Pohl agreed to represent Bradbury and offered advice on how to slant for the three highest paying science fiction pulps—*Astounding, Amazing,* and *Thrilling Wonder.* But Bradbury remained wary of slanting, especially when the highest rate was still only a penny a word. In February 1940 Pohl became editor of both *Astonishing Stories* and *Super Science Stories* for a subsidiary house of Popular Publications, and he soon became more of a "first refusal" editor than an agent. One of the first stories that Pohl refused was Bradbury's fanzine story "The Pendulum." Bradbury immediately appealed, maintaining that *FuFa* had no measurable circulation and therefore "The Pendulum" would not violate Popular's no-reprint rule. Pohl remained firm and Bradbury tried again with Pohl's fellow Futurian Donald A. Wollheim, who was about to start up *Cosmic Stories* and *Stirring Science Stories.* But Wollheim had even stronger antipathy for recycled fanzine material and wrote the young author a harsh editorial rejection.

By early 1941 Pohl had rejected at least four stories, but these would be the last of Bradbury's direct pulp submissions.[4] Julius Schwartz had now agreed to represent him to the pulp prozines as a full-time agent with no editorial ties. Bradbury's work was improving, yet stylistically he was still under the influence of Burroughs and H. G. Wells, Lovecraft and Poe, and the recent exotic romances of Frederic Prokosch. Thomas Wolfe had exploded into his life in the fall of 1938—the very first book he bought with money from his newspaper stand was Wolfe's *The Web and the Rock.* He soon read Wolfe's earlier novels *Look Homeward, Angel* and its sequel, *Of Time and the River.* Within a year, he was reading Wolfe and Steinbeck in equal measure.[5] Steinbeck's rebellious and often melodramatic prose affected Bradbury in much the same way that Wolfe's more imaginative fiction had moved him, but in Steinbeck Bradbury also discovered a new model for articulating both the sacrifice and rebirth of America's new, economically driven migrations to the far West. These were powerful variations on his own experience; understandably, he was still unable to distance himself from these literary loves as he typed his own stories, and much of his work from this period was written in the style of one master or another.

His more specialized efforts at science fiction fared no better; he continued to find new models to imitate in the expanding prewar field of science fiction and fantasy magazines. Between 1939 and 1941 sixteen editorial letters from Bradbury appeared in the various prozines; with the exception of one in *Weird Tales,* all were in the SF&F publications. The *Weird Tales* letter, along with several others, promoted the artwork of his friend Hannes Bok, but most of the letters document his close reading of a wide range of pulps. He was now getting to know more of the professional writers, and occasionally Robert and Leslyn Heinlein would invite him to join an informal group of writers they hosted in their home. The so-called Mañana Literary Society offered Bradbury a better chance to get acquainted with writers such as Heinlein, Henry Kuttner, Cleve Cartmill, Leigh Brackett, Edmond Hamilton, and eventually Jack Williamson. Bradbury was still a bit overly enthusiastic, but his dedication to writing soon prompted Heinlein to suggest that he submit work to Rob Wagner's *Script*, a regional slick magazine that was regarded as a *New Yorker*–style publication by West Coast readers. Wagner didn't pay his writers, but he had persuaded William Saroyan and other up-and-coming writers to place stories in his magazine.

In the summer of 1940 Bradbury submitted a story to *Script* that he had thought up while visiting Charlie Hornig, who was now editing all three of his New York–based science fiction magazines from Los Angeles. They were joking about clichés when Bradbury decided to write an "article-story" about a man who attacks anyone who uses clichés in public. "It's Not the Heat, It's the Hu—" might have become just another variation on Bradbury's penchant for low comedy, but he put just enough controlled humor, pacing, and stylistic polish into the piece that it found a home in the November 2 issue of *Script*. This was a tremendous boost to his confidence, even if he was paid with only three copies of the magazine. Between March and July 1941, Bradbury placed two articles and two more of his humorous short fictions with Wagner. None of his *Script* pieces are remarkable, but together they document his ability to write humor in a more disciplined way than he had ever thought necessary for the amateur fanzine circle of readers. Nevertheless, he now realized that humor could carry him no further on the printed page without the added dimension of larger fictions, and for the most part he stayed away from anecdotal humor during the first fifteen years of his professional career.

He had now appeared in a professional magazine, but he had not yet been paid as a professional writer. Not surprisingly, the spring of 1941 proved to be a time of reflection and reassessment. His newspaper concession at Olympic and Norton provided his principal source of income, and major construction along Olympic disrupted both street and pedestrian traffic for many weeks. Without a story sale he would not be able to make the summer trip to Denver for the third WorldCon; he had missed the Philadelphia WorldCon the year before, and saw the Denver event as his best hope to renew contact with the broader science fiction community. In April he burned, by his own count, a million words of fiction—pages of description for the most part, for he retained another million words of plotted text and story ideas. There is no way to know how accurate these numbers are, but this was the reckoning he confessed to Jack Williamson at the time.[6] Nothing sold in the months leading up to the WorldCon, and Bradbury remained in Los Angeles.

Everything changed in August 1941, on his twenty-first birthday. Julius Schwartz and Edmond Hamilton had attended the DenCon and they continued west to spend the rest of the summer in Los Angeles, living just a few blocks from Bradbury's newspaper corner. They literally stumbled over him shortly after arriving, and Schwartz presented Bradbury with a check for "Pendulum," which had sold to *Super Science Stories* for $30.00. The transformation of this tale from its 1939 amateur publication as "The Pendulum" in *Futuria Fantasia* to a professional sale as "Pendulum" was a collaborative effort; in December 1940, Henry Hasse moved down to Los Angeles and suggested to Bradbury that they work on a few stories together. They decided to begin with "The Pendulum" in an effort to break the stalemate with Donald Wollheim and the other East Coast editors over its "reprint" status. Hasse's strength was in story development and editing; he set up a story-within-a-story frame, and added a touch of technology to Bradbury's original descriptions of the protagonist's failed time machine and his pendulum prison. The two soon sent Schwartz a rewrite with the shortened title. They split the $27.50 left after the agent's commission, and were soon gratified to see that their mutual friend Hannes Bok had drawn the story's title art for *Super Science*. Bradbury was now a paid professional, and the distinction meant the world to him.

Early Disappointments:
The Science Fiction Pulps

Through the late winter and spring of 1941 Bradbury and Hasse collaborated on four more stories, but in spite of Schwartz's continuing efforts, publication of these new tales would be a far more difficult proposition than it had been with "Pendulum." In October 1941, Schwartz finally placed "Gabriel's Horn" in the superhero pulp *Captain Future*, but even there it did not reach print until the spring 1943 issue. "Final Victim" was rejected three times by Ray Palmer for *Amazing Stories*, and Hasse, now married and living on the East Coast, began to pull back from both Bradbury and Schwartz.[1] In 1944 Hasse himself was finally able to place "Final Victim" with *Amazing Stories*, but Palmer's wartime shift from bimonthly to quarterly issues delayed publication until February 1946. Two more Bradbury-Hasse collaborations, "City of Intangibles" and "The Emotionalists," never reached print at all.

Bradbury was the first to realize that the short-lived collaboration had run its course, and in the summer of 1941 he arranged an amicable parting of the ways. Nearly thirty years later, he reflected on this relationship in an unpublished interview with his agent, Don Congdon. "Generally speaking, I'd come up with the idea first and we'd talk about it a lot and then I'd do a first draft and Henry would come in and mainly polish it, which was important—I learned about cutting, writing, from Henry that way. But I soon realized that we were a crutch for each other. He was using me as a crutch because he couldn't come up with ideas, I was using him as a crutch because I couldn't finish out a story."[2]

Fair-copy typescripts of the two unpublished Bradbury-Hasse stories survive, and in a few places show Hasse's final handwritten revisions. Although most of the collaborative work was done in earlier unlocated drafts, it's still possible in context to see how the work evolved. "The Emotionalists" is clearly a Bradbury "what if": what if Earthmen are descendents of an ancient Martian race, a highly rational and scientific culture that exiled its emotional "primitives" to Earth eons ago? And what if the last Martians, who have dwindled in numbers as their motivation for life has faded, decide that their last hope is to invade Earth and take over the "Emotionalist" inhabitants? Much of the opening technical detail and plot transitions are probably Hasse's, but the central question is clearly

Bradbury's: How do we balance scientific perfection and human values? For Bradbury, it is this balance that gives meaning to life in the modern world.

Hasse's imprint is less discernible on "City of Intangibles," a story that he had less to do with in its surviving form.[3] An Earth expedition to a star's innermost planet finds a marvelous mobile city that constantly moves just ahead of the sunrise to remain safely within the survivable temperatures of the planet's terminator line. The descendants of the original city builders are shape changers; the most effective description involves the city's caretaker-Intangible, who assumes the form of each Terran crewman in turn before revealing his true form to the expedition's commander: "But the figure had changed again, it was no one and nothing now. The face blurred like the surface of a clear stream suddenly disturbed; the features blanked out and left nothing but a dead white oval, a shimmer of energy covered the entire naked body, and the limbs seemed more frail than before . . . the figure paced away in the gloom like the going of a breeze." This eerie transformation bears all the stylistic hallmarks of a Bradbury composition.

The sole surviving typescript for "City of Intangibles" suffers from a lack of technical detail, another clue that it survives more or less as Bradbury sent it to Hasse in August 1942, with only a few points of revision penciled in Hasse's hand. But it has a continuity and structure that is superior to many of Bradbury's earlier science fiction stories and shows the effect of their original face-to-face collaborations in early and mid-1941. The true extent of that collaboration cannot be determined, yet there are significant developmental clues within these tales that point unmistakably to Bradbury alone. Although they remained unpublished, these two stories reveal early hints of the Martian culture that would begin to surface in Bradbury's stories of the mid- and late 1940s: an ancient and jaded race of shape-shifters, tired of life but nonetheless willing to defend themselves by taking on the forms and personalities of unwelcome interplanetary visitors.

Even though there is very little surviving "work-in-progress" evidence from these coauthored stories, a close study of all five of the Hasse collaborations bears out Bradbury's retrospective assessment. He was already finding his own strengths, and he would never feel the need to collaborate with other short-story writers again. Nevertheless, he had very limited success with any of his science fiction stories for the next three years. In March 1942 he sold a short "Probability Zero" contest piece to John Campbell for the July issue of *Astounding* ("Eat, Drink, and Be Wary"), but only one other Bradbury story appeared anywhere in print during the rest of the year—"The Candle," in the November 1942 issue of *Weird Tales*. It was a formula tale of the supernatural, and it gave Bradbury fits until Henry Kuttner showed him how to end it.

His break into the top-tier *Astounding* was equally tenuous. Campbell's monthly "Probability Zero" contest competition played into Bradbury's old passion for humorous anecdotes, and this diehard habit threatened to pigeonhole him in an obscure department of the field's most important magazine. Part of the problem was his enthusiasm for the more controlled humor he had discovered in the science fiction of Theodore Sturgeon and Nelson Bond. For a time he studied and imitated them, but these stories never sold.[4] Bradbury's stylistic leap into the weird tales genre was a more natural progression, but his inability to find his own ending for "The Candle" was an early indication of the trouble he would have with editors who required traditional genre fiction. Nevertheless, Bradbury would soon find his own style and his own peculiar range of off-trail subjects with a very effective and popular string of horror stories in the pages of *Weird Tales,* and the following year he extended his talent into the detective magazines as well. Not all of these stories are exceptional, but most reveal an unmistakable rise in quality.

With the exception of one actual story sale to Campbell for the September 1943 issue of *Astounding* ("Doodad"), the dozen or so science fiction stories that Julius Schwartz managed to sell for him during the war years appeared in lesser venues. He made only three sales to *Thrilling Wonder Stories* and just two more (besides the wayward Hasse collaboration on "Final Victim") to *Amazing Stories.* As descendants of the pioneering Gernsback magazines from the late 1920s, these two publications still had a certain cachet in the field, even if, under Oscar Friend's wartime editorship, *Thrilling Wonder* continued Mort Weisinger's trend toward the juvenile; but the rest of Bradbury's wartime science fiction sales went to the second-tier *Planet Stories* and such lower-echelon publications as *Astonishing Stories, Super Science Stories, Famous Fantastic Mysteries,* and the superhero story-pulp *Captain Future.* He wasn't writing the kind of scientifically grounded fiction that John Campbell wanted for *Astounding,* which had quickly become, under his editorship, the premier pulp in the science fiction field.

Campbell wanted writers who weren't afraid to be themselves, to project a style free of earlier influences. In October 1941, Campbell wrote to Jack Williamson on this point, observing that his newest *Astounding* authors—Heinlein, A. E. van Vogt, and Asimov—were his strongest contributors for just that very reason. This was a time when Williamson, Edmond Hamilton, Lester Del Rey, and Doc Smith rounded out the rest of Campbell's so-called stable of contributors for *Astounding.* Henry Kuttner broke into their ranks on a number of occasions, and he did so more frequently after his marriage to C. L. Moore led to very fine collaborations under several pseudonyms. Campbell valued Kuttner's ability to write-to-order in his solo work and found him equally valuable as a leading contributor to the fantasy-based companion magazine, *Unknown*. For *Astounding*, however, Campbell wanted adherence to the Wellsian strategy of extrapolation that had opened the door to twentieth-century science fiction, a strategy that Jack Williamson would describe in later years as "a single new premise logically and believably developed." Campbell expressed his own version in a more proscriptive way to Williamson in the fall of 1941, allowing somewhat for a wide range of styles among his writers: "Anything goes, so long as it takes one reasonable premise, one reasonable future background, and expands on those in a coherent, logical manner."

Wells resonated in a different way for Bradbury, offering an entry point to the world of ideas that was as appealing to the lover of scientific romance as it was off-putting to the hard science fiction writers and editors of the Golden Age. Four decades later, Bradbury would broaden this irony in a book review for the Los Angeles *Times*: "Wells, though less the darling of the intellectuals, was the most accurate of all those who tried their hand at guessing the future." But Bradbury's divergence from Campbell's hard science fiction writers is most clearly revealed through his abiding enthusiasm for *The Invisible Man*, which he has always loved above all other Wells titles. In more recent times, Bradbury's good friend Arthur C. Clarke observed that the significance of Wells's approach lay in his decision to downplay the hard scientific possibilities of invisibility and focus instead on the theme of invisibility as a basis for extrapolation: "If one could be invisible, then what?"[5]

Bradbury's innate attraction to wonderment and reverie, nurtured by his own experiences with literature and the visual arts, naturally focused on the same process of observing or imagining situations. Throughout his career, he attributed many of his story ideas to the simplest of thought experiments: What will a character do in a particular situation? What will happen? This approach also underlies many of Wells's most famous fictions, and explains part of Bradbury's love for these works. But in a far more significant context, Bradbury's willingness to begin each story idea with a "what if" that is completely unfettered by logical development would prove crucial to his developing writing process. The subtle example of Wells, combined with the prewriting strategies for unlocking the unconscious mind that he found in Dorothea Brande's *Becoming a Writer*, were already leading Bradbury toward a writing regimen tailored to his unique strengths as a prose stylist. He soon settled into a process of writing, revising, and submitting stories that would form the basis for a lifetime routine of creativity.

He formed these habits in a rich cross-cultural milieu as Los Angeles continued to be the destination for Americans uprooted by the final years of the depression, for Hispanic and Pacific rim immigrants, for the rapidly escalating numbers of transient military personnel, and for the increasing numbers of European intellectual refugees fleeing wartorn Europe. As these cultures mingled and sometimes clashed, Bradbury quickly became a keen observer of the fascinating range of people who constantly moved through the cross streets and boulevards of downtown Los Angeles.

The Road to Autumn's House

I'm a metaphor machine. In the nineteenth century, we had . . . Melville, Washington Irving, Nathaniel Hawthorne, Edgar Allan Poe, that's about it. And they spoke in tongues, they told stories, they told tales, they told metaphors. They had this ability—I have that. It's inborn, it cannot be taught. You can help people—say, "For Christ's sake, fill yourself up with motion pictures and poetry and essays, and art of all sorts, and just chock yourself full, and maybe they'll all collide with each other, and come out with a new metaphor." But there's no guarantee, no guarantee. — RB, 2002

8 Living in Two Worlds

Bradbury's first journey to a far metaphor may be an unpublished story title from his high-school days. "The Road to Autumn's House" is a schoolboy's vampire tale, but the title and opening lines provide a glimpse of the October Country that would emerge from his own childhood fears and desires as he created some of his most enduring stories of the mid-1940s. The title may also be perceived as a metaphor that invites an examination of his path to achieving a fully realized narrative voice of his own. His early activities with the Science Fiction League did not provide the breakthrough, nor did his two-year period of enthusiasm for the Technocracy movement. When it surfaced, his voice emerged first in his weird tales, written as he commuted between two very different neighborhoods of metropolitan Los Angeles.

In the spring of 1942 he moved with his family to Venice Beach where his father's employer, the local Bureau of Power and Light, settled them in a rental house attached to a power substation. Bradbury set up a work area in the garage, adjacent to the humming power equipment that reduced the high voltages to residential levels, and worked there off and on until his marriage in 1947. He had a variable arrangement for paying room and board to his parents right up to the time he left the double bed he shared with his brother Skip until he was twenty-seven years old. But throughout the war years he maintained a parallel writing regimen at a day-office he set up in the downtown Los Angeles tenement owned by the mother of his new friend Grant Beach. He would work there up to eight hours a day, and he sometimes spent the night there or at his Aunt Neva's home in Hollywood. Bradbury was medically disqualified for military service due to his poor eyesight; he wrote Red Cross blood drive copy for local media and settled himself into a writer's world of observation and composition. He soon set up a nearly invariable pattern of writing and revising a story each week and then sending it back East for Julie to circulate to the various New York pulp editors.

The tenement at 413 North Figueroa, situated just off the corner of Temple and Figueroa, was part of several downtown worlds that converged near that intersection. This was the approximate western edge of the original Hispanic pueblo, and the area still contained the plaza and other elements of the Sonoratown district that existed well into the twentieth century. But the Mexican Revolution of 1911 and the years of unrest that followed led to the Great Migration, and this small area of downtown Los Angeles received thousands of immigrant families. By the 1920s the new wave of settlement became known as México de Afuera, or Outer Mexico. Bradbury was about the same age as most of the children of these immigrants, and in 1942 he found himself living in the midst of their culture. It was a culture in transition, largely English-speaking yet still concentrated within the circumscribed roads that discouraged movement out and reflected the continuing segregation of the times. Downtown Los Angeles opened out south of Temple and east of Figueroa, and the Beach family's various properties were part of the older Victorian architecture of that area.[1] The rich white Angelinos had left this district generations earlier, but small businesses, clubs, and theaters attracted a wide range of customers from various cultures. Bradbury's family had lived a few miles south and west of these neighborhoods through his high-school years, in generally white working-class neighborhoods. Now he was writing and sometimes living above streets where a largely Mexican-American population also included Chinese, Filipinos, and other Asians.

The poorer neighborhoods were north along Figueroa and on beyond the city limits in the Chavez Ravine area. In 1940 parts of Chavez Ravine gave way to the Naval Reserve Armory, and the rich cultural mosaic of downtown Los Angeles faced yet another challenge as friction built between the sailors training at the Armory and some of the younger Mexican-Americans. Transient military personnel, now passing through in large numbers on their way to duty in the Pacific, were attracted to the business establishments and entertainment venues south of Temple Street, and Figueroa Boulevard provided the primary route across the Hispanic neighborhoods. The younger generation, already unwilling to accept the segregation imposed even on the native-born Mexican-Americans, resisted the new social pressure created by the military personnel who were constantly moving back and forth through the old neighborhoods.

Bradbury was by nature one who could not abide oppression of any kind, and he knew what it meant to be socially and economically isolated. He was accepted by the mixed culture of these neighborhoods and soon developed a wide range of acquaintances. Many of these people would inspire characters in his stories and novels; the three-story tenement owned by Mrs. Beach housed the endearing illegal immigrant of "I See you Never," the raggedy animal trainer "Masinello Pietro," all the young men of "The Wonderful Ice Cream Suit," and the great-hearted opera singer Fanny Florianna of his first detective novel, *Death Is a Lonely Business*. The quiet couple of "The Mice" rented an apartment in the Beach home itself, just below the ceramics studio that Bradbury had helped to build for his friend Grant. He experienced the good and the bad with these people, and sometimes there were tears as well as laughter. He never forgot the face of a young rich man sitting in a car out in front of the tenement; a few hours later the stranger was murdered in his townhouse a few blocks away, the victim of a crime that was never solved. Sometimes tragedy struck people he knew in and around the tenement itself—he never forgot the pathos and horror of a domestic homicide he witnessed, the wife crying for a priest, weeping over the dying man who had both loved and brutalized her.[2]

Bradbury experienced other terrifying moments during the so-called Pachuco riots of early June 1943. The Pachuco look was easily identifiable on the streets of Los Angeles—the zoot suits and broad-rimmed hats first associated with the flourishing jazz culture had been modified into the "drape" by some of the children of México de Afuera. This was not a widespread fashion, but some of the young men who adopted it became identified as Pachucos, a hard-to-define term generally applied to anyone who defied the continuing marginalization encountered by even more recent waves of immigration from Mexico.[3] Tensions between Mexican-American youths, many of whom did not wear the drape, and the growing numbers of servicemen stationed in the Los Angeles area first boiled over in late May 1943 along Venice Beach, just a few blocks from the Bradbury home on Venice Boulevard. The violence finally erupted on a large scale a week later, focusing on the neighborhoods between the Naval Armory and downtown Los Angeles.

Bradbury was astonished by the insanity of the situation. Much of the early rioting was centered on the intersection of Figueroa Boulevard and Alpine Street, only a few hundred yards north of Mrs. Beach's tenement. Over the weekend many of the rioting servicemen fanned out into East Los Angeles and south into the Watts neighborhood, but the last intense night of rioting played out just south of Temple along Main Street. Bradbury never forgot the fear, the unfocused hatred, and the uncontrollable events of those nights. It was in many ways a better lesson in the psychology of crowds and violence than he could ever learn from the books he was reading, and by October he had written "The Long Night," a fast-paced tenement murder mystery set in the midst of these events.

During the war years he lived and wrote in two worlds, spending many solitary daytime hours writing stories in the Beach's downtown tenement and significantly more hours out near the far end of the Red Car line, writing in the garage situated between the powerhouse and his parents' home in Venice. But the great entertainments were downtown and Bradbury's passion for the cinema led him to discover new foreign influences. In October 1942 he and Beach saw two Russian films at the Grand Theatre—The Battle for Siberia and The Golden Key, a partially animated feature known as "The Russian Pinocchio." The constantly shifting fantasy format of *The Golden Key* fascinated him with its range of live-action characters, masked children, marionettes, and stop-action miniature figures.

By contrast, the action of *The Battle for Siberia* barely interested Bradbury—he was there to hear the Dmitri Shostakovich soundtrack. He already had recordings of the Fifth and Sixth Symphonies, and the day after attending the two Russian films he listened to the first network broadcast of Shostakovich's Seventh, the newly composed "Siege of Leningrad" symphony. As the years passed, his early encounters with the works of Prokofiev, Rachmaninoff, Shostakovich, and their European precursors would continue to inspire his own basically neoromantic approach to creativity.

For a time in 1942 he joined an informal writing group sponsored by Virginia Perdue, a mystery writer he had met at the Heinleins' home the previous fall. During the brief time that he knew her, Perdue published the four mystery novels she would be most famous for, including *Alarum and Excursion*, *The Silent Stranger*, and *The Singing Clock*. She wrote for the very popular Doubleday Doran Crime Club series, and in August 1942 Perdue helped Bradbury make contact with a New York agent who specialized in the major market slick magazines.[4] Unfortunately, the timing of this opportunity was just off; he was still a year away from finishing such quality stories as "The Lake," stories that might have the legs to carry him to the major periodicals that he had unrealistically reached for on his own since his teenage years. Nevertheless, this fleeting opportunity made him realize that sooner or later, and with Julie Schwartz's blessing, he would develop enough quality stories to sign on with a major market agency.

There were four or five members in Perdue's writers' group, varying widely in both skill and background. One or two were published mystery writers like Perdue, but there was also Bradbury, in his last months as a street-corner newspaperman, and a sugar cane heiress from Hawaii. At times Perdue's critique of Bradbury's work was colored by her invalidism, for she had never recovered from a serious automobile accident years before. Bradbury unwittingly shocked her once with a story he had just written about immortality and reincarnation centered on a young boy's Midwestern experiences. The physical pain she constantly endured led her to dismiss the story out of hand. This incident made it all the more difficult for him to interact with her and the other more experienced writers, and he eventually left the group without fully developing "The Reincarnate" (it remained unpublished for more than sixty years).

The Perdue group experience didn't really help him find his own voice, and he still instinctively resisted genre formula writing. At this point Bradbury realized that if he was going to write original material, he would have to anchor his stories in what he knew better than anyone else—his own dark childhood terrors and passions. Probing these memories meant probing his subconscious mind, and his progress was hit-and-miss for a time. The experimental evidence survives in many fragment openings for abandoned stories and in unpublished poems that stand even closer to his unspoken sources of creativity. More than thirty poems survive from the war years, representing a form he would not attempt again in any systematic way for nearly two decades. Most are uncontrolled speculations about love and hate, life and death, and the gray zones in between. An exception is "god [sic] in small letters," which presents his early wariness of divine purpose with a controlled emotion reminiscent of Robert Frost or Dylan Thomas, two poets he would grow to admire:

> god in small letters.
> Don't capitalize, I ask it of you.
> One cannot believe when in one's box,
> All eaten and slick and white,
> That he (again the lower case)
> That he invented death
> As a means to pleasure.
> No. Do his name small.
> god.
> Like that.

He already knew Frost's work well and this 37-line poem continues in the controlled, almost detached tones of Frost's "Departmental" and "Design." Bradbury's concluding lines ("g-o-d- | that will be sufficient.") echo Frost's "Fire and Ice" (. . . for destruction ice | Is also great | And will suffice."). Here, at least, was influence rather than imitation—a fleeting flash of verse potential. After the war Bradbury tried, unsuccessfully, to place the poem in *The Sewanee Review*.

Other unpublished Bradbury poems seem to serve as a trying out of ideas (or perhaps afterthoughts) for such mature wartime stories as "The Emissary" and "King of the Gray Spaces." But during this time Bradbury's stories, rather than his very tentative verse, were the more fully formed children of his imagination, and he considered them to be living extensions of his own mind. In this process his typewriter became more than a tool, even more than a midwife. The almost mystical connection he felt between mind, fingertips, and keyboard went all the way back to the toy machine he had received from his parents in Tucson, and now that he was beginning to make a living from writing, the connection became even more vital to his psyche.

He carried his portable machine back and forth on the Red Car line between Venice Beach and downtown Los Angeles, but when he opened the case and set his fingers to the keys, it didn't really matter where he was. In the spring of 1942, he typed out an exercise in rhyming couplets titled "My Typewriter Wife." The governing metaphor is playful, but unmistakably establishes the machine as a partner in the creative process. He defines the workings of his "darling metal mate" in direct address, as

> A paradise of keys where stories dwell
> The characters who lurk within your womb
> That I push out, give birth, and kill, entomb,
> Line after night-black line, page after page.

The personifications that emerge from these metaphors underscore Bradbury's lifelong sense that each story he writes has a life of its own. Yet Bradbury would also continue to be deeply ambivalent about the lives of his fictions, and the images of pregnant death, entombment and disentombment in the verses of this poem rather starkly foreshadow the carnival juxtapositions of life and death that were already becoming signature elements of his fiction.

9

Reading about Writing

Bradbury's rise from raw and undisciplined talent to literary prominence was remarkably rapid. Once he discovered that he could write with conviction and power from his own hopes, fears, and experiences, he was able to find his way stylistically and break away from imitating the hallmarks of other writers. The process required a great deal of willpower and determination, but it also required the ability to discover new, more mature influences and use them in creative rather than obsessive ways. He came to these discoveries through three interrelated processes: his professional reading in the nature of authorship, his ever-widening range of literary reading, and the constructive criticism offered by other writers—trusted friends who believed in his potential from a very early age. Bradbury's texts reveal *what* changed in his work over a short period of time, and critics have told us for decades *why* this is important. But it's not clear *how* he reached his full power as a storyteller and prose stylist until one examines certain influences on authorship that he encountered between 1938 and 1944.

His professional reading can be traced back to 1938, when Bradbury purchased an unlikely high-school graduation present for himself—W. Somerset Maugham's The Summing Up. It was newly published, and it was a hard title to classify; a bright orange ribbon across the front of the dust jacket proclaimed that The Summing Up was "Not an autobiography nor a book of recollections, but the brilliant and provocative summing up of a great author's views on life and art." Maugham won him over immediately with his insistence that writers must be true to themselves above all else. Sixty-six years later, Bradbury's enthusiasm for Maugham remained centered on that maxim: "It was common sense. If you look at the book, here's a man of just straight common sense, who said, 'Go straight ahead—don't look left or right, don't listen to your friends, don't be political, don't be psychological, be yourself.' . . . A terrific man."[1]

If pressed to identify good books on writing over the years, Bradbury often included The Summing Up, for it had eventually provided the proper channel for his own strong sense of individuality. In its earliest manifestations, of course, irrepressible individuality had gotten him in trouble with science fiction fans across the country. However, Maugham's example helped him stay the course as he began to mature as a writer and as niche market editors were tempting him to slant his work for a particular perceived readership base. It was difficult at first, but Maugham's independence from genre rules and from creative conformity was, at its roots, a very healthy thing for Bradbury to hang onto. Near the end of the twentieth century, Bradbury looked back to Maugham as the source of his own method for finding a way between the perils of popular and high literary labels: "By describing the life of a writer as being in the middle of the road, half between the hack sell-outs and the literary intellectual snobs, and not participating in either of their low or high class fibs, he helped me establish myself as a true lover of writing. I went my way by myself, a lonely way but a fine one."[2]

Maugham's more direct influence on Bradbury begins with the way the older writer illuminated the periods and writers of English and European literature in *The Summing Up*. Here Maugham was the master teacher and provided Bradbury with his first glimpse of the larger literary traditions. Bradbury absorbed more from Maugham about English literature than he did about Continental writers, but he formed his own views over time. Where Maugham favored Swift among the Augustans, Bradbury eventually settled on Alexander Pope as his favorite writer from the two centuries between Shakespeare and the English Romantics.

Bradbury saw another self-reflection in *The Summing Up*—Maugham described his early personality as both pessimistic and life-affirming, a pattern that constantly surfaced in Bradbury's early work as well. Bradbury, a neo-Romantic, eventually became more optimistic on balance than Maugham, who embraced Naturalism and a belief in the entropic process. But at times Bradbury's postwar writing followed an unmistakably pessimistic arc, especially in certain dark science fiction stories of the late 1940s. This dual tendency in both writers offered an advantage in eventually fighting off the influence of literary critics. Later in life, Maugham realized that "the only thing that mattered to me in a work of art was what I thought about it." This was the lesson that Bradbury most enthusiastically took to heart from Maugham, a lesson that allowed him to detach his ego from the occasional bad reviews and even to take on the critics in such stories as "The Wonderful Death of Dudley Stone."

Finally, Maugham's definition of "reverie" in *The Summing Up* offered Bradbury a deeper look into his own creative impulses than he had ever found in print before: "Reverie is the groundwork of creative imagination; it is the privilege of the artist that with him it is not as with other men an escape from reality, but the means by which he accedes to it." During the winter of 1942–43, as Bradbury began to turn to his own life and emotions for creative inspiration, reverie became the means by which many of his characters perceived the world around them. Bradbury's appropriation of "reverie" echoed Maugham's further observation that, for the author, "His reverie is purposeful . . . it affords him the assurance of his freedom." Maugham also acknowledged the flip side of the coin, that the author may often be "unwilling to exchange its enjoyment for the drudgery and loss of execution."[3] Like Maugham, Bradbury would have to guard against this demon, as well as the demands of time, throughout his career.

Twenty years after reading *The Summing Up*, Bradbury sent the aging master a copy of his fantasy-based story collection *A Medicine for Melancholy*. In the spring of 1959 Maugham wrote back to Bradbury twice; he read the collection slowly over a three-week period and offered his unqualified endorsement: "I need not tell you that I enjoyed them. You have a very individual gift." The key words "individual gift" echoed the old Maugham maxim to be true to your own talent, and Bradbury found this comment most gratifying. Maugham's favorite story in the collection was "The Town Where No One Got Off," and he offered this closing observation in his second letter: "I have an idea that it would have given Allan Edgar Poe [sic] a peculiar satisfaction to write it himself." It was a high compliment from the 85-year-old writer, and perhaps one of his last literary judgments, for episodes of dementia would soon begin to cloud Maugham's final years.

The other key professional readings from this period focused on the writing process itself. In 1939, Bradbury read Dorothea Brande's *Becoming a Writer*, and in 1942 he read Lajos Egri's *How to Write a Play*. The following year he discovered Maren Elwood's *Characters Make Your Story*, and together these three books provided the insights by which Bradbury worked out his own maturing dynamics as a writer. The most important of the three was Brande, who maintained that the fundamental challenges facing the author are personality-based rather than issues of technique. *Becoming a Writer* is a prewriting study: "If it is successful it will teach the beginner not how to write, but how to be a writer; and that is quite another thing."[4] Brande also noted that writers of genius retain "spontaneity, the ready sensitiveness, of a child, the 'innocence of eye' that means so much to the painter," and in this observation Bradbury's fundamental genius as a writer is clearly reflected.

But the central thesis of Brande's book involves the notion that the maturing author must recognize the role of both the conscious and the unconscious mind in the creative process, and learn as well how to let these two forces work in concert. Her working metaphor appealed to Bradbury from the beginning—the concept that the writer is two-persons-in-one. Bradbury thus learned to restrain his conscious intellect, the mental component that made him a self-conscious, anxiety-ridden emulator of the masters, and to allow his creative unconscious to "flow freely and richly, bringing at demand all the treasures of memory, all the emotions, incidents, scenes, intimations of character and relationship which it has stored away in its depths"; once stimulated in this way, the conscious mind can then sort out the ideas with universal relevance from the too personal ones and begin the process of humanizing the characters. Yet the unconscious dictates the type of story and will take over from time to time as the story develops.

Brande was no Freudian and made a clear distinction between the unconscious and the subconscious, and her somewhat Jungian interest in plot and character archetypes appealed to Bradbury in ways that Freudian psychoanalysis did not. And once again, Bradbury found a writer who, like Maugham, taught him to embrace reverie: "All those naïve and satisfying dreams of which we are the unashamed heroes or heroines are the very stuff of fiction, almost the *materia prima* of fiction." Here Bradbury first learned that his hero H. G. Wells had also "led an intensive dream-life" that took other forms in his mature fictions.[5] Eventually, Bradbury developed the ability to project the insights and discoveries of reverie through the eyes of his own characters.

Many writers would have reservations about this approach, but for Bradbury, Brande's observations explained a great deal of his own tendencies and allowed him to harness them effectively. He would begin to look to his own memories for material, as he had done in high school with his dark mood piece, "The Night." And he was already learning another of Brande's points—to let the conscious mind deal with criticism from critics and rejection from editors. Some of his best and most highly regarded stories would leave a long trail of rejection slips before reaching the periodical and book-reading public because he rarely accommodated editorial views on targeted readership. This tenacity in the literary marketplace, due in large part to Bradbury's ability to shield his creativity from the trauma of rejection, was encouraged at a very early stage by Dorothea Brande.

Lajos Egri's *The Art of Dramatic Writing* has had a long history of influence on stage and story writers since its publication in 1946, but it was first published four years earlier as a shorter work titled *How to Write a Play*. Bradbury first encountered it in this shorter form between 1942 and 1944, and found it useful as a formal study of the writing process itself.[6] Egri defined the relationships between the components of all good dramatic literature—premise, character, conflict, and resolution—and demonstrated how the effective development of all the components depends in the beginning on a clearly articulated premise. By the end of 1944 he could write enthusiastically about Egri's book to his friend and mentor, Henry Kuttner: "I don't mind confessing that its simple, basic, resilient rules of dramatic and dynamic law have helped me many times in the past. He only points a direction and seems not to constrict one with irrational diagrams and rules and numbers and charts. He points out the simple realities of character, conflict and theme very successfully."[7]

Bradbury found Egri's insights on characterization very interesting, but over time he became less enthusiastic about the book's highly structured analysis of character. As he recalled more than six decades later, "He revolved around character a lot, but he was a little too technical. He made you think too much." Egri maintained that effective characters have a triune essence of physiological, sociological, and psychological dimensions, and that all characters change under the influence of conflict of one kind or another. *How to Write a Play* described the basic elements of creative writing primarily in terms of character, believing that everything should advance from a premise based on human behavior. This was a hallmark of good theater from the Renaissance on, and was akin to the standard way that horror and mystery writers work out plot and character interaction in advance. Bradbury learned a lot about human motivation from Egri's book, but he found the technical aspects of character development and plotting too constraining for his own freewheeling fantasies.

In 1943, however, Bradbury came across Maren Elwood's *Characters Make Your Story*, and found an approach to characterization that provided both a consistent strategy and a sense of freedom from traditional rules of writing. To this point he had not been able to let his characters do or say enough to advance the action of his stories and was too reliant on narrative description. Decades later, in retrospect, Bradbury recalled the single most important lesson he carried away from Elwood's book: "To let characters act, and explain themselves with action. So, instead of describing them, letting them act." In defining himself as a writer, Bradbury soon took this approach to characterization one step further—he came to believe that his characters, once created, operated on their own. It was a way of forcing his conscious mind to give way to his unconscious, and it soon became the way he would explain his writing process to the public. In countless interviews and presentations over the years, Bradbury has described the way that once an idea surfaces in his mind, the story just writes itself. This is more than a writer's mask, for success has made him a true believer. He has always been susceptible to the power of suggestion, and this gentle form of self-hypnosis is simply the way that he sustains his creativity through the first draft of nearly every story he has written since encountering Brande, Egri, and Elwood. He took a few useful points from each author as he began to find and harness his own strengths, and he eventually evolved a distinct approach to fiction; by the late 1950s, Bradbury would begin writing and publishing his own commentaries on the art of writing.

10

Early Mentors: Hamilton, Williamson, and Brackett

Brande believed that writers must take "every opportunity to study the masters of English prose writing." As he observed in an unpublished interview in 2002, Bradbury was still in the early stages of a process of literary education that ran roughly from 1934 to 1953:

> I read all the short stories in existence when I was between the ages of fourteen and thirty. And so I went to the library (I couldn't afford to buy the books) and I read all the short stories by all the great American writers, a lot of the Europeans, so that it all goes into your bloodstream. And then I read all the great essays over a period of time, and I read all the great poetry, starting back 200–300 years. So all these things go into your bloodstream, and they shouldn't be thought about, they should be part of the ambience of your character. And you learn from them secretly, then, when you write, the secrets they give you come out automatically in your writing.[1]

During the early 1940s, his own maturing reading interests were enriched from time to time by friends like Henry Kuttner, who introduced him to the fiction of Sherwood Anderson, Eudora Welty, Katherine Anne Porter, Willa Cather, Charles Jackson, and the short stories of William Faulkner. These discoveries had immediate impact—in spite of the fact that he was still terribly poor in 1942, Bradbury went out to the May Company's lending library and bought a discharged copy of Eudora Welty's A Curtain of Green for 35 cents. Kuttner also introduced him to the entertaining novels of Thorne Smith and the masterful dark fantasies of John Collier.[2] But Collier was one of Bradbury's few reading passions among the contemporary horror writers; he was beginning to turn out dark fantasies of his own by that time and kept away from the possibility of influence in that field. Consequently, he read very little of Blackwood, Coppard, Chambers, and Machen.[3] Leigh Brackett replaced his reliance on dictionaries and Hartrampf's Vocabulary with more sophisticated books for lay readers on semantics, including Stuart Chase's Tyranny of Words and Hayakawa's Language in Action. As a trigger for ideas, she loaned him the Barnes and Teeters study New Horizons in Criminology, which complemented his own discovery of Dr. Karen Horney's influential book on psychotic types.[4]

Both Kuttner and Brackett introduced Bradbury to the hard-boiled American detective writers. Bradbury fell in love with John Huston's film version of Hammett's *The Maltese Falcon* shortly after its October 1941 release, but the next year Kuttner persuaded him to read the original novel as well as *The Glass Key* and *Red Harvest*. He recommended both Hammett and James Cain to his young friend as "a counterpoint to Thomas Wolfe and such."[5] Bradbury liked Hammett to a point, but he found himself much more appreciative of Raymond Chandler. By late 1944 he was urging Kuttner to read Chandler's new essay in the *Atlantic Monthly*—the now classic study of crime fiction, "The Simple Art of Murder." Leigh Brackett had led him to Chandler's work, and his interest intensified in 1944 as she began work on the screenplay of *The Big Sleep*.

Her future husband, Edmond Hamilton, also significantly broadened Bradbury's reading horizons throughout the early 1940s. Hamilton had left college before graduating but he nonetheless had developed a formidable command of literature and history as well as a great capacity for memorization. Through him, Bradbury discovered Shakespeare's sonnets, Samuel Johnson, Alexander Pope, David Herrick, and many of the British neoclassical and Romantic poets. Hamilton also led him to Emily Dickinson, Alice Meynel, and the poems of Gerard Manley Hopkins and Robert Louis Stevenson. Together, they would go to Long Beach and survey the shelves in Acres of Books, one of the largest used bookstores in the region. But money was still tight, and most of the time Hamilton sent him to the library with reading assignments: "He recommended, then I'd go read them and come back." Beneath his reputation as a planet-smashing pulp novelist, Hamilton was deeply influenced by the Romantic tradition, and he reinforced Bradbury's own Romantic tendencies. His influence as a teacher continued until the postwar years, when Bradbury's future wife Marguerite McClure brought an equal command of poetry into his reading life.

To some degree, Ed Hamilton critiqued Bradbury's work in the early 1940s, as did Julie Schwartz. More often, though, Schwartz's long-distance comments took the form of reader responses as he concentrated on circulating and promoting Bradbury's stories in the New York pulp markets. Ross Rocklynne, who had critiqued a few of Bradbury's early stories during the 1939 NYCon, moved out to Los Angeles in 1940 and found much improvement in his young friend's work. During March 1943 Rocklynne critiqued a draft of "The Wind," and helped Bradbury through five or six drafts of "Promotion to Satellite" before that story reached print in the Fall 1943 issue of *Thrilling Wonder Stories*. The sentient storms of "The Wind" were inspired by two of Hamilton's weird tales, but Bradbury was also attracted to the sentient stars and galaxies of Rocklynne's "Into the

Darkness" series. His influence in revisions to "The Wind" may also have carried over into "The Meteors," one of the best of the unpublished Bradbury stories of the period.[6]

For a time, Bradbury received more direct feedback from Jack Williamson, one of Ed Hamilton's best friends within the far-flung science fiction writing community. In 1940 Williamson moved to Los Angeles from his native New Mexico highlands and remained there until he volunteered for military service in 1942. Bradbury was always amazed that Williamson, who had been a steady contributor to the pulps since his 1928 debut in *Amazing* at the age of twenty, would regard him as a friend. He found Williamson's fantasy and horror tales as fascinating as his science fiction; one of his reading highlights of the fall of 1940 was Williamson's now-classic werewolf novel, *Darker than You Think*.[7]

Sometimes he drove Bradbury to Robert Heinlein's Mañana Literary Society gatherings.[8] He also read Bradbury's story drafts during this period and once agreed to read the fruits of perhaps the most impractical long fiction concept that his young friend ever produced. Bradbury recently recalled Williamson's patience: "He lived about a mile away. So I trudge over to his apartment and knock on the door. He opened it, and he kept his face straight. I was there with the manuscript. Dreadful crap, you know—I wrote a novella about a totalitarian society controlled by music. It's a dumb idea, how can you control people with music? You can, up to a point—in a musical. But he read that thing and he criticized it."[9] Seventeen discarded pages from various episodes of the novella survive in the Albright Collection under the title "Black Symphony." The fragments suggest that the concept was probably influenced by Joseph O'Neill's *Land under England* (1935), which Bradbury bought in 1939. O'Neill's dystopic cave dwellers, survivors of old Roman Britain, are enslaved by means of telepathic mind control.

O'Neill's very eloquent and pointed satire (aimed at Hitler's spreading totalitarianism) struck a chord with Bradbury, but he already knew that his own variation was too uneven and fantastic to circulate. A surviving two-page fragment from "Black Symphony" offered a glimpse of things to come, however; in these pages, a teacher has broken free of the musical mind control and tries to read literature to his students. He chooses the Mad Hatter's tea party from *Alice in Wonderland*—if the students laugh, then he will have broken through the mind control. He fails, just as Montag will fail, in *Fahrenheit 451*, to reach Mildred's video-addicted girlfriends by reading them Matthew Arnold's "Dover Beach." This earliest known antecedent to a major scene from *Fahrenheit* was composed at least seven years before the next known *Fahrenheit* antecedent, the unpublished and largely lost novel *Where Ignorant Armies Clash by Night*. Small but effective scenes such as this one may explain why Williamson did not simply dismiss the largely unbelievable premise of the novella out of hand.

In spite of the uneven work displayed in "Black Symphony," Williamson saw potential in other Bradbury stories and never turned him away. Williamson no doubt sensed a kindred spirit in Bradbury, for both men shared an uneasiness in certain social situations. To some extent they were both still solitary and single-minded in their working habits, and Williamson had taken much longer to work through his own internal conflict with societal controls. Like Bradbury, Williamson found the archetype for this kind of egotism in H. G. Wells's *The Invisible Man*: "That conflict is the stuff of most fiction. I saw it in Wells, most clearly in the Invisible Man, who defies his world and dies. I think it energized all Wells's early fiction; his later work, done after he made his own successful compromises, is weaker for lack of its drama."[10] Williamson's take on Wells, so similar to Bradbury's view, sheds light on their own relationship—despite a twelve-year age difference, the established writer and the neophyte were both working through the sometimes destructive impulses of the creative ego. In 1940–41, Williamson was just finishing a successful regimen of psychoanalysis; Bradbury, who had not suffered such deep depression, continued to work through his creative challenges with his writing mentors.

From a psychological point of view, the most significant of his mentors was Leigh Brackett. She was five years older than Bradbury, and in 1940 she had just broken through with two stories in John Campbell's *Astounding Science Fiction*. Henry Kuttner had been instrumental in her breakthrough; he took time from his own writing (and from his consultations for the Laurence D'Orsay Agency) to work through drafts of her first science fiction stories. He also introduced her to the Los Angeles Science Fiction League writers and fans.[11] Brackett was an attractive tomboy from nearby Santa Monica and, like Bradbury, had grown up reading Burroughs, Haggard, and other masters of the adventure tale. She was already among the best in science fiction plot development and was branching out into westerns and detective fiction with promising results.

Brackett moved easily with the downtown SFL crowd as well as the more mature gatherings at Heinlein's Laurel Canyon home and Hamilton's bachelor's bungalow. The dynamic that soon developed between Hamilton, Brackett, and Bradbury followed an improbable course that, in retrospect, seems inevitable. In the beginning Brackett looked up to Hamilton, who had pioneered space opera and had published more well-plotted fiction than most of his peers over the previous fifteen years. In a short time, however, her own talents for story development led to success in a wide range of genre pulps and eventually in screenwriting. Although Hamilton spent most of the war years back East, their easy, noncompetitive relationship led to marriage in December 1946.

Bradbury's relationship with Brackett followed a similar but far more complex path. From the start, he looked up to her as a model of creativity who took an effective, common sense approach to story writing. She was a beach athlete with a passion for volleyball; her postcards to him were usually signed "Muscles." It was easy for Bradbury to bicycle from his parents' home in Venice Beach north along Ocean Boulevard to the Santa Monica waterfront where they met most Sundays from 1941 until the late summer of 1944, when screenwriting began to demand much of her time; privately, they called their partnership the "Santa Monica Muscles, Malts, Manuscripts and Ah Bergman and Bogart Society." Her constant drilling, like the reading assignments given by Ed Hamilton, was pivotal in Bradbury's development as an author: "Edmond Hamilton was my professor, and Leigh Brackett was my teacher. They taught on different levels. She taught me basic writing, and he taught me the classics."[12]

Ironically, her influence had a more immediate impact on his weird tales and his detective fiction than it did on his science fiction. There were lessons in plotting that he could apply immediately to the unique brand of creativity he was beginning to bring to bear in these other genres, but his science fiction was still derivative. The ideas were his own, but the stories that developed were not yet flowing from his own storehouse of imagination. He was forcing fantastic ideas into science fiction contexts, and he was not experienced enough to plot them out in convincing ways.

Not unexpectedly, Brackett herself became the major influence on his science fiction ideas, overshadowing Bradbury's earlier reading influences to a large degree. In 1951 he offered these measured reflections to both Hamilton and Brackett: "I think I owe Leigh several years out of my life for having read and helped me immeasurably with so many of my poorer stories back in 1942, 1943 and 1944. I have always realized that it was Leigh's help and friendship in those long years that turned my writing over into the black side of the ledger. My first successful sales to Planet, if you go back and read over them, were, you'll find, approximations of Brackett stories. By strengthening my plot lines and giving me direction, Leigh gave me the courage and belief in myself to later experiment and find my own forms."[13]

During these years Brackett was a dominant author in the pages of Planet Stories, and this quarterly published four of Bradbury's apprentice tales before he began to produce genuine originals in the field. Brackett's influence is most apparent in the situational challenges facing Bradbury's protagonists. Michael

Moorcock has observed that Brackett often championed the down-and-out hero caught in a situation where chances of success are slim to nonexistent,[14] and Bradbury's earliest *Planet Stories* sales share this characteristic as well—long odds face the heroes of "The Monster Maker" (Spring 1944), "Morgue Ship" (Summer 1944), "Lazarus Come Forth" (Winter 1944), and "Defense Mech" (Spring 1946). In some of Brackett's stories she also featured a disillusioned hero who unexpectedly finds new purpose and meaning in life. The reluctant heroes of her "The Stellar Legion" (1940), "Interplanetary Reporter" (1941), and "A World Is Born" (1941) resonate in the themes that Bradbury explored as he developed "Morgue Ship" and "Defense Mech" for *Planet*.

But Brackett's influence is also detectable in some of Bradbury's better science fiction. The invasive telepathic entities of Brackett's "The Demons of Darkside" (1941) probably sparked Bradbury's haunting tale "Asleep in Armageddon" (*Planet Stories*, Winter 1948); however, he would later realize that the full inspiration for his story centered more fully on Brackett's "The Sorcerer of Rhiannon," and in fact Bradbury's earliest draft of "Asleep in Armageddon" was composed shortly after the February 1942 appearance of Brackett's story in *Astounding*.[15] More speculative examples are no less intriguing. "Child of the Green Light" (1942) was probably one of the first Brackett manuscripts he read on the beach; the accelerated aging that threatens mankind in this story reached print just as Bradbury began to develop a Bergsonian thought experiment into his own time-compression tale, "Eight-Day World"—published as "The Creatures That Time Forgot" (*Planet Stories*, Fall 1946) and best known as "Frost and Fire."

The few gaps in their weekly working sessions were bridged by occasional postcards and letters. They do reveal that she critiqued his detective fiction as well as his science fiction, but there is little commentary on Bradbury's stories in her half of the correspondence, suggesting that all of the work occurred on the beach. Bradbury himself has noted on more than one occasion that her work occasionally went beyond advice; he has long credited her as the source for the opening 600 words in two of his stories—"The Scythe" and one of his first significant time travel stories, "Tomorrow and Tomorrow" (published in 1947, but composed in 1942). In both cases, he felt that he could not top her openings, and with care the transition points can be detected in both tales. He was able to return these favors during the fall of 1944 by stepping in as coauthor to write the final half of her novella "Lorelei of the Red Mist" (*Planet Stories*, Summer 1946) when she was hired by Howard Hawks to script *The Big Sleep*. They were the first to greet Ed Hamilton when he returned to the West Coast during the summer of 1946; at year's end Bradbury stood as best man when his two good friends were married.

11 "Chrysalis": Bradbury and Henry Kuttner

In terms of his overall development as a writer, Bradbury received his most intense mentoring from Henry Kuttner, one of the first professional writers that he had met when he joined the LASFL in 1937. Kuttner was a bit of an enigma—quiet, apolitical, and most of the time reticent about discussing his own work. His preference for pseudonyms slowed public recognition, and this habit exploded into even more intricate variations in bylines after his marriage to the very talented C. L. Moore in 1940; for the next eighteen years, until Kuttner's untimely death, the two wrote a wide range of collaborative stories and novels under various names. But from the beginning of his career, authors and editors in science fiction appreciated his range of work no matter what name he used in print. In the late 1930s his initial popularity in *Weird Tales* broadened into the science fiction pulps, and by the early 1940s he reached the top of the range with regular appearances in Campbell's *Astounding* as well as its newer fantasy-oriented companion magazine, *Unknown Worlds*. Later, in varying degrees of almost undetectable collaboration, the Kuttner and Moore brand of science-fantasy successfully combined Moore's vivid but controlled romanticism and Kuttner's ability to plot and pace fiction of any length.

It was Kuttner's mastery of plotting that proved most important to Bradbury, but Kuttner also passed on other lessons in his sometimes mysterious way of mentoring. At one point he got Bradbury's attention by telling him that he would kill him if he didn't stop writing purple prose. Kuttner's actual cure was only slightly less drastic than the figurative one: he made Bradbury type out stories from various science fiction pulps (especially *Amazing Stories*), word for word, and report back on the effectiveness of the plot, narrative hook, and pace of each tale.[1] He set to this onerous task out of respect for Kuttner's knowledge and experience, but soon gained valuable lessons in development from the elementary exercises. Bradbury also learned a valuable lesson about focus from Kuttner, a rather elementary lesson in behavior modification that removed one of the last aspects of immaturity from his writing habits. Thirty years later, Bradbury could still recall Kuttner's words: "You give away all your steam. No wonder you never finish your stories. You talk them all out. Shut up."[2] He soon locked into the habit of writing a first draft in a single burst of creativity—no more self-conscious discussions with other writers, no more second-guessing himself. His writing habit became a quotidian fever, rising each day without interruption from any other voices.

Bradbury never felt that Kuttner wanted to be a close friend, but he correctly sensed that this fellow graduate of Los Angeles High School believed in his potential and respected his enthusiasm. In fact, though, Kuttner's surviving letters to Bradbury from this period project a genuine friendship as well as growing professional respect, for Kuttner was apparently more easily intimate in his letters than in person. These letters, written after Kuttner entered military service in early 1942, document the first major opportunity for Bradbury as a science fiction author. By this time, the talent base of John Campbell's *Astounding* was disrupted when Robert Heinlein, Isaac Asimov, Jack Williamson, and Henry Kuttner took up wartime service of various kinds. This shift in Campbell's core author group meant that A. E. Van Vogt, Clifford Simak, Fritz Leiber, and the diminished Kuttner-Moore combination became more prominent in *Astounding*, and these were authors who, like Bradbury, were more interested in the human factor behind the machines of the future than in the workings of the machines themselves.[3]

Bradbury was aware of this situation, since his agent and his fellow writers kept him informed. But his work was still uneven at this time, and so far he had only been able to nibble around the edges of *Astounding*. With some help from his own contrived fan letters (penned under various names), he had won praise for the humorous short "Eat, Drink, and Be Wary" in the "Probability Zero" liar's tale column of the July 1942 *Astounding*. Finally, in May of 1943, Campbell bought "Doodad" for the September issue of *Astounding*, which would also include Bradbury's second and final appearance in the "Probability Zero" competition ("And Watch the Fountains"). Schwartz never indicated why the story sold, but it's possible that Campbell saw "Doodad" as an homage piece, or perhaps a respectful parody—it was, by Bradbury's own admission, a clever detective-story variation on A. E. Van Vogt's "The Weapon Shop" (Dec. 1942) and *The Weapon Makers* (Feb., Mar., Apr. 1943), highly popular *Astounding* selections that became classic "fixup" novels in the early 1950s.

But Bradbury's most significant encounter with Campbell occurred between his 1942–43 appearances in the pages of *Astounding*, and Henry Kuttner was to play the crucial role of mentor throughout this editorial adventure. In the fall of 1942, Bradbury sent Julius Schwartz a new story that seemed to have enough hard science quality to catch Campbell's interest. *Astounding*'s editor was indeed interested, but he also saw problems with length and narrative point of view and asked Schwartz to pass the story to Kuttner for a third opinion. The new story was a long one, 18,000 words at that initial stage of development, and was titled "Chrysalis."

This story would prove to be the prototype for the dark and menacing science fiction tales that Bradbury wrote with great regularity in the late 1940s and eventually brought together in both *The Martian Chronicles* and *The Illustrated Man*. Some, though, remained uncollected for decades, and "Chrysalis" itself did not appear in a Bradbury collection until *S Is for Space* (1966). In this tale, Dr. Rockwell takes charge of Smith, a comatose technician whose exposure to a new kind of radiation has caused his body to form a hard, shell-like chrysalis protecting deep and unseen changes going on within. Dr. Hartley, his initial physician, is convinced that Smith is devolving into a horrible monster, but Rockwell is certain that the radiation has triggered the next stage in human evolution. The ensuing arguments between the two scientists reveal two interwoven themes that would continue to resonate in much of Bradbury's later fiction: the hope that human evolution will allow us to reach beyond this planet and gain immortality in the stars, and the opposing fear of "Otherness" that dooms all contact with alien beings and even with future man. Rockwell's superman theory is elegantly extrapolated from Smith's blood work in the finest tradition of scientific romance, but the lack of scientific detail is offset by the suspense and misdirection provided by the tense and nearly lethal conflict between the two doctors. Hartley even attempts to murder Smith's mysterious chrysalis, revealing in the process that he himself is in the first stages of exposure. When Smith finally emerges from his chrysalis, he seems perfectly normal in every respect—a development that bewilders Hartley and deeply disappoints Rockwell. Only the reader observes Smith after he leaves Rockwell's desert clinic, moving out of sight, closing his eyes, and launching his new body slowly into outer space.

In Kuttner's words, Campbell felt that Bradbury had "mastered the mechanics of writing pretty thoroughly already."[4] But Campbell felt that the material warranted only about a 6,000-word treatment, and he was also unhappy with the multiple points of view that surfaced in the first submission. Kuttner, on the other hand, thought that the story nearly justified its length, and needed cutting only in the dialog passages that diminished the suspense generated in the first half of the story. But he also offered detailed advice on how to solve the point-of-view problem, speaking often in the plural to indicate that Kat Moore was taking an active role in this critique.[5] Initially, Bradbury's third-person narrative moved through the eyes of all the characters in succession, and even moved to Smith himself after he emerges from his chrysalis. This approach gave away too much too early, and in successive drafts Bradbury shifted the third-person point of view almost entirely to the limited omniscience of Rockwell.

It was an important but complicated learning process, and Bradbury occasionally objected to limiting the story to a single viewpoint—it seemed too much of a concession to Campbell, who bound his writers over to many of his own writing conventions. Kuttner advised Bradbury to take the long view: "When you write for Campbell, never use the superman's viewpoint. He objects, feeling that a human can't write about a superhuman except indirectly. In other, less specialized cases, use your own judgment . . . Rules are made for one purpose: because if you follow them, you're taking the easiest path. Maugham or Cain can use several viewpoints and do it well; but it's harder for less experienced writers."[6]

As a young writer, Bradbury was learning to walk the line between unrestrained individualism and the effective use of technique. Kuttner, like Brackett, could show Bradbury how to follow a method without surrendering creativity and soon confided as much to his young friend: "I object to forced rules in writing. They tend toward artificiality. Stick to the rules, but vary from them when it seems best for story value. I myself figure I learned the principles only so I could forget them when necessary."[7]

Even after months of revision that brought "Chrysalis" down to 8,000 words, Campbell still felt that it was too long for what the material warranted, and he never bought the story. But it was now a fine science fiction tale, and in January 1944 it sold to *Amazing Stories*, where it appeared, after the wartime backlog cleared, in the July 1946 issue. The cross-country distances between the two writers made it impractical to work closely on other story drafts, but Kuttner would continue to offer significant feedback on Bradbury's published horror and science fiction stories until 1946. Then, like Leigh Brackett, Kuttner could see that his job was done. Bradbury went on to write excellent dark science fantasies of his own in the late 1940s and has acknowledged that two of his best-known tales of this period, "Zero Hour" and "The Veldt," also owe a great deal to the Kuttner-Moore influence in terms of tone and shock effect. In a very real sense, Henry Kuttner encouraged Bradbury to write some of the best science fiction that he would attempt outside of the *Martian Chronicles* group of stories. He now had the ability to focus on writing instead of talking about writing and to channel his passion into an effective writing regimen. In later years, this became a mantra for him: "You've got to save that passion—don't talk about it, go do it, and don't intellectualize it. Don't plan ahead, but surprise yourself."[8]

There would be some regressions, especially with his science fiction stories, but during the war years he was in the midst of a rapid and unmistakable rise in the quality and appeal of his writing. The first quality stories would emerge from his typewriter keyboard more quickly than his publishing record has ever revealed. And at the same time, Bradbury's own reading of literature would broaden out in unexpected ways. The barest outline of this reading record can be found here and there in some of his published interviews. His unpublished correspondence and the often signed and dated volumes in his personal library, however, illuminate a far greater portion of his wartime reading discoveries. Bradbury's evolving method for generating ideas and his constantly expanding reading life are inextricably woven together throughout the war years; under examination, these elements of his intellectual life reveal the inner makings of a largely self-educated writer during his most crucial period of development.

12 A New World of Reading

Once Bradbury began to tap into his reservoir of life experiences, he had the basis to sustain and advance his own evolving style and vivid metaphors. He had always had a gift for metaphor, a gift enhanced from the beginning of his career by his fascination with sensate experience. During those years Bradbury accumulated scientific books that helped him convey sensation: "Books on the olfactory sense, books on the construction of the eye and the phenomena of seeing, books on the ear, books on the tactile sense. So I educated myself to all of my senses, and that's one of the reasons why my books are memorable, because I make you reach out with your hand, and with your nose, and with your ears, and with your eye, and with your tongue."[1]

The road to all his mature fiction was paved to a large extent by a great wartime shift in his personal reading agenda. The most surprising transition in his reading is also the least known—his sudden and permanent shift away from reading new science fiction sometime in 1944. Within the genre he continued to read only work by Brackett, Hamilton, Ted Sturgeon, Nelson Bond, the now almost inseparable blend of Kuttner-Moore, and Fritz Leiber, whose early fantasies for *Unknown* and his novel *Gather, Darkness!*, featured in the May 1943 *Astounding*, had already become Bradbury favorites. He developed an enthusiastic friendship with Leiber at war's end, finding in Leiber's fiction the same blurring of distinctions between fantasy and science fiction that he admired in the work of Brackett, Kuttner, and Moore. Even these very selective readings in the work of his peers diminished in a few more years; there was no arrogance in this, only a need to find his own way as his unique approach to writing fiction continued to mature. Bradbury maintained an abiding enthusiasm for light horror and dark fantasy, but for the most part he concentrated on extending his reading of mainstream modern and contemporary British and American authors in all genres during the final years of World War II and beyond.

He navigated from discovery to discovery by browsing bookstores and by reading the prize story annuals published by Martha Foley and other editors. By 1944 he was also reading books and anthologies recommended by Arkham House editor August Derleth, who was now following Bradbury's career in *Weird Tales* with great interest. Over the next several years Derleth would solicit and publish

Dark Carnival, Bradbury's first story collection, and although Bradbury would quickly grow beyond Derleth's world, his early letters to his newfound publisher reveal much about his broadening reading and maturing tastes in literature. As he worked more deeply into the canon of certain authors, he developed the ability to make comparative judgments. He had spent precious earnings to purchase Eudora Welty's *A Curtain of Green* two years earlier, but by the summer of 1944 he found her next collection, *The Wide Net*, to be "bewildering and confusing." For the first time, he turned to a literary journal—*The Kenyon Review*—to validate his opinions of contemporary fiction, and he gained confidence in finding that experienced reviewers came to similar conclusions about Welty's latest work. He began to read the *Saturday Review of Literature* with great regularity during his bookstore evenings and began to learn more about the enduring qualities of literature from the SRL essays of Clifton Fadiman.

In July Bradbury bought and read a secondhand copy of *Roundup: The Stories of Ring Lardner*. He also read the stories of Jesse Stuart, finding them "immensely human, amusing, and vital," and later that summer he consumed two volumes of stories by Katherine Anne Porter, *Flowering Judas* and *The Leaning Tower*. He found her stories incredibly stimulating and felt that Porter's advantage over the still-developing Eudora Welty was the result of a "surer, finer, more polished approach and style resulting from her long, leisurely years at the craft." Both Derleth and Henry Kuttner had recommended Porter, but Kuttner remained the stronger influence when it came to recommending mainstream novels and stories. In addition to Porter and Welty, Kuttner had recommended Willa Cather and Sherwood Anderson. As the summer of 1944 progressed, Bradbury continued to read these major authors as well as the work of Sinclair Lewis, Ernest Hemingway, and John Dos Passos. For some of the American masters, he went to the significant expense of purchasing older works that had stood the test of time. In August he bought two early Steinbeck novels, *To a God Unknown* and *Tortilla Flat*. In September he secured a portable Modern Library edition of Anderson's *Winesburg, Ohio*. In October he sealed his love for the late Thomas Wolfe by purchasing *The Face of the Nation*, a posthumous compilation of Wolfe's most poetic prose passages from the four novels that would come to represent his major canon works.

This was not the first time that Bradbury bought a topical compilation to accelerate his command of a beloved writer. These Bartlett-like collections operated, in a most Bradburyian way, as surrogate teachers. Two years earlier, during the summer of 1942, he had purchased a similar volume of Shakespearean quotations topically arranged and indexed by the eminent British scholar and stage director George Rylands. *William Shakespeare: The Ages of Man* offered him a way to study Shakespeare's core ideas far more effectively than *Hartrampf's Vocabulary* had offered a younger Bradbury a way to study the English language or Mortimer Adler's *How to Read a Book* had offered him ways to read for content. He was once again schooling himself, but he was also trying out a memory-based approach to the transmission of literature. From here, it would take only a small leap of the imagination to fashion the book people of *Fahrenheit 451*.

As the summer of 1944 progressed, Bradbury went on to read a number of titles by contemporary writers of less critical acclaim than Hemingway and Steinbeck, including such Kuttner recommendations as Charles Jackson's *The Lost Weekend*, E. B. White's *One Man's Meat*, and Thorne Smith's final and perhaps most delightfully absurd novel, *Rain in the Doorway*. Bradbury read *The Lost Weekend* fully a year before Billy Wilder's Academy Award–winning film made the central character, if not the novel, a cultural archetype. But Bradbury found Jackson's next best-selling book, *Brainstorm*, disappointing; in spite of his single-minded desire to become a best-selling author in his own right, he was now sophisticated enough to realize that excellent sales do not always reflect enduring literary qualities. Neither Kuttner nor Bradbury liked the best sellers *Mildred Pierce* or Kathleen Windsor's *Forever Amber*, although Bradbury read only the first three pages of the latter title before placing it back on the bookstore shelf. Bradbury was also disappointed by Lloyd Douglas's *The Robe* and Franz Werfel's "recent metaphysical journeys." His love of exotic fiction also became more discriminating but was no less central to his reading passions, and as he read the major works of American and British fiction he also enjoyed Richard Hughes's child's-eye view of piracy, *A High Wind in Jamaica*.[2]

Bradbury's summer 1944 reading strategies were validated and perhaps focused by the August 5 *Saturday Review of Literature*. It was, in fact, the *Review's* twentieth anniversary issue, and it offered a ranking of the midcentury American novelists as well as survey articles of the nation's major literary and scientific writers. This issue offered a broader perspective on earlier articles that attacked (Bernard DeVoto) and defended (Sinclair Lewis) the American writers of the interwar period. The *Saturday Review of Literature* provided content for some of his letters to Derleth, Kuttner, and even Julius Schwartz, whose high-school friend Norman Cousins was now editor-in-chief. Cousins had been responsible for much of the *Review's* wartime growth, and in its pages Bradbury found crucial context for the ideas he was forming about contemporary American fiction.

There were other literary judgments to consult, of course, and Martha Foley's *Best American Short Stories of 1944* and other anthologies allowed Bradbury to cast an even wider reading net. This strategy formed a large part of his plan to read the short stories of well-known contemporary writers. Foley's 1944 collection seemed to Bradbury to be the best of the series so far; he was most taken by Gladys Schmitt's "All Souls'," Lionel Trilling's "Of This Time, of That Place," and "the charm and quaint economy of Jessamyn West's 'The Illumination.'" Even before finishing the volume, he also commented to Derleth about the selections by Edita Morris and Dorothy Canfield; clearly, Foley's policy of moving beyond the male-dominated lists of "great authors" helped Bradbury to appreciate a wider range of writers from the earliest days of his professional career. Over the decades Porter, Welty, and West all remained perennial favorites on his reading list. The simplicity and directness of West in particular appealed to him, as did her kindred spirit as another author with Midwestern roots. During these years he also came to appreciate the works of Edith Sitwell and, to a point, Karen Blixen, writing as Isak Dinesen, whose novels and stories he found fascinating but too rococo to become a reading passion for him.[3]

Not all of his reading was mainstream; he read westerns (but saw more on screen than he read), yet the one he loved the most transcended its genre boundaries. Walter Van Tilburg Clark's *The Oxbow Incident* reinforced his own desire for integrity of authorship—there were deeper psychological insights here than in the formula western, thoroughly grounded in real-life situations. Bradbury's highly emotional response to the novel was centered on the way that Clark reversed the western formula by showing the complex trail into authoritarian tragedy that touched both the historical West's frontier violence and the present world's drift into total war. Bradbury would follow similar reversals of convention in the horror and weird tales that emerged from his unique fantasy landscape during and after the war years.

Darker fictions also continued to interest him as a reader. He read Derleth's Arkham House anthologies *Beyond the Wall of Sleep* and *Sleep No More*, and was deeply gratified to see his own story "The Lake" selected for Derleth's Rinehart horror anthology *Who Knocks?* He was also finding that the inspiration for his dark stories drew at least as much from the more subtle tradition of terror tales as it did from the sometimes gruesome hallmarks of horror. This distinction was what Bradbury appreciated most in the films of Val Lewton, whose innovative genre movies produced for RKO offered something different from the archetypal monster horrors that Lewton was expected to produce. Instead of trying to follow the horror formula that was working so well for the rival Universal Studio, Lewton worked with RKO directors such as Jacques Tourneur to produce terrifying films where the title creature is seldom directly seen.

Bradbury was impressed by Lewton's first three films, all directed by Tourneur: *Cat People* (1942), *I Walked with a Zombie* (1943), and *The Leopard Man* (1943). Between 1942 and 1946 Lewton produced (and to varying degrees wrote) nine significant terror films that were perfect examples of the minimum of suggestion that Bradbury was beginning to develop in his own narrative fiction. Bradbury considered *Isle of the Dead* to be the perfect example of Lewton's plot strategy: "[He] made you wait for an hour, for the one scene that *counted*. . . . There's only one moment that terrifies you, but the rest is leading up to that."[4] Lewton is perhaps best remembered as the filmmaker who left much of the terror to the viewer's imagination, and this would be a quality that Bradbury would strive for, sometimes unevenly but more and more effectively over time, in his best dark tales.

Bradbury was also beginning to discover new masters of narrative terror, and the greatest of these wartime discoveries was Cornell Woolrich. During the 1940s Bradbury rarely missed an issue of *Ellery Queen's Mystery Magazine*, and he discovered Woolrich in the fall 1941 issue, which contained a reprint of "Dime a Dance." Woolrich began to show the full possibilities of noir terror in the series of crime novels that he wrote (under various names) throughout the 1940s, and Bradbury followed his Hollywood successes as well. *Black Alibi* (1942) was soon transformed into Val Lewton's classic terror film *The Leopard Man* (another Bradbury favorite). Over the next five years, Bradbury saw at least seven more films adapted from Woolrich's mid-1940s fiction, but he found the novels even more frightening—he later described them to William F. Nolan as masterpieces of suspense, mood, and character development.[5]

He read Woolrich's novels through *Rendezvous in Black* (1948), and this novel is probably the best example of the Woolrich plot formula: the protagonist's fiancée is killed the day before their wedding while walking to their usual rendezvous, but the cause is as shocking and unexpected as the result—an empty whiskey bottle, dropped from a chartered airplane by a group of drunken businessmen returning from a hunting trip, kills her as she crosses the street. The authorities consider it a terrible and untraceable accident, but the grieving protagonist spends years identifying the businessmen and exacting his own special revenge on each one. *Rendezvous in Black* is not a well-known title today, but Bradbury has remembered the plot across six decades. It was the unexpected, terrifying turn in the everyday lives of everyday people that Bradbury found so fascinating in Woolrich's fiction; he would carry off similar effects in some of his own very unique crime stories of the mid-1940s.

Crime fiction, however, was only a transitional phase in Bradbury's growing development as a fantasy writer. He was not prepared, nor really even suited, to write in this dark vein forever. But a few of the best "light" horror and fantasy writers of this period provided reinforcement for the credo that was beginning to form in his own mind—a growing conviction that fantasy, good fantasy, provided a much needed contrast and relief from the dark realities of our age. His most significant discoveries of the 1940s included the gentle fantasies of Robert Nathan, whose work was skillfully translated to screen during the 1940s in such films as *The Bishop's Wife* and *Portrait of Jenny*. By far the greatest influence in this tradition, however, was John Collier. In 1942, in one of his frequent excursions through the books that had been discarded from the Macy Company's store library, he purchased a copy of Collier's story collection *Presenting Moonshine* for twenty-five cents. During his summer 1944 reading rampage, he purchased the more comprehensive collection *A Touch of Nutmeg and More Unlikely Stories by John Collier*.

Six decades later, in his 2003 introduction to a new edition of *Fancies and Goodnights* (by far Collier's most popular and enduring collection), Bradbury observed that Collier's stories are deliberately set in an artificial world remote from social arguments: "The stories here are not serious, and thank God for that. We live in a world that has grown too serious, and we are inundated with sad news." In a 1972 review of Knopf's *The John Collier Reader*, Bradbury was even more pointed in his charge: "This book is not relevant, thank God, except to the condition of human wit, the comedy of expectations run afoul, and the beauty of those fantasies that explain reality better than the realist ever can."[6] Throughout his career, Bradbury would both defend and practice the carnival tradition in literature as a relief from realism and naturalism. He felt that one of Collier's main strengths rested in the way he "saw the irony in human encounters and the fun in putting it down." It was a quality that Bradbury would also appreciate in the work of Roald Dahl, Shirley Jackson, Nigel Kneale, and Stanley Ellin—authors that he would eventually anthologize or adapt for television during the 1950s.

13 An Emerging Sense of Critical Judgment

Even as he took the first steps toward defining himself more broadly as a fantasy writer, Bradbury continued to read and study the great fiction writers of his time. In 1943, still not earning enough from his stories to owe income tax, he had purchased a copy of Hemingway's *To Have and Have Not*. During July 1944, he began to work systematically through the short stories of Hemingway, and found it tough going at times. His comments to Derleth indicate that Bradbury, reading without the perspective of postsecondary literary studies, had trouble maintaining objectivity in assessing an author's work. For Bradbury, the literary work and the author were always one inseparable entity, a conviction that went all the way back to his earliest association of love, security, creativity, and imagination with the libraries that preserve literature. This would always be the main point of distinction between Bradbury and the Modernist ideal of impersonality in fiction—for the High Modernists, the author was expected to disappear into the work. By contrast, Bradbury's own view was that the literary work is the expression of the author. In terms of style, mood, character, and content, Bradbury would always demand the tangible presence of the author, and therefore he was at his best in judging the hallmarks of the Romantic classics.

Early in his career, this close association of author and work interfered with his ability to compare or rank more contemporary writers effectively; he confided to Derleth that at times he preferred "the somewhat diluted brutalisms, sadisms and morbidities" of James M. Cain's *Serenade* to the Hemingway stories. He was looking for a glimpse of the author's soul in every word he read, a method that might drive less impassioned readers to distraction. But this approach was already leading Bradbury to explore the inner workings of the author's mind: "Hemingway strikes me as a man who has a steel grip on his mind and is afraid to let go, for fear of finding out that he is nothing but some species of lovable, sentimental, ordinary jelly-fish underneath. He seems a little too preoccupied with being hard, and that fairly well indicates a lot of secret goings-on in his mental life."

He was only guessing at the vulnerabilities beneath the stoic exterior of Hemingway's prose, but he would soon realize that the fear of random violence, the unexpected wound or injury that negates all the strengths of character and experience, was closer to the mark. Over time, Bradbury developed a more mature sense of the complexities of Hemingway's life, and understood better than most how physical pain from an accumulation of such injuries muted Hemingway's creativity. But even in the mid-1940s, Bradbury was beginning to see the price that many of his new reading loves paid for the fame that they enjoyed. He read Steinbeck's *Cannery Row*, *The Moon Is Down*, and *The Pearl*, sensing that one of his favorite prewar authors was in eclipse, if not decline. He knew of Steinbeck's marital troubles and drinking, and he also knew that others paid a similar price for fame. Leigh Brackett, who worked with William Faulkner on the screenplay of *The Big Sleep*, had told Bradbury of the great writer's extended and solitary drinking. Late in 1945, he would remark to Derleth, "God, are there no *happy* big-time writers?"

Another one of his new reading passions had health problems of a different sort. Aldous Huxley was now in his mid-40s, but a corneal infection at the age of sixteen had led to keratitis punctata and permanently impaired eyesight. Bradbury was greatly interested in the British and European expatriate writers who settled in Southern California before and during the war, and he absorbed Huxley extensively; in the years after high school he read the principal works, including *Antic Hay*, *Eyeless in Gaza*, and Huxley's first "American" novel, *After Many a Summer Dies the Swan*. The last novel's philosophical exploration of individualism would play into Bradbury's own search for authorial identity, but Bradbury soon discovered an odd little book that Huxley published in the fall of 1942, *The Art of Seeing*.

This slim volume offered a discussion of the Bates method of eye treatment framed within the context of Huxley's own success with Bates exercises in improving his own damaged vision. Bradbury was instantly fascinated by the Bates premise, as explained by Huxley, that sight is linked to both the physiology of the body and the psychological processes of the mind. The exercises were promoted as relevant to most ocular impairments, and even though Huxley was by nature farsighted and Bradbury nearsighted, *The Art of Seeing* offered Bradbury a way to overcome one of his greatest fears as a writer—the fear of blindness that had haunted him since his earliest years. He soon discovered that Huxley's eye therapist lived just a few blocks away on Venice Boulevard, and he contacted her for screening. He responded well to the initial testing and preliminary exercises—not because of any physiological factors, but largely because of his strong susceptibility to the power of suggestion. The Bates system was based on relaxation exercises that were closely related to the technique of self-hypnosis, so Bradbury was, in effect, relieving stress and anxiety as well as resting his eyes. Huxley's instructor referred him to Olive Brown, who eventually wrote her own testamentary book on the method; for six months in 1944–45, Bradbury worked with her to strengthen his eyes and to learn how to relax before continuing on his own to round out a full year of therapy.

Even though no permanent improvement resulted, his eyesight stabilized—his vision had grown progressively weaker from age eleven to twenty-four, but he would never need a revised prescription for the rest of his life.[1] There is, of course, no provable medical connection, but there's no doubt that this year of daily relaxation and sunning stimulated his creative muse. At Christmas, Bradbury noted in a letter to Henry Kuttner that he'd had "a helluva swell time during the past year discovering all kinds of art forms in my relaxation periods." He enjoyed Matisse and Dali and was beginning to appreciate the work of Van Gogh, which he had previously detested. He was now able to understand Picasso's work, although he found the more recent pieces featured in *Life* magazine to be a disappointment. The relaxation periods also led him to work more often in the ceramics studio he had helped to build for Grant Beach: "I've done some water colors, sculptured some strange little modernistic men and women in clay, designed some interesting plates and painted their motifs in underglaze. . . ." The Bates method was never accepted in mainstream ophthalmology, but Bradbury's discovery of it through Huxley's *The Art of Seeing* sparked experiments in painting that would continue for the rest of his life.

Bradbury found Huxley's next book, the novel *Time Must Have a Stop*, to be more bewildering than stimulating. It was perhaps too short a book to accommodate everything Huxley intended with the plot, and Bradbury sensed this from the moment he read the liner notes. He explained his reaction to both the "blurb" and the novel itself to Kuttner: "I wondered how in hell he could accomplish the transition from Sebastian the boy to Sebastian the man in three hundred pages. He didn't. The abrupt transition in the last chapter, from boy to man, was quite a jolt for me, anyway, and the book did not convince me of a darn thing." His almost boyish way of expressing criticism still surfaced at times in his correspondence, but he had nonetheless hit on the novel's major structural flaw. Bradbury also confided to both Derleth and Kuttner that he did not understand Huxley's metaphysics. This would become less of a problem as Bradbury came to understand the Eastward-turning philosophy of Huxley's close friends, Gerald Heard and Christopher Isherwood; for now, though, he received a copy of *Brave New World* for Christmas 1944, and this gift, along with his subsequent reading of Huxley's essays and later novels, solidified Huxley's place in Bradbury's pantheon of authors.

Bradbury was beginning to understand some aspects of the great turn-of-the-century changes in American literature that led from romanticism to realism and on to the more subjective experiments of Modernism. He was also beginning to sense the earlier but parallel transitions in modern art into such subjective forms as impressionism, expressionism, and surrealism. Yet he remained unfamiliar with many of the Continental writers of that crucial transitional period, and had not yet read many European writers of any period. Kuttner suggested Rousseau as a philosophical foundation, and Bradbury agreed to "look him up," shorthand for a trip to the public library's encyclopedias. The great exception, however, was Thomas Mann. Bradbury revered all Nobel laureates, and was fascinated that Mann was living in Santa Monica, just a few miles up the shoreline from his parents' home in Venice Beach. His love of short fiction led him to Mann's shorter works first; by early 1945 he had read English language editions of two of Mann's best-known novellas, *Death in Venice* and the antifascist *Mario and the Magician*.[2]

Kuttner introduced him to the pastoral and pantheistic fantasies of Jean Giono, who wrote about country life in the Provence region of southern France. By 1950 Bradbury would find the contemporary fantasies and children's stories of Marcel Aymé more interesting, but during the war few European writers other than Mann, Giono, and Arthur Koestler caught his interest.[3] By contrast, his knowledge of contemporary American fiction was rapidly expanding through his new reading regimens, and he was learning more and more how to discriminate among the contemporary mainstream writers. During the war years, he began to sense that Frederic Prokosch, one of his first contemporary favorites, would settle into an obscurity that his popularity with readers and authors did not yet reflect.

Prokosch had everything that Bradbury had initially wanted for himself when he dreamed of becoming a writer during and just after high school. His first two novels, *The Asiatics* (1935) and *The Seven Who Fled* (1937), were intoxicating tales of Western travelers passing through the exotic lands of Asia after the First World War, just as cracks began to appear in the European colonial empires of the East. Endorsements by Mann and André Gide, along with strong marketing from his publisher (*The Seven Who Fled* won the 1937–38 Harper Prize), led to great critical acclaim in America and overseas. His quick succession of novels and poetry volumes was rewarded by a 1937 Guggenheim Fellowship for creative writing.

Few contemporary novelists meant as much to Bradbury in the years after high school; the dark prewar broodings about modern civilization that surfaced in the final chapters of *The Asiatics* struck a chord with him, and as early as 1940 the novel had provided both mood and character motivation for "The Piper," perhaps Bradbury's best fanzine tale. Prokosch lays out his mystical novel through the eyes of a young and well-educated but penniless American who has traveled from the Middle East all the way across Asia to Indochina, relying solely on luck and the kindness of strangers. By novel's end, the subtle and often deadly colonial frictions between East and West that shape all of the nameless narrator's travel adventures are overshadowed by an even darker view of man's fate. The dying Dutchman De Hahn, who has crossed paths with the American traveler throughout the novel, offers a broader interpretation of the death and suffering that has defined the largest continent all through its history: "We're all Asiatics. . . . We're lost, the race is dying. What's ahead for us except a dark age? . . . Yes, that's what I see at the end of this sinister tunnel. Darkness. The dark ages coming over us like an ocean. These voices of warning and exhortation and disgust that you hear everywhere, what are they but sighs before the real storm arrives?"[4]

Bradbury's own voice of "warning and exhortation" became manifest in the Piper, a character that he transformed from his initial 1940 fanzine version (a Venusian exile living on Mars) to his far darker 1943 prozine form as the last Martian, returning from exile to seek revenge on the alien colonial masters who destroyed his people. His piping calls up primitive creatures from beneath the Martian surface that are literally dark and shapeless manifestations of Prokosch's dark ages. There is clearly less of Blake's Romantic "Piper" in Bradbury's final version and more of the darkness that Bradbury absorbed from Prokosch's first two novels. Indeed, the fatalism of The Asiatics, almost Conradian in its subtlety, is grimly reinforced by the nihilism of The Seven Who Fled. These seven Europeans, political refugees who must travel from Chinese Turkestan across the high deserts, barren plateaus, and towering mountain ranges of Central Asia toward various sinister and elusive outposts of civilization are almost all killed or enslaved by the despair, indifference, and will to dominate that represent (at least in the West) consequences of the Modernist crisis-of-values. As the rumors of war that inform both novels turned into the actual flashpoints of World War II, Bradbury responded with his own lament for a world that had lost its ability to reason, to love, or to know joy. In terms of mood and purpose, "The Piper" reflected the influence of Prokosch in ways that Bradbury could easily recall nearly sixty years later:

He was very ornate in many ways, very mandarin, very strange. He was otherworldly, he "traveled" all over the Far East, to places he'd never been. And later on, when he [actually] traveled, his novels got less interesting. The imaginings of a writer are more important than the realistic stuff they do. And he was a good example of that. He was romantic, he took me to the Far East, he took me all over China, the Middle East, Iran, Iraq, Persia, and I think "The Piper" was influenced by his romanticism. It was Mars, in a way. So my Mars, and my environment in "The Piper," is pure Frederic Prokosch.[5]

Although William Blake's piper still provides the dominant image of the story, the modernist themes of exile and loss of the homeland and its cultural past undoubtedly derive from Prokosch. "The Piper" certainly reflected recent history, but it also ran against Bradbury's neo-Romantic impulse to somehow create a new mythology to live by in the modern world. Therefore it was, perhaps, more important for Bradbury to break away from Prokosch's influence than it had been, a few years earlier, to break away from the stylistic influence of Poe and Lovecraft and Burroughs. Bradbury had none of the advantages or education that Prokosch had turned to popular fame, and in 1949 he failed in his own attempt to win the Guggenheim Fellowship for creative writing that had come so easily to Prokosch a dozen years earlier.

Clearly, Bradbury was fascinated by the way that Prokosch's unrelieved darkness played out in the novels; he even named the protagonist of "Pendulum" after Layeville, one of The Seven Who Fled. But he could not linger in this darkness himself—his own reveries and stream of consciousness were very different, at once fearing death but always affirming life. Bradbury was still several years away from discovering that he was not of the temperament of the Modernist world that Prokosch had been privy to from birth. He was a neo-Romantic at heart, in many ways self-educated, but he soon saw that Prokosch's style and sensibilities were not his own. The influence would continue to echo in subtle ways, however; "The Piper" was the first of several masks—some literal, others metaphorical—that Bradbury would develop in the early postwar years to work out his frustrations with a world that seemed to be unraveling in front of his eyes. For now, though, he was able to avoid the trap before it pulled him in. This had been his first serious skirmish with Modernism.

The systematic reading that he had begun under the mentorship of Leigh Brackett, Edmond Hamilton, and Henry Kuttner had become, as the war entered its final year, a more elaborate plan that incorporated the recommendations of literary critics, literary magazines, and major anthology editors. Bradbury continued to write every day, composing through the morning hours, usually revising in the afternoons. But his relaxation periods, initially undertaken as part of the Bates eye exercises, opened up more time for reading and broader artistic studies. The library continued to be his college, and at the end of 1944 he summarized his plans to Kuttner in this way: "All in all, I'm trying to give myself a liberal education in politics, psychology and art. I've often wondered whether attending college would help my writing, but, from what I read, more good talent is broken in short story classes, than is ever made."

14 On the Shoulders of Giants

There were Modernists who appealed to Bradbury in more mature ways than Prokosch had done, and there were in fact abiding lessons that he could take away from some of these other writers. The lessons that Bradbury had learned just after high school by reading Somerset Maugham's autobiographical *The Summing Up* led him quite naturally into Maugham's fiction, and he would eventually purchase more than forty volumes of Maugham's novels and stories. Sometime between 1938 and 1944, he read *The Painted Veil* (1925), and it remains his favorite above all other Maugham titles.

In its subject, *The Painted Veil* was, like the Prokosch novels, a close study of the mysterious East. What Bradbury discovered in Maugham's sense of the Far East extended themes he had found in Prokosch and in Joseph Conrad—the concept of Otherness, an Otherness so different that it defies understanding by the uninitiated. Bradbury was also inspired by Maugham's narrative technique; the eighty-chapter sequence that shapes this rather short novel foreshadows the chapter dynamics that Bradbury would use in writing his own mid- and late-career full-length novels. As early as 1947, Bradbury typed a brief but very telling narrative mantra: "Keep chapters to FOUR pages. No more than EIGHT pages. The purpose of a chapter is to contain ONE IDEA! And ONLY one! See Jane Austen! See Tolstoy, Dostoevsky!"[1]

Maugham's *The Painted Veil* also illuminates the subjects that Bradbury would turn to in the years immediately following World War II—the exploration of marriage and the psychological intricacies at work in any domestic relationship. Through writers like Maugham and Hemingway, Bradbury would find the encouragement to create his own stories of men and women and their relationships; within a few years, his carefully crafted third-person narrative of a loveless marriage produced two first-rate interlocking stories in this tradition—"The Next in Line" and "Interval in Sunlight."

During 1942 Bradbury encountered the even more subjectively narrated *Thunder on the Left* by the American critic and novelist Christopher Morley. The third-person narrative of this novel shifts between various couples and single adults who return to a favorite childhood vacation estate to find, unexpectedly, that time has taken a great toll on both the memories and the relationships that the vacationers collectively share. Bradbury loved the elements of fantasy woven into the limited omniscience of each vacationer, and the unconditional endorsement he offered to Edmond Hamilton rings true beneath the self-conscious and unsophisticated style he adapted when venturing a literary opinion to one of his mentors: "It's one of the neatest human documents, interspersed with fantasy, I've ever read. Morley has a fine sympathetic ability for psychiatric detail, he portrays the human frailties so well, I'm certain you'll remember the yarn long after you've read it."[2] Morley's subject matter would have its greatest impact on Bradbury's Green Town trilogy of novels and novelized story cycles, but Thunder on the Left, like The Painted Veil, also provided Bradbury with narrative insights as he turned to the very different style of domestic fictions that he would write throughout the late 1940s and early 1950s.

The narrative models provided by Maugham and Morley were reinforced by Thornton Wilder's The Cabala (1926), a novel that Bradbury read shortly after high school and reread, by his own admission, eight or nine times over the years.[3] It was Wilder's first novel, full of exotic characters inspired by his year as a student of archaeology at the American Academy in Rome. As the novel progresses, there is the implication that the members of the cabal are modern shades of the Olympians themselves—philosophical archetypes who have known all the great writers of all the ages of man. The Cabala clearly offered a glimpse of the immortality of authorship, and indeed Wilder quotes Oedipus at Colonus to remind readers of the alternative: "to the gods alone old age and death come never. But all else is confounded by all-mastering time."

Bradbury would return again and again throughout his career to reread this novel. Wilder's personification of literature through his characters is certainly half-cousin to Bradbury's book metaphors, where authors become their own works. His use of metaphorical masks in The Cabala reinforced what Bradbury was also learning from the multilayered characters of Maugham's The Painted Veil and Morley's Thunder on the Left. These figurative masks, along with the primitive masks that Bradbury would soon begin to collect, were forerunners of the exotic silver and gold masks of his Martian stories. And the moral issues that each of these authors explored in one way or another provided grist for the values debates at the heart of his best postwar science fiction.

As important as the Maugham, Morley, and Wilder titles would become for Bradbury, two newer novels stood out from all of the other books that Bradbury read during the war years—the English translation of Arthur Koestler's Darkness at Noon (1941) and Ayn Rand's The Fountainhead (1944). Both titles came into Bradbury's hands during 1944, capping a remarkable year of literary discoveries. On July 10th, he bought a copy of the American first edition of Darkness at

Noon, which was based on Koestler's re-creation (from memory) of his original German-language manuscript, lost during his dramatic escape to England from occupied France in 1940. For Bradbury, *Darkness at Noon* revealed the common element of tragedy that linked the dictatorships of modern times. He already knew, in political and economic terms, what he disliked about the Axis powers, and Bradbury could foresee a postwar world in which Stalin would demand global power and influence on a similar scale. But in ethical terms, Koestler cut to the essence of the inhumanity central to all dictatorships, regardless of political orientation. In the novel, the fallen Commissar Rubashov hears it from his first interrogator Ivanov, one of his oldest friends: "a collective aim justifies all means, and not only allows, but demands, that the individual should in every way be subordinated and sacrificed to the community—which may dispose of it as an experimentation rabbit or a sacrificial lamb."

After the war, *Darkness at Noon* helped shape Western intellectual and political attitudes toward Communism, but it didn't take that long for Bradbury to realize that Koestler really understood the Stalinist system in ways that had never before reached the general reading public in America. What Bradbury found most fascinating about *Darkness at Noon* was what it revealed about the so-called Moscow public "show trials" of 1937. Koestler first presents the bizarre mix of puppeteer-like procedural comedy and life-and-death consequences of these trials through the way Rubashov is interrogated by Gletkin, his second interrogator. Rubashov characterizes Gletkin as the ultimate example of the new generation, "born without umbilical cord" to tie them to the original party visionaries, and thereby free to interrogate with "correct brutality." Rubashov soon sees that there is no need of actual evidence to prove a charge.

Taken together, these ethical insights inspired Bradbury to begin one of the great achievements of American literature—a novel centered on the Modernist crisis-of-values that would evolve, over a period of six years, into *Fahrenheit 451*. Decades later, in an unpublished note, Bradbury established the full literary context of that inspiration: "People have often asked me what effect Huxley and Orwell had on me, and whether either of them influenced the creation of *Fahrenheit 451*. The best response is Arthur Koestler." He felt that Koestler, writing during the opening stages of the Second World War, was one of the few writers who chose to come to terms with the magnitude of the Soviet tragedy: "From that time on to the Gulag revelations, only a few perceived the intellectual holocaust and the revolution by burial that Stalin achieved. . . . Only Koestler got the full range of desecration, execution, and forgetfulness on a mass and nameless graveyard scale. Koestler's *Darkness at Noon* was therefore . . . true father, mother, and lunatic brother to my F.451."

Bradbury's metaphor is right on the mark, for *Darkness at Noon* resonated in his imagination throughout the evolution of *Fahrenheit* and its precursors. When the specter of censorship and the climate of fear began to spread across America in reaction to the rising postwar Soviet empire, Koestler's most famous novel inspired a half-dozen Bradbury book-burning stories and the *Galaxy* novella "The Fireman." Rubashov's interrogation sessions with the enigmatic Ivanov, his first interrogator, echo in very different and original ways through Fireman Montag's interviews with his demonic Fire Captain. Finally, after seeing Sidney Kingsley's award-winning 1951 dramatization of *Darkness at Noon* in New York, Bradbury was inspired to take up "The Fireman" once again and transform it into his enduring first novel, *Fahrenheit 451*.[4] "I left the theater, unknowingly, with child. Various short stories and the novel were inevitable."

In revealing the underlying terror of the show trials, *Darkness at Noon* became the great cautionary tale for Bradbury. It fueled his own subsequent confrontations with intolerant authority, or with those who denied the existence of intolerance. And it didn't matter how the tyranny was anchored politically—over the next two decades, Bradbury would take on those on the right who advocated the Red Scare's climate of fear, those on the left who refused to believe the blood purges and Gulags of the Stalinist era, and those of any persuasion who failed to see the great human tragedy of China's Cultural Revolution.

If *Darkness at Noon* affirmed Bradbury's sense of the sanctity of the individual, Ayn Rand's *The Fountainhead* affirmed Bradbury's still-evolving belief in his own creativity. The novel reached the bestseller lists during the Fall 1944 book season, and came into Bradbury's hands at a time when his most reliable source of income—the editors at *Weird Tales*—were pressuring him to slant his work toward traditional ghost and vampire stories. The timing couldn't have been better. "It was the right age. I was twenty-four, and I needed to believe in my own character, to hold still in spite of people doubting me, or [doubting] me being a science fiction writer—and I wasn't really a science fiction writer anyway. I was a fantasy writer, and most of my stuff that established my career was in *Weird Tales*. . . . So when I read *The Fountainhead*, it gave me courage to just stand and say to people, 'Go away and leave me alone.'"[5]

This was the kind of discipline that Henry Kuttner had been trying to get Bradbury to practice for several years: "No wonder you never finish your stories. You talk them all out. Shut up." In Rand's iconoclastic architect Howard Roark, Bradbury found unwavering reinforcement, an ironclad resistance to seeking criticism of a work-in-progress: "Never ask people. Not about your work." It wasn't Ayn Rand's Modernist aesthetic stance, or even her philosophical system of Objectivism, that attracted Bradbury. It was, quite simply, her protagonist's unwavering belief in his own work, no matter how far it might vary from the mainstream. He had already encountered the appeal to individualism in Huxley's first American period novel, *After Many a Summer Dies the Swan*: "Good is a matter of moral craftsmanship. It cannot be produced except by individuals." Huxley offered a Modernist context, but in Rand's Howard Roark Bradbury found one of the great neo-Romantic protagonists of modern times—in certain ways, a kindred spirit.

Bradbury felt the kinship in the way he himself had to respond to the pressures of his own professional world, the analogous pressures of agent, editor, publisher, and reading public. Bradbury was nearly two years into his first reputation as a gifted new stylistic talent in the pages of *Weird Tales*, but he was still making a half-cent a word on those stories. After the war, as he prepared many of these same stories for publication in *Dark Carnival*, he still reacted with heat when his publisher and friend, August Derleth, prepared the *Weird Tales* acknowledgments for the new collection:

> Year after year *Weird Tales* has tried to break me down into a hack writer. They rejected tale after tale because it was too off-trail, "we want stories with ghosts and haunts and terrible creatures in them." I was god-damned if I'd write about ghosts and haunts and dark necromancies. The Watchers was one of the few commercial yarns I did, and I'm ashamed of it. . . . They kept insisting to Julie that I do formula, formula, formula. . . . They prefer to have those terrible Matt Fox horror covers in place of a few well-done Boks. Well, I don't feel I owe them a damned thing except constant pressure to cheapen my work, and I don't feel grateful to them for that.

Bradbury felt no ill will toward his editors, but they were not able to stand up to the publishing executives at Short Stories, Inc., who wanted inexpensive formula work from contributors. This pressure increased after John Campbell's *Unknown Worlds*, the only serious competitor, became a casualty of the wartime paper shortage. Like *The Fountainhead*'s Howard Roark, Bradbury was always on guard against a culture trying to hamstring his creative potential for the sake of commercial gain, especially while he was making next to nothing from his stories. As an idealistic young writer, Bradbury's fundamental conception of creativity found reinforcement in Howard Roark's definition of the meaning of life: "Your work. The material the earth offers you and what you make of it."

For Bradbury, Howard Roark also represented the disciplined act of leaving the stylistic influence of others behind. Roark has one mentor early in the novel, the pioneering but isolated Modernist architect Henry Cameron. When illness and exhaustion lead Cameron to retire, he trusts Roark to burn everything—even his plans for great buildings yet unbuilt. Later, during the rare moments when he has to work for other firms, Roark earns his living by working out the technical challenges of assigned projects, staying away from design elements where others would inevitably try to alter his unconventional style. Bradbury's reading of The Fountainhead coincided with his own decision to turn away from reading the science fiction, horror, and fantasy works of all but a very few writers. He wanted no stylistic influences, especially at a time when he himself was being pressured so strongly by certain editors to write in established genre formulae.

Rand's great romance with uncompromising creativity provided the novel's overarching attraction for Bradbury. The established architects and reviewers end Roark's first attempt to launch his own business, but not before he fights with all his might to make it work. Bradbury identified closely with Roark's sense of authorial integrity, and the importance of not selling out for money. It was an issue of identity—like Rand's architect, Bradbury was in love with the work that his hard-earned talent was beginning to produce; in Bradbury's case, he maintained the strength of his convictions by regarding each new story as a precious child. To tamper with a story under pressure from editors was a crime against a child. He now knew how his friend Hannes Bok felt as he painted covers for the science fiction and fantasy pulps, agonizing over whether he should paint what he felt or paint what he thought his editors would want.

For many authors this is not a moral issue, but rather a matter of deferring full artistic freedom until a more secure situation arises. But on this point, Bradbury preferred not to delve into situational ethics. In reading The Fountainhead, his own vivid imagination identified with the sculptor Mallory's abiding nightmare: a culture that can recognize the best, but doesn't want it, and will go to any lengths to destroy it. Mallory describes it in stark terms: "That's horror. That's what's hanging over the world, prowling somewhere through mankind, that same thing, something closed, mindless, wanton, but something with an aim and cunning of its own." This fear, in a very discernible way, is the flip side of the Wellsian paranoia—the Invisible Man's desire to control the world—that Bradbury had always found so fascinating. He recognized at an early age that a culture can slip away from its ethical anchor by destroying, or even by simply ignoring, its art and literature—a lesson that would eventually lead Bradbury to write a novel and create a title metaphor around the temperature at which book paper burns.

15 The Road to Autumn's House

During the war years most of Bradbury's maturing process, both self-taught and mentored, went on beneath the surface of a publication history that was rapidly bringing him to public attention as an unusual new talent in two niche market genres—the weirds and the detective pulps. Throughout the early and mid-1940s, Bradbury's relationship with the editors and publishers of *Weird Tales* was as privately frustrating for the young writer as it was publicly successful. The legendary Farnsworth Wright had been Bradbury's initial contact at *Weird Tales*, but before his first story appeared, Wright had been forced to retire by his failing health. Wright had also been under pressure from executives at Short Stories, Inc., the syndicate that had purchased *Weird Tales* from Popular Publications in 1938, to hold the half-cent-a-word line with most of the magazine's contributors. After Wright's sudden departure in 1940, Bradbury had reacted with youthful emotion in a letter to Henry Hasse: "*Weird* without Wright? That's like bacon without eggs . . . What will *Weird* become? A nursery rhyme booklet for tired tots?" He offered a more measured but no less passionate response six years later to August Derleth: "I can't for the life of me see how you can defend *Weird Tales* since Wright was so crudely removed from his job a few years ago and a newer, cheaper policy instigated. I shall never forgive the money men at the head of *Weird* . . . for treating Wright the way they did." *Weird Tales* joined the growing list of pulps that he continued to collect, but no longer read.[1]

Nevertheless Wright's successor, Dorothy McIlwraith, and her associate editor Montgomery Buchanan probably accepted as many Bradbury stories as they rejected. He worked well with them, but bridled every time they used an acceptance letter to caution him: "'This is the *last* one' they always wrote me, 'Your next story will have to be formula.'" With the help of Henry Kuttner, his first *Weird* appearance ("The Candle") was traditional, yet he managed to publish another twenty-four stylistically original off-trail stories in the pages of *Weird Tales* between 1943 and 1948. As often as not, his editors gave in to Bradbury's talent and growing popularity with readers and had the luxury of accepting (and sometimes even refusing) stories worthy of the quality magazines. One such refusal, "The Man Upstairs," appeared in the March 1947 issue of *Harper's*. Even his pulp sales showcased his talent in ways that other writers could admire; Henry Kuttner always had a fond place in his heart for "The Scythe," featured in the July 1943 issue (he may have known that Leigh Brackett wrote the opening paragraphs).

Bradbury appearances in *Weird Tales* soon came to be expected by readers, but they knew nothing of the restrictions placed upon him. Owner William J. Delaney had long since narrowed the scope by eliminating science fiction, and only the very few remaining writers from the old days received more than the minimum rate for stories. In fact, Delaney never really reformed the magazine's compensation formula in any meaningful way; by 1948 Bradbury had appeared in many major market magazines, two O. Henry award volumes, and two *Best American Short Story* annual anthologies, but still received only $30.00 for each of his three *Weird Tales* appearances that year. Yet Bradbury always worked hard to maintain good relationships with his editors, and he kept his perspective throughout his wartime dealings with Wright's successors: "I hold nothing against Buchanan and Mac, I hold plenty against the system." [2]

He developed a much warmer relationship with his detective pulp editors, and between 1944 and 1948 Bradbury published sixteen stories in their magazines. With the wartime suspension or outright demise of a number of the fantasy and science fiction pulps, Julie Schwartz had little trouble convincing Bradbury to try his hand at detective fiction. During the summer of 1943 Schwartz's good friend Mike Tilden was hired as editor of *Detective Tales*, a magazine that privileged strong and emotional characterization. Schwartz knew that this emphasis would play to Bradbury's developing stylistic strength without raising the usual editorial demand to slant or write to formula. Tilden could also offer 1¼ to 1½ cents per word, a significant improvement over the rate at *Weird Tales*. Bradbury responded with enthusiasm, placing five stories in *Detective Tales* and three more in Popular's companion title, *New Detective*. Ryerson Johnson, editor at *New Detective*, closed Bradbury's first sale in the genre, purchasing "The Long Night" during January 1944. The story appeared in the July issue, along with Johnson's assertion that "Bradbury is the most promising writer I have ever read."

By the end of the year Tilden had moved up to a managing editorial position at the Popular Publications offices on 42nd Street in Manhattan, where he oversaw both *Detective Tales* and the far more sensational *Dime Mystery*. During the 1930s Popular Publications had turned *Dime Mystery* into the first of the "shudder" pulps by featuring stories in the French Grand Guignol tradition of visualized terror. The occasional gruesomeness in his narratives and his still-developing, emotionally charged style clearly came from the same fascination with carnival and gothic literary roots that fueled writers in the Grand Guignol tradition, but Bradbury's work contained none of the sadistic and gruesome tortures typical of *Dime Mystery*'s "shudder" pulp heyday; during the war years the magazine was toned down considerably, and Bradbury was eventually able to place five original stories and two reprints in *Dime Mystery*, written with some "grue" but with more of the spectacle elements of carnival found in some of his best weird tales as well.

Alden Norton, editorial director for Popular Publications and editor of *Flynn's Detective Fiction*, bought "Yesterday I Lived!" for the August 1944 issue of *Flynn's* before the wartime paper shortage forced Norton to discontinue the magazine. This story, along with "The Trunk Lady" (*Detective Tales*, Sept. 1944), offers the best combination of plotting and imaginative power found in Bradbury's wartime crime and detective tales. From his vantage point as editorial director, Norton liked both of these stories very much, as did Henry Kuttner, who felt that both stories showed restraint, "lack of which was about your worst enemy in the old days. The handling of the villain in 'Trunk Lady' was especially delicate and unpleasant, and both yarns had a touch of freshness and ingenuity that you could never get by writing for the fantasy books alone. I'm glad you're branching out."[3] He would reach his peak in crime fiction just after the war with "The Small Assassin" (November 1946), his last original story for *Dime Mystery*, and "The Fruit at the Bottom of the Bowl" (1948), published for Fiction House's *Detective Book* as "Touch and Go."

His progress was, nonetheless, unpredictable in traditional genre terms. Both Tilden and Ryerson Johnson were willing to excuse the inconsistent plots to publish the high-impact style, but Bradbury's approach never really sold Norton. In turning down "Where Everything Ends," a story of murder in Venice Beach, Norton reiterated his concerns to Schwartz: "As I've told you many times, if this Bradbury guy can combine undeniable talent for good writing with a few plots that can really hang together, he will be astoundingly good."[4] His Popular editors quickly found that Bradbury, by the very nature of his creative process, was unable to conform to logical notions of crime plotting at all. His instinctive need to trick his subconscious creativity into action—that is, to let his characters tell their own stories—reflected what he had learned about the unconscious from Dorothea Brande, rather than the ratiocinative strategies of Edgar Allan Poe. As much as he loved Poe's Inspector Dupin, Bradbury would never compromise this process.

There was a richer tapestry of creativity than the publishing record reveals for the war years—at least thirty-eight Bradbury stories from this period circulated under Schwartz's entrepreneurial stewardship, but failed to sell. The unsold detective stories within this group often had original and creative premises but were weakly plotted; others had structural flaws or character motivation problems and involved well-worn situations that were simply not worth the trouble of fixing up: "Remember Helen Charles" centered on a revenge plot, "Who's Little Corpse Are U" involved a cocktail party murder game-gone-awry, and "The Cricket Cage" offered an exotic Caribbean setting for an otherwise predictable murder mystery. One of these, however, was original and off-trail enough to interest Alden Norton in early 1944, who found it well-written but too vaguely plotted to publish in Popular's stable of detective pulps. "Where Everything Ends" added an unusual complication: the unseen murderer cannot be tracked because he moves through the canals of Venice Beach and awaits victims beneath the drains along the canal walls. Forty years later, Bradbury developed this twist into the core of *Death Is a Lonely Business*, the first of three interrelated detective novels that he furnished with memories of Venice Beach, downtown Los Angeles, and the Hollywood studios that he knew so well.

Through his years living, off and on, in the Hispanic community of Los Angeles, Bradbury had developed into a keen observer of people. Through the advice of Brackett, Hamilton, and Kuttner, and through his own ever-widening reading loves, he developed his own distinct style and method. In fact, he developed into a significant talent far earlier than his wartime publishing record ever revealed. The breakthrough didn't just happen one week in the summer of 1945, when he sent three stories out to three major market magazines. His relatively weak publication record in 1942 belies the fact that he had already written such distinctly Bradburyian weirds as "The Wind" and "The Crowd" a full year before they reached publication in the pulps, as well as such important later stories as "The Lake" (1944) and "Chrysalis" (1946).

His 1943 compositional records show that even more enduring stories were written while he was still publishing intermediate quality work in the pulps. That year alone, Bradbury composed first drafts of "The Small Assassin" (1946) and his first significant *Martian Chronicles* story, "The Million Year Picnic" (1946), as well as two of his first Green Town stories, "The Night" (1946) and "The Man Upstairs" (1947). Two of his first three breakthrough slick publications—"The Miracles of Jamie" (April 1946) and "Invisible Boy" (Nov. 1945)—were complete by mid-1944. Although some of these required months and even years of intermittent revision, they were nonetheless breakthrough works-in-progress from a very early date in his career, indeed far earlier than anyone has ever guessed.

"How may a race of people, " I asked, "banish every worry?
It seems a prodigious task."

"We have all that we wish to eat," said my guide. "We have
music and wine and food and love of living."

"And no quarrels?"

"Over what?" he asked.

"Love."

"Everyone loves everyone else in Luur-uh--lur. There are
no matings. We have our moods. Sometimes we go out alone
and sit in the forest and contemplate the trees or the brooks
like crystal in our glades. We gather at nightfall and play
our symphonies as the moon waxes and wans, we dance, we feast,
and we do not worry."

"If only the world were like this," I sighed.

"The world is like this," corrected my companion. "Someday
you will realize that all of the lands are like this. For a
time anyway there is no care, no toil. You realize it not now,
but when you leave this land and return to your home country,
then it shall come to you why this place is so beautiful and
necessary to everyone on the earth."

"Have many others such as myself been here before?" I
asked.

"Everyone in the world," he replied, and his voice was
strangely sentimental, his eyes were seeing far off things.
"Everyone in the past and the present and even the future has
come here. And they will continue journeying to our borders
to stay for an hour, a day, no longer perhaps, but yet they
have their brief stay of happiness."

The voice of the imagination. Bradbury transformed Hannes
Bok's whimsical tempura figure into the character Kuahdo,
Leif's guide through the lost island of the unpublished
"Lorelei" (July 1938). This surviving typescript page
reveals how Lorelei emerges as a master metaphor for the
imagination. Author's revisions and a caricature of Leif
appear in the final paragraph. Bradbury's stencil of Kuahdo
(inset) became the cover art for the first number of *Futuria
Fantasia* (Summer 1939). From the Albright Collection;
courtesy of Ray Bradbury and Donn Albright.

Any Time After Twelve
a collection of
WEIRD--STORIES!
made by
Ray D. Bradbury

A science-circle publication
illustrated by VIRGIL FINLAY
thirty of them
on manila-colored paper-$3.00

Satan's Palimpsest
by Seabury Quinn

The Defense Rests
by Julius Long

Clicking Red Heels
by Paul Ernst

He That Hath Wings
by Edmond Hamilton

Fane of The Black Pharoah
by Robert Bloch

Return to The Sabbath
by Robert Bloch

Uneasy Lie the Drowned
by Donald Wandrei

Globe of Memories
by Seabury Quinn

The Black Stone Statue
by Mary. E. Counselman

Mother of Toads
by Clark Ashton Smith

Incense of Abomination
by Seabury Quinn.

The Mannikin
by Robert Bloch

The Graveyard Rats
by Henry Kuttner

At The Time Appointed
by Loretta Burrough

The Purple Cincture
by H. Thomspon Rich

The Statement of Randolph Carter
by H.P. Lovecraft

Shambleau,
By C.L. Moore

The Kelpie
by Manly Wade Wellman

Hellsgarde
by C.L. Moore

Pickman's Model
by H.P. Lovecraft

The Waxworks
by Robert Bloch

The Feast in The Abbey
by Robert Bloch

Date in The City Room
by Talbot Johns

The Lonely One
by R.D. Bradbury

Fortune's Fools
by Seabury Quinn

Return to The Sabbath
by Robert Bloch

six by Bob Bloch
four by Seabury Quinn
. . . .
 . . . .
  . . . .
   . . . .
    . . . . . .
     . . . . .
      . . . .
       . . .
        . .
         .

A collection of weird stories
to read at night..anytime after
twelve.

Bradbury's outlines for a two-volume anthology of stories selected from the pages of *Weird Tales*, c. summer 1939. Duplicated entries for C. L. Moore's "Shambleau" and for Robert Bloch's "Return to the Sabbath" indicate the tentative nature of the project. With the exception of "Shambleau" (1933), the stories listed here represent Bradbury's favorite originals or reprints from January 1935 to April 1939 issues of *Weird Tales*. The proposed imprint ("A science-circle publication"), the illustrations, and the pricing are speculative,

All Through The Night
  a second volumn
  of WEIRD TALES:
  made through
  Ray D. Bradbury

The Inn: by Rex Ernest

Dread Summons: Paul Ernst

Secret of Sebek: Bob Bloch

Eyes of the Mummy: Bob Bloch

Quest of the Starstone: Kuttner and Moore

The Canal: Everil Worrell

The Treader of The Dust: Clark Ashton Smith

In A Graveyard: By Eando Binder

A Rival From The Grave: Seabury Quinn

THEY: Robert Barbour Johnson

Return To Death: J. Wesley Rosenquest

The Satin Mask: August W. Derleth

Shambleau: C.L. Moore

It Walks By Night: Kuttner

but suggest a joint venture with LASFL support. Forry Ackerman owned both pages for many years. The outlines represent one of the earliest titled book projects planned by Bradbury, but there is no evidence that the proposal moved beyond this early stage of brainstorming. From the Albright and Miller Collections; courtesy of Ray Bradbury, Donn Albright, and Greg Miller.

Caricaturist and still life artist Fritz Zillig produced this profile of Bradbury
on Olvera Street in downtown Los Angeles around 1940.

The one-hundredth meeting of the Los Angeles Science Fiction League occurred in 1940, just as the organization refashioned itself as the Los Angeles Science Fantasy Society (LASFS). A center closeup from one of the photographs taken that evening isolates Bradbury at front right; to his left are Jack Williamson, E. E. "Doc" Smith, Walt Doughtery, and Robert Heinlein. From the left, the back row includes Forry Ackerman, Edmond Hamilton, prozine editor Charlie Hornig, and fan Vic Clark. In the background is a Robert Fuqua painting. Courtesy of Ray Bradbury, Donn Albright, and the LASFS.

A posed photo (top) with Ray Bradbury (R) and Julius Schwartz reviewing a story, Los Angeles, summer 1941. Schwartz and Edmond Hamilton had driven on to Los Angeles after the 3rd World Science Fiction Convention in Denver and settled into a hotel near Bradbury's newspaper corner at Norton and Olympic. Schwartz was now Bradbury's agent and critiqued a few of his story drafts before heading back to New York. Below: Edmond Hamilton and Bradbury (L), summer 1941, each clowning with examples of the other's work; Hamilton endures a Bradbury typescript, while Bradbury holds a copy of *Captain Future*, a hero pulp built largely around Hamilton's serial prose, at arm's length. Throughout the 1940s, Hamilton's reading advice and command of mainstream literary traditions extended Bradbury's reading passions deeper into British and American poetry and prose. Photographs from the Albright Collection; courtesy of Ray Bradbury and Donn Albright.

"BRADBURY" — BY
BENNETT WADE

This sidewalk sketch of Bradbury was created by the Olvera Street artist Bennett Wade around 1941. Bradbury and his friends often enjoyed the performers and artisans of this downtown area during the late 1930s and on through the war years. From the Albright Collection; reproduced by permission of Donn Albright and Ray Bradbury.

3,200 words
July 9th, 1943

FAMILY OUTING

Somehow the idea was brought up by Mom that perhaps the whole family would enjoy a fishing trip. But they weren't Mom's words; Timothy knew that. They were Dad's words, and Mom used them for him, somehow.

Dad shuffled his feet in a clutter of Martian pebbles, and agreed. So immediately there was a tumult and a shouting, and quick as jets the camp was tucked into capsules and containers, Mom slipped into traveling jumpers and blouse, Dad stuffed his pipe full with trembling hands, his eyes on the Martian sky, and the three boys piled yelling into the motorboat, none of them really keeping an eye on Mom and Dad, except Timothy.

Dad pushed a stud, the water-boat sent a humming sound up into the sky, the water shook back and the boat nosed ahead, and the family cried, "Hurrah!"

Timothy sat in the back of the boat with Dad, his small fingers on top of Dad's large hairy ones, watching the canal twist, leaving the crumbled place behind where they had landed their small tourist rocket.

Dad had a funny look in his eyes as the boat went up-canal. A look that Timothy couldn't figure. It was made of strong light and maybe a lot of joy. It made the deep wrinkles laugh instead of worry or cry.

So there went the tourist rocket, around a bend, gone.

"How far are we going?" Robert splashed his hand. It looked like a small crab jumping in the violet water.

July 9, 1943: the earliest known page from a *Martian Chronicles* story-chapter, composed prior to Bradbury's development of the larger *Chronicles* concept. No other pages have been located, but "Family Outing" eventually reached print in the Summer 1946 issue of *Planet Stories* as "The Million Year Picnic." During the summer of 1949, Bradbury revised this tale into the final story chapter of *The Martian Chronicles* (1950); in the process, he made a half-dozen substantive revisions to the opening page and greatly expanded the fourth paragraph. From the Albright Collection; courtesy of Ray Bradbury and Donn Albright.

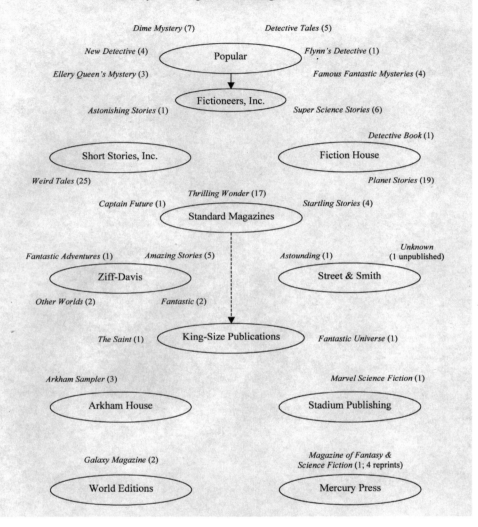

Bradbury, the Pulps, and the Digests: 1942-1954

Dime Mystery (7)   *Detective Tales* (5)

New Detective (4)   Popular   *Flynn's Detective* (1)

Ellery Queen's Mystery (3)   *Famous Fantastic Mysteries* (4)

Fictioneers, Inc.

Astonishing Stories (1)   *Super Science Stories* (6)

Detective Book (1)

Short Stories, Inc.   Fiction House

Weird Tales (25)   *Planet Stories* (19)

Thrilling Wonder (17)

Captain Future (1)   *Startling Stories* (4)

Standard Magazines

Fantastic Adventures (1)   *Amazing Stories* (5)   *Astounding* (1)   *Unknown* (1 unpublished)

Ziff-Davis   Street & Smith

Other Worlds (2)   *Fantastic* (2)

The Saint (1)   King-Size Publications   *Fantastic Universe* (1)

Arkham Sampler (3)   *Marvel Science Fiction* (1)

Arkham House   Stadium Publishing

Galaxy Magazine (2)   *Magazine of Fantasy & Science Fiction* (1; 4 reprints)

World Editions   Mercury Press

The early Bradbury universe. Bradbury and his first agent, Julius Schwartz, had to negotiate the ever-changing galaxies of pulp magazines and editors throughout the war years. Despite his postwar major market success, Bradbury and his new agent, Don Congdon, continued to place at least a few original stories in the genre magazines until 1954. Bradbury sales totals are indicated in parentheses with each title. The vast majority of these early sales represented first serial publication; in later decades many of the digests and pulp revivals would reprint Bradbury classics, but very few originals. British, Canadian, and Australian magazine printings are not included here.

The electric company compound at 670 Venice Boulevard where Bradbury lived with his parents and brother from the Spring of 1942 through the summer of 1947. Bradbury's garage office window (above, far right) looked out onto the utility substation and the humming machinery that often powered his imagination deep into the night. The view from Bradbury's office (below) centers on the high green windows of the substation. Both views were taken in October 2007, long after the compound had been sold to private owners. The house and garage were demolished to make way for urban development in 2008. Photographs by the author.

Part III

The Fear of Death Is Death

The incense of the church is in the road and you rush through it but do not leave it behind, it is all of Mexico, it is everywhere with that other cool fear and that shadow and that smell of charcoal October. . . . Tomorrow you will go on and on over the vast strange country in the October smell in your car. And the smell is always with you. The watch ticks on your wrist, your heart ticks in your throat. You smell the smell. The smell of death.

— RB, October 26, 1945

16 Exploring the Human Mind

Even as his sense of the rich possibilities of unfettered literary creativity grew, Bradbury also worried about having an adequate understanding of the human experience. He could always generate word associations for potential story subjects, but what kinds of characters would emerge and run off with his stories? His rapid and unconventional successes in weird tales and detective fiction opened up new possibilities and led him to readings far beyond the fiction field. Leigh Brackett, already an accomplished detective writer, loaned him her copy of the Barnes and Teeters text on *New Horizons in Criminology* in 1944. But Bradbury had also collected a number of scientific references on his own, and the most important of these was Karen Horney's influential first book, *The Neurotic Personality of Our Time* (1937).

She published three more books before the end of the war, but it was Horney's first study of neuroses that Bradbury found most useful for his own exploration of personality disorders. It was designed to be useful to professionals and at the same time completely accessible to lay readers, and the book would prove to be more interesting than the 1938 Modern Library edition of *The Basic Writings of Sigmund Freud* that Bradbury had also acquired after his high-school days. Freud provided a good grounding, though, and helped him understand the sometimes tenuous boundary between full-blown psychotic pathologies such as paranoia and the less distorted (and far more common) personality disorders of the neurotic. Freud had helped put Bradbury's own fears and anxieties into perspective by observing "that the border-line between the nervous, normal and abnormal states is indistinct, and that we are all slightly nervous."[1] Horney reinforced Freud's general observations on this point, noting that normal people continually work under threshold anxieties, thanks in no small part to the culture-generated anxieties of the technological age. But *The Neurotic Personality in Our Time* also presented Bradbury with a full definition of the causes of neurotic behavior and the resulting deformations of character. Through her work Bradbury came to understand the often destructive cycle of anxiety and hostility that underlies all neuroses.

Unlike Freud, Horney did not focus on child psychology or the origins of the neurosis, but rather on the neurotic personality itself. She examined four ways that the neurotic tries to protect against anxiety (seek affection; offer submissiveness; gain power over others; withdraw from the world). Horney felt that the greatest drives in neuroses were the craving for affection and the craving for power and control, but Bradbury's characters, both in his genre fiction and in the broader fantasy fiction that followed, represent the full range of neurotic behavioral manifestations. Bradbury's early anxieties were no doubt heightened by his fertile imagination, but they were nonetheless the normal or basic anxieties that Horney describes as disproportionate fears of "death, illness, old age, catastrophes of nature, political events, accidents."[2] The neurotic sometimes assumes sentient hostility in the face of such anxieties, and Bradbury effectively used this pathology as his point of departure in such early stories as "The Wind" and "The Crowd."

For the most part, he let his stories stand for themselves, and he first made this point in the autobiographical essay that accompanied his story "The Poems" in the January 1945 issue of Weird Tales: "There's really not much a writer can say about himself that he hasn't already said in the story, unwittingly. The kind of people in his story, their beliefs, their fears, their reactions, their tastes, are pretty indicative of the author's mind; even if some of the people in the yarn appear to be exact opposites." On a very elementary level, he was not afraid to be specific: "So, fears, prejudices and premonitions and all the rest, I imagine you pretty well know me from my stories. The refusal to meet death inherent in the theme of 'There Was an Old Woman,' 'The Ducker,' 'The Reunion' and 'The Scythe.' The escape motive apparent in 'The Sea Shell,' and in this newest story, 'The Poems.'" But he was not about to probe any deeper into his own mind for the benefit of Weird's readership, as he noted implicitly in speaking of "The Pendulum," his first pulp sale: "Only Freud could tell you what a pendulum could possibly mean in my life; perhaps the fear of passing time, growing old, death; perhaps some subtle movement, balance, or rhythm."[3]

Bradbury remained most fascinated with the psychology of children, for he felt that his early success was inextricably linked to that very strange world that he remembered so vividly. He already had some grasp of the Freudian view that anxiety originates in childhood and infantile experience, and his Modern Library Freud included The Interpretation of Dreams and Three Contributions on the Theory of Sex. There is no evidence that he ever read the work of Melanie Klein, whose controversial conclusions on pre- and postnatal memory, the birth trauma, and neonatal impulses for hate as well as love would seem to presage the most famous of Bradbury's crime stories, "The Small Assassin."[4] It was through his ever-broadening reading, and through his careful observation of people, that he came to understand what happens when parents, and even other children, try to break a child's will.

From his reading and from other cultural influences, Bradbury also encountered Carl Jung's conception of the unconscious, but this trail is more difficult to illuminate. By 1944 he had read about Jungian archetypes in Philip Wylie's *Generation of Vipers*; Horney's study, which touched on persona and the Jungian sequence of individuation, may also have had an impact. A decade later, as he began working for John Huston on the *Moby Dick* screenplay, he felt confident enough to ask his director if he wanted a Freudian, Jungian, or literary approach (Huston, he quickly discovered, wanted Bradbury's approach). But the influence of Jung was already woven into Bradbury's work, as extensively documented in William F. Touponce's studies of the role of reverie and individuation in *Fahrenheit 451*.[5] Although Freudian manifestations of conflict can be found throughout his early fantasies and off-trail weird tales, Bradbury was fundamentally more attuned to the psychological balance inherent in Jung's work. Besides, Freud had little to say about creativity, while Jung had a great deal to say about the artistic temperament and the creative potential of the human psyche.

His exploration of psychology would continue intermittently into the 1950s and 1960s, but even these early basic readings were stimulating him to write on broader themes. Henry Kuttner, ever the close reader of Bradbury's early professional work, had been worried that his young friend focused all too often on only two themes: "refusal to grow up, and fear of death," conceding that the latter might at least be "symbolic of maturity, perhaps."[6] As the war moved into its final year, though, Bradbury was beginning to focus on themes that certain other writers were also exploring: how do we know what is real, and how do we know what is human? These were the themes that distinguished writers like Van Vogt, Simak, Leiber, and Theodore Sturgeon from the writers of space opera adventures and hard science fiction. This sensitivity was what genre historian Mike Ashley would call, many years later, "a softer, more human approach. . . . the incidents in their stories were not necessarily explicable in scientific terms." And it was also central to the science fantasies of the Kuttner-Moore collaborations. Bradbury was closer to Kuttner than to any of the others, and in spite of the geographical distance between them, Kuttner remained his best and most perceptive critic for some time to come.

By the summer of 1944 Kuttner had completed his eighteen months of active duty with the medical detachment at Fort Monmouth, New Jersey, and was able to move with his wife and writing partner, Kat Moore, to a house along the Hudson River north of New York City. Kuttner missed tequila more than any of his other Southern California indulgences, and throughout December 1944 he coached Bradbury through the very tricky business of shipping alcohol cross-country under wartime restrictions. After several frustrating attempts at mastering the intricacies of railway express mail, Bradbury finally succeeded in sending the tequila through to Kuttner as "bubble bath cologne." To Kuttner's delight, Bradbury had intuited that Mexican tequila was superior to the cheaper Cuban brands; in fact, his young friend had finally, at the age of twenty-four, learned to drink socially. It was in this context that Bradbury's deep reading on neurotic types radiated out into other anxiety-producing behaviors, including alcoholism.

Kuttner, sometimes a heavy drinker, had found Charles Jackson's The Lost Weekend very fine writing and thoroughly believable. It was clearly autobiographical, and reflected an understanding of alcoholism that transcended the psychological and sociological explanations of the day. In early March 1945 he recommended it to Bradbury, who found that Jackson's fictitious Don Birnam manifested interesting character traits long associated with alcoholism, including narcissism, latent homosexuality, and a deeply buried death wish. There are elements of all these traits in Birnam's disjointed adventures and stream-of-consciousness memories as he falls through a five-day "weekend," trying desperately to gauge how long he can remain high before he must slowly ease off and let his body recover for the next bout. Bradbury speculated that the alternating scenes of public and private drinking revealed, among other things, that drinking offers an escape valve for the latent homosexual in some men.

Kuttner agreed that drinking could bring out such latencies, but suggested that drinking actually brought out a broader sexual behavior: "You could call it masculine-gregariousness, the Army instinct, the herd instinct excluding women—or fraternal love." Bradbury wondered if repressed homosexuality in the military culture might express itself as sadism, using The Brick Foxhole as a recent literary example. From his experience, Kuttner had not seen a problem in the Medical Corps, where nursing provided a sanative emotional release no matter what the personality of the corpsman or nurse: "It's axiomatic that everybody's part male and part female, depending on the chromosomes or something, and it's rather like using both hands on the piano. One hand is generally predominant, carrying the tune, but the other hand gives the balance, counterpoint, or whatever." It was a metaphor that resonated for Bradbury, who would always look for the common denominators of the human condition, the leveling factors that could sweep away the intolerance inherited from earlier times.

Both Kuttner and Bradbury found great relevance in the way that The Lost Weekend revealed the primary limitations of psychoanalysis. In flashback, Don Birnam reveals how he discovered that his analyst, "the foolish psychiatrist," would never be able to know him or help him: "What the doctor knew he knew academically, according to rule and case. His own varied experiences in life had taught him nothing about himself and therefore others. . . . The human being was lost sight of . . ." Kuttner also found this insight played out to great effect in Mary Coyle Chase's *Harvey* and recommended that Bradbury see a performance when the Broadway stage production went on tour. "It's a vicious satire on psychiatrists, and might have been written by a more objective Thorne Smith." In coming years Bradbury would weave a wide range of psychoanalytical scenes through his stories and novels, some subtle and chilling and others satirical or simply humorous.

But in 1944 his suspicion of analysis was outweighed by the fear that he might have gone just about as far as his talent could take him and that his success would peak in the pulps. If he could afford it, there was professional help close at hand. His friend Grant Beach occasionally had his own analysis sessions with Dr. J. M. Nielson, a well-known psychiatrist who figured prominently in the criminal court system and sometimes testified at high-profile trials.[7] Beach arranged an appointment; Dr. Nielson urged patience and prescribed a Kuttner-like reading regimen: the author biographies of the Encyclopedia Britannica. Bradbury found that, with exceptions (the most significant for Bradbury being Charles Dickens), most of the great literary figures had to wait a long time for recognition, and a significant number never achieved fame during their lifetimes. This realization was reinforced by his ever-widening readings in the social sciences: "The more I read, the more I realized we can't help one another. The way you help yourself is by working every day of your life—no matter what your work is—and gradually you look over your shoulder and look back at what you were the year before. And so you teach yourself."[8]

17 Exploring the Human Condition

Even as he broadened his horizons by reading more books than he had ever read before in a single year, Bradbury realized that he also had to broaden his experience with the world beyond books. In July 1944, Kuttner suggested a trip East: "You're apt eventually to get insular out west, and it might pay you to spend a month or two in Manhattan, seeing editors and writing." It was the logical next step professionally, but Bradbury wanted to wait until he had made the jump to the major market magazines. Instead of looking East, he looked South. Later that summer, Bradbury found a way to expand his contact with Hispanic culture back toward its source, journeying from the México de Afuera—the "outer Mexico" of Los Angeles—down into Mexico itself. He was selling one or two stories a month to the pulps by this time, and had enough money for preliminary trips north to Santa Barbara and east to Lake Arrowhead, and even to Yuma, Arizona. His friend Grant Beach soon came up with the idea of a longer tour through southern California, visiting the historical sites on both sides of the border. Using Beach's automobile, the two cut a great clockwise path east to Palm Springs, south and west through the border towns of Ensenada, Calexico, and Mexicali, and back up through San Diego to tour each of the 300-year-old Spanish missions along that portion of the coast.

One evening they crossed over from Calexico to Mexicali, and an entirely new carnival world opened up before their eyes: a small circus set in the midst of a locust plague. Bradbury was captivated by the tiny venue, where all the grounds workers doubled as performers. When he returned home he felt compelled to write a travel article about this magical experience, and sent a small narrative sketch to Mike Tilden about "one of the most intriguing, hilarious, outré circuses I've ever seen. . . . a microcosmic satire on our huge American tent shows." This bit of local color captured the kind of fantastic merging of landscape and culture that was slowly drawing Bradbury deeper into the strange and alien world he had discovered south of the border:

> . . . the crickets jumping and dying by the thousands in the Mexican shop windows, the dust winds at noon, the circus perched like a clown's hat on an adobe hill, the antique camels stumbling about the one ring inside—propped

up by performers on all sides to keep them from collapsing outright, the torn top of the tent with the stars shining through, the little buck-toothed Indian ballerina who is shot skyward clenching a rope with her teeth—to the impossible height of fifteen feet above the ground!—at which moment the entire tent sags and buckles dangerously because of her suspended whirling!

Bradbury thought that Tilden might send the idea across the hall to *Argosy*, which now accepted nonfiction submissions for its new slick-paper format. The proposition didn't pan out, but Bradbury never let the experience slip away. He would eventually publish two pieces based on this memory, the essay "Mexicali Mirage" (1974) and the story "That Old Dog Lying in the Dust" (1997). Bradbury wrote this story in the late 1940s, and for a time he considered placing it in *The October Country* (1955); a companion piece, "You Must Not Touch the Cage," finally reached print in 2009.

As he began to explore the multiplicity of cultures in the region, Bradbury continued to explore as well his own personality—who he was, and what he believed in. As he observed in a Christmas Day 1944 letter to Kuttner, "like most guys who try writing, I'm honestly looking for some philosophy which correlates the old religiosity with the newer precepts of science." An editorial by Sterling North in the Dec. 2 issue of the *Saturday Review of Literature* had reinforced Bradbury's growing sense that the wartime boom in novels exploring faith and the modern crisis of faith were out of step with events in the real world. The tone and content of the piece struck a chord with Bradbury—he was annoyed by Franz Werfel's perennial bestseller *The Song of Bernadette* and the movie adapted from it, and was outright disappointed that one of his favorites, Somerset Maugham, had recently written novels centered on the Catholic Church and its history. As the decisive events of the final year of the World War began to unfold, Bradbury found North's rather one-sided argument persuasive. North believed that turning to religion in a war-ravaged world signaled a return to the outdated mythologies of the past, subordinating ethics to what he called the conflict between "black and white magic": "Never in the history of mankind have we been so in need of an ethical pattern. But war destroys ethics, while awakening myth. And the results of our ignorance and fear and superstition lie all about us in a shattered world."[1]

Although Bradbury felt that the emphasis on traditional faith in contemporary literature and film distracted from what he called the "real, factual, scientific problems" of the day, he was not quite willing to fully endorse North's view in his own reasoning; he confided to Kuttner that "Faith isn't enough to solve our problems, though it may help." But at this stage in his life, with the final events of the war playing out in very bloody advances across Europe and the Pacific,

Bradbury's sense of faith centered on ethics, and in particular on a belief in peace. He had read a chapter in Thomas Dewey's *The Case against the New Deal* (1940), and in the months after Dewey's defeat in the presidential election of 1944 this brief reading provided Bradbury with a tangible, if rather secular, basis for belief. He explained it this way in his Christmas letter to Kuttner: "[A]s Dewey points out . . . the trouble with our civilization is separation of means from end. We talk a hell of a lot about peace, but when a problem arises which we can handle objectively, our beautiful ideas are not set in operation."

Bradbury had voted for Roosevelt, but he did not fully trust a government that had tacitly condoned the rise of Franco in Spain and continued to trade with the Axis powers in the years leading up to the outbreak of war. He never forgot that his family was a working class family that had barely scraped through the Great Depression, and he sympathized with the dockworkers and other laborers of the late 1930s who were often caught up in the behind-the-scenes manipulations of the big business interests and labeled "Communists," whether they were or not. He admired the politics of Henry Wallace, whose progressive economic policies had angered party conservatives and cost him a second term as Roosevelt's vice president. Bradbury's preference for Wallace echoed his old Technocracy views: "Roosevelt is too much of a politician at times. Admittedly he helped somewhat in the depression, but the glaring fact is that it took the war to return those eleven million unemployed to work. I like Wallace and his clear, sensible thinking in regard to production and distribution. We've lived under an economy of scarcity too long, it's about time we lived under an economy of abundance instead."

Bradbury's lifelong tendency to simplify an argument to its essentials evolved in this way from his working-class roots. Through his teens and into his middle twenties, he often oversimplified his argument in ways that exhibited a naiveté about politics and economics. But as the postwar years transformed into a bipolar arsenal of terrifying proportions, Bradbury's judgment matured in ways that inspired some of his most effective sustained writing, including many of his Martian stories and *Fahrenheit 451*. Even as early as Christmas 1944, he knew what was coming: "The same old spheres of influence, you may notice, have begun in the last six months." Bradbury may not have gone to college, but he had indeed read the papers he sold during those four years at his corner newsstand, and he continued to study current events all the evenings he spent reading books and magazines in the bookstores. As he closed his Christmas diatribe on international spheres of influence, he offered Kuttner another broad but nonetheless compelling generalization: "All of which reminds one of the oil situation in the Middle East, where our oil companies are fussing around. As long as business enterprises have control of our government, Christ Allmighty, we're going to have war." These words were more than prophetic—they could easily have been written in the first decade of the twenty-first century.

His views on the causes of the present war, as well as his evolving sense of the challenges facing the future postwar world, were also influenced by Philip Wylie's controversial best-selling Jeremiad, *Generation of Vipers* (1942). Bradbury read it over the winter of 1943–44, but it was by no means his first encounter with Wylie's wide-ranging work. Here was another contemporary writer who, like Jack Williamson, shared Bradbury's passion for H. G. Wells and, in particular, for *The Invisible Man*; in fact, Wylie had written his own novel-length variation on this theme (*The Murderer Invisible*, 1931), and had coauthored the screenplay for James Whale's now-classic 1933 motion picture adaptation of Wells's *The Invisible Man* for Universal. Wylie's famous collaboration with Edwin Balmer, *When Worlds Collide* (1933), was one of the very few stand-alone science fiction novels that Bradbury read or owned outside of the pulps.[2] To some degree, he was also influenced by Wylie's periodic engagement with the notion of the superman; among Wylie's explorations of this theme were *Gladiator* (1930), a novel that paved the way for Superman and other superhero comics, and *The Savage Gentleman* (1932), considered the inspiration for the pulp fiction Doc Savage. Wylie revisited the idea of the superscientist in *Generation of Vipers*, and Bradbury's cumulative reading no doubt played into his extended revisions to "Chrysalis" as he reworked it during and after Henry Kuttner's 1942–43 long-distance tutorials on that story.

Although his influence on popular culture was significant, Wylie's impeccable education and formidable powers as a persuasive writer paved the way for his rise to prominence as a well-traveled social critic. Wylie's position throughout *Generation of Vipers* was iconoclastic—he felt that America and the rest of the world's democracies had invited the present war. His style was eloquent, and his charges dramatically wide-ranging; he indicted the shortcomings of science, modern education, church and state, and America's obsession with motherhood. Wylie's famous criticism of "Momism," as he called it, would be debated for decades, but Bradbury was far more interested in what Wylie had to say about how humans think. Early on in *Generation of Vipers*, Wylie noted that "the writer—or anybody else—will come upon the notion that his psyche operates in many ways besides those of verbalized logic, and the logic of mathematics." This spurred Bradbury's recurrent desire to learn more about psychology and the ability to think outside of logical patterns.

Like Bradbury, Wylie felt that moral sensibility had moved further into decline as Americans came to live "too objectively and with too little subjective awareness." In a later chapter, Wylie presented the central irony with even more bluntness: "Our civilization, as this book is designed to demonstrate, suffers from *not* being rational and from not knowing that it is irrational." For a subjective alternative to this logical roadblock, Wylie turned to personified instinct—Jungian archetypes of the hero, the wise old man, and other universal characters found in the mythologies and legends of all cultures: "For the archetypes are the picture-memory of the wisdom of the breed and there are as many of them as there are human qualities and problems. . . . The pattern of nature, inexorably implanted in human instinct, completely expressed in thousands of years of legends, is the compelling pattern of existence."[3]

Bradbury's continuing interest in psychological studies now had an applied example of a Jungian model of behavior that reinforced his own instincts of compassion and engagement as a writer. This approach addressed a central concern of Bradbury's, one that surfaced in many of his letters during the war years: how to give the individual a sense of identity and purpose in a world dominated by special interests and totalitarian states. Wylie's central concern was to take away the usual excuses, beginning with the metaphorical wall of denial: "the wall which keeps us from seeing that the reason for our planetary paranoia lies inside each single individual—and not in the system. . . . You have made the choice of folly, along with the rest. . . . But all the old archetypes are functioning. You know it, somewhere in the dark depths of yourself. . . . Ignorance is not bliss—it is oblivion" (41–42).

From Wylie and other authors of this period, and from his own soul-searching, Bradbury would develop lifelong views about living with the choices we make as individuals. Self-reflection was the key, and over time Bradbury's separate peace with his Baptist upbringing would parallel Wylie's own secular context: "Christ asked only that you set truth first ahead of all other fealties, and that you examine yourself, not your brother, with its light" (304). The title allusion to Matthew 12:34 reflects the core revelation of the book: "either make the tree good, and his fruit good; or else make the tree corrupt, and his fruit corrupt; for the tree is known by his fruit. O generation of vipers—!"

Wylie also offered the goal of improving an educational system that often failed to teach students "the simple distinction between real objects and arbitrary ideas, between real laws and mere opinions, between facts and . . . prejudices" (80). This observation also hit home; in Bradbury's mind, education always centered on libraries and museums, where the books could speak for themselves. But he was always on the lookout for books that could fill the gaps in his own education, and another 1944 reading discovery provided the first detailed overview of Western civilization that he had yet encountered. In August his mother gave him a copy of Lewis Mumford's *The Condition of Man* for his twenty-fourth birthday. The book was a new release, and as one might suspect the gift represented a specific wish-list selection rather than Mother Bradbury's own reading passions. In fact, Mumford's masterful prose and his insightful cultural criticisms were already known to Bradbury. Works such as *Technics and Civilization* (1934), the first volume in Mumford's "Renewal of Life" series, offered a more humanistic alternative to the Technocracy movement that had engaged Bradbury during the prewar years. "Technics" was an overarching term that Mumford had grown from its Greek root *(tekne)* to show that technology, as a tool of society, is incomplete without the human dimensions of art and craftsmanship.

In *The Condition of Man*, the third volume in the "Renewal of Life" series, Bradbury found a broad interdisciplinary survey of Western thought and culture, as well as creative goals for the new age that might open out of the global conflict. The deep cultural history at the heart of the volume was more important to Bradbury than Mumford's postwar game plan; the first ten chapters provided his first systematic reading of the philosophies, the aesthetics, and the science of the last twenty-five hundred years. It was a great preview, but it was dense—well written, accessible, but dense. Bradbury would also need to *see* the history of the Western world to feel the full impact of the Ages; that experience would come exactly a decade later, in Italy, under the brief but indispensable tutelage of Bernard Berenson.

Bradbury may not yet have been aware of *The Brown Decades* (1931), Mumford's early study of urban American life and architecture, but by the 1950s he would encounter the *New Yorker* essays that Mumford had written on these subjects for nearly thirty years. Over time, Mumford's interdisciplinary approach to art and architecture provided a context for Bradbury's enthusiastic discovery of Frank Lloyd Wright's place in twentieth-century American design. By then, Mumford's work was already part of a broader pattern of influence—in the later 1940s *The Condition of Man*, along with Wylie's *Generation of Vipers*, Joseph Wood Krutch's *The Modern Temper*, Albert Jay Nock's *Memoirs of a Superfluous Man*, and the early essays of Loren Eiseley would help Bradbury begin to articulate his own misgivings about the way mankind might handle future advances in science and technology.

18 With the Blessings of His Mentors

Between the fall of 1944 and the summer of 1945, Bradbury earned quiet recognition of a most personal kind, and it meant the world to him—one by one, his mentors told him that he was now a seasoned professional, rapidly approaching the time when he could become a major market writer. For various reasons none of his three closest writing friends had taken this route themselves, and their blessings reflected an implicit pride that their younger friend had found his own remarkable narrative voice. Leigh Brackett knew it first because she had read most of his submissions during their Muscle Beach Sundays in Santa Monica; his potential was apparent to Brackett during the weekly critique sessions, and successive drafts grew even stronger as they circulated from editor to editor under Julie Schwartz's watchful eyes in New York.

Brackett's blessing came first, in the unexpected form of a trial by fire. During the summer of 1944 she was moving into screenwriting and was soon contracted to come up with an original story and screenplay for Republic's B-picture line of horror films. The result would be *The Vampire's Ghost* (released May 1945), which to her credit proved to be one of the better films in the Republic genre series. But in late August, her recent noir novel *No Good from a Corpse* landed her an even shorter deadline with Howard Hawks to collaborate (with William Faulkner and Jules Furthman) on *The Big Sleep*. By September 1944 she was working on the set at Warner Brothers and asked Bradbury to take over her most important pulp deadline—the final half of a 21,000-word novella she had under contract for *Planet Stories*.

It was, in a way, poetic justice. In the spring he had urged her to try her hand at a full-length novella for *Planet*, and she provisionally called it "Slaves of the Burning Sea." By the time she handed it over to Bradbury in September or October, the first half of the novella had evolved into "Red Sea of Venus," a warrior-tale of the last battle between two rival Venusian civilizations ruling opposite shores of a misty-red ocean. It was still pulp fiction, but it was a challenge—Brackett had no outline and left Bradbury with a single sentence of advice on plot resolution.[1] But she was the best author writing for *Planet Stories* at that time, and had a well-developed narrative at midpoint when she turned it over to Bradbury. Somehow, he managed to work this unforeseen project into his demanding writing schedule; between October 1944 and February 1945 he completed the novella, providing unexpected plot turns as well as two horrifying armies of living dead from beneath the ocean.[2] These new elements could have formed a recipe for disaster, but by this time he knew Brackett's work so well that he was able to control the effects with great restraint. The final version, published as "Lorelei of the Red Mist," remained true to Brackett's vision; in fact, the transition is seamless and would perhaps remain undetectable today if she had not revealed the transition point in her late-life homage to the collaboration: "I'm convinced to this day that he did a better job with the second half than I would have done. Bradbury's section begins with the line, 'He saw the flock, herded by more of the golden hounds.'"[3]

The second blessing came from Edmond Hamilton, her future husband, writing to Bradbury on December 31, 1944, from his family home in New Castle, Pennsylvania: "You always did have the 'knack' of writing—I don't know just what to call it, but a person either has it or doesn't, and you do. Jack [Williamson] does, too. I don't and wish to God I did, but have been able to compensate for it by a strong faculty of plotting and a certain amount of craftsmanship gained from experience. But you've added to the ability to pour it out, the ability to shape a story and make it flow smoothly to a satisfying conclusion, and that's what you needed most, so you are all set now." He knew that Bradbury's talent was a special one, different from his own master plotting abilities that had made Hamilton one of the most prolific and widely published genre authors of the 1930s and 1940s. In his shy but sincere manner, he also made a humorous comment that foresaw exactly what would happen to Bradbury over the next year: "Whenever any of you youngsters come along with enough talent to eclipse us completely, you write yourself right up into higher realms and deliver us from your ruinous competition in the pulps."

The third blessing came from Henry Kuttner, but not before Kuttner offered a characteristic chastisement for one of Bradbury's last attempts to land a story with Campbell's *Astounding Science Fiction*—a long 42-page typescript titled "From Now On." It was inevitable, perhaps, that Bradbury would eventually try his hand at his favorite Wellsian subject: invisibility. The passing tail of a comet has left everyone to discover, at dawn's first light, that all animal life has become invisible to the naked eye. The Remington family soon finds it impossible to locate each other except by voice, because all clothing, food, and drink slowly become transparent at first touch. The world around them suddenly grinds to a halt, and then slowly begins the almost inconceivable task of adjusting to how life will be "from now on." Campbell, who had published Bradbury's "Doodad" in 1943 and had almost taken "Chrysalis," received "From Now On" in early

March 1945 and once again asked Kuttner for advice. The narrative successfully (if unevenly) achieved a low-key humorous tone reminiscent of Kuttner himself, but for the most part it lacked character development. It seemed to his mentor that Bradbury's new story was similar in style to Gerald Heard's "The Great Fog," which also lacked a strong dramatic basis. On March 26th, Kuttner offered his opinion of "From Now On," noting in the first place that the story was "pure style and trick writing . . . a lot of one-sentence paragraphs . . . you just haven't acquired the sound basis of experience, of humanity, that can let you do that."

"From Now On" certainly followed H. G. Wells's "what if" formula, and like Wells's romances it offered only a vague backdrop of scientific cause and effect. This aspect put him on shaky ground with Campbell from the start. But Bradbury's story was no imitation; he moved the narrative vigorously forward into an emotional examination of differences—racial, marital, and generational differences—in a new world of disembodied voices, a world where appearance and clothes and facial expressions no longer existed to be judged. It was one of the first Bradbury stories to circulate that directly addressed issues of race. Mr. Remington is the first to realize what has happened: "Praise the Lord, you can't tell a man's color by stroking his arm . . . all the Jews and Negroes and Orientals are no longer races but one word—men." The central metaphors were not original or sophisticated at all, and he only touched on the actual intercultural tensions at play in the modern world. But in terms of Bradbury's development as a writer, this story lays out a path for several of his best (and most controversial) Martian tales, "The Other Foot" and "Way in the Middle of the Air." Other stories of race were already in his file drawers, but most would have to wait many years to reach print.

"From Now On" offered a very emotional glimpse of a brave new world, but this story would never reach print even though Kuttner saw some signs of promise in it for the future: "I think it very probable that a variation of this style will show up in your novels. But you'll have a stronger basis, there will be fewer infelicities, and you'll have something important to say." The story's evolving dialogues between father and daughter, husband and wife did indeed show signs of the interactions that Bradbury would build into his better fictions to come. He was, in some ways, already beginning to write his way out of his chosen genre, and Kuttner offered a gentle reminder that Bradbury should concentrate on the story rather than the genre scaffolding of science fiction: "You write best when you write simply. Then it's really fine writing."

Nevertheless, Kuttner's long-awaited blessing would soon follow, triggered by a story that delved even deeper into the racial issues that were beginning to surface more and more in his unpublished typescripts. On July 25, 1945,

Kuttner offered his critique of "The Big Black and White Game," Bradbury's first breakthrough sale to a major-market magazine. It had sold two weeks earlier to *American Mercury* for $125, four times what he was receiving from *Weird Tales*. The story emerged from Bradbury's childhood memories of a lakeside resort, where "Big Poe" and the serving staff team of Black baseball players outplay the resort's all-White team of hotel guests. Kuttner's critique was very positive: "This is your best story so far. . . . You've achieved excellent suspense, the writing is extremely smooth and vivid and unpretentious (very vital), and you've succeeded quite admirably in what you set out to do." Kuttner (and Kat as well) wanted to see "Big Poe, a sympathetic character, achieve a moral victory rather than a physical one." But in general, the restraint shown here was a major breakthrough, similar to "The Lake" and "King of the Gray Spaces," which had gone to niche market magazines when they could have made it to this level. "The Big Black and White Game" was Bradbury's forty-fourth professional story to reach print, and it was a turning point in more than one sense.

With this story, Kuttner gently set Bradbury off on his own—not in so many words, but simply by offering his own perspective on the advice he had provided for Bradbury over the past five years. "I want you to remember something I've always tried to point out: that no critic is infallible. The best thing a writer can do is to get several critical opinions, consider them, and then go ahead and do as he damn pleases, making use of any of the opinions if he finds them acceptable. Never take my word for gospel, or anybody's, in the matter of writing." Bradbury was already beginning to learn this lesson from his reading of *The Fountainhead*, and now he was hearing it sotto voce from one of his best mentors. Perhaps both men sensed that the time was right; they remained good friends, but subsequent letters from Kuttner (which continued at least until 1952) center more on their lives and less on the details of their writing. At the same time, editors beyond the niche market magazines began to sense the consistent quality in Bradbury's submissions. Late in the year, Martha Foley selected Bradbury's "The Big Black and White Game" for the *Best American Short Stories of 1946* anthology volume, an honor he had dreamed of since his high-school days.

Kuttner would reinforce the transition in a letter dated October 13, 1945. In it he went so far as to advise Bradbury to quit questioning himself: "You're a good writer, and will be a better one, but lay off this soul-searching stuff. Take a good, close gander at your soul and then sit back and be satisfied. As long as you're paying for your bed and board and paying your own bills, then you're the one who's responsible to yourself and it's your opinions that are important. That's exactly why I've so often told you that my literary criticisms must be considered as one man's opinion, and that it's your own final judgment that's important."

19 New Stories and New Opportunities

Bradbury was, in many ways, already beginning to make his own developmental decisions, and during the spring of 1945 he wrote his first quality novella-length story. He had written long stories for both the detective and the science fiction pulps, but only one of these, the long-labored-over "Chrysalis," had staying power in the genre. That story had probed our natural fears of otherness and the superhuman in our own species; now, he chose to investigate what makes us human from a very different angle through the novella "Eight Day World," which sold to *Planet Stories* in early June 1945. At 15,000 words, this novella sold for $219 and helped Bradbury reach both a new genre status and a new financial plateau in the pulps. "Eight Day World" would reach print a year later in the Fall 1946 issue, as "The Creatures That Time Forgot."

The inspiration for this story followed a fascinating trail. In May of 1945, Bradbury purchased a copy of Bertrand Russell's new and comprehensive *A History of Western Philosophy*. His reading of Mumford's *The Condition of Man* the previous year had, to some extent, prepared Bradbury for Russell's more specialized masterpiece, but working through *History* was nevertheless a challenge. He made it, though, and an examination of that volume today still reveals where Bradbury turned down the corners of pages 800–803, exactly where Russell made reference to the influential French philosopher Henri Bergson. Russell's passage highlights Bergson's continuing importance to both modern philosophy and modern physics: "The two foundations of Bergson's philosophy are his doctrines of space and time." This revelation led Bradbury to Bergson's *Time and Free Will* (1910) and in particular to the chapter titled "Real Duration and Prediction." The library trail to this book is long gone, but one of Bergson's seminal thought experiments provided the creative spark for one of Bradbury's best and longest early tales:

> And in that book, he had a section where he imagined—he was talking about time, and how strange it was in very different shapes and forms. He said, "If you lived in a world where you were born and grew up and grew old and died in nine days, how would you know it?" Especially if it happened to you in a different time context. Things shifted. The way you know is lack of knowledge.

You wouldn't have enough time to accumulate knowledge to make changes, whereas, in our world, we have a lifetime to grow up, get knowledge, and change things. That idea fascinated me, of a world where people realized that if they stay, if they are stuck in that world, they would be destroyed. So then, what are you going to do? You've got to find a hero who would change things so you would go back to normal time.[1]

The result was a highly emotional tale of colonists who have been trapped for generations on a planet that has accelerated human metabolic rates to fantastic levels; people are born, grow to adulthood, age, and die within eight days. The blazing hot days and the arctic nights leave only a few minutes at dawn and dusk when the people can leave the caves they inhabit to gather the plant life that grows incredibly fast during these short daily interludes. Against all odds, a young man and woman manage to collect enough knowledge of the past to escape from the planet and its metabolic nightmare. It is, understandably, a fast-paced plot, but action provides only a portion of the novella's strength. The power of Bradbury's first novella is found in his haunting and highly emotional descriptions of the constant presence of death, which has all but extinguished the qualities of love and hope that make us human. In "The Creatures That Time Forgot" (better known as "Frost and Fire"), and in many of the Martian stories that followed over the next few years, Bradbury settled into an easy accommodation with the science fiction genre—science fiction would serve as a setting, a backdrop, or a situation for stories about people, their hopes, their fears, their aspirations, and their inspirations.

As Bradbury began to extend his fiction into novella-length work, he also began to revisit his prewar dream deferred—the possibility of adapting his stories for radio and film. First, though, he composed an original radio play for the CBS show *Dr. Christian*, a series reflecting small town life that, along with *Vic and Sade*, appealed to his own childhood memories of life in Waukegan. Nelson Bond, whose *Blue Book* stories regularly entertained Bradbury during the war years, had won the *Dr. Christian* script competition for 1943, and Bradbury would try, unsuccessfully, to win the 1945 prize. At about the same time, however, his success in the detective pulps led to his first breakthrough into radio. In March 1945, Bradbury began to send stories to Young & Rubicam, the New York advertising firm that handled the writing talent for NBC's very popular *Mollé Mystery Theatre*. The firm had already approached Schwartz for stories by two other authors he represented—Robert Bloch and the late Stanley Weinbaum. Bradbury's first submission was "Killer, Come Back to Me!" (*Detective Tales*, July 1944), which had been the first Bradbury crime yarn to reach print. Eventually Frank Telford, Young

& Rubicam's director for the Friday night *Mollé* show, approached Schwartz and Mike Tilden of *Detective Tales* for permissions.[2] It was a slow process, involving another writer for the adaptation, but on May 17, 1946, the show aired nationally, featuring Richard Widmark in the lead role. It was the beginning of a significant Bradbury radio presence, spanning the final decade of radio's golden age.

At the same time that he was first reaching out to the radio world, Bradbury also made his first Hollywood connections as a writer. Sometime during the fall and winter of 1944–45, Leigh Brackett introduced him to Erline Tannen, her representative with Myron Selznick's film agency. Through Brackett's connections at Republic, Bradbury was soon offered the writing assignment for *Catman of Paris*. The film was to be directed by Lesley Selander, who had most recently worked with Brackett on *The Vampire's Ghost*. Although Brackett's film turned out to be better than most of Republic's mediocre horror films, Bradbury was concerned that Republic's B-productions did not stand up well against the better horror features produced by Universal at the time. He sensed that his initial reputation as a screenwriter would be completely dependent on Republic's very limited studio budget and decided to pass, for the time being, on his first chance to enter a studio through the front gate.

Over the next year or so he would consult Tannen whenever the smaller studios sniffed around the rights to his published stories. In September 1945 Brackett sent Tannen "The Big Black and White Game," and she remained interested in his work for some time. By now Bradbury's stories had fans throughout Hollywood, but during the mid- and late-1940s none of the larger studios were interested in backing his older genre fiction. Periodically, when producers like the King Brothers showed interest in a quality Bradbury story such as "The Lake," Tannen could provide the advice he needed; but Bradbury still did not have a literary agent in New York to advise him as he began to break out of the genre pulp markets. Kuttner and Schwartz both recommended Ed Bodin, and Kuttner also recommended the Saunders Agency; Bradbury had seen Bodin's agency ad in *Writer's Digest* and decided to engage him on a short-term basis. During the fall of 1943 Bodin circulated a few Bradbury stories, but without success.[3] By late 1944, Bradbury turned to Arkham House founder August Derleth as an unofficial advisor.

Derleth had come to appreciate the unique perspective and style that Bradbury brought to the pages of *Weird Tales*, and in early 1945 he drew Bradbury into his circle of authors by giving him the green light to develop his own story collection for Arkham House. This arrangement also provided Bradbury with opportunities to appear in anthologies that Derleth edited for other publishers in New York; in return, Derleth asked for more control of Bradbury's reprint rights than mainstream publishers might have done with established authors. But then, Bradbury was still trying to establish himself, and Derleth was an honest, if dominating, publisher-editor.

Schwartz and Kuttner cautioned Bradbury about Derleth's required half-split on all reprint rights.[4] Bradbury, looking forward to his first book and perhaps a series of anthology appearances, was willing, for the present, to agree to Derleth's terms. But he had managed to reject, after some serious thought, Derleth's June 1944 suggestion that he change his name to something more dramatic than "Ray Bradbury." Today, the mind boggles at the possibility of a world without "Ray Bradbury," but Derleth had thought the name was too "hail-fellow-well-met." The young writer considered Ray Douglas Bradbury, Douglas Bradbury, and R. D. Bradbury before adapting a fellow Midwesterner's nonchalance toward Derleth and concluding, "I guess I'm too darn used to just plain Ray Bradbury."

But the lack of an agent continued to be a problem. As early as July 1944 Bradbury had asked Derleth if he knew any writers' magazine publishers who might serve the purpose over the short term. Bradbury's idea was to find a publisher who could provide, at least for a time, an editor-mentor: " . . . is there any particular one whose editors will go somewhat out of the way to offer constructive criticism? I've submitted to STORY in the past, but Burnett is so deluged with mail that he finds it impossible to take time out on any specific author; and I'd like to find an editor whose mail-sack is smaller and who will shake hands and trounce my stories good when they need it." Story magazine editor Whit Burnett, one-time husband of Bradbury's favorite mainstream anthologist Martha Foley, was unable to make the time. Although Derleth did not ask for the role, he became a de facto advisor for Bradbury through the middle 1940s.

It was a relationship that would, at times, test the patience of both men because Bradbury was determined to move beyond genre labels. His early July 1945 sale of "The Big Black and White Game" to American Mercury was a breakthrough, but only consistent success would give him the confidence he needed. Then, within a matter of days, Bradbury sold three stories to the major market slick magazines: Collier's ("One Timeless Spring") and Mademoiselle ("Invisible Boy") in late August, and Charm ("The Miracles of Jamie") in September. These three unexpected sales brought him checks totaling $975, a windfall that he did not have to share with an agent. Bradbury had never seen so much money anywhere in his life; for a few days, he cashed out the $500 he had received from Collier's in hundred-dollar bills, just to see them in his hands and show to a few trusted friends.[5]

The catalyst, however, came from an unlikely source. Kuttner had advised him to submit to the slicks as early as February 1944, but for more than a year

Bradbury found himself too unsure to make a systematic attempt to break out of the genre markets. Then suddenly, during the summer of 1945, his friend Grant Beach offered some characteristically blunt advice: take the best unpublished new stories and send them out to the slicks, scattershot, without trying to match a story to a particular magazine's fiction profile. The advice was also characteristically self-serving; for some time Beach had wanted to take an extended trip into Mexico to find masks and ceramics for the Los Angeles Museum and for his own studio, but he needed a companion with the means to share expenses. Suddenly, Bradbury had the means to travel, and although he had no real interest in exploring Mexico, he felt an obligation to Beach for sparking his breakthrough sales. It was, though, more complicated than the simple sense of obligation that Bradbury has always described. He had, in fact, sent out stories to the major market magazines from time to time throughout the winter and spring of 1945, just as Kuttner had urged. He would have made the breakthrough, with or without Beach's advice, in short order; but Beach had critiqued his story drafts throughout the war years and Bradbury valued the insights that welled up from Beach's deep passion for psychology and philosophy.[6] The rapid sequence of sales merely intensified these unspoken obligations. Bradbury knew he had to make the trip; what he couldn't know was that Mexico would have a profound impact on his writing for decades to come.

20 | Life and Death in Mexico

The logistics of the trip would be complicated by Bradbury's abiding fear of automobiles—the multiple-fatality accident he had witnessed shortly after moving to Los Angeles in 1934 remained a recurring nightmare, even though he had managed to release some of the effects by writing "The Crowd." More recently, his fear of long-distance auto travel led him to back out of a family vacation to Arizona at the very last minute.[1] Nevertheless, the Mexico trip soon proved to be a watershed moment in his career—it would provide material for some of his best fiction of the late 1940s and early 1950s, and it would radiate on down the decades into *The Halloween Tree* and beyond; but the trip would also prove to be one of the most challenging and traumatizing personal experiences of his life.

During the last week of September 1945 Bradbury set out as map-reader and companion in Beach's late-1930s V-8 Ford sedan, heading east all the way across southern Arizona, New Mexico, and Texas to the border crossing at Laredo. They proceeded into Mexico through a great swarm of locusts that seemed to underscore the completely alien nature of the adventure in Bradbury's mind. But this highway offered the only direct passage to Monterrey, Lenares, and the citadel towns of Mante and Valles. In these towns the two men discovered the buying power of their dollars and were able to stay in excellent hotels. Their route continued south between the Gulf of Mexico and the eastern slope of the Sierra Madre Oriental, where they began to purchase the masks that Beach had come to find. For Bradbury, the change in terrain was striking. "When you cross Texas in the heat, everything is silver and yellow and white. It's nothing. And then you get to the Mexican border, and you begin arriving in jungles and everything turns green. And then you pass those little towns and hit an orange wall, a yellow wall, a blue wall, a red wall . . . all the colors of the rainbow begin to hit you from the walls and the buildings. So color becomes part of your life, color enters your imagination."[2]

Beach and Bradbury proceeded through Tamazunchale and on up to the central plateau of Mexico. The strangeness never ceased to amaze them both: "We saw a spider so big we actually got out of the car to examine it. It was bigger than one of my hands, and quite furry."[3] By October 9th they had reached Zimapan, where Bradbury began to compose a few mood pieces on his typewriter. His subjects were studies in contrast, as he would recall more than sixty years later:

> One night, walking through the streets of Zimapan, this woman came around the corner, and she was carrying over her shoulders two pans of charcoals. The two brains of charcoal were whirling rain in the wind—fireflies from the charcoal. So I put that in The Halloween Tree. I always remembered it. And in that very same quarter of Zimapan, I looked in the front of someone's house, and there's a beautiful lady, a young girl, sitting at a blue piano playing Beethoven. We stood outside the house looking at her with her long dark hair, and she's playing on a piano that's blue. These things stay with you forever. It's amazing.[4]

A two-page typescript survives, dated the night of their arrival in Zimapan, and it includes Bradbury's description of the woman balancing those very same braziers of charcoal, "breathing red, like pink brains glowing and thinking, balanced on gliding carriers, passing." But even as he recorded these beautiful snapshots of life, he was already beginning to discover the abject poverty all around him, and he could sense the low regard for life implicit in such an environment. Bradbury felt at home with the children of México D'Afuera in Los Angeles, but he never found the same comfort in the land of their fathers. Mexico was, at times, a dangerous place, and his own latent fears of death moved a notch closer to the surface of his mind.

The two travelers soon reached Mexico City, and for the next eighteen days they would remain there, exploring the urban culture and taking short day trips and overnight excursions through the region. They first stopped at the home of Jorge Escotto and his mother. Escotto had lived for a time in Mrs. Beach's Los Angeles tenement before returning to Mexico City, where he was about to graduate from Medical School. Their house turned out to be too small for visitors, but Bradbury had another contact through two American women, friends of his Aunt Neva, who were staying at Siento Seis Lerma, a large house contracted by Smith College for students spending their third-year study abroad program in Mexico. The Smith women were still in studies at Guadalajara, and for the month of October the rooms were available to private visitors.

Bradbury and Beach made day trips to nearby historical sites and cities. On one excursion Bradbury had himself photographed at the garden wall of Emperor Maximilian's Palace; another time they took the highway east out of Mexico City all the way to Vera Cruz on the Caribbean coast. He was amazed by a ghostly port town close to Vera Cruz, the harbor long since silted in and dotted with stranded, rusting freighters. This dead zone would provide the setting for his story, "Where All Is Emptiness There Is Room to Move." A longer five-day adventure led through the grand estates of Cuernavaca and on south to Taxco and Acapulco. Back in Mexico City, Bradbury did no shopping and very little sightseeing. Instead, he spent most of his time seeking out the murals and paintings of José Clemente Orosco, David Alfaro Siqueiros, and Diego Rivera. He was also fascinated by the Church of the Blessed Virgin, where worshippers approached the altar on their knees.

By now, though, the trip was beginning to take on a darker mood. It began with Beach himself, who projected an almost constant ill humor. He did not have Bradbury's natural ability to converse with new acquaintances; furthermore, Beach had been sick with strep throat through much of the trip, and he expected Bradbury to find him medicines and doctors along the way. He also expected Bradbury to handle all of the room arrangements and service the car in each town, even though Bradbury did not speak Spanish and had never driven an automobile. This was one of many contradictions in his character, for Beach knew Spanish well enough to handle these negotiations with ease. In Mexico City Bradbury began to suspect that there was more to Beach's behavior than physical discomfort could explain; the mail that Mrs. Beach and his parents forwarded from home included "Invisible Boy" in advance copies of the November *Mademoiselle*, but Grant tried to stop him from showing the story to their friends at 76 Lerma. He began to sense that Beach was jealous of his achievements; eventually Bradbury would discover that his friend was a secret writer who was becoming increasingly bitter over his own lack of success.[5]

Bradbury was also troubled by the intercultural tension he was sensing almost every day in Mexico. It really didn't matter if the contact was urban or rural—there was always, it seemed, an underlying coldness that was all the more chilling because it was not personal at all. Throughout his career, he would write stories in response to the twin tragedies of poverty and racial bias. But Mexico almost overwhelmed him, and the only way to deal with the experience was to write— without delay. His first telling survives in the form of a three-page typescript fragment, dated October 26, 1945, intended as the opening of a novel concept titled *The Fear of Death Is Death*.

> You go into Mexico, and there it is, the smell of death. It is there with the smell of church incenses and the cookings of many foods. You live in an effluvium of death. The air is one part melancholy. The wind is one part dirge. . . . It drips from the eaves of your window on rainy Mexico City afternoons and it is in the opening groan of the door, and everybody sings and there is bright dancing, but, nevertheless, you are living with death.

You feel it when you are once over the border, it is there and nothing you can do with the throttle or money or your mind will put it away from you. The tall towers of the churches lie across your path all the way from Nuevo Laredo to Mexico City to Acapulco, blue shadows that are cool stratas across the hot baked completeness of Mexico. And you feel the feeling and know the knowing of the cool thing that lies across your path.

He would work on this novel, in one form or another, for eight more years, never finishing it, but eventually producing seven published stories that all touch on some of the darker aspects of the journey.

Bradbury's focus now turned back to the original goals of the trip, for they were about to leave Mexico City and head west for an extended tour of the Tarascan Indian culture. On October 29th they set out for Toluca, spent the 30th in Morelia, and arrived in Patzcuaro on the 31st to join in the coming celebrations of El Día De La Muerte. During the traditional midnight boat ride across Lake Janitzio, he met Madame Man'Ha Garreau-Dombasle, wife of the French ambassador to Mexico. In decades to come she would promote his work within French literary circles, but her greatest impact on his life came the next morning in Patzcuaro, when she suggested that Bradbury and Beach continue far to the north to study the mummies of Guanajuato.

First, though, they had to fully explore the local area, for Patzcuaro and the native town of Uruapan to the west were in the heart of the old Tarascan culture. He soon discovered the shop of Señor Cerda, a master craftsman whose masks were different from those he had yet encountered anywhere on the journey. In eastern Mexico, the masks had been representations of Conquistadors and Indian or African faces; here, Señor Cerda's masks were more imaginative—exquisite little miniatures carved from balsa—and Bradbury bought several dozen. Within a year and a half, nine of these would adorn the dust jacket of Dark Carnival as part of a photographic collage.

On Monday the 4th they viewed the many fine masks in the museum at Uruapan. The next day, Bradbury and Beach visited the newest natural wonder on the planet, the Paricutín volcano, which had recently engulfed the village that gave it its name. On Wednesday the two set out for another perspective of Paricutín, this time from the old village church; they climbed into the tower from the original lava flow, which was level with the church bells. Later in the day, they returned to Patzcuaro and started out for the nearby waterfalls. But Beach's mood had once again turned dark, and Bradbury walked back to their lodgings while Grant continued up to the falls on horseback. In town, alone, Bradbury checked the train schedules; for the first time, he began to think seriously about leaving Beach and returning home to Los Angeles on his own.

On Thursday November 7th Beach drove them north along the eastern shore of Lake Champala en route to several days in Guadalajara. They were fascinated by the mummies preserved in glass cases at the Guadalajara museum, which provided a preview of the most famous concentration of mummies in all of Mexico. On Wednesday the 13th they arrived in Guanajuato, where the arid climate and unusual soil chemistry preserved the many mummified corpses disinterred when families failed to make the annual payments for burial space. That evening they shopped for pottery and climbed to El Pípila's monument for a view of the town. The next day, Bradbury and Beach visited the famous catacombs. Bradbury's trip notes barely begin to describe the trauma: "The mummies! In the catacomb. Christ, what horrors! Brrrrr." Bradbury has told the story more often, perhaps, than any other true-life tale, both in print and in interview. A recent private conversation shows almost no variation from the content of his earliest accounts: "It made me afraid of life! I got to the end of the catacomb. It was a hundred feet long, there were mummies on each side. They were wired against the wall—a hundred mummies here, a hundred mummies there. I got to the far end and I turned, I looked back—it's a hall of mummies. I said, 'Jesus Christ, I don't want to go back!' I was terrified. It was a horrible, horrible thing. So Grant managed to get me back through, and I was a wreck by then."

This was a Jamesian "vastation," producing a terror almost beyond words. But Bradbury had to find words in order to survive, and this gallery of mummies quickly resurfaced at the core of his early realistic masterpiece "The Next in Line," completed within months of the experience. "The Candy Skull," one of his last stories for the crime pulps, also centers on the mummies of Guanajuato, and the ultimate test of human compassion at the conclusion of The Halloween Tree requires each of the boys to sacrifice a year of life to help Joe Pipkin escape from the catacomb. Bradbury and Beach immediately left town, canceling plans to explore San Miguel Allende, and headed for San Luis Potosi—the first town on the route back north to the United States.

Bradbury's departure from Guanajuato may not have been as simple as the log entry indicates; in fact, a significant variant soon emerged from his own storytelling subconscious. The horror of "The Next in Line" is heightened when the automobile breaks down, forcing the American couple to remain one more night in Guanajuato and listen to the relentless hammer-tapping of the coffin-makers. At the end of the story, only one of the two central characters will awaken from the terror. Bradbury no doubt did hear the coffin-makers in Guanajuato during the night *before* visiting the catacombs; given his highly pitched Poe-esque imagination, the chilling irony of Guanajuato's death cycle was already having an effect. However, Bradbury's brief log indicates that, in reality, the car had broken down in Guadalajara several days earlier, but not in Guanajuato. The conflation of the two events became great fiction, however, and over the years it also became reality for Bradbury—the imagined extra night in Guanajuato has embellished every subsequent telling of the real-life events. For Bradbury, growing the mythology in his own mind could sometimes become a vital part of the writing process.

On the way to San Luis Potosí, Bradbury and Beach passed a scene that reminded the young writer once again of the poverty that seemed to surround him at every turn in the road. In 2002 he remembered it this way in a private reflection: "Everywhere you went, the . . . things you threw away were the things they picked up. Going from Guanajuato, . . . we saw a crashed airliner by the side of the road. They'd never taken it away. Too much bother. But the ants were taking it away. Like those films—you see the ants, the leaf ants, they're picking up bits of leaves, and they're walking and walking. Well, this airliner was invaded by ants. You pass by, and there are peasants coming to get a piece of aluminum or an engine part or a piece of glass. That airliner will be gone a year later. You don't bother to take it away. The people will take it away."[6] The beautiful things he had written about in Zimapan were now enveloped within the overwhelming sadness he felt for Mexico. This feeling was already apparent in the more somber passages he had written later on, in Mexico City. His writing about Mexico would move between these sentiments, and he would slowly develop variations on the good and the bad of his Mexican odyssey. But first, he had to get home, and more than two thousand highway miles still separated him from Los Angeles.

Beach drove them back north, retracing their original route back through the border crossing at Laredo. They made it to El Paso on Sunday the 24th and crossed back over into Ciudad Juarez for one more day of shopping in Mexico. Gas was cheaper south of the border, but when Bradbury accidentally overfilled the tank Beach's temper flared white-hot. All of his self-indulgent frustrations came together at once: he was exhausted from driving every day on challenging roads, and he expected Bradbury to handle all of the other aspects of travel. He made no allowances for the challenges of a strange land and unfamiliar language, and he lashed out at every perceived mistake. Beach's repressed writer's jealousy undoubtedly played into this flare-up, and now Bradbury had reached his own breaking point as well. Their friendship was beginning to unravel; Bradbury wasn't yet fully aware that it was the beginning of the end, but his subsequent actions that day foreshadowed the inescapable conclusion.

It was a hot afternoon, and while Beach napped, Bradbury quietly gathered some of his belongings and set out for the bus station. He had left eight weeks of purchases and his typewriter with Beach; leaving the typewriter was a calculated risk, for this was the machine he had purchased secondhand in the fall of 1937 and hundreds of his earliest story typescripts had emerged from it. Two days later, on Tuesday November 26th, Bradbury arrived in Los Angeles and explained the situation to Mrs. Beach. Grant continued on in the Ford with the rest of the baggage and purchases; along the way, he pulled to the side of a bridge crossing and threw Bradbury's typewriter into a river.

Transitions: Bradbury and Don Congdon

The early months of 1946 were challenging for Bradbury, both personally and professionally. For Christmas, Beach presented Bradbury with a copy of Edwin Seaver's latest anthology, *Cross-Section 1945: A Collection of New American Writing*, but there was now a somewhat unfathomable jealousy in Grant's approach to Bradbury's career. This tenseness further aggravated the growing sense of stagnation that Bradbury felt about his own prospects. The nine weeks away from Los Angeles had significantly slowed his writing schedule—he had nothing under review with the major market magazines, and during the first three months of 1946 Schwartz was able to sell only one of the pulp market stories he was still circulating for Bradbury. To add insult to injury, that sale went to *Weird Tales*, for "The Smiling People," and netted only $31 at the usual penny-a-word rate.

In spite of these challenges, however, there were developments that boded well for the long term. He was still establishing the contents and revising stories for *Dark Carnival*, which he had promised to deliver to Derleth in April. *Who Knocks?*, Derleth's latest anthology for the major New York publishing house of Rinehart, would include "The Lake," Bradbury's first anthologized story. But a wider range of anthologists were now interested in Bradbury's work. The previous year, Oscar Friend had requested "The Jar" for a projected Leslie Charteris anthology under his well-known "The Saint" (Simon Templar) series imprint. Bill Spier, director-producer of the popular *Suspense* radio program, was also considering several Bradbury stories for a *Suspense* anthology. Neither of these projects worked out, but Bradbury did win a place for "The Watchers" in *Rue Morgue No. 1*, the first Rex Stout mystery annual, for 1946 publication.[1]

At the same time, Bradbury's four major market magazine sales from the summer of 1945 led to even greater opportunities. In early November, while Bradbury was still in Mexico, New York agent Jacques Chambrun wrote asking to represent Bradbury. Chambrun, who represented Bradbury's beloved Somerset Maugham in America, had just read "Invisible Boy" in *Mademoiselle*. Leland Hayward, the agent-husband of film star Margaret Sullavan, did Chambrun one better by contacting Bradbury in Mexico City with the same request. But Bradbury did not yet know enough about these agencies, or indeed about any agency, to make a commitment, and he politely declined both. Various New York publishing houses were also interested in contacting him—between August 1945 and March 1946, Bradbury received three direct requests—from Lippincott, Farrar-Strauss & Company, and Simon & Schuster—to submit a novel or story collection of his own. Two of the letters came from names that Bradbury recognized: editor-publisher Whit Burnett of *Story Magazine* and *The Story Press* made the Lippincott offer, and Roger W. Straus Jr. initiated the Farrar-Straus bid.[2]

But the earliest of the three offers came from Don Congdon, the most recent editorial hire at Simon & Schuster. He was no newcomer to publishing, though, having spent nine years with Lurton Blassingame's agency and a year as an associate fiction editor at *Collier's*. In July 1945 he moved into the book trade with Simon & Schuster, but a month later his friends at *Collier's* tipped him off to a new major market talent named William Elliott. Bradbury had submitted all three of his late-summer slick sales as William Elliott, fashioning the name from the Modernist poets William Carlos Williams and T. S. Eliot. On August 27th Congdon wrote "Mr. Elliott" to see if he had a novel or anything of length for Simon & Schuster to review. Bradbury was already arranging to have the three slick sales published under his real name, and on September 11th he revealed his identity to Congdon in a letter that also outlined his first plans for a novel. It involved the sometimes unbridgeable differences between adults and children, and it would eventually evolve into the *Summer Morning, Summer Night* materials that produced both *Dandelion Wine* and *Farewell Summer*.

Congdon wrote back on the 18th with interest, comparing Bradbury's idea favorably with Henry James's *The Turn of the Screw* and Richard Hughes's *The Innocent Voyage*, a novel Bradbury had already encountered under its original title, *A High Wind in Jamaica*. Bradbury received Congdon's letter on the 20th, just before he set out for Mexico, and he didn't have to wait very long to discover that Congdon was won over as a fan; a letter forwarded to Bradbury in Guadalajara praised "Invisible Boy," which Congdon read while Bradbury was on the road.[3] In December, Bradbury forwarded the typescript of "Homecoming," his finest piece of fiction to date. In his January 3, 1946, response, Congdon suggested several slicks, in descending order of probability based on his own experiences in the New York magazine market: "The vampire tale, Homecoming, is a fine piece and I can't understand why it hasn't sold somewhere." But that was just the problem—Congdon soon learned that Bradbury wasn't represented by anyone beyond the pulp field.

For the time being, Bradbury continued to rely on August Derleth for occasional guidance, especially on the stories destined for *Dark Carnival*. Over the next two years Bradbury would give up control of reprint rights to Derleth in a way that a represented author might have been able to avoid. But Bradbury was reluctant to let Derleth shape his newer work, for there was always the danger that he would come to regard Bradbury as one of a number of Arkham House "properties." Instead, he began to show his new stories to Don Congdon for criticism and advice. Even though Congdon was not an agent, he believed in Bradbury enough to work with him even before he had any book-length work ready for review. In this unofficial capacity, Congdon's influence and contacts in the slick magazine world would help secure major sales for some of Bradbury's best new fiction during 1946.

Spring began well for Bradbury. By this time Congdon had read all four of the major market stories that had financed Bradbury's Mexican excursion, but he was more interested in "Homecoming," Bradbury's unsold story of the Elliotts, a supernatural clan of vampires, werewolves, shape-changers, and other fantastics modernized into a semisecluded Midwestern family. Bradbury had already received rejections from *Harper's Monthly*, the *Saturday Evening Post*, and *Collier's*; the story was now at *Mademoiselle*, and had been there since January. In early March, Congdon took the liberty of passing his copy of "Homecoming" to Innes MacCammond, editor-designate for a projected Marshall Fields national weekly magazine that was as yet only known in publishing circles as *Project X*. MacCammond and his staff quickly became very interested in Bradbury's work; although they declined this story, the heat of competition helped secure an offer from *Mademoiselle*.

"Homecoming" was making headway at *Mademoiselle* even before Congdon used it to establish *Project X*'s interest in Bradbury. The story seemed too unusual for *Mademoiselle*'s readers, but Truman Capote, a staff favorite who was just beginning to make his own mark as a short-story writer, singled it out from other submissions. Margarita Smith, *Mademoiselle*'s assistant fiction editor, shared Capote's enthusiasm but initially saw no way for Bradbury to tailor the rather long "Homecoming" narrative for their readership. "Invisible Boy," Bradbury's first *Mademoiselle* story, was shorter and remained firmly grounded in folklore presented through a child's imagination, thus requiring somewhat less of a leap into the fantastic.

Congdon's actions were crucial in breaking the impasse. He had known Rita Smith for some time, and they often talked of Bradbury; Congdon's news of MacCammond's interest prompted Smith and fiction editor George Davis to buy "Homecoming" directly from the author on March 27, 1946. In the end they found a way to accommodate this engaging Halloween fable—it seemed better to theme the entire October 1946 issue around "Homecoming" than to lose a good Bradbury tale to the competition. The new *Mademoiselle* sale represented a major milestone, for he now had a repeat sale to a major-market slick. Julius Schwartz, who had only been able to secure one new pulp sale for Bradbury since January, was elated: "That's the important sale. The first might have been a freak, but now that they like you enough for a follow-up, it looks like you're in. Keep punching at them."

It was a big sale in another sense as well, for the $400 payment would not have to be shared with an agent. This was the first top-dollar offer since his four-sale mainstream magazine breakthrough the previous summer, and after the expenses of the Mexico trip it was a welcome windfall. Furthermore, Bradbury was now known in an ever-widening range of publishing markets, and this also meant increasing reprint sales. Checks for anthology reprints of "Skeleton" and "The Watchers" came in, and August Derleth would soon anthologize three more Bradbury weirds. Even his first major market sales were now in reprint demand; a condensation of his first *Mademoiselle* story—"Invisible Boy"—sold to *Story Digest* for $150. Although Bradbury would always resist editorial cutting, this was four times what his pulp reprints were bringing in. Finally, four months after returning from the emotionally exhausting Mexico trip, he was writing and selling again. But there would be unexpected consequences; suddenly, in early April 1946, the professional jealousy that he had sensed in Grant Beach's behavior during the Mexican journey became manifest as Beach now began to tamper with his incoming mail.

Bradbury still enjoyed the good will and friendship of Mrs. Beach and the people who lived in and around her properties at Temple and Figueroa. The lives and personalities of these people inspired many of his stories of this period, prompting Bradbury to continue to work in his tenement office a few days a week and to receive his professional mail there. But all of this changed suddenly, when Beach intercepted a most unexpected honor—a letter from Martha Foley asking Bradbury for permission to place "The Big Black and White Game" in her *Best American Short Stories* anthology for 1946. Beach, masquerading as Bradbury, sent a response declining the honor. Fortunately, Foley mentioned the surprise refusal to Charles Angoff at *American Mercury*, and Bradbury was soon alerted by a telegram from Angoff urging him to reconsider.[4] Beach was unable to intercept the wire, and Bradbury belatedly accepted an honor that lifted him to a new plateau of literary recognition.

Bradbury wasted no time in confronting Beach, who admitted the deceit. Within a few weeks it soon became apparent that Beach was also withholding at least some of the mail from Julius Schwartz concerning Bradbury's radio breakthrough with "Killer, Come Back to Me," and he feared the same for his correspondence with August Derleth. Bradbury was at a crucial stage of work on *Dark*

Carnival—Derleth had just extended the rolling deadline for book submission into June—and by early May Bradbury decided he had no choice but to change his professional address to his parents' house at 670 Venice Boulevard.[5] He still lived there except for occasional evenings at the tenement or at Aunt Neva's, and he already had his cramped but familiar corner office in the family's detached garage. For the next year and a half, the garage and the humming power station across the yard would be the sole center of his creative world.

22 The Power of Love

One constant throughout this major transition in Bradbury's daily work schedule was his need to read—an almost visceral need that was only slightly less of a reflex than breath itself. On April 24, 1946, while reading in Fowler's Bookstore, he met Marguerite McClure for the first time. As a responsible employee, she felt the need to keep an eye on the young man with the suspiciously large overcoat and book satchel; as a writer, his response to the attention was to ask for a store copy of *Who Knocks?*, Derleth's new Arkham House anthology, so that he could show her "The Lake," a reprint of his first quality story. For the moment, luck was with him—"The Watchers," his only other anthologized story so far in print, would have given her a far darker impression of this strange young writer. He also told her of his other recent anthology sales, including his selection for Foley's *Best American Short Stories*. She was amazed to find out that he was a legitimate author and not a thief; for his part, Bradbury was amazed that she paid him any attention at all.

A romance quickly developed over the next few weeks, recoverable today only from fragile memories, a few book inscriptions, and the barest fragments of calendar notes. On the 2nd of May, a Thursday, he bought a copy of Edmund Wilson's *Memoirs of Hecate County* from her at Fowler's. Soon, though, he wouldn't need to hide behind books to be with Marguerite. Within a week they were dating; in early June, the young couple celebrated their first month together with two beach trips sandwiched around an excursion to Griffith Park, a ride on the merry-go-round, and their first movie date—*The Postman Always Rings Twice*, from a favorite James M. Cain novel, was playing at Lowe's State Theater downtown. On June 20th, Bradbury bought Cyril Connolly's *The Unquiet Grave*, and wrote on the endpaper, "Maggie and Ray engaged."

Who was this Marguerite M. McClure? Bradbury immediately found a love of literature in her that was more studied than his own. The complementary nature of their literary passions was symbolized, though by no means established, by a fascinating coincidence: his first preschool book had been the Bates and Price *Once upon a Time*, a foundational fairy-tale primer; her first book had been the companion Bates and Price volume, *A Child's Book of Myths*. If fairy tales embodied Bradbury's abiding fascination with childhood loves and fears, mythology embodied McClure's lifelong interest in history and the Classics. As a child she preferred history to all other reading, and this first passion was perhaps the secret to her more scholarly and methodical reading discoveries. She loved the American and English poets and storytellers that he adored, but she also knew European literature and loved this tradition even more than the Anglo-American. Yet these were complementary experiences, not conflicting, and a new literary synergy began almost from the moment they met—in fact, his purchase of Kafka's *The Castle* dates from one of their first bookstore excursions over to Brentano's.[1] Two talents helped her master this wide command of the Humanities—she could read fast, and she retained all that she read.

Her father was a restaurateur who provided a good home for his family in the Lienert Park neighborhood of town. Here Bradbury saw a level of prosperity that he had not known in his own life; it was all a strange new world for him, but this strangeness did not diminish the first great love he had ever known. Marguerite returned his love with equal passion, bridging the differences by exploring literature with him and encouraging his writing in ways that made the rest of the world seem far away. Many of their dates included bookstore excursions from Fowler's, where she worked, on to the other shops that he had frequented for years—Brentano's, the May Company book department, the Satyr Book Shop, Bullock's, Martindale's in Santa Monica, and Pickwick Books in Hollywood. He called her Peg and Peggy sometimes, and soon settled on Maggie.

His relationship with Maggie developed during a year of creative enrichment that centered on the visible metaphor of the powerhouse, just fifty feet from the window of his garage office. From 1942 to 1945, he had split his office time between the Figueroa Street tenement downtown and the garage of the Venice Beach home his parents rented from the Department of Power and Light. There was a nine-foot-square office walled off in the southwest corner of the garage, creating a small room with a window facing the powerhouse just to the west. Bradbury kept an old Underwood typewriter here along with a new portable Royal he purchased to replace the machine that Beach had destroyed. By the late spring of 1946 the garage had become his primary writing home; he was now free of the downtown distractions that used to interrupt the two or three crucial hours needed for his fingertips to release the first draft of a story.

The Muse was the key to beginning every story, however, and Bradbury sensed early on that the powerhouse offered a prime source of inspiration. But he needed to make the powerhouse his own creative domain first, and during the war years he pushed perhaps too hard. This failure first surfaced in an abandoned introduction for *Dark Carnival*, probably written in the early summer of 1945 as he gathered together the stories for this first collection. *Dark Carnival* was eventually published without an introduction at all, but in the discarded draft he described the story that had so far eluded him:

> I have a perfectly fine Power House next door to my studio in Venice, California and this Power House is a huge, malignant, hulking monster of a building, with frosted green glass in its high thin windows and immense coils and elbows of wire and tubing acluster with electrical sputtering, sparks and worms. All of this is just a dozen paces away as I write this, and yet with a quiet steadfastness that is the special quality of brick and concrete, the Power House has withstood onslaught after onslaught of my typewriter, and still the walls stand, I have no story. I have put dependent writers into it and let them live, I had inserted old maiden ladies through its huge metal doors to see what they might find to fear in it, but as yet no character has acted as the catalyst. The Power House and I are not on writing terms. I fully intend to attack and attack again and again, and one day I shall have a story about this Power House, for it is good stuff. It needs only for me to find a person to react to it in a way so original and horrifying that I will be delighted and immediately sit me at my typewriter and type forth the adventure. But not this month, perhaps not this year. Eventually, one night, I'll enter the Power House, via my typewriter, and scare the living guts out of myself. Then you shall have your story, and only then.

The powerhouse became a symbol of the broader worlds of theme and character that were not yet consistently his, and for a time this humming edifice continued to deny him entry. In a private note to himself, Bradbury admitted that it "persists in being an unresolvable object, there is no catalyst at hand in my brain which will turn the power house from what it is into a highly incredible story . . . I take a character and put him inside it and nothing happens. I put three characters inside and nothing happens. The powerhouse hums a humming melody on one key, one note, and does nothing, not even to me."

The breakthrough began early in September 1945, in the midst of his three rapid-fire sales to major market magazines. In these three stories—"One Timeless Spring," "Invisible Boy," and "The Miracles of Jamie"—Bradbury had evoked fear and anxiety only as background for broader emotions, thus allowing each of the central characters to negotiate a crucial moment of initiation into the adult world. When these three stories sold, Bradbury's confidence grew and the powerhouse began to yield up its secrets. An old folder of unpublished writer's notes contains two pages describing how the powerhouse suddenly played into

Bradbury's idea for a new story: "a woman who never believed in God before, finds God." He made the connection in the final days of the Pacific war, after the unimaginable power of two atomic bombs had changed the world forever:

> Then one night, coming home late, depressed at the war news current in 1945, I looked at the POWER HOUSE wires going out to all the world around me, giving light, and a concept of God came to me, that for every light that was put out, another could come on, the power was there, unceasing and steady, and what seemed like death was simply a ceasing of power at one small point, while light and life were reapplied in another room a few miles distant. Everything balanced suddenly. I had my story. I went into my work room at one in the morning and finished the first draft of POWER HOUSE, a wealth of imaginative detail stored and utilized and put on paper because I had the patience to wait a number of years for the POWER HOUSE to fill me with itself. While writing the story I didn't have to stop and think WHAT IS THE POWER HOUSE? I *knew* what it was in every part of myself, I knew how it looked and how it sounded, and how it smelled, and most important of all, I knew what it meant to me. In my personal discovery I had discovered the core and being of the story I wished to write. And in the story I placed my woman, who did not know God, in a Power House in an Arizona desert on a night when her mother was dying, and herself wondering Why, Why? What is the answer? How can one accept death? The POWER HOUSE taught her, as it had taught me.

On July 23, 1946, just a little more than a month after his engagement to Maggie McClure, Bradbury completed "Powerhouse." Over the next six months it received nine rejections from major-market magazines before finally selling to *Charm*. "Powerhouse" would become an award-winning story, an O. Henry prize-winning selection that confirmed Bradbury's staying power in the major literary markets, but its origins pinpoint an equally important period of creative development. He now knew that every story would have mainstream potential as he continued to broaden his exploration of the emotions that extend from childhood into adult life—the dark and mysterious as well as the wonderful and enlightening. He would continue to write beside the Power House until he married Maggie in late September 1947. During the two years between his first major market sales and his marriage, Bradbury wrote his best short fiction of the decade—Mexican stories, small-town Midwest remembrances, and the science fiction tales that he would shape into *The Martian Chronicles* and *The Illustrated Man*.

23 | From Arkham to New York

Throughout 1946, Bradbury had to navigate the increasingly complicated process of bringing *Dark Carnival* to publication. Derleth had originally expected to list Bradbury's first book as an Arkham House release for the summer or fall of 1946, but Bradbury's continuing revisions resulted in an actual publication date of May 1947. At first, his work evolved predictably enough; Bradbury's original 1944–45 concept (*A Child's Garden of Terror*) stabilized under the *Dark Carnival* metaphor, which was powerful enough to absorb the constant changes in content. By the end of August 1945, *Dark Carnival* was on the Arkham House list of fall 1946 releases; the contract was finalized by the end of the year, with manuscript submission scheduled for February 1946. But Bradbury was still writing new stories for the collection, and he was able to persuade Derleth to extend the submission deadline to April and eventually to June 1946.

Bradbury was beginning to alter his concept of the collection from a survey of his best weird tales to a record of his movement away from the pulps and into mainstream American periodicals. He continued to move older or less successful stories out of the collection, replacing them with newer, better weird tales that had not yet appeared in magazines. All of the older stories that remained were revised, some extensively, and Bradbury completely rewrote "The Wind." He was able to use the evolving *Dark Carnival* collection to signify that a literary author had emerged from a genre where writers were often seen as entertainers rather than authors; through this process, he gave the collection a tremendous new range in tone.

Bradbury took the same view in developing a dust jacket, but this process moved along much more quickly. He had initially wanted a carousel-and-midway composition for the cover, but after his return from Mexico in late 1945 he became convinced that an excellent photographic collage effect could be achieved by using some of the delicate little masks he had purchased from Señor Cerda in Patzcuaro. In December 1945 he went to the Los Angeles Art Center and arranged to review the work of a half-dozen photographic art students. Bradbury was immediately drawn to the work of George Barrows, a young photographer from New England who had recently established himself in California as a cover illustrator for George Leite's experimental *Circle* magazine. By March Derleth had approved one of the two covers that Bradbury and Barrows submitted. Bradbury was relieved, for it allowed him to retain the *Dark Carnival* title—the masks in the collage emerged out of an image of a carousel horse in motion.

This visual focus was even more important now, for he had decided to withhold the original "Dark Carnival" title story from the collection. He sensed that this carnival story, subsequently published as "The Black Ferris" (1948), had the potential to anchor another project entirely, and the Barrows dust jacket provided the sleight-of-hand necessary to cover the loss. But the photographic collage and its Art Center pedigree also allowed Bradbury to further deemphasize the low-carnival carousel-and-midway origins of some of the older stories and underscore the more literary carnival that the more recent stories in the collection promised.[1] As much as he loved their work, he was determined that none of his favorite pulp cover artists would be involved with his book at all.

By June 1946 Derleth finally had the promised twenty-nine-story typescript in hand, and agreed to move the publication timetable back to accommodate a spring 1947 release. At Bradbury's request, he also reluctantly agreed to minimize the copyright page references to the pulp origins of these tales, but not without cautioning his young friend that it might jeopardize copyright protection on the individual tales. It was a good point, but Bradbury remained adamant about minimizing any references to the stereotype of low-carnival entertainment that broader market readers and critics always associated with *Weird Tales*. He knew he was becoming more than a niche-market entertainer, and this conviction is evident in his rejoinder to Derleth's cautionary note: "In closing, then, I hope you'll let me take the responsibility for the castrated copyright page, for in the event of any literary pilfering, it shall be I, not you, who will some time later be heard crying in a high, eunuch's soprano."[2]

Derleth never understood Bradbury's desire to refashion previously published material. He still viewed *Dark Carnival* as an anthology of what Bradbury had done in the pulps, and he resisted the young writer's sense of the collection as a representation of what he was becoming. He was used to controlling more specialized genre authors, and he was also used to authors who shared his somewhat antiquated sense of the genre traditions. Henry Kuttner, who knew Derleth well but had deftly managed to avoid falling under his control, provided Bradbury with some perspective. Kuttner observed that Derleth's expectations for Bradbury probably came from memories of his own early career in the late 1920s and early 1930s: "Look at August Derleth. He began rather like you, sold easily at an early age, got into the novel field, the slicks, etc.; and milked his subjects dry. He never leaves Sauk City mentally. There is now a fatal sterility about his work; he has reached the limits of his cosmos, and he won't go outside of it." Kuttner also felt that these midcareer limitations affected Derleth's broader genre tastes, and he had expressed this view to Bradbury almost two years earlier: "August is a queer fish; he loathes s-f and modern fantasy without discrimination. . . . And the Arkham House books have got fearful pannings from the critics—more or less justified, since Derleth's selections for the anthologies were too esoteric and specialized. Fantasy has moved with the times, but Derleth apparently has not."[3]

Kuttner felt that there was more to the Bradbury-Derleth relationship than just author-publisher friction, for Derleth's midcareer decline as a writer was perhaps an even more important lesson for Bradbury to understand: "I think it's good for you to go ahead and immerse yourself in writing now, writing what you want and how you want. But don't forget the future. If you grow and mature, your work will too, automatically . . . I would not be so emphatic if I weren't forcibly struck by the parallel between your career and Derleth's."[4] Bradbury was indeed at a crossroads where he would have to choose between continued isolation and more engagement with the outside world, and Kuttner knew it:

> You must expand, or your writing will suffer. It'll be a long time before you reach your limits, but while you're still elastic, you should expand. Your Mexico jaunts are an excellent idea. But they are a line of least resistance, in a way. You have got a comfortable microcosm in which you can enjoy yourself, do what you want, and write what you want. And that's swell, for a while. It gives you the opportunity to flex your literary muscles, experiment, and write.
>
> But you must have things to write about. You must get 'em before you use up the material you already have. You should reach out for new things before you have any limits. Right now, you are in exactly the same position that Derleth was in fifteen years ago. New things and people and experiences are vitally necessary for a writer. That's why I think you should visit New York.

Bradbury's trip to New York and back occupied the entire month of September 1946.[5] Bill Spier's purchase of radio rights to Bradbury's unpublished ventriloquist tale "Riabouchinska" for the CBS *Suspense* program brought in $350 over the summer, and this windfall allowed him to make the entire trip by train. He took Union Pacific's *City of Los Angeles* into Chicago for a seven-day layover that served several purposes. First he visited two writers he had recently met but had long admired—Fritz Leiber and Robert Bloch. Bradbury met them just two months earlier, when they came out to Los Angeles for the Science Fiction Convention. He found Bloch's brilliant and morose humor a match for Kuttner's; by virtue of this new friendship, he soon began to receive some of the entertaining but unprintable round-robin stories that circulated between Bloch, Kuttner, Leiber, and E. Hoffmann Price.[6] Bradbury arrived in Chicago on the 6th, spending the night at Leiber's Southside home before moving on to Milwaukee for a weekend with Robert Bloch.

He spent the 9th and 10th of September at August Derleth's Sauk City home, which also functioned as the publishing headquarters of Arkham House. Here Bradbury reacquainted himself with the gentle hills, grasslands, and forests he knew so well from his childhood summers in southern Wisconsin, and enjoyed hiking the countryside with his host. His final goal before boarding the *Pacemaker* out of Chicago was to reconnect with hometown friends and relatives in Wauke-gan and to coordinate the projected spring release of *Dark Carnival* with the local media and bookstores. On Friday the 13th Bradbury finally arrived in New York, where Don Congdon was already setting up meetings and cocktail hours with magazine editors and book publishers. Congdon was just finishing up his first year as an editorial talent scout for Simon & Schuster, and during the next two weeks he was able to secure a verbal commitment from the house to publish Bradbury's evolving Green Town novel. Bradbury decided against signing a con-tract, though, for he sensed that the additional pressure would only complicate his slow and uncertain progress toward writing sustained works of long fiction.

On Monday the 16th Congdon introduced Bradbury to Innes MacCammond, who immediately bought "The Next in Line" for USA, the projected Marshall Field weekly initially known as *Project X*. This tale had grown out of his deeply disturbing experience with the mummies of Guanajuato the previous fall, and the substantial $500 check was sweet compensation for the fact that *Mademoiselle* had passed on it a month earlier. MacCammond turned down "The Cistern" and "The Man Upstairs," but this freed Bradbury to show "The Cistern" to *Mademoi-selle*'s George Davis the very next day.[7] Davis took it under strong consideration, and hosted a cocktail party for Bradbury that evening along with Rita Smith, his assistant fiction editor. Smith's sister, the novelist Carson McCullers, provided Bradbury with a lasting memory of the evening; he would later describe this encounter in a letter to Derleth: "I met Carson McCullers in New York, as well as Charlie Addams, the cartoonist, and Sam Cobean, of the *New Yorker*. I was kept constantly inebriated by all and sundry. McCullers is a fey, pale, pouty, stocking-gawky girl with a bang-fringe hair-do and ploppy ways; I waltzed her wildly about George Davis' . . . house. She is quite neurotic."[8]

Bradbury found himself celebrated throughout his first full week in New York. On Monday evening, John Shaffner of *Good Housekeeping* had taken him out for cocktails; Tuesday culminated in the *Mademoiselle* party; and the next day Charles Addams and Sam Cobean took Bradbury to lunch at the Hotel New Yorker. Ad-dams had already taken a liking to Bradbury's strange "Homecoming" family, for these characters were created in the same spirit as his own weird "Addams

Family" cartoons in the pages of the *New Yorker*. In fact, "The Homecoming" was about to debut in the October issue of *Mademoiselle* with an original Addams color illustration. Bradbury arranged to buy the original, paying $300 to Addams in payments spread across the next year.[9] At some point that week Bradbury also met the two editors who would be most instrumental in his rapid rise to critical prominence. He offered Martha Foley an explanation of the events that almost cost him his place for "The Big Black and White Game" in her *Best American Short Stories* anthology and found that she had a particular fondness and enthusiasm for the unique style and strong emotions of his work. He also met Hirschell Brickell, who would soon anthologize "The Homecoming" as one of the O. Henry anthology stories of 1946–47.[10]

On Friday the 20th he broke away from Congdon's tour of the top-tier magazines to visit Julius Schwartz and some of the pulp editorial offices, where he still had more than a residual interest in publishing. Although Julie was now three years into his pioneering role as a late Golden Age comic book editor with DC comics, he still maintained an active folder of Bradbury's unsold pulp submissions. In spite of his growing success in the major magazine market, Bradbury was still selling more than half of his new stories (and many of his better ones) to the pulp editors who had come to depend on his talent. Since more and more of these sales were to the science fiction pulps, he was willing to accept the quick money that these sales brought him.

During his ten days in New York Bradbury met Frederic Danay, half of the famous *Ellery Queen* writing and publishing team, who was well aware of his crime and weird fiction. He also met editors at *Collier's*, *Good Housekeeping*, and *Harper's*. *Collier's* Larrabie Cunningham had already published "One Timeless Spring," and by the end of the year Katherine Gauss would buy "The Man Upstairs" for *Harper's*. He also met *Charm's* Jane Rice and Oliver Claxton, who had published "The Miracles of Jamie" in the April issue; two years later, they would buy "The Silent Towns"—Bradbury's first major market sale of a Martian story in the United States.

He also visited Paul Payne, the new *Planet Stories* editor at Fiction House, who found Bradbury's latest science fiction stories to be even better than the ones that his predecessor, Wilbur Peacock, had bought in 1944 and 1945. It also helped that a spirited discussion of Bradbury's stories was evolving in *Planet*'s fan letter column. The initial letter was from Chad Oliver, then a young fan destined to become a prominent academic and science fiction author in his own right, but *Planet*'s editors let the debate run on across several quarterly issues. Such actions by Payne and Peacock at Fiction House reinforced Bradbury's own sense that he was putting his best effort into every story he wrote, never aiming at any one market.

Another high point was his first face-to-face meeting with Jack Snow, a promotional writer at NBC radio who shared Bradbury's love of child psychology, children's literature, and especially the works of L. Frank Baum. Snow was so impressed with Bradbury's *Weird Tales* success that he initiated a correspondence with him in early 1944. By the fall of 1944 he was promoting Bradbury's first serious foray into the radio world with his two Johnny Choir stories—"The Ducker" and "Bang! You're Dead!" Snow was able to sell two NBC executives on the idea of developing both of these Bradbury weirds for the juvenile program *Adventure Ahead*, but the series was canceled before anything developed. He was fourteen years older than Bradbury and had published in *Weird Tales* himself during the late 1920s. Monty Buchanan, who effectively controlled sales at *Weird Tales* during the 1940s, had recently published three more of Snow's ghost fantasies, so Snow arranged an evening out with Bradbury, Buchanan, and magazine illustrator Ronald Clyne.[11]

He spent several evenings showing Bradbury how much the Manhattan of 1946 had changed since the 1939 NYCon; in private, he showed Bradbury his collection of Baum's works and presented him with a copy of *The Magical Mimicks in Oz*, the first of two Oz books that Snow would author during the 1940s. This was not his first literary favor for Bradbury, however; through his publishing connections, Snow had been instrumental in placing Bradbury's "The Watchers" in Louis Greenfield's first *Rue Morgue* anthology. During the summer of 1946, Greenfield had proposed publishing a collection of Snow's stories, and Bradbury readily agreed to write the foreword. He would leave New York with galleys of the new Snow collection, titled *Dark Music and Other Spectral Tales*. He would also leave with a new appreciation for two of Snow's favorite composers—Hector Berlioz and Gustav Mahler.

He arrived home on September 29th after enjoying a roundabout rail journey through Atlanta to New Orleans, where he picked up the Southern Pacific's passenger service on through El Paso to Los Angeles. Maggie greeted him with the new books she had purchased for the personal library she would soon merge with his own very different one. These included a two-volume *Alice in Wonderland*, poetry by Robert Herrick and William Blake, the *Viking Book of Poetry*, and more novels by Kafka. Like her fiancée, Maggie appreciated the art of the book as well as the contents; while he was away, she had purchased a finely bound copy of *Madame Bovary* for herself, and a near-perfect first edition of Katherine Anne Porter's *Flowering Judas* for Bradbury.[12] It was, in all respects, a wonderful homecoming. Now, back in his office garage on Venice Boulevard, he was more motivated than ever to transform *Dark Carnival* into a collection that he would be proud to showcase at any level.

24 Obsessed with Perfection

In some ways, Bradbury's public reputation was growing faster than he could handle psychologically. He now had a taste of the high-pressure world of radio production, and he had attracted the attention of major market publishers, editors, and agents on both coasts. His September 1946 train journey to New York and back also opened up the world of transcontinental rail travel to him at a time when the wartime restrictions on transportation were disappearing and passenger rail service was regaining its appeal. A few months before his trip to New York he bought Maggie a first edition of The Hucksters to show her the world of trains and media hype that he was beginning to know.[1] Frederic Wakeman's best-selling "insider" story of a radio advertising executive's rise and fall centers on the New York and Los Angeles entertainment hubs and two of the elite passenger trains that connect them—the Twentieth Century Limited between New York and Chicago, and the Super Chief between Chicago and Los Angeles. Bradbury had taken the less glamorous Southern Pacific passenger service for the western leg of his recent journey home, but in the years to come he became a great fan of Santa Fe's Super Chief and its rival, Union Pacific's City of Los Angeles.

If the Super Chief ("the train of the stars") symbolized his newfound ability to reach the Eastern literary markets in person, his continuing major market sales symbolized his growing popularity with mainstream editors and readers. In November, Martha Foley reprinted "The Big Black and White Game" in Best American Short Stories and included two other Bradbury titles in the volume's Roll of Honor. Before the end of 1946, George Davis and Rita Smith bought "The Cistern"—Bradbury's third sale to Mademoiselle in little more than a year. In early January, Harper's bought "The Man Upstairs" for the upcoming March issue and ABC's World Security Workshop aired his one-act radio play, "The Meadow," on their national network. But he was still learning to handle himself in this new world, and he was trying to manage without the guidance of an agent. The lack of official representation in Hollywood was becoming a problem as well. Just before his New York trip, he was sought out by the King Brothers, who had parlayed their film projector manufacturing business into a B-level motion picture production company during the war years. In mid-August 1946 Maurice King wrote Bradbury with instructions to telephone him at his studio office; King, who had no idea that Bradbury still lived with his parents, had been surprised to find no telephone listing for the young writer.[2]

The King Brothers were interested in "The Lake," but not as a feature film property; instead, they wanted to use this story as an episode or, at most, as a continuing motif in Monogram's *The Gangster*, a film centering on a declining crime lord whose control of the beachfront numbers racket is slowly slipping away from him. Bradbury's story of a young girl who drowns but seems to return years later to rebuild her little sand castle would no doubt have complemented the highly emotional psychological noir drama at the heart of the Daniel Fuchs screenplay, but this was not to be. Bradbury turned to Erline Tannen, Leigh Brackett's agent, who had helped with the ill-fated Republic negotiations two years earlier, and asked her to make the call for him from her office at the Selznick Agency.[3] She relayed Maurice King's initial offer of $500 to Bradbury, who instructed her to counter with $5000 and not to go below $2000. The King Brothers found this position absolutely unacceptable—Monogram was marketing *The Gangster* for release as an A-grade film through United Artists, and money was tight. Bradbury broke off negotiations; as welcome as the money would have been while courting Maggie, he felt that he had to protect the potential option value of his stories even if he really didn't know just what that value was.

His own inexperience and lack of representation also played a part in this debacle, and he was thankful that Julius Schwartz was still circulating his new stories among the New York pulp editors. But Bradbury was sending fewer and fewer selections East, for he was gradually becoming obsessed with perfection. He worked the only way he knew how—by instinct, writing rapidly from sudden insights, often producing a story draft within a few hours, and always revising the entire work many times before circulating the result. It was not a formula that necessarily worked for others, and sometimes his convictions led to conflict with the few writers he considered intimates. There was now a tendency to judge where he had once simply observed and learned. This tendency began to surface in the fall of 1946, after his intoxicating experiences in New York.

During that trip he had reconnected with Hannes Bok, whose brilliant but erratic successes as a pulp illustrator and cover artist had led to professional sales of his own fantasies. In the old days, when Bok wrote only for his own entertainment or for the occasional fanzine appearance, they had not had many writer-to-writer conversations. But now they were both professional writers, and in November 1946 Bok wrote—in his inimitable offbeat style—to find out whether they shared any techniques: "[T]ell me (if thou wilst) do you write more or less first draft, Ray, or do you do several versions & choose the best one afterward? Practically everything I ever wrote was hot from the typewriter (a la Jack

Woodford's advice)—and I didn't like it, but it sold. Whereas every tale I'd sweat over, revising like mad, got bounced. I'm curious; thought maybe it'd lie in your experience to explain."

Jack Woodford's *Trial and Error* had been one of Bradbury's first readings in the art of writing, and he found that most of Woodford's tips on initial composition fit his own spontaneous and un–self-conscious habits. But Bradbury was coming to believe that careful revision, sometimes over a period of weeks or even months, was preferable to immediate circulation "hot from the typewriter." He preached the need for revision in his response, and Bok soon rejoined with a dissenting analogy from the lessons he had learned about art from Maxfield Parrish: "Thanks for your explaining your writing-method. I've never tried the second, third and fourth draft method: reason is a carry-over from drawing. Once I sent Parrish a bunch of quick sketches outlining picture ideas. M. P. told me to frame the sketches, that he never makes them, since you put all your feeling into the sketch, and the picture itself, a mere copy of the sketch, lacks life. I found this to be true, and got to the point where I never could do a sketch—every picture was finished from the start."

Bok's analogy is historically significant, for Parrish never documented or commented on his interactions with the few artists he mentored. More to the point, however, Bok was making it clear that he would continue to write as he painted, never revising or rewriting in any substantive way. Bradbury tried to bring his friend around to a longer view of the writing process by recommending one of the books that had helped his own technique a few years earlier—Lajos Egri's *How to Write a Play*. Bok good-naturedly but firmly rejected Bradbury's advice, noting that Abe Merritt and H. P. Lovecraft often went final from first drafts. He knew, without any particular regret, that he was doomed to remain in the pulps and began to fulfill his own prophecy by completing and publishing two novels that his good friend Merritt had left unfinished at his death.

This difference of opinion left no scars; Bradbury knew that Bok's legacy would rest not with his fiction, but rather with his unique style of pulp magazine cover art and interior illustration. Bok was now living in seclusion in a poor district of Manhattan on the outskirts of Harlem; Jack Snow had met him through Ron Clyne and had offered Bradbury a plausible explanation for this eccentricity: "I think Bok has been hurt dreadfully in some manner and that he fears the world. He hides himself in Harlem and delights in the association of the lowest class people. Don't you see—he's safe that way—he cannot be slapped down any further." Throughout these personal trials, however, Bok remained very fond of Bradbury, Forry Ackerman, and the other SF&F writers and fans he had met in Los Angeles before the war. As they renewed their friendship in the fall of

1946, Bok was very pleased to discover that Ray had found someone like Maggie McClure, and was elated that they were engaged to marry. In spite of his exotic lifestyle, he could appreciate this milestone event and offered congratulations in his usual zany way: "Ackerman predicts the collapse of civilization within five years. I hope you and Maggi [sic] will be members of my clan."

There was only a hint of intolerance in Bradbury's friendly exchanges with Bok, but his growing need to distance himself from his own apprentice writing was beginning to spill over into an increasingly vocal desire to distance himself from the work of less gifted friends. This surfaced more stridently as he prepared to write the foreword to Jack Snow's *Dark Music and Other Spectral Tales*.[4] Snow had warned him that some of the stories had a weakness in plot; he tended to write prose-poems, and some of these thinly plotted mood pieces dated back to his late teens and early twenties. Snow had wanted to include only twelve of his best stories, but Louis Greenfield insisted on twenty. Even before meeting Bradbury in New York, Snow revealed a reluctance to revise: "My only criticism of them now is that they are weak in plot. That couldn't be improved by re-writing and if I attempted it I would wind up with a different story." This view was similar to Bok's and it evidently predisposed Bradbury to be wary. Shortly after he returned from New York, he read the galleys and immediately notified Snow that he couldn't possibly write a foreword. His exact words are unknown, but on October 30th he offered Derleth a summary of his rationale: "I told him I thought Louis Greenfield showed poor taste in encouraging the publication of a book that was patently unpublishable without great sections of rewriting and much elimination of entire stories."

Bradbury didn't have to hold back with Derleth, who had recently written to Monty Buchanan demanding that *Weird Tales* publish no more of Snow's short stories. But Bradbury had no professional axe to grind: "I could only be truthful to him. I offered to help him on his future rewrites if he wished my criticism. I said I could not honestly write an introduction to the book, knowing it would hurt Jack in the end." Unfortunately, Bradbury's sincere desire to do the best by his friend could not hide his distaste for a writer who did not give every story the best possible effort. He did not yet know how to pull his punches, and the lack of a response from Snow was beginning to make him feel guilty: "I am very sorry to have hurt him. I did not think he would react so childishly to my letter. I understand his hurt feeling, but he should not be bitter toward me, I could only say what I honestly felt. It made me feel very strangely; I am only 26 years old and Jack is 40. Somehow it seems quite horrible that I should dare to tell him his stuff was not ready. I told him to take it to Chris Morley; and that I was sure Chris would back me up on it, would say the stories were too trite, too full of clichés and much, much too underdeveloped. I'm willing to back my critical analysis up against any other person in this affair."

The rapidly shifting emotions of these comments—ranging from remorse, to uncertainty, and on to outright defensiveness—show just how unsettled he was by Snow's silence. On November 4th, Snow wrote a very mild reply thanking Bradbury for the obvious sincerity of his comments. But he went on to make the crucial distinctions that represented the heart of the matter: "You are a literary craftsman with ambitions to become a skilled and recognized artist in the field of letters. I have no such ambitions. I want to write because I enjoy it. I want to write the things that I can do with the greatest facility—and I want to make money. All of this is possible with no great reputation. I believe *Dark Music* will be a fair to middling collection of fantasy tales. That's all I hope for it." Louis Greenfield agreed to drop two stories and overstamped all of the dust jackets with a bar of red ink to remove Bradbury's name.

Bok's prose *was* uneven, and (in spite of Christopher Morley's surprisingly favorable review) Snow's new collection *was* overburdened with his early apprentice work. Bradbury was developing good editorial instincts, but he was also beginning to show the impatience of a driven writer obsessed with perfection. He knew a good story when he read it, but it would be a few years yet before he developed the critical perspective needed to write a foreword or an introduction for a story collection or anthology. On a more personal level, this impulse led him to continue to revise circulating stories and even the contents of his own first book. And all of this contributed to the growing tensions between Bradbury and Derleth as *Dark Carnival* went through presswork.

25 Dark Carnival

Dark Carnival soon cost Derleth more in press corrections than all his previous Arkham House titles combined (or so he told Bradbury). But there's no doubt that Bradbury pushed as hard as he could to update it as it moved toward the May 1947 publication date.[1] In December, with the book in galley composition, he replaced "The Poems" with a newer story, "The Coffin"; during March he cut two stories from the page proofs ("The Watchers" and "Trip to Cranamockett") and tried to make significant revisions in seven other stories. Derleth allowed the less invasive revisions Bradbury had marked in proofs for "The Homecoming," "The Crowd," "The Night," and "The Wind," but he refused the more substantive rewriting Bradbury had prepared for the magazine appearances of "Homecoming," "The Man Upstairs," and "Cistern." This unpublicized decision would confuse scholars for decades—all three of these stories would appear in major market magazines in a *later* stage of revision than the versions that subsequently appeared in *Dark Carnival*. Bradbury finally made his peace with the contents, however, and offered his final prepublication assessment in a letter to *Ellery Queen*'s Frederic Dannay: "There isn't an actively bad story in the thing. There are a few that missed the target, certainly, but nothing that fumes in the hot sun. . . ."[2]

In spite of the fact that Derleth relied heavily on catalog subscribers and independent bookstores for sales, *Dark Carnival* secured some prophetic commentary from reviewers after its May 1947 release. Anthony Boucher's brief 120-word notice in the *San Francisco Chronicle* was nevertheless an important endorsement by a respected multigenre critic and editor. Boucher had been following Bradbury's rise in the pulps as well as his major market breakthrough and already considered him a mainstream talent: "He's not only a fantasy writer; he is also a writer, period, and there's no telling what may come of this still very young man." The midsummer 1947 issue of *Book-of-the-Month Club News* contained an even shorter notice that was just long enough to announce Bradbury as "a new author of real talent" whose first genre collection "has none of the old-fashioned spooks and weary werewolves." Neither the brevity of the notice, nor its formulaic endorsement, could detract from its significance, for *BOMC News* reached an incredibly broad cross section of mainstream American readers.

The *Chicago Sun*'s notice offered nothing more than a summary of contents, but Will Cuppy devoted a large portion of his regular genre column to *Dark Carnival* in the *New York Herald Tribune Weekly Book Review*. Cuppy felt that Bradbury was already "suitable for general consumption" and predicted that, with practice and better characterizations, he would someday move into John Collier's league as a contemporary fantasy writer of enduring stature. The most insightful critical comments, however, came from England, almost a year in advance of the British edition. Arthur Hillman's "Phenomenal Bradbury" appeared in the fourth issue of Britain's *Fantasy Review*, but he extended his commentary well beyond the magazine's genre boundaries. He felt that Bradbury had now joined a vanguard of other writers—Bloch, Kuttner, Nelson Bond, and John Collier—who were already successful practitioners "of the macabre in the modern vein."

Yet Hillman also thought that Bradbury's spontaneity and stylistic brilliance represented a new level entirely: "But there is an air of the self-conscious in the modernity of these writers; they seem to be striving for effect, to assert even aggressively that the weird tale can be modern. Bradbury's tales, on the other hand, are not simply patterned in a modern mould: their very foundations are laid in the minute now passing. The sparkling prose is not just an outward façade; it is the very bricks and mortar of each streamlined edifice in this book." Bradbury would always pay a price for his spontaneity and the high intensity of his emotional engagement, however; there was still an inconsistency in his work that was largely masked by the careful revisions and frantic last-minute reconfigurations of *Dark Carnival*, and most of the reviewers were not familiar enough with his wider body of work to qualify the careful showcase that Bradbury had placed before them.

Publication, and these few but generally positive reviews, did not bring an end to the marketing friction between author and publisher. Bradbury continued to push against Derleth's control of reprint rights as he tried to arrange further magazine and anthology appearances of the *Dark Carnival* stories. To their credit, the two men never lost trust in each other, and they maintained friendly relations even as Bradbury moved further and further away from the specialized market represented by Derleth's Arkham House volumes. Over time, critics and writers alike came to see *Dark Carnival* as a creative turning point for both the author and the genre he was rapidly leaving behind. Darrell Schweitzer, like Arthur Hillman, saw it as an influential departure from the neo-Gothic tradition, moving "away from haunted English country houses, dark forests, and monsters (Lovecraftian or traditional), toward big cities and their suburbs, and into the mind." Even though Bradbury focused on his own experiences and read only sparingly from the works of early-twentieth-century masters, both Stephen King and Clive Barker would come to regard *Dark Carnival* as a vital bridge between the fantastic tradition and contemporary fantasy fiction. In their own way, the stories of *Dark Carnival* were as groundbreaking as the more specialized dark fantasies that had appeared in *Unknown* just as Bradbury was breaking into the pages of *Weird Tales*—Jack Williamson's *Darker than You Think*, Fritz Leiber's *Conjure Wife*, and L. Ron Hubbard's *Fear*.

Many of the *Dark Carnival* stories would influence more contemporary fantasy writers through the pages of *The October Country* (1955), Bradbury's final reconfiguration of his best weird tales. But before the ink was dry on the few reviews that *Dark Carnival* generated, Bradbury's original concept had already spun off other projects. During the summer of 1946, in the midst of stabilizing the contents of *Dark Carnival* for an exasperated August Derleth, he saw the British film *Dead of Night*, Ealing Studio's only venture into the horror genre.[3] Bradbury came out of the theater convinced that the writers and directors at Ealing who had woven five stories into a sustained and sophisticated horror film for *Dead of Night* could do the same thing for *Dark Carnival*. In the spring of 1947 he sent a copy of his new book to the production staff at Ealing but never heard back. However, Bradbury learned that Ivan Foxwell, who had connections at Ealing, was in Hollywood, and he arranged to meet him during July 1947. Foxwell was impressed with Bradbury's collection, and after returning to London he circulated *Dark Carnival* among British filmmakers for at least a year. He confessed to Bradbury that the austere postwar conditions in the British Isles had set the critics as well as the major film distributors against dark subjects, and the lesser distributors followed suit in discouraging such productions.[4]

Over time, however, these stories became the basis for enduring literary success. In all, Bradbury's original idea for *A Child's Garden of Terror* would radiate out through *Dark Carnival* and on into the stories that became book chapters of his Green Town trilogy (*Dandelion Wine*, *Farewell Summer*, and *Something Wicked This Way Comes*), more than a dozen Elliott family story-chapters destined for *From the Dust Returned*, and dozens of other child-centered narratives of the 1940s and 1950s. Some of these later stand-alone stories, such as "Zero Hour" (titled in manuscript as "The Children's Hour"), "The Miracles of Jamie," "The Screaming Woman," "The Veldt" (first published as "The World the Children Made"), "All Summer in a Day," and "Hail and Farewell" would come to rank among his most enduring tales. Many of these stories would be loosely framed within the worlds of science fiction; by the mid-1950s Damon Knight, a friend from the prewar fanzine days, would take him to task for inverting the normal science-fantasy goal of expanding the imagination: "Bradbury's subject is childhood and the buried child-in-man; his aim is to narrow the focus, not to widen it; to shrink all the big frightening things to the compass of the familiar: a space ship to a tin can; a Fourth of July rocket to a brass kettle; a lion to a teddy bear."[5] For Knight, this inversion was what distinguished Bradbury from true science fiction writers; but it was also what initially attracted younger science fiction writers to Bradbury, including such British innovators as Brian Aldiss and J. G. Ballard.[6] And it would have an even greater impact on such late-twentieth-century heirs to the horror tradition as Stephen King and Clive Barker.

As soon as he began to break out into major market prominence, the cultural pressure to label and classify Bradbury grew even more intense. How would he stand up to a broader critical scrutiny? In Mexico, he had gathered the material for some of his best psychological realism, and his true Modernist triumph in reverie and character development would evolve over the next seven years into such enduring stories as "The Next in Line," "And the Rock Cried Out," and "Interval in Sunlight." Bradbury discovered his narrative genius in the use of metaphor and, perhaps most fully, in his ability to weave reverie into character consciousness—his one truly Modernist technique. But he was, first and foremost, a fantasy writer working intuitively, beyond all genre boundaries and methods; in 1946, as he began to move out of the niche-market magazines, the high literary scene was still dominated by Modernism. Could he address the Modernist crisis-of-values? Could he address the Atomic Age? How would he, finally, be forced to define himself as a writer? And how would publishers, editors, critics, and reviewers try to define him?

One way or another, Bradbury would have to confront Modernity intellectually if he wanted to take his place in mainstream literary culture. The transition out of the science fiction field would be a tough one in the years after the war. He had to fully transcend all of the genre labels, at least in his own mind, even as the critics would continue to try to limit him with such labels. And he would have to succeed with book-length fiction without losing his identity and integrity as an author. Clearly, the next few years would be the most crucial of his career. He had developed masterful and unique ways to reflect on his own past and to wonder about Earth's future. The central challenge would be to create characters that could come out on the other side of the Modernist crisis-of-values, scarred but able to face what Robert Penn Warren would call, in *All the King's Men*, "the awful responsibilities of time."

Part IV

The Tyranny of Words

[B]y the time I met my wife Maggie I was 25 and . . . I began to make plans to sell out. . . . I wanted to sell out in the worst way because I wanted to be with her, but the wonderful thing about creativity is that once you get an idea that's decent, even though you may want to commercialize it, you can't. I tried to be commercial and it never worked, because my intuition was so powerful always in my life, I could never be a commercial writer.

— RB to Don Congdon, 1969

26 Lifetime Partnerships

Bradbury and Maggie were hoping to be married soon, and for a time he may have considered securing their future by selling out to the formula-minded pulp editors. Such a thought stands in sharp contrast to the unwavering arguments for quality writing that he was leveling at Bloch, Bok, and Snow. It also lacks contemporary documentation; his confession appears only in reminiscences of later decades, and by then he had convinced himself that his intuition, rather than good judgment, had blocked the impulse. The correspondence of the period suggests that he never really considered selling out at all, but financial challenges continued to plague Bradbury until the breakout year of 1950 secured his future with the major trade publishers. Even with the occasional slick sales, reprints, and two radio sales, Bradbury's income was less than $3000 for 1946. With economies this could represent a livable income for two, but only if he could manage to sell consistently. There would be dry spells, however, and one of the longest came in 1947.

In April Hirschel Brickell announced Bradbury's first *O. Henry Prize Stories* selection (for "The Homecoming"), but over the next five months sales would be few and far between. The situation was aggravated when Marshall Fields's USA magazine folded in August without publishing a single issue. This development left Bradbury without a magazine publisher for "The Next in Line," the best of the newer stories that he had inserted into *Dark Carnival*. That summer he also learned that two of his recent reprint sales to Donald Wollheim—"Homecoming" and "The Man Upstairs"—were delayed indefinitely when Wollheim's new *Avon Fantasy Reader* series fell victim to paper shortages. Avon did get these stories into print eventually, but the long delay ended his plans to place a number of other *Dark Carnival* stories in subsequent *Fantasy Reader* issues.[1]

Bradbury was still offering to the major market magazines without an agent, and this too was cutting into his potential sales. Derleth had obligated Bradbury to the Otis Kline agency for overseas negotiations involving *Dark Carnival*, but Kline's people had been unwilling or unable to follow through on Bradbury's request to offer the individual *Dark Carnival* stories for serialization in the British magazine market. Kline did secure Hamish Hamilton for the British edition of *Dark Carnival*, but Hamilton's larger interest, thanks to a tip from Congdon delivered through Katherine Gauss at *Harper's*, was really focused on Bradbury's new Illinois novel. Bradbury was unwilling to trust this new novel project to Kline's agency, and in early July he notified Derleth that he was considering either Curtis Brown or the Marion Ives agency for all future projects.

During the summer of 1947 he asked Don Congdon for guidance.[2] Congdon recommended a wider range of proven agencies, including Ives, Matson, Brant, Mavis McIntosh, Russell & Volkenning, and the well-known Harold Ober. But in the same letter Congdon revealed that he'd be leaving Simon & Schuster on the first of September to join the Harold Matson agency, and asked if he could represent Bradbury in all markets. By this time Bradbury had come to trust Congdon as an advisor, and he readily agreed to the arrangement. Congdon immediately asked Bradbury to provide him with summaries of his sales and copyright details so that he could study this history during his final weeks as a Simon & Schuster editor. But in the intervening weeks Bradbury would need the help of both Congdon and Derleth to generate more income. He and Maggie had set their wedding date for September 30th, and time was of the essence.

By July Bradbury had to face the reality that paper restrictions and other postwar economic hardships would result in an abridged British edition of *Dark Carnival*. Ten of the twenty-seven stories were scheduled for omission, but Bradbury succeeded in restoring three of the best: "The Lake," "The Night," and "The Dead Man." He was ambivalent about the date of British publication, for he still believed that he might finish the Illinois novel in time to have it published ahead of *Dark Carnival* in that market. But he desperately needed the $400 advance promised by Hamilton and continued to ask Derleth for updates. The irony is apparent in his July 2nd letter: "So I'm living on sunlight and fresh air. Ah, the literary life. I always wondered what it would feel like to be an O. Henry Award nominee. Now I know. Broke!"

Nevertheless, the O. Henry announcement had brought Bradbury the kind of literary recognition that he had only dreamed of—finally, the academic world was beginning to show interest in him. In June the *Kenyon Review* offered to print a notice of *Dark Carnival*, and in August *Epoch*, the new Cornell University quarterly, accepted "Interim," a time travel story that explored the same "ages of man" issues that were at the heart of the evolving Illinois novel. *Touchstone*, another new literary quarterly, published "El Dia De Muerte," one of the dark reveries that were beginning to emerge from his long trip to Mexico. He knew that such recognition would mean a great deal in the long run, but these publications did little to fix his more immediate problems. *Epoch* offered literary status but no payment; *Touchstone* paid for and published Bradbury's story in the inaugural number, but quietly folded after the second issue.

He managed to pull through the summer of 1947 by sending some new stories to the pulps, but only after deciding to shift his entire strategy for pulp submissions. In May he sold two of his most recent weirds, "Touch and Go" and "The Coffin," to the detective pulps.[3] He already had a three-year run of success in the crime genre, and the pay was about two cents a word—double what he could expect from Weird Tales. This irritating contrast only served to underscore Bradbury's growing sense that he had little more to contribute to this form of fiction. Monty Buchanan would be able to coax only two more original stories out of Bradbury for Weird Tales—"Fever Dream" and that all-important progenitor of Something Wicked This Way Comes, "The Black Ferris."

This adjustment in his sales strategy was only the beginning of a much more significant shift in Bradbury's pulp profile. Given his rapidly rising status, editors in both the weird and detective fields were now willing to stretch the rules to secure practically any Bradbury tale, but during the spring and summer of 1947 he wrote almost exclusively for the science fiction pulps. The stories he was now offering to Paul Payne for Planet Stories were stronger than his 1944–45 run of appearances in that magazine; he was also offering better science fiction stories to Sam Merwin for the more prestigious Thrilling Wonder Stories, a market he had only cracked twice during the war years. The increasing quality of his particular brand of science fiction, along with his more general need to turn back (at least temporarily) to the pulps for a steadier source of income, had sparked a return to the genre that had nurtured his original desire to become a writer.

He suddenly saw his career coming full circle: During the early war years, his more rapid mastery of the weird genre had delayed his development in science fiction; in fact, he would later confide to Anthony Boucher that his entry into the field was an accident, the result of successive rejections from the science fiction magazines. But his particular brand of humanized science fiction stories continued to evolve all through his Weird Tales years and can be traced through such quality stories as "King of the Gray Spaces," "The Million Year Picnic," "Chrysalis," and "The Creatures That Time Forgot." Now, as he sensed that his creative wellspring of weird tales was running dry, Bradbury returned to his original course as a science fiction writer.[4]

A thematic pattern soon developed in his newer science fiction stories. His new novella "Pillar of Fire" may have triggered his subsequent interest in discovering a mythos that could compensate for the loss of traditional systems of value as mankind moved, in fits and bursts, toward the space age that the technological achievements of the recent World War seemed to make possible. "Pillar of Fire" had projected a future utopia where imagination no longer exists; as the graveyards of Earth are reclaimed and the bodies consigned to incinerators, the exhumation teams unintentionally release William Lantry, a last representative of the living dead. He tries to invoke the supernatural literatures and superstitions of his own twentieth century to make men fear and obey him, but these powers have no effect in the twenty-fourth century, where books and libraries no longer exist. When he is finally tracked down and destroyed, the last vestiges of fantasy and imagination are lost forever.

The decline of literature and human values in an increasingly rational society would soon become a recurring theme in Bradbury's fiction, eventually leading to *Fahrenheit 451*. But during the spring and summer of 1947, Bradbury began to focus a separate search for a space-age mythos on one of the oldest loves of his creative life: the planet Mars. He spent many hours in his garage office, contemplating the day-and-night humming of the dynamos in the adjacent powerhouse and developing in his imagination an ancient race of silver-masked Martians.[5] These jaded but mentally powerful creatures had been evolving in his mind for more than a year, but now he extrapolated four distinct and fully formed stories from a single Wellsian "what if" situation: What would happen if expeditions from Earth encountered these Martians and their exotic ways? Editorial reactions soon validated his sense that these four stories were quality pieces. Paul Payne took "Mars Is Heaven!" for *Planet Stories*; Leo Margulies accepted "—And the Moon Be Still as Bright" and "The Earth Men" for *Thrilling Wonder*; and *Mademoiselle*'s Rita Smith was giving "Ylla" serious consideration. Bradbury did not yet know the larger consequences of what he had created, but eventually these four tales would become the opening chapters of first contact in *The Martian Chronicles*.

Although he was primarily targeting the pulps once again, the *Mademoiselle* gambit was part of his continuing crusade to place a science fiction story in the slicks; in fact, during July he sent another new Martian story, "The Long Years," to the *Saturday Evening Post*. This story played off of an earlier Martian "what if," the same one that had produced "The Million-Year Picnic": What would happen if wars back on Earth threatened to end the human settlement of Mars and thereby destroy mankind's chance to reach the stars? Taken together, these six stories would mark out a pattern of inquiry for many of the Martian stories that followed—stories centering on first alien contact, the fear of otherness, the desire for colonial exploitation, the successive waves of settlement, the effects of prolonged isolation, and the haunting risk of failure at every turn.

Bradbury was beginning to articulate a new myth for man, projected on Mars from the frontier myths of Earth's past, the present apocalyptic potential of the emerging Cold War powers, and the first stages of the worldwide postcolonial conflicts to come. His quest for values centered on ways to take imagination, as well as technology, out to the stars; in this way, Mankind could restore divine creativity to what Bradbury perceived as a Deistic universe—fashioned by the eternal Watchmaker, but left to run on its own. This cautious optimism did not carry over into his personal reality, however; both of his major market submissions were eventually returned unsold. For now at least, he was unable to follow his friend Bob Heinlein's breakthrough sales of science fiction to the *Saturday Evening Post*. He continued to write to Derleth for news about the British advance payment for *Dark Carnival*, but it remained unclear when the contract would be finalized. On September 24th, however, Bradbury received a most welcome wedding gift from Derleth—an early royalty check that was really an advance on projected American sales. He was genuinely touched, and in return he offered to waive the reprint fees for several stories that Derleth was considering for his new quarterly, the *Arkham House Sampler*.

Ray Bradbury and Marguerite McClure were married on September 30th, 1947, with Ray Harryhausen standing as best man. Bradbury was emotionally ready for this step, but he remained concerned for their financial security. Two weeks earlier, he had revealed to Derleth just how worried he was about supporting a wife and family. "When I contemplate my financial future, small as it is, I grow somewhat faint. I don't know why in hell I'm marrying at this time, unless of course it has something to do with love, which it undoubtedly has, because I'm simply flat. I'll have to get to work on some pulps. It's all very well to be in the Cornell quarterly, but it hardly puts anything in the stomach. They say you can live on milk for years; I'll have to look into it." At the age of twenty-seven, he was leaving the security of his mother's dinner table and the bed he had shared all his life with his older brother Skip. But he was most certainly in love, and he deeply treasured the passion and intellectual companionship that Maggie brought into his life.

Mother Bradbury had found a rental bungalow for the newlyweds just a block off of the Venice beachfront, at 33 Venice Boulevard. Although he was only moving a half dozen blocks west from the house at 670 Venice, the change of environment was monumental for him. He was leaving a home where he was dearly loved, but where he had never been understood. His parents hardly knew the interior world of his imagination, and Skip, who was four years older, never understood it at all. Skip's tolerant contempt of his younger brother's unwillingness to fight back when bullied by outsiders had slowly faded as the two boys became men, but understanding never came with age. Shortly after his marriage, Bradbury wrote a two-page sketch of their relationship, closing with a final ironic reversal: "Somewhere between high school and college I became older than Skip. I ran on ahead of him. When he was twenty-one and I was seventeen, he began coming to *me* for advice. He began to imitate me. After all the years of trying to follow in the cleat-prints of his track and football shoes, I was amazed to see him trying to put on my glasses and read my books. But he never succeeded. And we were never brothers again." It wasn't a matter of estrangement; he had simply left Skip's world behind, and sadly enough Skip would never be able to appreciate the immensity of that journey in any measure. His parents left his garage office intact for a time, since there was little room in the new bungalow for all of his files. These were all natural stages of growth and departure, and Skip would eventually negotiate similar departures when he married and moved away. But the powerhouse was a different matter entirely—where would Bradbury find a new creative metaphor for his muse? The answer came to him two weeks before the wedding, indirectly and implicitly, through a brief confessional reverie he wrote on his mother's birthday:

> I have had days of unaccountable depression in which I sat in my studio and looked out along the burnt meadow to where the ice factory makes its hushing, cool sound of constantly pouring water, and then over to the Doll Factory in whose windows I have never glanced, and I have torn up page after page of bad stuff written during the morning. Then I lock up my typewriter, fling my leg over my brother's bicycle and ride, clicking gently, for the thing has a free-wheeling mechanism on it, all down to the sea. I find great refreshment in the sea, it is so irrevocably old and it says to me, little man, what are your problems? Fifty years from now where will you be? And I have been here forever, passing between man and earth in passionate exchanges and gentle redistributions.

This was his farewell to the vibrating energies of the powerhouse, no longer dominant among the neighborhood attractions. The rest of the single-page composition opens out into a pensée, a prose poem describing the even greater dynamo of the nearby ocean:

> Naturally, in California, the sea is certain to be of a more quiet aspect, for there are eight months here when we see no cloud in the sky. We may have vapors and mornings of mist that hang over and occlude vast territories of sky, but these whisper down only futile little moistenings upon sidewalk and snail, rose bush and bus-top. On many evenings when the wind is right you can smell the sea pouring over Los Angeles in invisible waves, subtle and vanishing. But there is no thunder, no downpour, no lightning. There is always the summer season, with certain days which take onto themselves, for an hour or so, the sound and the feel of autumn, some mock autumn which the next day is denied by a sudden hot summer again. And so you cannot expect too

much of our sea here on our shore; it will not be as violent, it will comb in in curves and foamings, it will rear and crash, but it is, after all, a California sea. It is enough, however, for me.

This self-contained cycle of the California shoreline mapped out Bradbury's small wedge of it, and gently invoked the ocean as his new metaphorical muse. Here was all that the once solitary writer needed for encouragement—he easily adjusted his writing routines to the new dynamics of married life in the Venice Beach bungalow. Maggie had resigned from Fowler's and for a couple of months worked for an advertising agency before settling into a permanent position editing a company newsletter for the head office of Abbey Rents, a regional medical equipment rental chain. Evenings and weekends, they often walked through the neighborhoods of Ocean Park, years before the Pacific Ocean Park amusement complex replaced the older shoreline communities. Bradbury would often nap in the mornings after Maggie left for work, and then ease into the day's writing. He would finish up around noontime, and walk a hundred yards to the beach and let his Muse relax.[6]

Before long he appropriated the pay telephone in the parking lot of the adjacent gas station, and gave out that number to all of his Los Angeles and New York contacts. Leigh Brackett and Edmond Hamilton soon returned from a summer of writing near Ed's family in Western Pennsylvania, but instead of moving back to Arcadia they settled into a beach-house that Leigh's grandfather owned—just two blocks south of 33 Venice Boulevard.[7] Every Thursday evening, Bradbury and his wife would visit his old friends. Maggie and Hamilton both had a passion for the novels of Thomas Love Peacock, and soon had Bradbury hooked as well. Hamilton would recite Yeats and Shakespeare's sonnets and instruct him on the works of George Bernard Shaw and the poetry of Robert Frost. Money was short, but it was a grand time.

27 The Illinois Novel

Bradbury was now represented by Don Congdon and the Matson Agency, but a few of his earlier direct negotiations finally brought in some much-needed cash. In October he received nearly $200 from the *New Yorker* for "I See You Never," a story from his Figueroa Street tenement days that had been declined by the *New Yorker* more than two years earlier. And there was luck on the home front as well; on November 13, 1947, a Mel Dinelli adaptation of his unpublished noir ventriloquist fantasy "Riabouchinska" marked Bradbury's debut on the CBS radio show *Suspense*. Bill Spier soon bought two more unpublished Bradbury stories, and adaptations aired during the show's 1948 summer and fall seasons. "The Screaming Woman," the story of a woman buried alive told from the point of view of the children who hear her but cannot get anyone to believe them, starred Agnes Moorhead and Margaret O'Brien. "Summer Night" was even more suspenseful—Bradbury's old high-school mood piece had now fully emerged as the story of a woman who must find her way home through the Green Town ravine on a night when the Lonely One has already killed once. Although Bradbury was pleased with the *Suspense* adaptation, he regarded the piece as a story-chapter for the new Illinois novel.

In fact, Bradbury's new professional relationship with Congdon was most important for the opportunity it provided to develop and market the Illinois novel. This project, focusing on the vast emotional and intellectual gulfs that separate children from adults, was growing out of the stories he was beginning to write about his Waukegan childhood. The earliest of these was "The Night" (1943), another variation on his ravine mood piece that finally reached print in the July 1946 issue of *Weird Tales*. By this time Bradbury had begun to outline the novel and write brief mood pieces or vignettes of the people and neighborhoods that he was loosely adapting from his childhood memories. It's clear from these surviving but very fragmentary concept materials that the thematic inspiration derives from one of Bradbury's favorites—Christopher Morley's 1925 novel, *Thunder on the Left*.

In interviews, Bradbury has occasionally acknowledged the impact of *Thunder on the Left* and has mentioned (without elaboration) that it was indeed a source of inspiration for his first Green Town novel. He had been impressed with the internal monologues and reveries of Morley's novel when he first encountered it around 1940. The first chapter of *Thunder on the Left* centers on a child's birthday party in a turn-of-the-century vacation home on an island off the coast of New England. The children make a pact never to grow old, but there are dissenters among them. Martin, celebrating his tenth birthday, takes the next logical step: they must find out what the adult world is really like, "that Other World, the thrillingly exciting world of Parents, whose secrets are so cunningly guarded."[1] Martin and the other children quickly settle on the language of war to describe their strategy:

> "We must find out," Martin said, suddenly feeling in his mind the expanding brightness of an idea. "It'll be a new game. We'll all be spies in the enemy's country, we'll watch them and see exactly how they behave, and bring in a report."
>
> "Get hold of their secret codes, and find where their forces are hidden," cried Ben, who liked the military flavor of this thought.
>
> "I think it's a silly game," said Phyllis. "You can't really find out anything; and if you did, you'd be punished. Spies always get caught."
>
> "Penalty of death!" shouted the boys, elated.
>
> It's harder than being a real spy," said Martin. You can't wear the enemy's uniform and talk their language. But I'm going to do it, anyhow." (12)

Martin's decision becomes his unspoken birthday wish as he blows out the candles on his cake, and the rest of the novel reveals the consequences. Twenty-one years later, as adults, some of the same characters return to the vacation house for a weekend with their own spouses and children. "Mr. Martin," a handsome and engaging but somewhat childlike stranger, unexpectedly arrives, and transforms the weekend into a confusion of adult passions and childhood emotions. But darkness lurks beneath the surface throughout Morley's novel, for as the adults begin to explore the long-repressed emotions of childhood, their own children are endangered through a chain of events triggered by Martin's arrival in future time. At the last moment he sacrifices his dream of never growing up and closes the breach in time by returning to the birthday party.

By the early 1950s Bradbury had developed the same childlike pattern of war metaphors to structure the opening chapters of the Illinois novel, but this pattern was not fully realized until Bradbury published the original core plot as *Farewell Summer* in 2007. The process began in 1945 as Bradbury experimented with his own warlike version of early childhood rebellion in one of his first major market magazine stories, "One Timeless Spring." His first *Collier's* story offered up a nostalgic look back at the last gasp of "acceptable" boyhood rebellion as it dissolves away into the discovery of the fairer sex. He chose a child's metaphor to inform Douglas Spaulding's sense that growing up was a form of dying—the food his parents fed him, the candy the town merchants sold him, and the knowledge that the teachers revealed to him were simply variations on a "poison" designed to destroy the child in the process of creating the adult. Douglas tries unsuccessfully to warn his friends: "You play and run around and eat, and all the time they're tricking you and making you think different and act different and walk different. And all of a sudden one day you'll stop playing and have to worry!" The final dose of adult poison strikes Douglas as he walks alone through the town's deep and shadowy ravine and encounters his school friend Clarisse Mellin. She takes the opportunity to offer Douglas his first adolescent kiss, causing his simple metaphor of poison to dissolve into far more complex sensations: "I knew it was all over. I was lost. From this moment on, it would be a touching, an eating of foods, a learning of language and algebra and logic, a movement and an emotion, a kissing and a holding, a whirl of feeling that caught and sucked me drowning under. I knew I was lost forever now, and I didn't care. But I did care, and I was laughing and crying all in one, and there was nothing to do about it, but hold her and love her with all my decided and rioting body and mind."

As "One Timeless Spring" was beginning to establish a wider market readership for him in the pages of Collier's, Bradbury began to explore the deeper complexities of child-adult relationships through a novel-length concept of his own. In the process he was drawn back to an aspect of Thunder on the Left that fascinated him—Morley's notion of time and relationships. His own holistic sense of human nature was forming around the belief that we should never lose the child in the adult. Morley's keen sense of this very same struggle, presented through the internalized reveries of the main characters, focused in on the fundamental tensions that Bradbury was developing for his new novel. Like Bradbury's Douglas Spaulding, Morley's young Martin was painfully aware of "the whole secret infamy of childhood; the most pitiable of earth's slaveries; perhaps the only one that can never be dissolved." Morley's adults know the flip side of this slavery, the anxiety of passing time, an anxiety that forces Morley's George Granville to think of children as a race all their own: "People pretend that children are just human beings of a smaller size, but I think they're something quite different. They live in a world with only three dimensions, a physical world immersed in the moment, a reasonable world, a world without that awful sorcery of a fourth measurement that makes us ill at ease" (149).

Morley's insight would provide the Wellsian "what if" from which Bradbury would extrapolate the core dynamics of his own Green Town world. His earliest known list of volume contents, titled The Small Assassins, was probably prepared in 1945; by the end of the year, seven of the twenty-four chapter titles had been drawn off as stories for *Dark Carnival*, but the original concept persisted. On September 11, 1945, he described the idea in his first letter to Don Congdon; this letter remains unlocated, but Congdon's September 18th response placed the new idea squarely in the tradition of James's *The Turn of the Screw* and Richard Hughes's *The Innocent Voyage*—comparisons that gratified Bradbury's library-based conception of authorship. A few years earlier, the pirate-children of *The Innocent Voyage* (the American title of *A High Wind in Jamaica*) appealed to Bradbury in the same way as the children of *Thunder on the Left*, for Hughes also built on the imaginative premise that children were distinctly different creatures from adults. The strange psychological inversion of Hughes's novel (nice pirates, predatory children) fascinated Bradbury, and the emerging awareness of the life force experienced by Emily, the eldest child-pirate, foreshadows (in both point of view and tone) Doug Spaulding's similar awakening in the opening chapters of *Dandelion Wine*.

Fortunately, the original concept for Bradbury's novel survives in three pages of notes, prepared in the same way that he sometimes outlined story concepts to try out on Julius Schwartz during the early and mid-1940s. Bradbury used ellipsis points throughout the concept, a technique that served to emphasize that, at this early stage of thinking, the outline was intended to convey mood, themes, and situation rather than elements of plot progression:

> I WANT TO WRITE A NOVEL ABOUT . . . a small town and the adults and children who live in that town . . . a novel concerning the vast psychological differences between children and their parents . . . each group, whether children or adults, handled as if they lived in a separate world . . . the children strange, wild, calm, silent and by turns excitable individuals living under their own laws and beliefs . . . the parents unable to comprehend and a bit afraid of the children. I want to get the feel of the small town, the strange wonder of the children, the bewildered suspicion of the adults into the story.
>
> THE CONFLICT IN "the small assassins" IS GOING TO BE . . . between the children and their environment, their parents . . . and between the parents ideas of what the children should be and what the children really ARE . . . the conflict of making children fit into standards and moulds, making ladies and gentlemen out of untrained little creatures. And the children resentfully hating the idea of growing up . . . and the adults themselves wishing again to be children but not able to go back, and are frustrated . . .

During the rest of the 1940s, Bradbury would write a number of Green Town stories, but most of these would be held back from publication as he shopped the larger novel concept. The evolving plot centered on a summer war between Douglas Spaulding's "Blue Army" of boys and the "Gray Army" of town elders headed by Colonel Quartermain. The novel's title, however, shifted several times during the early years of development. Bradbury soon took the original *Small Assassins* title and transferred it to a story-in-progress that for three years had been circulating as "The Baby," but would soon become a popular Bradbury horror story as "The Small Assassin." This shift led Bradbury to re-title the Green Town novel as *The Winds of Time* before settling on *The Blue Remembered Hills*, a more nostalgic title inspired by two stanzas from A. E. Houseman's *A Shropshire Lad*. By 1947 Bradbury had finally decided on *Summer Morning, Summer Night*, a title that suggested the war between youth and old age that had become the central conflict of the novel. Over time, however, Bradbury's determination to build a seamless Green Town novel from finely crafted short stories would generate the longest writer's block of his career. In the mid-1950s, he would finally achieve a separate peace by working with his Doubleday editor to pull out seventeen of the story-chapters that were nonessential to the core plot, bridge them along with three newer stories, and successfully publish this novelized story cycle as *Dandelion Wine*. The original novel, however, would take a full six decades to evolve from concept to publication, finally reaching print as *Farewell Summer*.

Bradbury's ongoing struggle with the novel form does not diminish the quality of the individual stories that emerged during the late 1940s and early 1950s. He was continuing to experiment successfully with internal psychological narratives, and at times in his Green Town stories his reveries would reach beyond Christopher Morley's more self-conscious example in *Thunder on the Left*. In terms of the power of language, Morley's interior monologues are sometimes compared to those of Virginia Woolf, but in terms of impact and tone Bradbury had a more instinctive command of reverie than Morley's more distanced poetic voice could allow. He would soon show this command of subjective reality in his longer Mexican stories, and in such Green Town classics as "The Whole Town's Sleeping," "The Last, the Very Last," and two stories that first reached print among the untitled chapters of *Dandelion Wine*—"The Tarot Witch" and "Green Wine for Dreaming." Morley's sense of the effect of time on relationships would also seed Bradbury's imagination during this period, confirming his own sense that life, like writing itself, was a richly complex weave. As Morley's narrator observes, a holistic sense of wonderment is essential, "for life is all one piece, of endless pattern. No stitch in the vast fabric can be unraveled without risking the whole tapestry. It is the garment woven without seams" (93).

Bradbury's view of life was evolving along similar lines. He was already writing stories of time and memory, about old men and women who have become living time machines, about husbands and wives facing the consequences of decisions long past, and about the time and distance that creates the cold terror of loneliness for the first men who venture into outer space. And he was continuing to take a similar path in his writing style, ignoring reductionistic genre rules and traditions whenever they interfered with his own intuitive approach to writing. He continued to minimize the art of plotting, for his Muse worked best when the characters seemed to write their own stories. He would continue to use the loose framework of science fiction, or the weird tale, or even the occasional backdrop of noir crime, but he was writing about people rather than about science, or terror, or detection.

28 Bradbury and Modernity

Bradbury's early work on the Illinois novel coincided with the development of two novel concepts that would not reach print in any form for sixty years. Only fragments of *Masks* (1946–1947, 1949) and *Where Ignorant Armies Clash By Night* (1947–48) have ever been located, and until these fragments were pieced together for small-press limited editions in 2006 and 2008, the importance of these unfinished novels to Bradbury's early development remained largely unknown.[1] Behind the scenes of his award-winning success with major market magazines, his own search for a writing identity in long fiction moved for a time beyond the psychological novel he was writing about his Illinois youth. This search, along with the rising anxieties triggered by the rapidly polarizing postwar world, aggravated his instinctive disillusionment with modernity and led him, finally, to take on Modernist themes directly.

His own close reading of modern American fiction told him that this contemporary anxiety had its roots in the broader sense of alienation that was so apparent in much of the fiction written between the two world wars. Bradbury had been born and had grown to maturity during the interwar years, and he had a firsthand experience with the dislocation and constant uneasiness that working-class Americans knew perhaps better than those who commented on it. The recent war fully vanquished America's immediate foes, but unresolved social issues at home, the world's equally unresolved colonial dilemmas, and the growing dominance of Soviet totalitarian rule in Eastern Europe left Bradbury with a deep sense of uncertainty, disappointment, and unease as he prepared to tackle the subjects of mainstream novelists for the first time. For Bradbury, the great model for the crisis-of-values novel remained Arthur Koestler's *Darkness at Noon*, which offered a terrifyingly accurate assessment of the rise of modern totalitarianism that seemed to predict, as well, the greatest threat to the future of the postwar world. First, however, he would explore the roots of modern alienation and despair by looking deep into the human soul. He would take his favorite ambivalent metaphor—the masks that sometimes hide and sometimes project human passions—to study both the predators and the victims of modern society.

In April 1946, Bradbury began to develop *Masks* as a second psychological novel project.[2] But his approach would prove to be very different from the psychological underpinnings of the Illinois novel—*Masks* represented his first sustained attempt to directly engage the Modernist themes of isolation, alienation, the loss of values, and the decline of traditional sources of wisdom. As William F. Touponce has observed, Bradbury would eventually develop masks to enhance the social criticism of *The Martian Chronicles* and to convey the central psychological insights of *Something Wicked This Way Comes* and *The Halloween Tree*.[3] Initially, though, the title metaphor for *Masks* was inspired by the Indian artifacts that he and Grant Beach had collected in Mexico during the fall of 1945; what Bradbury now knew of the mask-making craft would provide a distant background for portions of the planned novel, but the concept centered on the metaphorical masks of modern civilization. This project got off to a slow start, however, and Bradbury did not have enough material to send to Don Congdon until the summer of 1947.

A surviving outline of short chapters or thousand-word "intervals" for a 50,000-word novel probably dates from this earliest phase of work. The concept soon grew into a long narrative of intervals, but in all only seventy typescript pages survive. A thirty-page continuous run begins with William Latting, master of masks, moving from his luxurious apartment to a rundown boarding house where he exposes the inner lives of a wide range of friends, acquaintances, and strangers. He also torments them with masks that expose their greatest fears and passions. This run of pages carries through just fifteen brief episodes, but the last nine of these were only in narrative outline form at the time that Bradbury sent the ribbon copy to Congdon. At this stage of work, Bradbury's concluding episode has Latting realize, when confronted with the mask of his own youthful face, that he has lost all the qualities that had once made him human. He is now a broken man, and takes his own life.

Almost all of the episode fragments are dark—some masks hide physical disfigurement or inner depravity, others externalize incestuous desires or project predatory battles for sexual dominance in relationships. There is a fascinating interval where Latting imagines every creative knife stroke of Señor Cerda, the Mexican master craftsman who fashions Latting's masks from his little shop in faraway Patzcuaro. But his increasing bitterness toward society would eventually lead to trouble with the police, court appearances, psychological evaluations, and a downhill slide toward self-destruction. In the final pages of the 1946–47 long narrative fragment, Bradbury outlined how Latting might degenerate into bitterness and psychosis: "He realizes upon what a thin skin of ice we are all skating within our civilization, with gestures and facial expressions to cover up our great inner foulness."

There is also a sense of paranoia in many of these episodes, a mood intensified by the increasing threat that outsiders will take the masks away. In one startling reversal of this theme the mask-wearer, now named Roby, offers a subtle threat to those who would take away his masks. Roby suggests that he will be far more dangerous to the others if he has to blend in without his masks as just another face in the crowd. The implication is that Roby's various masks provided clues and warnings about his behavior patterns. "[N]ow I'll be back among you, as always, with no masks of the wooden sort, only my face as it is and then you'll have no protection." This variation suggests the kind of social paranoia that was a hallmark characteristic of the early years of the Cold War. Bradbury's fragmentary attempt to reverse this scare tactic back onto the mob itself would be fully developed in some of his better cautionary tales of the early 1950s.

A dozen discarded pages of a *Masks* radio script also survive within the seventy pages of fragments. The first page of the script includes Bradbury's notation that this form of *The Masks* was "a play for the World Security Workshop." On January 2, 1947, ABC's World Security Workshop aired Bradbury's *The Meadow*, an award-winning one-act radio play adapted by Bradbury himself from a then-unpublished story of the same title. It is likely that he adapted *Masks* as a radio play at about the same time; these fragments have the same kind of "big idea" tone that surfaces in *The Meadow*, and both of these scripts are inspired to some degree by what Bradbury would later call the "great notion" radio shows of Norman Corwin, who (first as a broadcaster and later as a friend) was a great influence on him throughout the 1940s. Indeed, all of the *Masks* fragments have a moral tone and social purpose that suggests they were written almost simultaneously with "Pillar of Fire" and other stories that would lead, eventually, to *Fahrenheit 451*. *Masks* reveals a society that reads only superficial literature or advertising copy, a culture that forces people to find identities that are, as Bradbury described it in his project outline, "the most convenient and profitable in life."

But the more direct path to *Fahrenheit 451* led through the second of these unfinished dark novels—*Where Ignorant Armies Clash by Night*, which survives only as a thin shell of what it might have become. It appears to have begun as a radio drama before evolving into a fully outlined novel concept, but only fragmentary drafts of a few episodes have been located. These all focus on a nightmare inversion of traditional values in a future world where violent death provides the best way out of a ravaged landscape, and "Assassin" is the most noble of professions. There is very little evidence that *Ignorant Armies* ever moved beyond the developmental phase; however, the chilling cult of Assassins, and the ritual of burning books and fine art, shows Bradbury moving unmistakably toward some of the pivotal scenes he would reprise in a different future world for *Fahrenheit 451*. The closest corollary in *Ignorant Armies* is the ritual reading of Matthew Arnold's "Dover Beach" and the subsequent burning of Arnold's works as a warm-up to the destruction of perhaps the last copy of Shakespeare. The Assassin finds that he cannot take this ultimate step of cultural annihilation and becomes a fugitive from the mob that wishes to destroy the art of the past. For *Fahrenheit*, Bradbury would refine this image into the scene where Fireman Montag reads "Dover Beach" to his wife and her friends. This scene would become a pivotal point of no return for Montag in all three versions of Bradbury's masterpiece—the unpublished "Long After Midnight," "The Fireman," and *Fahrenheit 451*.

Bradbury came across Louis Untermeyer's insightful headnote to "Dover Beach" in his copy of Simon & Schuster's popular *Treasury of Great Poems*.[4] From Untermeyer Bradbury knew that Arnold defined poetry as "a criticism of life," and understood that Arnold's enduring hallmark was the "ethical, earnest and melancholy" nature of his verse. Thus Arnold's "Dover Beach" became the ideal instrument of self-torture for the nihilistic Assassin caught in a crisis of values, and the final line of the poem became the title of this early unfinished novel. The *Ignorant Armies* title would not carry over into the subsequent *Fahrenheit* sequence of texts, but the poem itself would become a touchstone by which Bradbury's protagonist Montag tests those around him.

Leigh Brackett's carefully crafted noir detective fiction also seems to have encouraged Bradbury as he explored what he described in one opening fragment of *Ignorant Armies* as "the dissatisfied, disillusioned, restless spirit of modern man." During the final war years Bradbury had read her first published detective novel in manuscript, published in 1944 as *No Good from a Corpse*. It would land her on the scriptwriting team for *The Big Sleep* later that year, and it centered on a detective who was dangerously close to seeing death as a value greater than life. The detective's last line of dialog closes the novel with this observation: "There's an old saying . . . that of all things, never to have been born is best."

The phrase is as old as Western philosophy, but Brackett's ability to build a full novel around it resonated with Bradbury as the postwar world continued to develop more and more efficient means of mass destruction. This philosophical endgame surfaces in one of the earliest narrative fragments of *Ignorant Armies*, as an old man instructs a boy on the meaninglessness of life: "If Life has no Value, then give Death a Value. Peace. Peace from worrying, peace from wondering. Death is positive and restful. It is the only value we can be sure, be certain of. Therefore let our word be of all things, never to have been born is best." Bradbury eventually developed a very short story under this title before abandoning the *Ignorant Armies* project; it is the only fully articulated stand-alone story in the manuscript nest, but it's unlikely that it was ever circulated for publication.

But one set of *Ignorant Armies* page fragments would eventually evolve into a published story as "The Smile" (1952). In addition to the embedded manuscript evidence, content also ties this story to *Ignorant Armies*. Both "The Smile" and its antecedent pages depict a nihilistic ritual of destruction in a postapocalyptic future—the few remaining symbols of art and civilization are destroyed in ceremonies designed to vent anger and to remind the survivors that the values of past ages had betrayed them. The young boy's fascination with the Mona Lisa (and his single-minded urge to capture a symbol of its beauty) has its origins in a fleeting encounter with an unlikely source of inspiration—Disney's animated film adaptation of *Pinocchio*. Bradbury had seen the film years earlier, but the unrestrained destructive energy of the boys during the Pleasure Island interlude (including a fleeting shot where the boys vandalize the Mona Lisa) stuck with him and slowly evolved in his mind into a dark future that had all but extinguished man's ability to be human.

By 1948, it appears that both of these nihilistic novel manuscripts had become creative dead-ends. On the individual level, the modernist defiance of conventional behavior that Bradbury explored in *Masks* became an inexorable descent into madness and death. And the result was no better when he tried to imagine an entire postapocalyptic world as he developed *Where Ignorant Armies Clash by Night*. His creative instincts, grounded in the Romantic's love of myth and supernaturalism, could not simply mourn the loss of traditional values in the Modernist fashion; the more extreme Postmodernist viewpoint, which celebrated the destruction of traditional forms of culture, was even more unthinkable for Bradbury. He had to have hope, he had to find a life-affirming mythos for the times, if he was to develop sustained works of novel-length fiction. And it was now becoming clear to him that the best way to find a life-affirming myth was to create one.

The first step had been to recognize the problem, and in this process he was in accord, to some degree, with his old friend Robert Heinlein. Although Heinlein first matured as a writer in John Campbell's hard science fiction cadre of writers at *Astounding*, he was moving into more humanistic concerns with his postwar fiction and would eventually observe that "realism in our times is a misnaming for the literature of defeat."[5] Bradbury's solution would take longer to articulate in its fullest form, but it eventually came down to denying the tragedy that invites us to die and affirming the tragedy that helps us to live.[6]

This insight went all the way back to his childhood cinema encounters with Lon Chaney's *Phantom of the Opera*, *The Hunchback of Notre Dame*, and *The Unholy Three*, where the audience could experience the tragedy of unrequited love but emerge from the cathartic effect purged. For Bradbury that kind of unhappy ending was justified, but he found no such uplifting qualities in the work of many modern novelists and dramatists. He soon saw this viewpoint reinforced through his 1948 appearance in the *Best American Short Stories* annual, where series editor Martha Foley criticized the postwar proliferation of what she called the "forced unhappy ending." The larger creative view that Bradbury was just learning to embrace during this period was effectively captured in Foley's invocation of Max Beerbohm: "What is all this talk of happy and unhappy endings? It is a matter of the inevitable ending."[7]

Bradbury had nevertheless learned a great deal by trying to write long fiction in a modernist vein. The mimetic impulse to copy, taken to extreme forms in darker manifestations of naturalism, would not be Bradbury's way. Instead, metaphor would work for him in long fiction as it always did in shorter works, providing an essential tool for his imagination to work with reality to form something new and magical out of the old order of things. But his experimentation with High Modernism—the Eliot and Pound strategy of mocking traditional prophets and values—had not been wasted, for both of these fragmentary novels can be used to track a significant shift in the early development of his book-length prose. In 1949 he returned once again to *Masks* and went so far as to apply for a Guggenheim grant to complete it. In spite of positive letters of support from August Derleth, Norman Corwin, Martha Foley, and Mark Schorer, Bradbury failed to win the grant, but the synopsis that he apparently submitted with his Guggenheim application package reveals a complete refashioning of the project:

My novel THE MASKS would concern itself with the life of one man who through the use of a large collection of masks that he had purchased or had manufactured, or carved himself, reveals the inner lives of his closest friends. Confronting people on the street, in businesses, or in his parlor, with representations of themselves, he reveals to them the parts they are playing in the world. He examines, with his Masks, the process whereby people shape their personalities not to their heart's desire, but to the expectancies of their friends and the demands of business and society. Through his Masks he hopes to prove that each person is in reality many persons, assuming identities which are the most convenient and profitable in life. He proves that life is a rehearsal, a fitting-on, a discarding of roles and parts, for some the Mask fits well and happily, for others it is a burden, it smothers, and only through the wit and mimicry of the Man and His Masks, can they find their way to their true selves.

The terrifying confrontations with Freudian taboos were gone, as was the great foulness of brute emotions. There was no longer a downward spiral to suicide for the protagonist. Surviving fragments for both an opening and an ending appear to date from the period of this late reconception of the novel, but there's little evidence that Bradbury was ever able to produce this more life-affirming version at all.[8] Although this work remained on some of his projected title listings well into the 1950s, the failure of his Guggenheim proposal, his continuing need to support himself through the short-story form, and his subsequent contract obligations for other book-length projects effectively ended his work on *Masks*.

Where Ignorant Armies Clash by Night was based on an even more severe crisis-of-values concept, and it proved to be completely unsalvageable in that form. But the novel's elite caste of professional Assassins has duties that anticipate those of Bradbury's Firemen—including the ritual burning of books and art treasures. Montag would be faced with many of the same challenges, including a world where literature of any enduring value, and the informed life that such literature nourishes, was not tolerated in any form. Here again was the choice to conform or die, but Bradbury would give Montag a third option—to find, through ordeal by fire and water, a sanctuary. The Book People would give Montag a purpose, and a way for Bradbury to bring a largely tragic work of long fiction to a redemptive conclusion. This achievement, born out of the ashes of two failed novels, would resonate in all of the sustained novel-length fiction he would ever publish.

29 Modernist Alternatives

Bradbury was still, first and foremost, a short-story writer. The Illinois novel was slowly emerging from a growing nest of Green Town stories, and a wide range of niche market and major market magazine editors were interested in new Bradbury tales. The darker themes and moods of the two failed novels lingered in certain kinds of short stories he was writing, however, and reflected his deep ambivalence toward an increasingly destabilized world. How could he and Maggie consider raising a family as a strange new form of Cold War between East and West accelerated an arms race with potentially un-imaginable consequences? He never developed a Postmodernist dislike of where technology and science had brought the world, but he always remained wary of where science may lead mankind in the future. This predictive urge led him to use his science fiction stories to work through some of the issues left unresolved in the failed novels. Many of these stories were dark and ranged across all kinds of science fiction settings.

Ten of these dark science fiction tales are, for the most part, unrelated to the fragile crystal cities and the exotic masked Martians that Bradbury would eventually bridge into the larger narrative of The Martian Chronicles. These ten are remarkably dark situational extrapolations, completely unrelated to each other yet clearly sharing the despair and isolation found in the two unfinished crisis-of-values novels. But the darkness in these stories centers more directly on a powerful sense of loneliness, made all the more chilling by the lack of any familiar source of strength or system of belief to balance the horror of the unknown. These were all written in the 1946–48 period and slowly worked their way into print over the next several years. Some are science fantasies, but all are built onto the conventional scaffolding of science fiction.

Even a cursory sequence of summaries, offered in the order of initial publi-cation, provides a sense of the darkness pervading much of Bradbury's lesser-known output of this period. What if Mars is a barren quarantine planet for people who have contracted the "blood rust" of a polluted Earth? "The Visitor" introduces a new resident who can provide wish-fulfillment illusions, until the greed of his fellow prisoners leads to his death. What if a space pilot crashes on an uninhabited planetoid and only has to await the ship dispatched to rescue him? "Asleep in Armageddon" describes the ghosts of ages past who take over his dreams and drive him to a sleep-deprived insanity (they'll be waiting for the rescue crew as well). "The One Who Waits" is an ageless entity in a Martian well, a mind invader who destroys a crew of Earthmen, one by one. "The Lonely Ones" are the two Earth astronauts who temporarily lose their slim grip on sanity when the prospect of continued isolation on lifeless Mars becomes too much to bear. "A Blade of Grass" is set on Earth, but is no less grim than the other tales: nurturing any life forms, even something as small as a blade of grass, is a capital offense in Earth's far distant future, where the dominant robot culture has long-since eradicated all known plant and animal life.

"Holiday," "Payment in Full," "Purpose" (better known as "The City"), "Death Wish" (better known as "The Blue Bottle") and "No Particular Night or Morning" round out these ten, which are distinguished from other Bradbury stories of this period by their science fiction trappings, their unrelieved darkness, the lack of any familiar points of reference, and their relative obscurity within the Bradbury canon. Only three of these tales would make it into *The Illustrated Man*, the collection eventually designed to showcase the best Bradbury science fiction not included in *The Martian Chronicles* cycle of stories. In most cases, Bradbury showed a marked reluctance to collecting these stories until many years later, if at all. These stories all represent downward spirals toward death or insanity, without any of Earth's wondrous technologies to rescue the protagonists or, at the very least, to explain and comment on the tragedy.

Other dark science fiction stories, based more firmly in the ancient Martian culture he was creating in his own mind, found their way into *The Martian Chronicles*, including tales of exploration ("Ylla," "The Earth Men," and "Mars Is Heaven!" revised as "The Third Expedition"), exploitation ("The Martian"), and abandonment ("The Off-Season," "The Long Years"). They would all be woven into the larger mythology for living that was beginning to peek out of some of these stories, and the most prominent of these was "—And the Moon Be Still as Bright," the story that Bradbury would eventually transform into the fourth expedition chapter of *The Martian Chronicles*. The dialectic that emerges from conversations between Captain Wilder and his renegade crewman Spender centers on a question that Bradbury would later describe this way: Do we go to Mars as suppliants, or as conquerors? The crew sees no value in the fragile treasures of the dying Martian culture, and even Captain Wilder feels that displacement of the old culture is inevitable. Spender feels otherwise, and is willing to kill his own shipmates if this will buy a little time for the old culture to survive.

Bradbury has always maintained that the central insights of "—And the Moon Be Still as Bright" were sparked by Joseph Wood Krutch's *The Modern Temper*. He purchased a copy of *The Modern Temper* in January 1947, about the same time that Byron's "So, We'll Go No More A-Roving" jumped out in his mind as the perfect evocation of loss that he wanted to bring into his next Martian story. Maggie had read the poem to him, and the first stanza's closing line quickly became the title. By late March, the tale was complete and sold to *Thrilling Wonder Stories* that summer, billed as a novelette. "—And the Moon Be Still as Bright" represented a direct rejoinder to Krutch's summary of the modern temper that philosophers since Kierkegaard and Nietzsche had struggled to define. Krutch did not engage these philosophers but attempted instead a very personalized examination that Bradbury's Muse found irresistible.

The Modern Temper was written in the 1920s and reflected Krutch's doubts that mankind could avoid nihilistic destruction by finding new myths to live by. Krutch's articulation of a "tragic fallacy" in modern man—that our appreciation of the great life-affirming tragedies of past literary ages disguises our inability to produce such works about our own age—provided the immediate basis for Bradbury's next creative move: the archaeologist Spender finds that the Martians had, after their own crisis of values, eventually restored belief in art and the other necessary illusions that give meaning to life within a seemingly indifferent universe. Krutch's concern with man's increasing detachment from the animal is echoed in Spender's revelations to Captain Wilder: "The animal does not question life. . . . Man had become too much man and not enough animal on Mars, too, one day. And man realized that in order to survive they would have to forgo asking that one question any longer: *Why live?*" [emphasis Bradbury's]. Through Spender and other character masks of the period, Bradbury was beginning to pinpoint his own focus for realism: the fundamental truths that help us live meaningfully rather than die in despair.

Krutch's concern for the ecological implications of consumerism reinforced earlier Bradbury readings, including Lewis Mumford's *The Condition of Man* and Philip Wylie's indictment of consumerism in certain chapters of *Generation of Vipers*. Bradbury was, in fact, developing a strong distaste for the new explosion of consumer culture and commercialism that seemed only one degree of absurdity away from the hot-dog stand on Mars at the center of "The Off-Season," which he also credits Krutch with inspiring. Both of these tales appeared in *Thrilling Wonder Stories*, and Bradbury's resurgence in the pages of this venerable pulp was aided by a shift in the magazine's editorial vision. As Mike Ashley observes, *Thrilling Wonder* adapted *Astounding*'s evolving approach and added writers "with a sense of wonder at a more human level" while continuing to solicit science fantasy and space opera. Sam Merwin, who had replaced Oscar Friend as editor in late 1944, was largely responsible for TWS's return to prominence by deemphasizing the juvenile elements of both format and contents, a strategy that paralleled Bradbury's own maturing vision as a science fiction writer.[1]

Another group of stories that eased Bradbury through his impasse with Modernist themes involved the relationship stories that he wrote but rarely published during the late 1940s and on into the early 1950s. This grouping centered on the strange new world of marriage that he was beginning to explore in fiction even as he settled into married life with Maggie. For the most part, these stories were inspired by his observations of other couples beyond his family circle, and show a fascination with the subtleties of married life. This fascination often led him to explore the anatomy of conflict in relationships that degenerate into struggles for dominance, and many of these studies never evolved past the first page of a fragment opening. There are a remarkable number of abandoned openings for such stories, and almost all of these date from the late 1940s.

One of the earliest is a failed attempt to write a "powerhouse" story about an unsuccessful writer who has left his wife for the sanctuary of the old powerhouse. The single fragment page has the darkness that informs many of these fragments; the writer describes marriage as "An empty vacuum. Into which I hopefully dropped a stone and from which no echo was forthcoming." By the end of the page, the metaphors become even more predatory: "'It was a marriage to a boa-constrictor,' he said to the walls. 'One of her coils at a time, until I was trussed and helpless. I never moved, from one day to the next. It was marriage to fly-paper. Fly-paper anointed with the finest stickiest effluvium of sickeningly—'" And here the fragment ends. Bradbury eventually developed more subtlety in completing and revising a few of these fragments; "A Touch of Petulance," completed around 1950 but not published until 1980, is perhaps the best, a time travel story where a middle-aged wife-killer goes back to warn his younger self about what is to come. Here, time travel is merely a device; as Bradbury more recently observed, "It's not a dark story about the future, it's a dark story about a marriage."

His two most powerful domestic fictions grew out of his extended Mexican journey of 1945. The American couple portrayed in "The Next in Line" and the prequel, "Interval in Sunlight," draw on the complex and sometimes tense relationships he saw among his fellow travelers in Mexico, presented against a backdrop of death and poverty: "None of us belonged in Mexico; it wasn't the right place to be." His earlier reading of Maugham's and Hemingway's fictions on the relationships between men and women came back to his mind now, especially as his increasing interactions with writers, Hollywood personalities, and the New York publishing scene allowed him to observe more relationships than ever before in his life. The result was a fusion of all these influences into the psychologically abusive husband traveling across Texas and deep into Mexico with a wife who has slowly, over the years, withdrawn into herself.

By April 1946 he had written the terrifying conclusion to the journey as the wife sees her destiny in the lines of mummies stored beneath Guanajuato, and as she finally becomes, through heart failure, "The Next in Line." In July he wrote his first draft of a prequel, "Interval in Sunlight," by providing a back-story to the relationship as the couple travels across Texas and deep into Mexico. These two long stories, and a few fragmentary bridges toward an unfinished novel, represent the high point of Bradbury's experimentation with realism. The subjective reality of the third-person narrative emerges from the wife's point of view, and the moments of reverie, unspoken thoughts, and lost opportunities for resolution resulted in one of the most fully developed characters to emerge from Bradbury's fiction prior to *Something Wicked This Way Comes*.

Bradbury would later observe, in a letter to Don Congdon, that the husband's motivation is chillingly casual—he's simply bored with the marriage, and lets the challenging circumstances of the journey kill his wife: "He hides the murder in his own heart from himself under a swarm of inconsequential detail, the details of the trip, the rooms, the gas and oil problems of the car, the breakdown of the car. All of these, interfering, prevent their escape from the environment which, by frightening her, will destroy his wife. . . . The true horror of the story then lies in the reader's recognition of the fact that the husband is letting Mexico kill his wife . . . knowing his wife's mortal fear of the country, and it's effect on her bad heart."[2] Mexico is killing her in stages, and the inaction of her husband reveals what Bradbury would come to call "the nightmare lying just beneath the surface of the husband-wife relationship."

Only two other tales of this period rise to such a level of sustained inner realism, and once again they represent two halves of a single narrative thread. "The Whole Town's Sleeping," adapted to radio for *Suspense* as "Summer Night" (1948), first reached print as a Bradbury terror in, of all places, the September 1950 issue of *McCall's*. It had evolved from Bradbury's original high-school mood piece about the ravine back home in his Waukegan neighborhood, and by the mid-1940s the deadly potential of the ravine had become manifest in the character of the Lonely One, a serial killer first described in the child narrative of "The Night" and brought fully into play as Lavinia's silent and unseen assailant in "The Whole Town's Sleeping"; the ravine is the natural shortcut home from her evening at the cinema, but it is also where the Lonely One strangles his female victims. She braves the ravine, falling deeper into a state of terror as she runs home, oblivious to the fact that the Lonely One is not behind her in the ravine, but in her house, waiting for her return.

In time, "The Whole Town's Sleeping" became the most suspenseful chapter of *Dandelion Wine*. If "Mars Is Heaven!" was becoming his hallmark science fiction story, "The Whole Town's Sleeping" slowly began to carry that status among his tales of terror. The typical Green Town opening, full of small talk among Lavinia's girl friends, slowly gives way to the internalized terrors of her own mind, presented in the third person as her cavalier attitudes give way to the darker side of her own imagination. In the early 1950s Bradbury carried the effect over into "At Midnight, in the Month of June," an overlapping sequel that tells the story and its aftermath from the deeply disturbed consciousness of the murderer himself. This sequel is, in effect, one long sustained reflective reverie; only a few words pass between the murderer and the counterman of the all-night diner where he sits, sipping milk, reflecting on his latest victim.

Although Bradbury never merged these two Green Town stories into a larger work, they nonetheless represent, like the two masterful Mexican tales, a sustained success with dark, naturalistic forms of realism that he would rarely attempt again. For the most part, his forays into Modernism would be thematic rather than formal, focusing on antimaterialist yearnings for lost values, his evolving and complicated mythos of loss and triumph in the ever-expanding space frontier, and his always ambiguous encounters with death. He would try these themes out across a wide spectrum of genres with little regard for established method, sometimes referring to himself as a magical realist, but always preferring the transformative vision of the Romantic tradition to the harsh, maskless face of raw realism.[3]

30 Finding His Own Way

As Bradbury worked through his Modernist impasse, he was also expanding his presence in radio. In May 1947 Jack Snow recommended Nelson Olmsted's Chicago-based NBC storytelling broadcasts to his friend, and Bradbury wasted no time getting a copy of *Dark Carnival* to Olmsted's network office. Chicago was in decline as a major NBC hub—most of the nationally broadcast shows originated on the coasts, but Olmsted still reached a number of network affiliates with his daily fifteen-minute morning story readings. During the 1947–48 season, he broadcast four Bradbury stories: "The Night," "The Miracles of Jamie," "One Timeless Spring," and "Powerhouse." Only the first of these was from *Dark Carnival*; Olmsted found Bradbury's major market magazine stories to be much more appealing to his perceived audience base: "Radio has had more than its share of public criticism concerning horror shows and most networks are scared to death when it comes to producing such programs."[1] Fortunately Bradbury still had strong support from Bill Spier at CBS, who managed to air house adaptations of two more dark Bradbury tales during 1948.

But Olmsted's cautions echoed the concerns Bradbury was beginning to hear from the major market magazine editors. His early postwar success in the slicks came with stories that were basically realistic ("The Big Black and White Game," "The Miracles of Jamie," "One Timeless Spring") or with a few dark fantasies ("Homecoming," "The Man Upstairs," "The Cistern") that the slicks were willing—very occasionally—to take a chance on. Rita Smith at *Mademoiselle* had taken three Bradbury stories, but began to draw the line at stories about Mars. The science fiction bias was quite strong with most of the slicks, and throughout the late 1940s Bradbury's science fiction and dark fantasies were rejected by major market editors who almost always enjoyed the submissions, but found them "wrong" or "not quite right" for their readers.

This was a code, of course, for the fact that major market editors had a very narrow definition of readership tastes. Congdon provided a broader perspective that helped Bradbury see that national magazines wanted to avoid subtlety, or in fact *any* kind of imaginative departure from everyday realism that might require too much reader insight—the editorial catchphrase was always something like "don't make the reader work too hard." Outside factors, such as occasional paper shortages and the rising postwar costs of publishing in general, forced editors to appeal to the broadest base of readership. Bradbury was also sending a lot of stories to major market women's magazines, including *Woman's Home Companion*, *Good Housekeeping*, *Charm*, *Today's Woman*, and the venerable *Ladies' Home Journal*. *Charm* would eventually become the first slick to publish one of his Martian tales, but for the most part this range of readership was not the place to send dark fantasies or the grim kind of science fiction he was now writing, and there were many rejections from this quadrant of the magazine market as well.

Bradbury continued to write his own kind of story, refusing to slant for the slicks as, for the most part, he had refused to do for the pulps. But there were creative factors that he could, with experience, control, and some of his editors joined Congdon in making suggestions. In May 1947 John Schaffner at *Good Housekeeping* rejected "The Illustrated Man" and took the opportunity to offer some friendly criticism. For some months Schaffner and Innes MacCammond over at the ill-fated *USA Magazine* offices had been trading Bradbury stories back and forth, and both men had found "The Illustrated Man" to be too complicated for easy reading. Schaffner felt that the ending was excellent and the overall concept strikingly original, but that the story, as submitted, suffered from over-writing and too many extra effects: "In short, I think you overplay your hand. This appears to me to be an outgrowth of your natural exuberance and it is something which a little self-criticism will easily take care of, I know."[2]

Bradbury did downplay the magical elements of "The Illustrated Man" in subsequent revisions, creating a tighter tragedy around the alienation, despera-tion, and fear of otherness at the heart of this carnival murder story. It would eventually become Bradbury's first appearance in *Esquire* (1950), and although it is distinct from the famous Prologue/Epilogue concept that structures *The Illustrated Man* story collection (1951), this tale became a perennial anthology favorite. But both Schaffner and MacCammond were concerned about the uncharacteristic carelessness that crept into some of the 1947 submissions as Bradbury pushed perhaps too hard for sales on his own in the months before his marriage. Here, too, was a natural exuberance that was the inevitable consequence of a writer working in the *Fountainhead* tradition, going his own way and writing to please himself. It was his chosen way of insuring consistent quality and integrity in his fiction, but this process worked best only so long as he could maintain some degree of authorial distance during the revising process. Distanced and dispas-sionate revision didn't always happen with the stories, though, and for now Congdon had the good sense to let Bradbury work it out for himself.

Occasionally, other writers offered suggestions as well. Besides the old core group of Brackett, Kuttner, and Hamilton, there weren't many new writer-friends who had this kind of connection with Bradbury, but Fritz Leiber was one. He had greatly enjoyed *Dark Carnival*, and early in the winter of 1947–48 he wrote a long critique based on the background structure of the stories: "It's the frame of reference of your stories that I want to talk about now—the laws and unlaws of the worlds they're laid in."[3] Leiber felt that most of the stories were consistently set in effective situational contexts, an obvious but essential imaginative element that all readerships require. Like their mutual friend Henry Kuttner, Leiber felt that this was more than a mere matter of definition, for "the world of the story may be an extreme variant on the worlds of previous stories, it may even be practically unique—and still give that feeling of a 'world' behind the tale, a whole set of facts, postulates, hints, and suggestions that tie together consistently."

Leiber found that *Dark Carnival's* three off-trail vampire stories were consistently grounded in a humorous world where the reader is invited to take a look at the vampire's side of things to discover many of the same hopes and fears and joys that inform the daylight world of ordinary people. In many of the other stories, Leiber found the real world effectively lightened by "poetry and oddity" or compellingly darkened by insanity. Still other *Dark Carnival* tales opened out into the world of the traditional ghost story before concluding with very original Bradburyian twists. But Leiber felt that other stories, including such enduring titles as "Skeleton," "The Crowd," "The Wind," "The Scythe," and to some extent "The Small Assassin" exploded beyond any frame of reference, and this was probably due to an inability or unwillingness in revision to rein in the flow of creativity. At times excessive elements of dark humor or irony diminished the larger realities at the heart of a good Bradbury idea. It was, essentially, the same problem that Schaffner, MacCammond, and Congdon had already pointed out, but it was useful to hear it from a friend who was already a proven master of the fantastic.

Soon, however, with Congdon to take on the time-consuming and often worrisome tasks of promotion and circulation, Bradbury's creative focus rebalanced, and the Martian stories, along with many of the other darker science fiction tales, generally sold to the pulps with little or no need for revision. Even the criticism he received from the slick editors as they declined his stories was often useful. The conscientious Rita Smith at *Mademoiselle* spent a long time reviewing "Ylla," a strange but beautiful love story of first contact with Mars, before returning it with comments that both Congdon and Bradbury found worth considering. Why did these masked Martians, humanoid but different from Earth's humans in every conceivable way, use rifles? Bradbury realized that his exotic vision of an ancient Martian culture was unfinished in many of its details. In the months that followed, he gave his Martians unique bee-stinger weapons unlike any Earth weapon or imagined ray-gun. He eliminated the cobwebs that Ylla used to pull in household dust, and created instead a magnetic dust swarm for her cleaning rituals; he also gave her a table of upwelling Martian lava in which to prepare hot foods. But the story, as fine as it was becoming, remained unsold.

His frustration with the failure of the major market magazines to take his new science fiction stories was overshadowed, however, by the impasse he had reached with his attempts at long fiction. The longer he worked at the Illinois novel, the harder it became for him to pull these Green Town stories into a unified novel structure. Throughout 1947 he looked for external financial support that might help him focus on the task at hand. Bradbury had considered using Congdon's residual influence at Simon & Schuster to ask for an advance, but he never really had enough of a manuscript to justify in his own mind an advance or, for that matter, even a contract. Congdon's contacts at William Morrow were also interested, but they too needed to see more progress. Later, in the fall of 1947, Bradbury tried fiction-wary *Life Magazine* and even explored the possibility of using radio or film development of some of the Green Town stories as a way to break the writing block. To this end he met with Norman Corwin, and, through Bill Spier, Orson Welles to see if this was at all possible.[4]

But nothing developed from these efforts, and Bradbury remained in stalemate with his most promising novel concept. This became even more frustrating as the two dark novel projects, *Masks* and *Where Ignorant Armies Clash by Night*, moved almost inevitably toward dead ends. His good friend Robert Bloch, no slouch at psychoanalysis, was of the opinion that Bradbury's dilemma was tied up to some degree in his distinctive disdain of writers who slanted or wrote for income rather than for the muse. For almost a year he had been recommending a wide range of authors for Bradbury to read, urging Maggie to use her bookstore connections at Fowler's to get *The Men of Good Will* series by Jules Romains, *I Claudius* and *Claudius the God* by Robert Graves, Karel Capek's *War with the Newts*, and Charles Finney's *The Circus of Dr. Lao*. Both Bloch and Kuttner had been after Bradbury to read William Gresham's tough but compellingly written new noir novel, *Nightmare Alley*. Bradbury soon read *Nightmare Alley* and apparently met Gresham and his wife, the poet Joy Davidman, when Gresham worked briefly in Hollywood. But Bradbury's expressed dislike of *The Circus of Dr. Lao*, a Bloch favorite, prompted Bloch to observe that "I get more angles on you from your criticism than I do on *Dr. Lao* . . . I think you expected too much of *Lao* and therefore you expect too much of yourself."

Bloch himself made no secret that he often slanted his own work. Both Bradbury and Leiber were disappointed at Bloch's undisguised strategy of writing, as Leiber called it, "to make money by catering to current trends and some of the mean appetites of the mob." Yet both men also knew Bloch's capabilities as a writer, and Bloch had established a rapport with Bradbury that gave weight to his analysis, expressed in an August 1947 letter. Like Kuttner, Bloch encouraged Bradbury to attempt long fiction with far less restraint and caution than he had so far exhibited: "I urge you with all sincerity to get to work, write a book, write two—three—four books, just as a matter of course. Don't worry about 'wasting' an idea or 'spoiling' a plot by going too fast. If you are capable of turning out a masterpiece, you'll get other and even better ideas in the future. Right now your job is to write, and to write books so that by so doing you'll gain the experience to write still better books later on."

Bloch's words were heartfelt, and arose from the same instincts that had led Henry Kuttner to offer similar advice to Bradbury during the war; in fact, Bloch had learned from the same source—"It took years for Kuttner to pound that into my thick skull," he confessed to Bradbury in the same letter. Bloch's further summary also seemed to echo their mutual friend: "Naturally, I have no right to preach to or at you, except the self-assumed one of interest in you and friendship for you. But I want you to do novels, and there is not the slightest doubt about your being able to do them successfully from both a commercial and an artistic standpoint. The danger—and I feel it is a real one—lies in waiting too long and developing an attitude about the importance or gravity of a novel-length work."

As compelling as it was, however, this kind of advice did not quite fit Bradbury's intuitive approach to writing. He did not yet feel comfortable forcing his unconscious fount of creativity to compose beyond the 3,000- to 5,000-word bursts that he was now adept at producing. From his perspective, this was the only way to guard against the kind of self-conscious writing that constantly threatened to extinguish his originality as a storyteller. But another kind of self-consciousness was preventing him from weaving these story-length threads into any sustained form of long fiction. Bloch focused in on this side of Bradbury's dilemma in his August 1947 letter: "But if you wait, and prepare, and keep a solitary vigil, and you anoint yourself as the Bridegroom, chances are you will be too self-conscious to do a workmanlike job."

Bradbury's drive to quality in long fiction would never settle for the "workmanlike job," however, and the dilemma remained. The best reinforcement of his own vision for fiction came from an East Coast friend he had corresponded with for some time, but had not yet met—Theodore Sturgeon. Bradbury had been a fan of Sturgeon's kindred gift for emotionally charged prose since discovering him in several 1940 issues of *Astounding*, and his enthusiasm had not waned in the years since he had turned away from reading the pulps. For his part Sturgeon greatly admired Bradbury's originality, and during the late winter of 1947–48 he offered his long-distance friend a literary perspective on his talents in terms that resonated with Bradbury's lifelong dream of joining his literary loves on the library shelves: "Forgive this dutch-uncle tone, but lissen: there is only one Bradbury, and like a few—Gerard Manly Hopkins, P. G. Wodehouse, James Branch Cabell, and a coupla more from widely separated fields—you can't be imitated; you're an original. (This is unlike Hemingway, Saroyan, Herman Wouk, Farrell, Steinbeck, and yards and yards of others—particularly Damon Runyan—originators, perhaps, but quite imitable.) One characteristic of the true original is that he does his work his way. (Alec Wilder is one in music; Emily Dickinson was one in poetry.)"[5]

Any writer opens up to imitation, and Bradbury would eventually see his share of imitations and parody-tributes; but the quality of his ideas and his metaphor-rich style had already developed into a very personal authorial signature. Sturgeon went on in his offbeat style ("The Kinsey Report aside, I *love* you!") to profess his enthusiastic jealousy for a writer who had avoided a moneymaking approach to writing: "I let myself be forced into markets for which I didn't care particularly; I forced my styles into preformed molds. As far as I know you have never done this." Arthur C. Clarke, their near contemporary, would later maintain that Bradbury and Sturgeon, above all other influential science fiction writers, were masters of distinctly original styles deeply grounded in highly emotional yet carefully controlled prose. Both would reach major milestones of book-length fiction in 1950—Sturgeon with his novel *The Dreaming Jewels*, in which he offered the first fictional reference to Bradbury's *The Martian Chronicles*, published just two months earlier that same year. But the *Chronicles* evolved as a novelized cycle of stories, and as early as February 1947 Bradbury revealed to Congdon his very real fear that he might die before ever completing the Illinois novel.

Congdon reassured him, noting that many writers went through this kind of anxiety.[6] But he already saw how Bradbury's instinctive preference for the short-story form was holding back his development as a novelist. Even before he left Simon & Schuster, Congdon cautioned him that, if he wanted to sustain his major market success, he'd have to work on character development to a degree not normally required in the pulp market. There was another problem, though, that surfaced as Bradbury sent Congdon more and more of the short pieces intended for the far larger fabric of the Illinois novel. This was a growing tendency to write short-short stories that were little more than scenes or fragments, glimpses of Green Town and the people who lived there.[7] As they circulated, editors also felt that they were too slight to sell, and as a result only one identifiable Green Town story, "The Summer Night," reached print during the final three years of the 1940s. He was, like Mark Twain, feeling his way toward sustained long fiction by doing what he knew best, but for a time these reminiscent Illinois stories were coming to the surface only in very brief bursts of writing.

31 | The Anthology Game

The development of the Illinois novel was also slowed by Bradbury's increased focus on the science fiction stories he was writing and revising with more and more frequency. In spite of Congdon's influence with a wide range of editors, these stories were still not selling to the major magazines at all. By the spring of 1948 he could claim, altogether, only nine slick appearances and two appearances in literary magazines. What sustained both his spirit and his reputation during this period was his almost phenomenal success with the premier award anthologies of the day. Martha Foley's selection of "The Big Black and White Game" for the 1946 *Best American Short Stories* annual (for stories published in 1945) and Herschel Brickell's publication of "Homecoming" in the *O. Henry Prize Stories of 1947* was soon followed by subsequent appearances in both of these award anthologies. "Powerhouse," his second sale to *Charm*, placed third in the *O. Henry Prize Stories of 1948*, and "I See You Never," his first sale to the *New Yorker*, appeared in *Best American Short Stories* that same year. Foley also included four other Bradbury titles in the volume's list of "Distinctive Short Stories in American Magazines"; these four titles, along with the featured "I See You Never," represented all of Bradbury's slick and literary magazine sales of 1947. He was not hitting these magazines nearly as much as he wished, but when he did, it was noticed.

Bradbury's first *O. Henry* appearance was made all the more remarkable by the amount of praise and recognition he received for *not* winning one of the top three story prizes. The most experienced judge, juvenile fiction author Muriel Fuller, had spent fifteen years working with Herschel Brickell and Doubleday on the *O. Henry* annual volumes and had voted "Homecoming" the third prize; Norma Long Brickell, who assumed Fuller's editorial duties late in the selection process, upgraded the vote to second place. But the other two judges failed to concur with these combined recommendations, and "Homecoming" appeared in the 1947 volume as part of the general prize-winning field. In relating these events, Herschel Brickell's introductory essay gave far more space to praising "Homecoming" than to discussing any other story in the volume. He cited Fuller's praise of Bradbury's powerful imagination, "the originality of theme and the brilliant carrying out of the concept." Brickell himself noted how the story invoked "the shades of Irving, Poe and Hawthorne," and spent more than a page lamenting the failure of his judges to award one of the three prizes to "Homecoming."

The spectral shade of the atomic bomb also loomed over the editorial process; one of the jurors, Struthers Burt, observed that "Not a single one of these stories presents a ray of hope for things as they are . . . Here is not the age-old revolt of the artist against things as they are, with the underlying implicit belief that they can be better, but a sort of grim acceptance that 'the American Dream,' personally and otherwise, has gone badly askew." Brickell himself felt that Bradbury's fantasy, and its closing promise of another dark family homecoming in 1970, might also play subconsciously into the world's newfound fear of the atom:

> Much may be made of the symbolism of the presence in the story of a being touched with human frailties amid his unearthly crew of relatives; little Timothy who cannot drink blood with enjoyment and satisfaction, who cannot fly, and who is probably cursed with mortality. Is Mr. Bradbury merely telling us a tale, and doing it well enough to cause us to believe what he says, or is he really saying that Timothy, in his curious plight, stands for the human race at the present sad moment? Who'll be at Salem in 1970 if all goes well with the plans for atomizing us in the meanwhile, excepting the goblins and ghoulies, the witches and warlocks—not poor Timothy, and not us, either.

Brickell would have the pleasure of awarding Bradbury a third-place prize in the following year's *O. Henry* volume for "Powerhouse," which offered a comforting counterpoint to Brickell's technological fears through its life-affirming view of cosmic consciousness and purpose. By contrast, Martha Foley settled on the simple tale "I See You Never" for Bradbury's second *Best American Short Stories* appearance because it exhibited the kind of carefully developed situational tensions that she found in the best short fiction of 1948. Like Brickell, however, she found a correlation between the deep worries of the postwar world and the stories she had selected for her 1948 volume, "[f]or there is in them definitely a feeling of tension, of expectancy, of breathless awaiting of the unknown. Perhaps a psychiatrist would say they show an 'anxiety neurosis.' Writers reflect the emotions of their countrymen, and therefore this must be a national attitude."

Whether he meant to or not, Bradbury had certainly tapped into a universal sense of anxiety in writing this story from his own memories of his years working around Figueroa and Temple, where a hardworking Mexican immigrant, living on a long-expired visa, was tracked down in Mrs. Beach's tenement and taken into custody by federal agents. As he was escorted out of Mrs. Beach's kitchen, her former tenant turned and offered a final desperate lament in his limited English: "I see you never!" This would be his only *New Yorker* sale, but it appeared in the second edition of one of the most critically influential midcentury class-room texts—the Robert Penn Warren and Cleanth Brooks high-school reader, *Understanding Fiction*.

Bradbury's appearance in the *Best American Short Stories* anthology of 1948 would have an even more immediate impact on his writing life. One of the other writers selected for that volume was Dolph Sharp, who was making a name for himself with his Jancie Brierman stories about Jewish life in New York. Sharp was a native New Yorker, but increasingly debilitating bouts with spinal arthritis led him to move his family to the Southwest and eventually on to Burbank. When "The Tragedy in Jancie Brierman's Life" landed him in the pages of the 1948 *Best American Short Stories*, he noticed that several other BASS selectees and honorable mentions for that year also lived and wrote in the Los Angeles area. The others included Bradbury and Elliott Grennard, a gifted jazz pianist, songwriter, and former music editor for *Billboard*. During the summer of 1948 Sharp brought in these and other local writers to form a variable core group of eight. Wilma Shore, who was becoming a regular contributor to the *New Yorker*, was also an early member.

The group soon included Sanora Babb, who wrote compellingly of her childhood dustbowl experiences among the Oto Indians of Oklahoma and the high plains farming towns of Kansas and eastern Colorado. The 1948 BASS included her on the Roll of Honor for "Reconciliation," and she would go on to win BASS selections outright in 1950 and again in 1960. Screenwriter Ben Maddow's "The Lilacs" also made the 1948 BASS volume's distinction list, and he was soon brought into the group as well. The architectural critic and writer Esther McCoy joined Sharp's group about the time that Martha Foley selected her 1949 *Harper's Bazaar* story "The Cape" for the 1950 BASS volume. In the early years the group also included Joseph Petracca, who wrote about the Italian neighborhoods of New York and occasionally broadened out into science fiction, and scriptwriter Joel Murcott, who would later, like Bradbury himself, write teleplays for Alfred Hitchcock.

Once Dolph Sharp brought the group together, it began a fairly stable life of its own. Sessions were scheduled for twice a month on Friday evenings, moving from home to home among group members. After midnight, the discussion melted into easy talk over beer and delicatessen snacks.[1] In the early 1940s Bradbury had been the youngest member of Virginia Perdue's writing group; he was also the youngest this time, but now he was the leading writer. It was never a question of dominance, however, or even standing first among equals. Everyone was on an even footing, and there was free give-and-take as they discussed each other's stories. Most of these writers were leftist liberals of one kind or another. Maddow had written left-wing documentaries in the 1930s and would always write from a social conscience perspective; he had recently scripted *Intruder in the*

Dust, and within a year he would achieve a lasting reputation as John Huston's cowriter on the script of *The Asphalt Jungle*. In the early 1950s Babb, Shore, and Sharp would join others to found the leftist poetry magazine *California Quarterly*. But politics meant little to the dynamics of the group, and many of the members from the early days, including Bradbury, would continue the group for decades. Bradbury would offer criticism in a collegial fashion, sometimes pointing out hard truths yet always encouraging at the same time. Yet he preferred to keep his own counsel in revising his fiction, and continued to write and revise in his own way.

An even more fundamental authorial interaction was also at play here, for Bradbury was now rubbing shoulders with mainstream American writers in the award anthologies. Some were favorites from before the war; others were major new writers like Jessamyn West and Truman Capote. These honors deeply gratified his library-shelf instinct for immortality and authorial companionship, but they also triggered a new idea in his mind: if he couldn't bring his science fiction stories into the major magazines, why not bring his favorite mainstream writers into science fiction? Throughout 1948, he considered how such an anthology, or even multiple anthologies, might be conceived. First, however, he would have to overcome the kind of judgmental bias against market-savvy writers that he had shown in his correspondence with Hannes Bok and Jack Snow and Bob Bloch. Writers who occasionally slanted to markets were often nonetheless writers of distinction, and Bradbury would have to learn to write more objectively about them if he wanted to have an impact as an editor.

The first chance came from his pen pal Theodore Sturgeon, who asked Bradbury to write the introduction to his first story collection, *Without Sorcery*. He set to the task in mid-February 1948 but had trouble from the start. Although he loved Sturgeon's work, he also knew that Sturgeon gave in to market pressures from time to time. His first draft was neutral in tone, encouraging but qualified, closing with a lukewarm endorsement to readers: "I believe you will enjoy reading *Without Sorcery*; it is a competent work trying to keep its balance in a literary environment where equilibrium seems a lost and irretrievable sense." As this sentence indicates, Bradbury was still focused on issues well beyond the task at hand; in fact, much of the draft focused on an issue dear to his heart at that moment: the rising threat of censorship and the leveling of talent that seemed, at least to Bradbury, to point to the imminent death of the imagination.

Large sections of this draft introduction reveal more about Bradbury than they do about Sturgeon. Although Bradbury was himself bringing the traditional subjects of the dark fantastic into the life and times of the modern world, he still deeply lamented the loss of values that seemed to be the central price of Modernity:

At the same time that the Holy Ghost was being exorcised by jubilant Darwinites armed with Flint Guns full of facts, the ghost of many a fine gothic tale was laid to rest. With our long withdrawal down the shingles of the world, as Matthew Arnold so hauntingly put it, we have lost faith not only in God but in God's opposites, the devil, the apparitions, the werewolves and warlocks. I cannot help but feel we have lost something essentially vital and stimulating in losing both things at once. Much savor has gone from life. This is not to say we would enjoy a hastening return to dark superstition, but then at least there was white Whiteness as well as the dark Dark, while today all is a vast and monotonous plain of unvarying grey.

This view, alluding with good effect to the shingled rocky shore and the darkling plain of Arnold's "Dover Beach," echoed his own recent novella-length masterpiece "Pillar of Fire," which would soon appear in the Summer 1948 issue of *Planet Stories* (its subject matter, almost by definition, consigned "Pillar of Fire" to the pulps in spite of themes and prose worthy of the major magazines). The draft introduction also anticipates the language of *Fahrenheit 451* and the great debates between Fireman Montag and Fire Chief Beatty. Another passage comments even more directly on the loss of the literary past: "Mr. Sturgeon, in line with the times, gives the horse laugh to the gothic structure. The sound of the avalanche is heard as that mighty tall dark architecture of the midnight Ages falls into heaped ruin. Is there a Poe somewhere ahead to pick among the kindling and re-start the fire?" This is a clear allusion to both "Pillar of Fire" and "The Exiles" (first published as "The Mad Wizards of Mars"), Bradbury stories that would pave the way to the central fires of *Fahrenheit 451*.

He was not totally dismissive of the five fantasy stories that Sturgeon had included among the tales of *Without Sorcery*, for he felt that "It" might stand as enduring evidence of Sturgeon's power as an imaginative writer ("It" would indeed). But Bradbury was not really writing about Sturgeon at all, and had, effectively, written himself into a corner. The impasse was broken, quite unintentionally, by Sturgeon's favorable March 5 response to the draft, in which he confessed his jealousy of Bradbury's integrity as a writer. Bradbury immediately set to work on a new introduction that expressed his own kindred jealousy of Sturgeon's ideas and imaginative genius, and this strategy soon released the crucial insight from his subconscious: he could write about other writers with the same style and commitment and emotional force that he brought to his own fiction.[2]

The final introduction was nothing at all like the earlier draft—it was now a balanced, startling, metaphor-rich dissection of Sturgeon's work: "[t]he most complimentary thing I can think to say of Sturgeon is that I hated his damned, efficient, witty guts. And yet because he had the thing for which I was looking, originality (always rare in the pulps), I was forced, in an agony of jealousy, to return again and again to his stories, to dissect, to pull apart, to re-examine the bones." This central structuring metaphor supported a full essay of literal and metaphorical observations about the stories in *Without Sorcery*, and gave Bradbury the breakthrough technique he would eventually bring to his work as an anthologist: Write like Ray Bradbury, regardless of the prose genre.

In spite of this breakthrough, Bradbury did not yet feel comfortable writing about his favorite genre from an anthologist's perspective. In June 1948 Bradbury's ongoing correspondence with August Derleth concerning Derleth's recent success editing the science fiction anthology *Strange Ports of Call* led to an offer that Bradbury simply had to refuse. Derleth was soliciting articles on the theme of "A Basic Science Fiction Library" for a special issue of his house quarterly, *The Arkham Sampler*. He had already asked for articles from authors such as A. E. Van Vogt, Clark Ashton Smith, and Theodore Sturgeon, as well as editors John Campbell of *Astounding* and Paul Payne of *Planet Stories*, and he wanted a Bradbury contribution if at all possible. For his part, Bradbury supported Derleth's attempt to distinguish, both in his essay campaign and in his anthologies, between literary science fiction and escape-adventure yarns, but he didn't feel qualified to contribute. In his response, Bradbury confessed to knowing very little about classic science fiction beyond his very selective reading of H. G. Wells. His own science fiction library was almost nonexistent; he no longer read the genre magazines and knew that his own future as an anthologist led in other directions.[3]

Bradbury's emerging idea for a mainstream literary anthology of science fiction stories began to center on his own favorite science fiction setting—the Red Planet. In December 1948, Don Congdon told Bradbury that editors at Harper's wanted to explore the possibility of having Bradbury edit a general fantasy anthology. He eventually proposed twenty-five stories by a range of mainstream and genre authors under the working title *Curiouser and Curiouser*. First, however, Bradbury used the Harper's opportunity to spring his Martian anthology concept on his agent. In return for agreeing to edit the general fantasy anthology, Bradbury proposed that a target group of contemporary writers be asked to write stories "concerning the first trip to Mars, the colonization of Mars by Earth people, or any aspect of later life on Mars, once colonized. What would [Evelyn] Waugh people do on Mars? How would Welty people react? Suppose Capote landed there? How different the reaction of Robert Lowry and John Collier, Margaret Shedd and John Hersey, Steinbeck and E. B. White."

He christened the project "*The Martian Chronicles. Edited by Ray Bradbury.*" In the same letter, he proposed *The Martian Poems*, a companion volume of thirty poems by thirty poets. Bradbury envisioned contributions by Marianne Moore, W. H. Auden, T. S. Eliot, Kenneth Fearing, Stephen Spender, e. e. cummings, Walter de La Mare, and others. "We would contact them and ask them to write poems as if they themselves were inhabitants of a Martian culture. An old culture, and a wise and beautiful one. There would be more than enough poetic freedom in the idea. Poems about Mars, the nights and days and temperatures and colours. Poems about love and hate and death, not far different from that on Earth." Here were the moods and images of his own Red Planet, a world that had emerged in fragments through a number of the stories he had written about Mars since the end of the war. The anthology was really a framework for commentary on our own world, more fantasy than science fiction, the prototype for a book-length concept of his own work that was perhaps already forming in his subconscious mind.

He went on to offer Congdon ideas about magazine serialization for the anthologized Martian stories and poems ahead of book publication, and offered to take less money for editing *Curiouser and Curiouser*, the fantasy collection that Harper's really had in mind. But this was a rather naive view, and it glossed over the monumental impossibilities of gathering work from such a broad base of popular storytellers and poets, nearly all of whom were under contractual obligations to other publishing houses. The Martian anthology project never developed, and Bradbury was not able to come to terms with *Harper's* on the general fantasy anthology either.[4] During the winter of 1948–49, the prospect of becoming an anthology editor seemed to be yet another creative dead end.

32 Paradise Postponed

Bradbury continued to publish short fiction at an impressive rate—eighteen new stories in 1947, twenty-one in 1948, along with an ever-increasing number of reprint sales. As he continued to find a new level of success in the postwar science fiction pulps, he soon became popular as a subject for fanzine articles and interviews. *Spearhead*'s "Ray Bradbury: An Appraisal" (August 1948) offered a fan's-eye view of his increasing popularity: his original style, his emotional power, and his penchant for capturing the impressionistic aspects of an autumn day or a lonely night. During the fall of 1948 LASFS's *Shangri-LA* reprinted Bradbury's first published interview—"The Market Is Not the Story," from the March issue of *Writers' Markets & Methods*.[1] This represented Bradbury's first chance to craft the writerly mask that he wanted associated with his work; it was founded on true articles of faith, such as his will to believe that slanting is a form of imitation, that "message" is secondary to true storytelling, and that "sincerity extends to the reader and improves the story immeasurably."

He bluntly declared that his method was simply to "sit down and write," but his earliest preserved interview also reveals a great deal about the process beneath this masking statement. The emotional blaze of his first draft captured idea, mood, and tension: "Revision is largely a matter of cutting to speed the pace and eliminate wordage that might be more important to the author than the reader." But revision required an inevitable degree of objectivity and analysis, and beneath the mask he found this quite boring. He handled this challenge somewhat obliquely in the interview, claiming that his habit of keeping many stories in revision simultaneously, over many months, was his way of avoiding creative dry spells. But his lack of enthusiasm for revision, which in years to come would spill over into his boredom with the galley and proof revisions of his books, surfaced more clearly in this interview than in many of his later statements on writing: "I carry a story forward when I feel like working on that story. When I'm not as interested in it as I should be I put it away and work on something for which I can show some enthusiasm."

For years his technique of substitution would provide a buffer against Don Congdon's requests for new stories, but it also underlines his abiding wariness of objectivity. In fact, this interview contained one of Bradbury's earliest public statements about his fundamental belief in writing as a purely emotional endeavor: "The fiction writer is, first, an emotionalist. Whether he admits it or not. A story is not successful through logic, or beautiful thinking, or by its appeal to the intellect, though these elements must be present. It succeeds in its appeal to the reader's emotions. Many of the best beloved stories are weak in plot and idea, implausible in conception. They are great because they get under the reader's skin, causing him to react sympathetically with the characters." He would eventually restate this conviction for a broader public in his introduction to *Timeless Stories for Today and Tomorrow* (1952). At its best, this focused appeal to emotions could make up for many sins of technique and result in little masterpieces of description, invocations of the past, and vivid encounters with the fundamental hopes and fears of humanity. In spite of occasional lapses of control and balance, and despite continuing efforts by critics, editors, and readers to paint him with genre labels, Bradbury would, within a few more years, become an acknowledged master of the short story.

But what about longer prose forms? His resurgent postwar success in the science fiction pulps, as well as his occasional successes with major market magazines and network radio, masked the very real and very private crisis he was facing in his efforts to publish any kind of book-length fiction. His inability to bring either of the Modernist crisis-of-values novels to completion was matched with similar frustration as he tried to fuse drafts of his Green Town stories into the still-nebulous Illinois novel. At the same time, he was also trying to forge some sort of book-length structure around "Homecoming," which was now widely recognized as one of his finest published stories. During the winter and spring of 1948 Bradbury had lobbied hard for a perennial Halloween gift-book concept with illustrations by Charles Addams. Congdon painstakingly negotiated the deal with Helen King at Morrow, but the commercial risk factor on such a book was high, especially given the price range commanded by an illustrator of Addams's stature. Bradbury and Congdon explored the possibility of sharing royalties with Addams to bring down the preprinting cost of $300 per illustration, but this would simply transfer the risk to the artist; in February Addams wrote back to decline taking that risk on a book that would probably never draw enough adult readership to sustain sales.[2]

That same month King persuaded Bradbury to develop a more ambitious "Homecoming" concept that would involve using the other two vampire "Family" stories included in *Dark Carnival*. At times working around Congdon, she soon convinced him to write several new "Family" stories for the illustrated book. Bradbury and Congdon then had to face an inevitable clash with August Derleth over the use of the *Dark Carnival* stories. After a lengthy and sometimes tense exchange of letters, Bradbury was eventually able to convince Derleth to compromise on his contractual reprint control of the *Dark Carnival* contents. This would turn out to be the true turning point in the relationship between Bradbury and his first editor-confidant; Bradbury's willingness to write even more "Family" stories for the new book convinced Derleth that there was no longer an exclusive reliance on stories first collected in *Dark Carnival*, and he eased back on the reprint fees. More subjectively, Bradbury's selection for both the *Best American Short Stories* and *O. Henry* prize volumes that spring forced Derleth to realize that Bradbury had long since outgrown genre publishers. By June the correspondence, always civil, had become warm and friendly again, and would remain so for the rest of Derleth's life.

Unfortunately, Congdon was not having similar success with Morrow's Helen King; she remained concerned that the high advance Bradbury wanted in return for writing a number of new "Family" stories represented too much of a risk. And there was also the problem of illustrations. With Addams effectively out of the picture, Bradbury suggested William Gropper and even sent a sample of his work to Morrow for consideration. Gropper's dreamlike perspectives and highly stylized figures opened out across a wide range of media forms, including cartoon illustration, painting, lithography, and etching. These talents played right into Bradbury's creative imagination, but Gropper's liberal political agenda was always controversial; Morrow's art director Frank Lieberman countered with the idea of illustrations by Mervyn Peake and had a British edition of *Dark Carnival* sent out from London to Peake's secluded home in the Channel Islands. Derleth had thought that Peake, in spite of his originality as an illustrator and his recent success as a fantasy writer with the first volume of the Gormenghast books, was too heavily gothic for the "Family" stories, and suggested instead the Connecticut illustrator Richard Taylor, who had published two books of his own that were similar in many respects to the Addams style. But Morrow's editors preferred Peake, who could work within their budget for an illustrated book.

The real sticking point remained the advance. It was a risky book no matter how it evolved, and Helen King remained firm on a $250 limit on the advance even if Bradbury wrote new stories for the book, encouraging him instead to take advantage of prepublication magazine appearances to make up the difference. She also indicated that the collection would not reach print until the fall 1949 book season—more than a year away. Congdon read between the lines and sent the proposal on to Ken McCormick, senior editor at Doubleday. The consensus that came back from Doubleday in early June 1948 was that the book was too narrowly focused and that Bradbury's off-trail conception of the vampire world would confuse as much as entertain. Bradbury was already manifesting his delightful tendency to upset genre rules in his writing, but he did not yet have the reputation to bowl over reluctant editors at the major book publishing houses.

Congdon knew this, yet he wanted to take one last chance on Farrar and Straus—he knew John Farrar fairly well, and Roger Straus Jr. had tracked Bradbury's magazine appearances since *Mademoiselle*'s George Davis had shown him tear sheets of "Invisible Boy" two years earlier. In his subsequent letters to Bradbury, Straus had encouraged him to submit a novel, so in October Congdon pulled out all the stops and sent three proposals for review: The illustrated "Family" book; an outline for the slowly emerging Illinois novel, now titled *Summer Morning, Summer Night*; and a wide-ranging collection of Bradbury tales brought together under the still-unsold title story, *The Illustrated Man*. By October Farrar and Straus indicated that they would publish the vampire book and take on the expense of commissioning Charles Addams for illustrations, but only if the novel-in-progress and the story collection were strong enough to make the risk worthwhile. Bradbury was proud of his new story collection, but his continuing disappointments with the big houses made him cautious. As he confessed to Derleth, "My only fear now is that *The Illustrated Man* will be a little bit of everything, and not enough of one thing, what with layers of s.f., weird, fantastic, and realistic fiction bundled together. I hope the diverse contents won't scare off certain groups of buyers. We'll see."[3]

This new collection harvested stories that he had written, for the most part, over the three years since the end of the war and that had not been included in *Dark Carnival*. Most had already appeared in various pulp and mainstream magazines, but all had received the same loving attention in revision; they were all quality stories, and as always Bradbury made no distinction between those that landed in the niche markets and those that achieved higher recognition in the slicks. Two of his award-winning stories were included, along with the original unpublished story version of his prize-winning radio play, "The Meadow."[4] He was stunned, therefore, when, in mid-April 1949, fully six months after receiving the multivolume proposal from Congdon, Farrar & Straus finally declined all three projects. On one level, this was a sign that the outline for the Illinois novel and the promising but unfocused new story collection were not yet strong enough to carry the financial baggage of the illustrated "Family" book. But it was the rationale for rejecting the story collection that angered Bradbury to distraction. Farrar and Straus declared the *Illustrated Man* collection uneven, but not because of the wide range of genres represented; instead, the reviewing editors relied on the magazine-publishing history behind each story to declare them, one by one, "pulp" or "quality."

This meant only one of two things: either Bradbury was wrong about the consistent quality of his published stories, or the serial history of every story in the collection had predisposed editorial judgment. The evidence in favor of the latter conclusion was overwhelming, and not just in Bradbury's mind. For years a wide range of magazine editors at all levels had conceded the quality of his stories and commented on his ability to write beyond niche market limitations. But the most compelling indictment of the Farrar-Straus position was in the prepublication history of circulation for many of these stories. He first vented his frustration in an April 21st letter to Derleth:

> Farrar-Straus rejected my book because the quality of the pulp stories in it, they said, was not on a par with my quality magazine writing. Ironic and ridiculous thing is that they like "Homecoming," "Invisible Boy," and "Power House" very much; all three stories appeared in quality magazines, but were originally written for—*Weird Tales!* . . . I wouldn't have minded a flat rejection from F-Straus, but this business of my pulp writing differing from my quality stuff is ridiculous. As you recall, "The Man Upstairs" was rejected by *Weird Tales* and sold to *Harper's. You* figure it out!

This rejection, after so many months of waiting, stung so deeply that he lashed out at his best ally—Don Congdon. In many ways, his comments reflected Congdon's exceptional competence as an agent and proven experience as an editor. Bradbury wanted Congdon to criticize and edit as well as market his work, just as Max Perkins had sometimes done for his stable of Scribner's authors during the 1920s and 1930s. It was a cry for help, but Congdon's long and measured response took an unanticipated turn by making a compelling case that Bradbury's stories, for the most part, didn't *need* criticism or editorial interference at all. Criticism was really beside the point—Congdon knew that his client and friend was set on writing to please himself, choosing science fiction and fantasy when the major magazine and book publishers preferred realistic situations, and sometimes writing beautiful but thin prose scenes and sketches when the market demanded fully plotted stories. These were points that Congdon had already made clear to Bradbury; he couldn't change Bradbury's subjects for him, and he couldn't change the way that publishers bought stories and book concepts at a time when there were too many works by too many authors clamoring for sales in an uncertain and economically constricted literary marketplace.

He also knew that Bradbury did not need an editor, observing that "my hand on the editing of your stories won't improve them to make them more salable, and you would be a sap to permit it. If you are anything, you are the way you write and the way you attack a situation." Both men knew that he had to continue writing his kind of stories, striving for excellence with every manuscript. The problem was not a need for editing, but a need for Bradbury to realize when his quest for excellence became a quest for perfection: "I have never seen you change a story drastically, or rewrite much. I believe that you write best on the first rush of creativity, and my hunch is that once written you should not go back and worry over stories or bother too much about polishing or blue penciling."

Excessive revision would continue to be a problem, off and on, for years to come, but in a larger sense Congdon reminded Bradbury that his subjects and his style represented his greatest strengths as a writer—consequently, his failure to fully break out of the niche markets was simply a reality of a marketplace that demanded entertainment over quality. He would finally have to accept this reality, at least for now: "My hope for you is based on your achieving, slowly at best . . . a reputation as the most exciting imaginative writer of fantasy in America. But it can only be slow when you write to please yourself. When and if you have a big name, magazines will begin to make some concession, but not much." Radio was already accelerating his recognition, but a major book contract remained the greatest hope for the future.

These were the right words at the right time, and Congdon's counsel allowed Bradbury to refocus his hopes on a more accurate assessment of his past successes and future potential in the marketplace. Overall, these insights provided crucial revelations about the true causes of Bradbury's Spring 1949 frustration, but they also implicitly echoed the words of Doubleday's senior statesman Ken McCormick from nearly a year earlier: "Isn't there some way that we can encourage this man to go on and write a novel rather than do the collection of short stories . . . ?" This question was all the more critical now, for Maggie was pregnant with their first child.

33 Broadening Horizons

Congdon had essentially advised Bradbury to stay the course and be more patient with a publishing culture that preferred formula over innovation. The insights that emerged from their April 1949 exchange of letters renewed Bradbury's confidence in his submissions, and he worked with Congdon ever more closely to shuttle his Green Town stories, his science fiction tales, and his fantasies in rapid succession through the offices of the mainstream magazine editors. Faith in this aggressive method, which Bradbury had naively tried on his own from time to time earlier in his life, now overshadowed his fear of rejection, and there were certainly plenty of stories to circulate. During 1948 Bradbury had more than sixty unpublished stories completed or in-progress, and in spite of a lull in productivity during the anxious early months of 1949, many of these were now circulating. By June 1949, Congdon had at least eighteen active story files; all told, these stories had already been reviewed 120 times by various major market magazine editors.[1] His exotic Martian story "Ylla," in the process of evolving through several stages of revision, was typical; over the previous two years, it had passed through *Collier's* (twice), *Cosmopolitan*, *Good Housekeeping*, *Harper's*, *Harper's Bazaar*, *Ladies' Home Journal*, *Maclean's*, *Mademoiselle* (three times), the *Saturday Evening Post*, *This Week*, *Today's Woman*, *Town & Country*, *Woman's Day*, *Woman's Home Companion*, and was now in London under review at *Argosy*. "Ylla" would soon go back for a second time to the Canadian weekly *Maclean's*, where it was finally purchased in a package with Bradbury's censorship fantasy, "The Mad Wizards of Mars."

He was constantly working with story collection concepts, and had begun to do so even before the Farrar-Straus rejection of *The Illustrated Man* in April. From his point of view, as well as from Congdon's, the only thing wrong with the collection was the scattershot range of subjects and genres, which prevented any kind of topical or thematic focus from emerging as a selling point. Story collections were hard to market in the present publishing crisis, but he nonetheless worked up a number of genre groupings, including his Martian stories, his stand-alone science fiction stories, and his fantasies. He also developed a collection based on his sales to the slick magazines and literary quarterlies, including his four award-winning anthology stories, but as yet he didn't have quite enough of these to fill out a volume. There was little prospect of a book contract of any kind, and this uncertainty was intensified by the fact that he had no major market story sales during the first half of 1949. Bradbury got by with a few pulp sales to *Thrilling Wonder* and the lower-tier *Super Science Stories*, and, thanks entirely to Congdon, his first four reprint sales to *Argosy* in London. Even with the welcome $261 boost from the *Argosy* sales, this income amounted to only fifty dollars a week through May, and soon Maggie would have to leave her job to prepare for the baby's arrival.

In spite of these financial uncertainties, Bradbury's interaction with younger writers was enriched when UCLA's writing group, known for want of a better name as the Bards, made contact. Harvey Edwards had already met Bradbury, and approached him on behalf of the Bards to solicit a story for *Copy*, the literary magazine they planned to bring out during the 1949–50 academic year. In this way Bradbury met the student editors, Sid Stebel and Russ Burton, and an abiding friendship was forged. Bradbury provided a new story, "The Highway," a very short tale of a simple Mexican peasant and his first encounter with the concept of a wider world. It appeared under the pseudonym "Douglas Spaulding" because Bradbury had already given the Bards "The Handler," a more familiar reprint, under his own name. The inaugural spring 1950 issue was also the last, but it had a remarkable moment of prominence nonetheless. Russ Burton, strongly liberal in his literary views, wrote a compelling publishing statement for the masthead titled "Why We Care" that won *Copy* a front-page review in the Sunday *New York Times Book Review* section.

Although the magazine folded, Bradbury came to value all three men as friends with whom he could discuss a broad range of literary and cultural matters. Burton and Stebel eventually joined Bradbury's professional writing group, although Burton found his true calling as a very successful Hollywood public relations agent. Stebel's twin gifts as both a writer and a teacher of writing eventually led Bradbury to rely on him as an advisor when he turned, in the final decades of the twentieth century, to writing his three interrelated and highly autobiographical detective novels—*Death Is a Lonely Business* (1985), *A Graveyard for Lunatics* (1989), and *Let's All Kill Constance!* (2003). But at midcentury, and for some years thereafter, many of Bradbury's private moments about town were shared with these three friends.[2]

In 1949 Bradbury also crossed a new threshold in his career by becoming a guest lecturer on writing. He was not particularly interested in (or even suited for) discussing techniques of writing because his techniques had little to do with traditional elements of craft. His working methods were highly intuitive, and his early presentations focused on the things he knew best—marketplace prejudices and the need to believe in one's self. One of his speaking texts may have been a ten-page typescript titled "A Young Writer I Know." He apparently intended it as an article, but it was never published and, moreover, it has the feel and diction of spoken language. He began by speaking of a package he had received from Julius Schwartz, containing thirty-two unsold stories—more than 125,000 words. The package offered a deeper look into his past than he had ever experienced; many of the stories were written in 1942, and, in various ways, all of them lacked the qualities found in the better stories that reached subsequent publication in the pulps. It also offered the perfect point of departure for a summary of what he had learned since.

A new authorial mask was at play in these lectures, and at first Bradbury shaped it by trial and error. His old fanzine friend Fred Shroyer provided the initial opportunities to try out this new mask; he was about five years older than Bradbury and had developed close friendships with Henry Kuttner and Robert Heinlein before entering an academic career in literature. He taught at USC and Los Angeles State College and participated in various writing groups. Bradbury first spoke informally to the Southwest Manuscripters in Redondo Beach, but the formal reading lecture he prepared for Shroyer's USC class didn't work at all until Bradbury threw down his text and began to speak extemporaneously.[3] "A Young Writer I Know" and other surviving narrative fragments on writing indicate that his early presentations focused on the need for originality in spite of the temptation to write for a particular magazine market. By this time, he had learned to qualify his bias against writing for money: "If both are honest in their aim, there need be no quarrel. One writes so as to enjoy life through the money therein obtained. The other writes to enjoy writing and literate things."

His only caveat was that one must be consistent. If he had once criticized Robert Bloch and Jack Snow for being consistently commercial, he now criticized literary writers who maintained what he regarded as a double standard: "Do not do as James Hilton has done, gone to bed with Hollywood while speaking of the high aims of Art . . . Do not on the one hand refuse to talk to writers who have written for *Collier's* (Katherine Anne Porter recently refused to meet me because she heard I had printed a story in *Collier's*), and on the other hand go to work writing scripts for a film factory in Hollywood under an assumed name." Bradbury did not hesitate to turn the mirror on himself, and in his new role he was surprisingly candid: "I have written only a handful of formula stories, and these, later, I was always sorry and depressed about. I put the same degree of honesty into my pulp writing that I did into my quality." In fact, many of his quality sales had been rejected by the pulps, a point which he always felt proved his argument about the integrity of his own work.

He had not yet had the chance to prove himself in the crucible of the Hollywood studio, but future events would show a strong pattern of resisting control of his talent as he worked, over the next three decades, at Universal, Twentieth-Century Fox, MGM, and Disney. John Huston and other independent producer-directors were attracted to his originality. Overall, the key to understanding Bradbury as a writer is to understand his passion for originality, and this conviction is stated most forcibly in one of his earliest talking papers on writing:

> I believe there was always one core of belief in me that burned from the time I was twelve on: I want to be different, to be different from everybody else, everybody else, different. When an artist has that, he either has everything or nothing. If, as Goethe says, he has imagination devoid of taste, he is indeed lost. If his ego rants, raves, blinds him too much, he is lost again. But if he continues wanting to be different, different, then no matter what happens to him, if he is forced to write for pulps, slicks, or radio and Hollywood, he will one day burst his bonds and be free. It is only that hard core of wanting to be different that separates the true artist, I believe, from the man who writes merely as a means of livelihood.

Beneath all of his authorial masks was the conviction that his instinctive drive to be different had made all the difference in avoiding the temptations of the marketplace. His long-term success in so many genres and media forms obscures the surprising number of projects he planned and wrote but that never came to fruition—sometimes because of uncontrollable external factors, but often because of his uncompromising desire to maintain the originality of a creative dream.

In the midst of these professional and personal milestones, Bradbury was, as always, on the lookout for new reading. His 1949 book purchases included Eudora Welty's story collection *Golden Apples*, as well as such classics as Whittier's *Poems*, Thoreau's *Walden*, and still more Poe—this time, *Tales of Mystery*. His growing interest in expanding his Mexican stories into a longer work of fiction probably led him to purchase Hans Otto Storm's *Of Good Family*, a book of stories and observations about Spanish America. The acquisition of the *Meditations* of Marcus Aurelius showed Maggie's continuing influence on their joint reading strategy; that year, they bought more books (at a slight discount) from Fowler's, her old employer, than from any other bookstore. On his own, Bradbury purchased Asimov's *Pebble in the Sky* and Jack Williamson's *The Humanoids*, a book that he had followed through much of its pulp serialization the year before; Williamson's humanistic speculations interested him greatly, but he was equally fascinated by the way that Simon & Schuster packaged *The Humanoids* for mainstream readership.[4] These were rare science fiction purchases, but the distinctly science-centered fiction of his friends, so far from his own work, prompted no anxiety of influence.

He also discovered Loren Eiseley, who opened up the interdisciplinary possibilities of anthropology to him with a single essay—"The Fire Apes." Bradbury immediately wrote to Eiseley, urging him to write book-length prose, for he found him to be a rare combination of poet, essayist, and scientist. Eiseley's metaphors, his prose rhythm, and his ability to convey sensation deeply influenced Bradbury's first sustained efforts to write essays nearly a decade later.[5] But in Bradbury's mind, it was the impact of his writing that elevated Eiseley above other scientific writers; "The Fire Apes" offered a simple yet profound cautionary tale about mankind's fleeting presence as master of the planet. What he had learned about mankind in reading Joseph Wood Krutch now expanded as he read Eiseley and as he continued to read Bergson, whose Creative Evolution would eventually inspire an unpublished Bradbury story.[6]

Not surprisingly, Bradbury's reading during the late 1940s reflected, to a significant degree, both the stress in his professional life and his abiding fascination with behavioral science. In the fall of 1949 he bought Marion Starkey's The Devil in Massachusetts, which analyzed the late-seventeenth-century Salem witch trials that had so nearly taken the life of his own ancestor, Mary Bradbury. He also read Richard Lockridge's A Matter of Taste, a particularly dark and gruesome book—not the sort of crime story that Richard and Frances Lockridge (authors of the "Mr. and Mrs. North" series) normally produced. He read Nelson Algren's The Man with the Golden Arm, but he found such searing realism of the drug culture diminished, in spite of the brilliant, almost naturalistic prose, by the lack of a traditional context of values to frame up the full magnitude of Johnny Machine's personal tragedy.[7] Bradbury also began reading the works of Dr. Frederic Wertham, including Dark Legend (1941) and a new 1949 title, Show of Violence, concerning the psychology of murder. These readings set the stage for Bradbury's 1954 encounter with Wertham's most famous study, Seduction of the Innocent, and, that same year, with Jacob Bronowski's Face of Violence—by far and away his favorite book on the darker side of the human soul.

In the midst of these new readings, Bradbury was still working out a myth to live by as a writer, and the despair he had manifested in the two unfinished crisis-of-values novels was beginning to reach the public in another form, as his string of dark science fiction stories slowly began to appear in the pulps. This mood was also evident to some degree in a few of the Martian tales and in the censorship stories that, since "Pillar of Fire," he was starting to write in reaction to the first political manifestations of the Cold War climate of fear. These shadows expanded into other, newer kinds of Bradbury stories as well.

His fascination with automata now led to three so-called "Marionette" stories that shared a dark sense of things to come.

Bradbury was beginning to write overtly about the nightmare side of the atomic age as well, and would do so intermittently through the mid-1950s. The first, and undoubtedly the best, was "The Last Night of the World," a deeply emotional but beautifully understated fantasy of a day when everyone on the planet awakens from the same dream, knowing with absolute certainty that the Earth would suddenly end during the very next night. The story is profoundly sad and represents Bradbury's measured response to public scientific speculation that the increasing yield of nuclear weapon tests might set the atmosphere of the entire planet on fire. History soon offered an ominous new variation on these metaphors—within weeks, Soviet scientists detonated Russia's first atomic bomb. It was a dark time indeed: the Bradburys had little money and little hope for the future of the world.

In his April 1949 letter, Congdon had suggested a trip East. It would be hard to imagine a less auspicious time for Bradbury to contemplate a transcontinental journey, but his friend and mentor Norman Corwin thought otherwise. During the late 1930s Corwin had created a pioneering new form of radio programming out of a rare intersection of literature and enterprise, and he knew what to do when he saw fortune in men's eyes. He was headed back to New York himself to air more of his recent United Nations programming features and offered to host meals if Bradbury could cover his own travel and lodging. Bradbury agreed because he knew that traveling to New York would help Congdon showcase the new assortment of story collections. In early June he set out by bus, all the more frustrating after the enjoyable train experience of his 1946 trip. He spent the 8th through the 19th in Manhattan, guided by Congdon's full itinerary of editorial visits by day and sleeping in the Sloan House YMCA by night—another concession to the realities of his bank balance, which was down to twenty dollars by the time he reached New York.[8]

There were other memorable moments. Finally, he was able to meet his enthusiastic correspondent Theodore Sturgeon, who was elated by his friend's continuing ability to avoid what he once described to Bradbury as the monumental leveling trowel of the literary critics.[9] They listened to Sturgeon's favorite recordings, and Bradbury was won over to the Bach fugues that he had been able to sample only in his beloved *Fantasia*. Hank Kuttner was briefly in town as well, and they were able to enjoy an evening at Fletcher Pratt's apartment with Harrison Smith of the *Saturday Review of Literature*.[10] He greatly enjoyed (and needed) these Manhattan moments with his friends, but there was little else to celebrate. During his final week in town, no publisher would commit to the Illinois novel or any of his story collection variations. And then he met Walter Bradbury, who simply had a better idea.

Although no relation, Walter Bradbury had known of Ray Bradbury for quite some time, and not just from Don Congdon. Doubleday published the annual *O. Henry Prize* volumes, and the house editors would not have missed his back-to-back selections the previous two years. Bradbury's vampire "Family" book proposal had attracted all three of the resident "spook" fiction fans—Walt Bradbury, Don Elder, and editor-in-chief Ken McCormick—when it passed through Doubleday the year before. Congdon arranged a dinner with the two Bradburys at Luchow's German restaurant on 14th Street, where the discussion seemed destined to follow all the previous publisher's meetings that week ("story collections aren't selling") when Walt Bradbury suggested that the Martian stories could be woven into some sort of tapestry, a "half-cousin" to a novel, for Doubleday's new science fiction imprint.

Suddenly, Ray Bradbury saw the simple *bricolage* concept of a Martian story collection, where the whole simply equaled the sum of the parts, transforming into a unified work more in line with Sherwood Anderson's *Winesburg, Ohio*. He had read the novel (on Henry Kuttner's recommendation) in 1944, and created a list of settlers (not unlike the grotesques of *Winesburg*) for a book to be called *Earthport, Mars*. Such characters had surfaced in various stories, but now, with Anderson's parallel fresh in his mind again, he saw how he might create his own novelized story cycle by establishing a chronological framework around some of the existing tales, which for the most part were predictive variations on Earth's colonial cycles of contact, exploitation, and lost empire. In terms of mood, metaphor, and character motivation, these stories reflected the pioneering history he knew from family stories and from literature—the bittersweet settlement of the American West. The three-way brainstorming conversation continued into the evening back at Congdon's Greenwich Village flat, and then Bradbury returned to the YMCA to work out the concept on paper. He had to do this almost entirely from memory; he'd brought just seventeen stories on the trip, and only two of them were Martian tales.[11]

Walt Bradbury wanted to see two novel concepts by the next day, when the three men met again—this time at Rockefeller Center, over coffee and doughnuts. Bradbury produced a pair of outlines: one for *The Martian Chronicles*, and another called *Frost and Fire*, a proposed expansion of his 1946 *Planet Stories* novella "The Creatures That Time Forgot." These were not, by any stretch of the imagination, true novels, but it didn't really matter—after final consultations at the Doubleday offices, Ray Bradbury suddenly had a combined advance of $1500 for two books, and started his bus ride home on Monday the 20th of June with the break he needed to establish himself in the major book market. In Chicago, he celebrated by turning in his bus ticket for a seat on *The City of Los Angeles*—the westbound run of the same Union Pacific Streamliner he had first enjoyed heading eastward, three years earlier.[12]

His bus-riding days were finally at an end, but his typescript preparation for the new book was just beginning. Maggie typed the final submission at home on the Royal, while Bradbury used the old Underwood in the garage at 670 Venice Boulevard to prepare revisions and structural transitions.[13] By early October he had stabilized the chronology around seventeen story-chapters and written thirteen bridging narratives. Here he turned to another beloved author for inspiration, modeling his bridges on the interchapters that Steinbeck had fashioned for *The Grapes of Wrath* to bring his immigrants to a new and dangerous land.

Throughout the summer Congdon had been concerned that Bradbury's desire for perfection might delay the submission of the *Chronicles*. He had seen this characteristic tie up stories for weeks and months on end, and was greatly relieved to receive the typescript on October 8th.[14] It soon became apparent, however, that Bradbury would view each new edition or reissue as a chance to perfect the *Chronicles* structure. He deleted two stories and two bridges from the typescript within a few weeks of submission and would continue to adjust the published contents for the next forty-six years. Six content variations resulted from this strategy, but the essential structure remains, in most respects, largely unchanged today.

34

The Miracle Year: Winter and Spring

The submission of the *Chronicles* typescript marked the beginning of Bradbury's *Annus Mirabilis*, which can be defined by the major works he submitted to publishers between the fall of 1949 and the fall of 1950—*The Martian Chronicles*, *The Illustrated Man*, and "The Fireman," the early novella form of *Fahrenheit 451*. The *Chronicles* proved to be the best thematic concentration of what David Mogen would later call "the lure of the space frontier" in Bradbury's entire oeuvre, a reaction to the sad close of America's westward adventure at the beginning of the twentieth century. Bradbury's inspiration, expressed many times, was the final section of Steinbeck's story-cycle, *The Red Pony*, and the grandfather's lament for the pioneering adventures that had ended at the Pacific Ocean: "But that's not the worst—no, not the worst. Westering has died out of the people. Westering isn't a hunger any more. It's all done." Bradbury expressed his breakthrough insight most succinctly in a 1980 interview with Mogen: "From now on there is no East and West, only up." This dramatic extension of Steinbeck's modernist lament for the lost spirit of the pioneer influenced all of Bradbury's best science fiction of the 1940s and the 1950s, the extremely humanized stories that many of his writing contemporaries never really thought of as science fiction at all.

But his readers were beginning to make little distinction between his science fiction, his fantasy, and his semiautobiographical Green Town stories. As promised, Congdon was finally beginning to break down major market editorial resistance to Bradbury's stylistic originality and his specialized subjects, and the first weeks of 1950 brought remarkable successes. The science fiction tales "There Will Come Soft Rains" and "To the Future" (better known as "The Fox and the Forest") sold to *Collier's*, where Knox Burger, the new fiction editor, cultivated a fruitful relationship with Bradbury by publishing six of his stories over the next two years. Stuart Rose finally took a Bradbury story for the *Saturday Evening Post*—it was "The World the Children Made," the tale of the deadly "virtual reality" nursery known best as "The Veldt." *Esquire* bought "The Illustrated Man," and provided a haunting color illustration by Stanley Meltzoff. *Coronet* published a condensed version of "Mars Is Heaven!"; counting two earlier Martian story sales to *Maclean's* and *Charm*, Bradbury now had eight science fiction stories headed for the slicks. During the same brief period, *Charm* bought "Miss Bidwell," and the *Philadelphia Enquirer* took "The Screaming Woman," two Green Town stories originally intended for the Illinois novel. Meanwhile, Bradbury sold four new stories to the science fiction pulps, three stories for radio adaptation, and four more anthology reprints.

Bradbury was now (along with Heinlein, Kurt Vonnegut, and for a time John Wyndham) among the first authors to place significant science fiction stories in the major market magazines. This milestone ushered in a new and dynamic pattern of sales that would continue for decades under Congdon's careful stewardship, a pattern that was impressively radiating out into constant reprint and adaptation sales. By the end of 1950, Bradbury would have twenty-seven anthology appearances in print, including two stories in *Invasion From Mars*, a mass-market Dell paperback edited by his idol, Orson Welles. By mid-1950, the new science fiction radio shows *Dimension X* (NBC) and *Escape* (CBS) were featuring Bradbury adaptations. His work was also featured on NBC's *Radio City Playhouse* and eventually on such writer-focused programs as NBC *Presents: The Short Story* and the *ABC Radio Workshop*.

Bradbury hit an all-time high with twenty-four new story appearances in 1950, but magazine reprints soon outstripped his new story sales. This trend, along with his ever-increasing anthology sales, would eventually be matched by the textbook appearances that began a few years later. Almost from the beginning, his magazine reprint history was no less prodigious. Bradbury's most significant second-serial magazine was British *Argosy*, which reprinted a total of seventy-one Bradbury stories over the next two decades. *Argosy* published four of the *Martian Chronicles* stories before the book itself was published, as *The Silver Locusts*, in Britain.

But Bradbury's most personal and rewarding reprint relationship also began at the outset of the *Annus Mirabilis* with the appearance of "The Exiles" (a revision of "The Mad Wizards of Mars") in the second issue (Winter-Spring 1950) of the *Magazine of Fantasy & Science Fiction*. This was the new digest-format brainchild of the West Coast writer and critic Anthony Boucher and editor J. Francis McComas, who ran the enterprise for New York publisher Lawrence Spivak's Mercury Press. F&SF was tailor-made for a writer like Bradbury, and through the 1950s this highly regarded magazine preserved his connection to the genre as most of the prewar pulps slowly died out.

Bradbury's early relationship with Boucher and McComas was even more significant than his publishing history with their magazine. Boucher had been following Bradbury's rise as a genre author for quite some time, but they had always just missed connections; they finally met in mid-July 1948 and Bradbury occasionally visited the science fiction group up in Berkeley that Boucher, Mc-

Comas, and journalist Don Fabun attended.[1] This group had a mature fan base and was writer-friendly, characteristics that were reflected in the group's subtle and sophisticated semiprozine *Rhodomagnetic Digest* and the annual award given under the group's tongue-in-cheek trade name: "The Elves', Gnomes' and Little Men's Science Fiction Chowder and Marching Society." It was an odd combination of intellect, humor, and humility, a far cry from the critics and profit-centered publishers he so deeply mistrusted. As reviewers for major newspapers, both Boucher and Fabun had received proofs of *The Martian Chronicles*, and in April Bradbury learned that he would receive the "Invisible Little Man" award from the Society at the 1950 annual award dinner.

First, however, Bradbury was scheduled for another publishing visit to New York. He arrived just in time for the official May 6th release of the *Chronicles*, and successfully navigated through six television and radio interviews with network affiliates.[2] The great accomplishment of the trip, though, centered on the worrisome *Frost and Fire*; the prospect of transforming his novella "The Creatures That Time Forgot" into a novel had run into the usual creative roadblock, and Bradbury wisely proposed an alternative to the contracted *Frost and Fire* concept. Instead, he would revisit his *Illustrated Man* story collection outline and present it as a showcase for the best of his other science fiction stories of the previous four years. Both "Creatures" and his other published novella, "Pillar of Fire," would have to be excluded to maintain the symmetry of the collection. After reading "The Illustrated Man" short story, Walt Bradbury felt that it was too much of a fantasy to fit the increasingly "other worlds" contents of the collection, and Ray Bradbury concurred. The contents would soon stabilize around three unchronicled Martian tales and several of the darker science fiction stories, including "Purpose" (retitled "The City") and the unsold nihilistic exercise, "No Particular Night or Morning." Others, such as "The Long Rain," were more typical Bradbury space yarns. At this point, the collection had a science fiction focus but no title story or unifying structure.

Bradbury returned to California in time to receive his "Invisible Little Man" award and make the keynote address at the Bay Area society's annual banquet. On May 22nd, at the India House Restaurant, he presented "A Few Notes on The Martian Chronicles" to the Little Men. He began by confirming what perceptive readers of the *Chronicles* might have already sensed—there was a darker purpose to conceiving the *Chronicles*, a hidden aspect of his desire to see how the new explorers and settlers would rise to the challenge of Mars as a new frontier. This was a desire to comprehend the incredible loneliness involved in reaching and sustaining life in a distant, hostile place. Bradbury's high degree of fascination with this subject is strongest in his early comments on the making of the

Chronicles, and his banquet address may offer the earliest evidence of all: "It was going to be about people and they were going to be lonely people. They could not help being lonely, for they were doubly damned; once by a civilization that yanked the base out from under their God, and tried to take their minds off their loss with nylon toothbrushes and V-8 engines, and again by the impossible total of miles between Earth and Mars."

Here, once again, was a hint of the agonizing loneliness and terrifying otherness found in the dark science fiction stories that lay beyond the specific plot line of the *Chronicles* family of tales. Here too was the quest for new Gods to replace what the modern world had stripped away and replaced with miraculous new technologies. Bradbury first made this underlying irony into an explicit observation in his address: "It is all very well to say that one would like to be one of the first Martian colonials, but quite another thing to awaken at midnight and find yourself, in reality, on the red planet sixty million miles from everything that means anything. It'll take a little adjustment. How much nicer if the colonials could look upon space as a cathedral, with God in His place, and all right with the universe, except that these colonials would be going into space that they had carefully sprayed with equal parts of philosophical cyanide and scientific DDT."

Bradbury's San Francisco address, published only for the extremely limited readership of the *Rhodomagnetic Digest*, was almost certainly the genesis for "How I Wrote My Book," a typescript dated Oct. 17, 1950.[3] This essay further documents the way that Bradbury felt about the *Chronicles* immediately after publication, before he had time to fully develop the authorial mask from which his better-known commentaries have radiated out into the public record. For most of his career, he has maintained that the Anderson-like grotesques of his 1944 outline were largely forgotten until Walter Bradbury brought them back to mind by guessing that there was some sort of creative center connecting many of the Martian stories written during the 1944–49 period. This is essentially true, with regard to the *Chronicles* as a whole,[4] but in his earliest articulations of the making of the book, Bradbury described in great detail how the original philosophy that grew out of the 1944 outline informed every "what if" that eventually came together to form the *Chronicles*. In his San Francisco address, he used the cartoon caricatures of *New Yorker* illustrator William Steig to make the connection between Anderson's grotesques and Bradbury's settlers: "Long before Mr. Steig, the illustrator, in my home in Illinois there was a man who prowled the streets in the year 1928, who was known as 'the lonely one.' I have never forgotten him. Some day his sons, or the sons of his sons, will go to Mars. Eliot calls them the Hollow Men. Call them what you will, but there they go, off to Mars, just for the ride, thinking they will find a planet like a seer's crystal, in which to read a magnificent future.

What they'll find, instead, is the somewhat shopworn image of themselves. Mars is a mirror, not a crystal." This philosophical core opened out into dozens of stories, written in no conscious sequence, but all of them were nonetheless motivated by the curse of this metaphorical mirror. In "How I Wrote My Book," Bradbury would expand on the theme that connected all the fragmented stages of creativity from 1944 to 1949:

> I followed that formula exactly. I wondered what Ray Bradbury would do if he were taken unceremoniously off and dumped 50 million miles from his safe, circumscribed little existence. I knew that I would be afraid of many things, loneliness, time, even existence, so far away. I knew that I would fear for not only Earth men, but Martians also, for Martians would be the first cousins to Indians and I recollected only too well what we had done to the Indians. There were both sides to be considered, the logistics of parceling up and crating off religion to Mars, and there was the racial problem to consider, and the problem of the sociologist who knows everything about everyone and would like to run everything with neat charts and graphs. I knew that I was suspicious of science, of the so-called advancements of our civilization, I suppose I knew that I was a trifle old-fashioned and romantic about some things, perhaps I imagined that man should slow down a little when he moved out into space, take life a little easier, enjoy himself. But Earth men, as now constructed, could not do that. He would have to take with him his hot-dog stands, his television, and his atom-bombs, and this very insistence upon "business as usual" would, in the end, trip him up, and bring his excursion to nothing.

The various confrontations between characters sustain these larger themes across all of the loosely connected chronicle-stories, but Bradbury still deferred one of the major transitions from story writer to novelist—character development. A decade later, as he began his first *Martian Chronicles* screenplay at MGM, he admitted as much to Don Congdon: "[W]hatever knowledge I had about characterization was pretty intuitive, and hidden from myself. . . . Most of the captains in *Chronicles* have no real past. Spender, also, when you come down to it, was an Idea in motion."[5] He was more successful in developing the structural elements of a novelized story cycle; he opened with four tales of first contact and bridged them into chronicles of settlement and exploitation. Finally, Bradbury placed his oldest Martian story at the end of the book, for in it he had found the redeeming moment of the entire saga—the closing scene of "The Million Year Picnic," when young Michael, a refugee from Earth's final atomic destruction, looks into the canal waters and says, "Where are the Martians?" As the image of the boy and his family reflects back from the canal's surface, his father says, "There they are."

WHAT IS MEXICO?

It is the smell of rain in the deep forests
It is the smell of rich earth in plowing
And the fresh warm odor of harvested grain.
Mexico is odors.

Mexico is also Time.
It is Ancient Time.
It is the old things lying in old places.
The Pyramid Teotihuacan,
The Pyramid of The sun.
The ancient carvings and sacrificial altars.
The old bronzes and gold things,
The fine turquoises and jet stones of long
Dead warriors.
The feather costumes of ancient dancers.
The masks.
It is the old towns,
The worn paths,
The oldest tree.
The bells from Spain four centuries past.
The dusty churches.
The cemeteries like frosted birthday cakes.
The catacombs and the dry rows of upright mummies.

Sometime after returning from his fall 1945 travels
through Mexico, Bradbury prepared an eight-page
proposal for "a travelogue in color film," with the
successive images expressed in the form of a concise
poetic catalogue. This page juxtaposes the masked
pre-Columbian culture with the Catholic overlay that
succeeded, but never overpowered, the ancient ways.
The final image on this page brings in the Mummies
of Guanajuato—his most terrifying memory of
Mexico. The inset photograph of Bradbury was taken
during October 1945 at Maximilian's palace, a few
weeks before the traumatic Guanajuato experience.

Portrait of Bradbury, September 1945, used in the Winter 1949 *Planet Stories* to announce a Bradbury story for the next issue. Bradbury appears to have circulated this photo with publishers during the late 1940s. From the Albright Collection (photographer unknown); courtesy of Ray Bradbury.

Ocean Park, 1948 (L to R): Ray Bradbury, Edmond Hamilton, Leigh Brackett Hamilton. These good times in Venice Beach and Santa Monica were short-lived; the following year, Bradbury's close friends would move east and settle into the rural community of Kinsman, Ohio. Brackett's return to screenwriting brought them back to California seasonally in later decades. Photograph from the Albright Collection; courtesy of Ray Bradbury and Donn Albright.

The nursery lay ready for their invasion. The walls hummed with a pink, almost sunset, perhaps sunrise, illumination. The foliage seemed prepared to propel forth all varieties of fauna at the tread of their small feet on the meadow-grass of the carpet. Now, the boy, for he was first through the cave door (the entrance to the nursery was camouflaged so as to appear part of a natural habitat) now the young lad, ten and briskly aware of all colours and sounds, entered on the run, to be followed an instant later by his sister, both screaming with exhileration and the not uncommon realization that both were very much alive.

Their mother stood in the door behind them, "You won't stay long here, you'll be ready for supper at six?"

"Yes, yes, mother!" they both replied, not looking at her, for she was a bother. Behind her, a glimpse of their rich big house could be had, white kitchen, leather and fire-hearthed living room, chintz curtains and all, a faint symphony playing, and then the door whispered shut, the children were alone with their nursery veldt.

And then the monsters crept forth. Yellow bears and purple tigers with lavender eyes and pink giragges with gold coin spots.

"I wish we could live here forever," said the boy. "And not go back in there, with them. I wish we could kill mother and father and live here forever and ever."

An early draft opening for "The World the Children Made," c. 1949. Bradbury would often start with a single-page burst of creativity triggered by a word association exercise—in this case, a nursery. All the basic plot dynamics unfold from this first prose snapshot: the oppositional tension between the parents' world and the children's world, with a Bradbury twist of patricide. Many such openings would go no further, but Bradbury grew this story into his first *Saturday Evening Post* appearance and, as "The Veldt," an enduring feature of *The Illustrated Man*. From the Albright Collection; reproduced by permission of Ray Bradbury and Donn Albright.

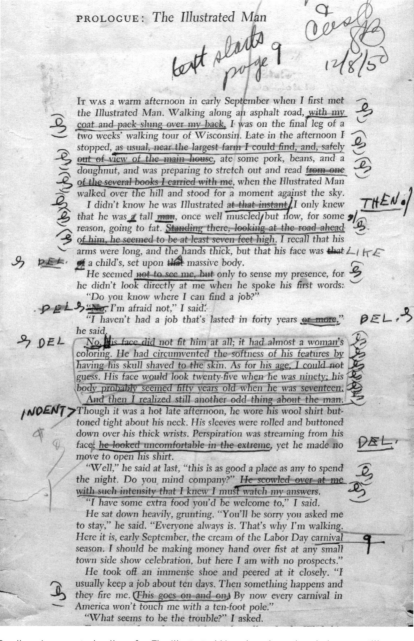

PROLOGUE: The Illustrated Man

text starts page 9
12/8/50

It was a warm afternoon in early September when I first met the Illustrated Man. Walking along an asphalt road, ~~with my coat and pack slung over my back,~~ I was on the final leg of a two weeks' walking tour of Wisconsin. Late in the afternoon I stopped, ~~as usual, near the largest farm I could find, and, safely out of view of the main house,~~ ate some pork, beans, and a doughnut, and was preparing to stretch out and read ~~from one of the several books I carried with me,~~ when the Illustrated Man walked over the hill and stood for a moment against the sky.

I didn't know he was Illustrated ~~at that instant,~~ THEN. I only knew that he was a tall man, once well muscled, but now, for some reason, going to fat. ~~Standing there, looking at the road ahead of him, he seemed to be at least seven feet high.~~ I recall that his arms were long, and the hands thick, but that his face was ~~that~~ LIKE of a child's, set upon ~~that~~ massive body.

He seemed ~~not to see me, but~~ only to sense my presence, for he didn't look directly at me when he spoke his first words:

"Do you know where I can find a job?"

~~"No,~~ I'm afraid not," I said. DEL.

"I haven't had a job that's lasted in forty years ~~or more,~~" DEL. he said.

~~No. His face did not fit him at all; it had almost a woman's coloring. He had circumvented the softness of his features by having his skull shaved to the skin. As for his age, I could not guess. His face would look twenty-five when he was ninety; his body probably seemed fifty years old when he was seventeen. And then I realized still another odd thing about the man.~~

INDENT > Though it was a hot late afternoon, he wore his wool shirt buttoned tight about his neck. His sleeves were rolled and buttoned down over his thick wrists. Perspiration was streaming from his face; ~~he looked uncomfortable in the extreme,~~ yet he made no DEL. move to open his shirt.

"Well," he said at last, "this is as good a place as any to spend the night. Do you mind company? ~~He scowled over at me with such intensity that I knew I must watch my answers.~~"

"I have some extra food you'd be welcome to," I said.

He sat down heavily, grunting. "You'll be sorry you asked me to stay," he said. "Everyone always is. That's why I'm walking. Here it is, early September, the cream of the Labor Day carnival season. I should be making money hand over fist at any small town side show celebration, but here I am with no prospects."

He took off an immense shoe and peered at it closely. "I usually keep a job about ten days. Then something happens and they fire me. ~~(This goes on and on.)~~ By now every carnival in America won't touch me with a ten-foot pole."

"What seems to be the trouble?" I asked.

Bradbury's corrected galleys for *The Illustrated Man* show how deeply he was still condensing the prologue motif to achieve the minimum of suggestion. His lightly penciled strikethrough lines are visible, along with his inked revisions. Doubleday's copyediting markup reinforces Bradbury's cuts with marginal deletion symbols. From the Albright Collection; reproduced by permission of Ray Bradbury and Donn Albright.

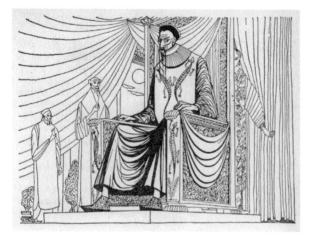

Joe Mugnaini's ability to convey the essence of Bradbury's stories is evident in these three headpiece illustrations from *The Golden Apples of the Sun* (1953): the foregrounded butterfly dominates the prehistoric dinosaur hunt in the background, for its unintended destruction will ripple down through time in "A Sound of Thunder" (top); and the chamberlains look for commands from their Mandarin, who looks in turn to his daughter, hidden behind the throne, whose wisdom will save the town of "The Golden Kite, the Silver Wind" (center). mankind's fantastic solar fusion scoop deploys from the super-cooled spacecraft of "The Golden Apples of the Sun" (bottom); Courtesy of Ray Bradbury and Diana Mugnaini Robinson for the Joseph Mugnaini Estate.

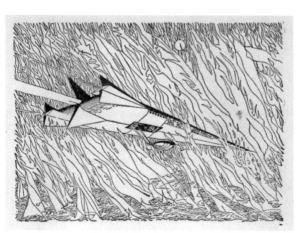

Long After Midnight (Summer 1950)	"The Fireman" *Galaxy* (Feb. 1951)	Fahrenheit 451 (Oct. 1953)
Leahy walked ~~across the room~~ over and shook Mr. Montag's hand.	Leahy shook Montag's limp hand.	Beatty shook Montag's limp hand. Montag still sat, as if the house were
"One more thing."	"Oh, one last thing. Once in his career, every fireman gets curious.	collapsing about him and he could not move, in the bed. Mildred had vanished
"Yes."	What do the books say, he wonders. A	from the door.
"Every fire man, ~~never having read a regular book,~~ gets curious."	good question. Well, they say nothing, Mr. Montag. Nothing you can touch or	"One last thing," said Beatty. "At least once in his career, every fireman gets an
"I imagine."	believe in. They're about non-existent people, figments. Not to be trusted. But	itch. What do the books *say*, he wonders. Oh, to *scratch* that itch, eh?
"What do the books say, he wonders. A good question. They say nothing, Mr.	anyway, say, a fireman 'takes' a book, at a fire, almost by 'accident.' A natural	Well, Montag, take my word for it, I've had to read a few in my time, to know
Montag, nothing you can touch or believe in. They're about people who	error."	what I was about, and the books say *nothing*! Nothing you can teach or
never existed. Figments of the mind. Can you trust figments? No. Figments	"Natural."	believe. They're about nonexistent people, figments of imagination, if
and confusion. But anyway, a Fireman steals a book at a fire, almost by	"We allow that. We let him keep it 24 hours. If he hasn't burned it by then, we	they're fiction. And if they're non-fiction, it's worse, one professor calling
accident, a copy of ~~Shakespeare~~ the Bible, perhaps. A natural thing."	burn it for him."	another an idiot, one philosopher screaming down another's gullet. All of
"Natural."	"I see," said Montag. His throat was dry.	them running about, putting out the stars and extinguishing the sun. You
"We allow for that." We let him keep it 24 hours. If he hasn't burned it by	"You'll be at work tonight at six o'clock?"	come away lost."
then, we burn it for him.	"No."	"Well, then, what if a fireman acci-dentally, really not intending anything,
"Thanks," said Mr. Montag.	"What!"	takes a book home with him?"
"I think you have a special edition of this one book called ~~Shakespeare's plays~~ the Bible, haven't you?"	Montag shut his eyes. "I'll be in later, maybe."	Montag twitched. The open door looked at him with its great vacant eye.
Montag felt his mouth move. "Yes."	"See that you do."	"A natural error. Curiosity alone," said Beatty. "We don't get overanxious or
"You'll be at work tonight at ~~eleven~~ six o'clock?"	"I'll never come in again!" yelled Montag, but only in his mind.	mad. We let the fireman keep the book twenty-four hours. If he hasn't burned it
"No," said Montag.	"Get well."	by then, we simply come burn it for him."
"What!"	Leahy, trailing smoke, went out.	"Of course." Montag's mouth was dry.
Montag shut his eyes and opened them. "I'll be in later, maybe."		"Well Montag, will you take another later shift, today? Will we see you
"See that you do," said Leahy, smiling. "And bring the book with you, then, eh, after you've looked it over?"		tonight, perhaps?"
"I'll never come in again!" yelled Montag, in his mind.		"I don't know," said Montag.
"Get well, said Leahy, and went out.		"What?" Beatty looked faintly surprised.
		Montag shut his eyes. "I'll be in later, maybe."
		"We'd certainly miss you if you didn't show," said Beatty, putting his pipe in his pocket thoughtfully.
		I'll never come in again, thought Montag.
		Get well and keep well,' said Beatty.
		He turned and went through the open door.

The fire chief's first warning to Montag was shortened sometime before the final (Sept. 1950) draft of "The Fireman." Bradbury greatly expanded and nuanced this passage during his summer 1953 expansion of the novella into *Fahrenheit 451*. (Texts: *Match to Flame* (Gauntlet, 2007): 371–72, 434–35 and *Fahrenheit 451* (NY: Ballantine, 1953, reset 1991): 62–63.)

The Miracle Year: Summer and Fall

The *Chronicles* story-chapters and bridges were now properly sequenced, but how would the critics and the reading public respond? A chance meeting with Christopher Isherwood at a Los Angeles bookstore in early July 1950 provided the critical breakthrough that Bradbury needed to bring *The Martian Chronicles* more fully into mainstream literary appreciation. Whether the bookstores would follow this lead was another matter, but the timing of Bradbury's review copy gift could not have been better; Isherwood had just agreed to write extended book reviews for *Tomorrow*, a new literary magazine. To his great surprise Isherwood quickly discovered that *The Martian Chronicles* was worth reviewing; by mid-July he found that visitors to his home spent more time reading Bradbury's new novel than talking. On the 25th he finished his review of the *Chronicles*, which appeared in *Tomorrow's* October 1950 issue. Over the next year he followed up his *Chronicles* essay with pieces on Katherine Mansfield, George Santayana, Stephen Spender, Robert Louis Stevenson, and H. G. Wells.[1]

Bradbury was thrilled to find himself elevated into such company by a discriminating author and critic, never admitting to himself that the short-lived *Tomorrow* probably did not have the broader market reach he had hoped for. But the Isherwood review was a great breakthrough nonetheless, and it initiated a form of literary acceptance that would provide much-needed confidence as he worked to transcend genre labels and his own uncertainties. Rather than dismissing the field outright, Isherwood's influential subset of the British expatriate community in southern California recognized distinctions of quality within the science fiction and fantasy genres. During the late summer of 1950 Isherwood brought Gerald Heard to visit the Bradburys' new but largely unfurnished Clarkson Road home. Bradbury began to take tea at Heard's small cottage, where he soon met Aldous Huxley and playwright John Van Druten.[2] They wanted to know how he wrote and where he got his ideas. Their interest offered the kind of gratification he had so far only received from Norman Corwin, and it made all the difference. Twenty years later, he would summarize the importance of this interest in his unpublished interviews with Don Congdon: "So people like this come along and put you in focus and calm you down and say . . . 'you don't have to fight so hard, you don't have to run so fast. You're doing fine. We accept you and we're accepted people ourselves.' They don't actually put it in those words but that's the calm feeling that comes out of it."

In spite of Heard's growing eccentricities (he firmly believed in UFOs and had written the first analytical study of the subject), he offered Bradbury more than his passion for Eastern philosophies. Bradbury was not drawn to Heard's beliefs, but he was drawn to his well-known studies of human consciousness and to such captivating Heard stories as "The Great Fog." Bradbury found many of the same qualities in Heard that he had always admired in Ed Hamilton: "a fascinating erudition, a knowledge of everything, with the Hamiltonian grace of modesty and good cheer."[3] Heard, now in his early sixties, was genuinely interested in Bradbury's life and career, and they soon became good friends. In early November he gave Heard a copy of *Dark Carnival* and a bound proof of *The Illustrated Man*, which Heard immediately read and compared to the scientific romances of H. G. Wells: "What HG did much to start but couldn't complete you are now, I am sure, bringing to its full maturity." Heard anointed Bradbury with the title of prose poet by virtue of the style that Bradbury exhibited in the *Chronicles* and now carried into the new collection: "The stories show again that you are a poet . . . with the power to raise not only a whole scene but a whole climate with a line or a phrase."[4]

Isherwood's friendship had a more public impact on Bradbury's career; over the next decade Isherwood would periodically lecture and write about his young friend and grouped him among such other emerging American writers as Norman Mailer, Truman Capote, and William Styron. Bradbury's qualities as a prose poet were eventually recognized by an even wider base of British literary figures as his science fiction grew in popularity abroad (in fact, his science fiction would always be more popular in Britain than his other chosen subjects). Isherwood probably led his cousin, Graham Greene, as well as longtime friends W. H. Auden and Stephen Spender, to Bradbury's work, for they all developed an interest in his fiction. C. S. Lewis discovered Bradbury through his correspondence with Tony Boucher and through the pages of Boucher's *Magazine of Fantasy & Science Fiction*, and found him to be "the real thing," a master of the delicate balance between science and fantasy.[5] Other British writers with a high regard for Bradbury's stories and books soon came to include Dylan Thomas, Kingsley Amis, Angus Wilson, J. B. Priestley and the increasingly popular Arthur C. Clarke, whom Bradbury would meet in 1953. Even the venerable W. Somerset Maugham read and enjoyed Bradbury's stories in the late 1950s.

The key to his more general popularity in Britain grew in large measure from the efforts of Congdon's liaison with the Matson agency's London partner, A. D. Peters. Through the Peters Agency, Bradbury stories were beginning to appear in *Argosy* and a number of other magazines and weekly newspapers. Peters representatives also negotiated a long and rewarding relationship for Bradbury with British publisher Rupert Hart-Davis, who purchased British rights to *The Martian Chronicles* in October 1950. Detective fiction writer Hugh Wheeler had passed a copy of the *Chronicles* to Hart-Davis, who was surprised to find literary quality beneath an off-putting science fiction title. As soon as he secured British domestic and Commonwealth rights, Hart-Davis wrote to Isherwood requesting an introduction. Isherwood declined—he never wrote introductions—but he did promise a second and completely new review for the London *Observer* timed to coincide with the British release. He also gave Bradbury first word of the British sale, beating both Congdon and the Peters Agency to the punch.

Hart-Davis remained concerned about the title, which seemed to mask the intrinsic literary merit of the book. He was certain that British critics would dismiss it unread and asked Bradbury to consider a title change: "A new title without any mention of Mars or planets or rockets would, I believe, help enormously to get the book into the same category as George Orwell's 1984." This concern ran parallel to Bradbury's embryonic campaign to remove the Doubleday Science Fiction logo from his future books, and they soon agreed on *The Silver Locusts* as a title. It was a metaphor that Bradbury had used to write (and title) one of the short interior bridging chapters; as a title for the entire book, it conveyed an elegant image of the rockets within the larger context of Bradbury's poetic imagination—an imagination that was always more concerned with truth than with facts.[6] Hart-Davis also allowed Bradbury to replace "Usher II," a story that the author no longer considered integral to the book, with "The Fire Balloons," a late galley cut that the author had come to regret as he reappraised the American edition.

Meanwhile, Bradbury had forged ahead with his second book under the Doubleday contract. On August 19, 1950, only four days after Doubleday's extended deadline, he submitted the story collection that had replaced the *Frost and Fire* novelization concept. His plans to separate the volume's content into distinct fantasy and science fiction sections had become problematic as he and Walt Bradbury began to weight the contents in favor of the best remaining science fiction titles, including four Martian tales that had not been incorporated into the *Chronicles*. He was still in search of a structuring device, and this emerged in early August in a form destined to give the collection enduring prominence. He created a new "Illustrated Man" concept in the form of a framing prologue-epilogue centering on a traveling narrator who offers the hospitality of his food and campfire to a drifter; the stranger is an illustrated man who has been banned from carnival work because his tattoos, under certain circumstances, become animated tales that foretell the future. As he falls asleep, the drowsy narrator sees one of the drifter's tattoos begin to move and tell a tale. Each story in Bradbury's collection emerges in succession from another tattoo as the narrator awakens from the preceding story-dream.

The Illustrated Man was published in February 1951, thus completing the modified conditions of his initial two-book contract with Doubleday. It bore the same title as the ill-fated collection proposal that Morrow had declined almost two years earlier, but the new prologue-epilogue framed up an entirely different mix of stories. His original tale of "The Illustrated Man," which involved a completely different tattoo artist, was held out of the collection; in the mid-1990s, with the prologue-epilogue framing device well established through four decades of sales and a feature film, Bradbury added his original tale as a nineteenth story in the Avon small-format hardbound edition that, ironically, remains in print as a Morrow reissue today—usually on the same shelf as the eighteen-story Bantam paperback, which, like Bantam's Martian Chronicles, has remained in print continuously since the early 1950s.

Although the reviews of The Illustrated Man were positive, this did little to break out from the limited marketing resources that Doubleday allocated to their science fiction line. Bradbury remained an enthusiastic campaigner for the recognition of science fiction as a legitimate mainstream literary movement, and one way to do this, from his perspective, was to get Doubleday to remove their science fiction logo from the new collection. Norman Corwin and Christopher Isherwood backed him, and Bradbury wrote his editor about this concern in mid-July, even before developing the title concept of the new collection: "I've worked so many years to be a 'literary' writer that I can't help but wince under the yoke of a label which doesn't exactly fit my shoulders, though I love and cherish science-fiction, as you well know." Walter Bradbury was able to get the imprint logo removed from the dust jacket and the binding, but it remained on the title page.[7] He was becoming a trusted friend and advisor, eventually second only to Congdon during the 1950s, but the logo debate proved the beginning of a decade-long frustration as Doubleday continued to market Ray Bradbury as a genre author.

Surprisingly, he made no adjustments to the American contents during press-work, but this departure from his earlier Dark Carnival and Martian Chronicles behavior was more the result of the short window of time before release; nevertheless he found, almost immediately, that some of the stories seemed weaker than others, and he chafed when the Bantam paperback went to press in the summer of 1952 with the contents intact. This was a contractual necessity, but he already wanted the weakest stories removed (these included "The Concrete Mixer," "No Particular Night or Morning," and "The Visitor"). Rupert Hart-

Davis, however, allowed him to take the first steps toward a fantasy concept with the U.K. edition; in addition to replacing "The Fire Balloons" with "Usher II" (completing a "swap" with *The Silver Locusts*), three other stories moved out of the British edition, and Bradbury's fantasy "The Playground" was moved in.[8]

In August 1950 Bradbury used his Bantam paperback advance on *The Martian Chronicles* to purchase a three-bedroom home on Clarkson Road near Westwood and Pico, a few miles south of the UCLA campus.[9] The detached garage soon proved to be an ideal place to work, for it contained built-in cabinets and room for all his files. But it was still cluttered from the move, and August was a hot month. Fortunately, Bradbury had discovered a typing room in the far cooler basement of the UCLA library, and for nine consecutive days that August, he retreated to the library machines (ten cents bought a half hour of typing) and attempted to follow up on the string of stories he had written in reaction to perceived restrictions on literary culture and freedom of expression as the nation's postwar anxieties began to verge on social paranoia. Koestler's *Darkness at Noon* had offered a model cautionary tale of totalitarianism, and his recent story "The Pedestrian" supplied the launching pad. He suddenly envisioned his solitary pedestrian, considered a dangerous deviant in a culture where virtual reality entertainments had replaced evening walks, in an entirely different role. This time, the cultural inversion of values included the walker himself—he was now a fireman named Montag, trained to burn books in a society addicted to contemporary multimedia entertainments.

During Bradbury's nine uninterrupted days at UCLA, Montag's journey of self-discovery grew into a 100-page typescript titled *Long after Midnight*. This journey took him from the glimmerings of truth and beauty that young Clarisse McClellan reveals in her simple conversations all the way to the Book People, who preserve the contents of burned libraries through memorization. Bradbury's earlier failed novel, *Where Ignorant Armies Clash by Night*, at last revealed its full value as a creative exercise; that past experience would help him avoid the same nihilistic dead ends in this new project. In September, after further stages of typed and handwritten revisions, Bradbury sent the novella on to Don Congdon in New York, who had it retyped and began to circulate it under Bradbury's new title, "The Fireman."[10] Within a week *Esquire* had declined and *Maclean's* reluctantly turned it down in order to avoid the perception of publishing too much science fiction. Further rejections came from *Collier's*, the *Saturday Evening Post*, and *Cosmopolitan*. Finally Congdon sent it to *Town & Country*, planning to submit it to *Astounding* if it failed to find a home in a major market magazine.

But while "The Fireman" was under consideration at *Town & Country*, Horace Gold expressed interest in the novella for *Galaxy Science Fiction*, a relatively new digest-format science fiction magazine that, along with F&SF, would survive the coming extinction of the larger-format pulps. In mid-October *Town & Country* declined and Gold immediately purchased serial rights for *Galaxy*. Bradbury made some revisions to the first half of the novella during November 1950, but refused Gold's suggestion to corrupt the memories of Montag and the Book People. Gold's idea was to render Montag unable to recall his texts without massive, Joycean juxtapositions of commercial ads and unrelated literary fragments—corruptions that the other Book People would be unable to repair or, sadly, even detect. Bradbury was convinced that such a pessimistic turn would destroy the restorative, healing conclusion that he had worked so hard to kindle out of the ashes of *Ignorant Armies*, and he published "The Fireman" without substantive changes in the February 1951 issue of Gold's magazine.

Congdon was encouraged by Bradbury's ability to stretch his comfort zone in short fiction to the 25,000-word length of "The Fireman." In early September, while "The Fireman" was still circulating, he suggested that Bradbury use this new work to anchor a collection of his novellas.[11] Bradbury gathered together tear sheets of "The Creatures That Time Forgot" and "Pillar of Fire" for the new book proposal, and Congdon added a ribbon copy of "The Fireman" typescript that he already had in hand. The idea was to sell the novella trio for mass-market paperback publication, a move that would avoid splitting the paperback royalties with a hardbound publisher and still get Bradbury's SF wider exposure than genre anthologies had so far provided. Unfortunately, publishers showed little interest in this publishing package. New American Library declined the novella trio in mid-September; Bantam had reservations about "The Creatures That Time Forgot" and declined the concept in mid-October 1950. Congdon had now exhausted the best options for an original paperback deal, so he presented the novellas to Walt Bradbury at Doubleday for consideration. But Doubleday was still hoping for an actual Bradbury novel, and deferred a decision for the time being.

In spite of these setbacks, Bradbury succeeded—quite unexpectedly—on another front. He had tried twice to sell Doubleday on his earlier idea for an anthology of new fantasy and science fiction stories solicited from the pens of American masters, but to no avail. Bradbury continued to feel that this was the best way to break down the broader market biases against science fiction, but he now realized that an anthology of existing stories would be far easier to sell. He prepared a new version of the project consisting of tear sheets of his favorite science fiction and fantasy stories by other authors, and Congdon sent it over to Bantam along with the Bradbury novella trio.[12] The novella concept was declined, but Bantam's Saul David showed strong interest in the anthology proposal. Bradbury soon sent Congdon a broader range of anthology selections as well as one of his own stories for David to review. As the concept evolved, Bradbury eliminated most of the pulp science fiction selections and moved toward light horror and fantasies published in a mix of genre and mainstream magazines. In a sense this project had come full circle in Bradbury's mind; it now closely resembled *Curiouser and Curiouser*, the anthology proposal that Harper's had requested (and eventually rejected) in 1949.

The paperback terms proved to be better than Congdon could have secured from a trade house, and Bantam also wanted a Bradbury introduction. By this time there was a great deal of support for Bradbury at Bantam, and not solely due to their contract for the *Chronicles*; Judith Merril, a house editor at the time, had already anthologized "Mars Is Heaven!" in her own first Bantam anthology, *Shot in the Dark*. Bantam founder Ian Ballantine, as well as Saul David and Stanley Kauffmann, also knew his work and were willing to bet that Bradbury could select and introduce an effective and popular anthology of his own. This was really the only path to editorial prominence for Bradbury, for he was now far more comfortable with the occasional fantasy and science fiction of mainstream writers than he was with the work of his genre peers. As he confessed to Derleth, "I have been so busy humanizing the science fiction story the last few years that I have forgotten the stars, and that's a hell of a thing to forget."[13]

Part V

The Last Night of the World

"The Last Night of the World" was written . . . because of our experimentations at Eniwetok, out in the islands, with the atom bomb, hydrogen bomb. The night before they dropped the bomb experimentally, there were all kinds of theories that maybe, when we dropped the bomb, the world would catch on fire, and we'd all go up. And Maggie and I brooded over this, and I'm sure we made love thinking of that. I was worried about all of us, and the future of the world. — RB, 2003

Critical Praise, Private Worries

Bradbury's Miracle Year had now run its course, from the fall 1949 submission of *The Martian Chronicles* to the fall 1950 sale of "The Fireman." The *Chronicles* had also won over a new British publisher who would market his books for the next quarter-century. During the summer of 1950 the editor of *The Writer*, one of America's oldest and most influential writer's magazines, asked Bradbury for an article on the technical challenges of writing fantasy and science fiction.[1] This was yet another important milestone, even though it would be six years before a more open-ended request, free of the genre-specific restrictions that were so foreign to his form of creativity, finally lured Bradbury into the pages of *The Writer*. These achievements were capped by his new Bantam anthology contract, which would allow him to project his own editorial judgment and influence into a process he had studied with passion since his teenage years: the process of shaping the literary canon of twentieth-century short fiction.

He had also successfully built a new story collection around his *Illustrated Man* framing device, and with the February 1951 release of that second Doubleday book he was beginning to solidify his reputation as a major market book author. This was what Congdon had been angling for from the beginning of their author-agent partnership, and it was now clear that Bradbury had made it through the dark spring of 1949 and emerged with a strategy—the concept of the novelized story-cycle—that might finally bring the Illinois stories together into a chronicle of their own. But there was a more commercial challenge that had to play out first—would the bookstores and critics lead mainstream readers to discover Bradbury, the perennial magazine favorite, as a literary author of quality books? And would he be able to transform "The Fireman" into a novel that might transcend, once and for all, the traditional genre fiction barriers?

By this time, *The Martian Chronicles* had already garnered a short legacy of reviews. The *Chronicles* received good commentary within the genre magazines from those insiders who were interested in his brand of science fantasy, including Sam Merwin (*Amazing Stories*), L. Sprague De Camp (*Astounding*), Fred Pohl (*Super Science Stories*), and the *Fantasy & Science Fiction* editing team of Anthony Boucher and J. Francis McComas. Major market periodicals published short but upbeat reviews by Rex Lardner (*New York Times*), Don Fabun (*San Francisco Chronicle*), and

Fletcher Pratt (*Saturday Review of Literature*). Two much longer and very positive reviews came out of Chicago from August Derleth (the *Tribune*), and Tony Boucher (the *Sun*). Fabun, Boucher, and Derleth all had personal, genre-related ties with Bradbury, but a broader literary judgment soon emerged from Christopher Isherwood's long review in *Tomorrow*. From the beginning, Isherwood chose to review Bradbury in the context of longer literary traditions, finding that in his earlier work he had already established a mastery of fantasy that equaled, but did not imitate, Edgar Allan Poe. For Isherwood, *The Martian Chronicles* offered an alternative to the "imaginative bankruptcy" of the realistic action story, but the book also avoided the conventions of hard science fiction: "His brilliant, shameless fantasy makes, and needs, no excuses for its wild jumps from the possible to the impossible. His interest in machines seems to be limited to their symbolic and aesthetic aspects."

Isherwood felt that the best science fiction and fantasy had an anthropological focus, and he believed that Bradbury's cultural judgment of the times was manifest in the failure of Earth's first wave of Martian colonization: "The immigration fails because, with its hot-dog stands and neon lights and gin and hymn singing and automobiles, it remains too obstinately American; it renames mountains and the forests and the rivers, but it never takes true possession of the planet; its settlement is only a camping party, not a real home." The true path to the stars is blazed by the few individuals who form the second wave—those who leave behind the postapocalyptic ruins of Earth and its "lopsided, labor-saving, thought-destroying mechanistic culture. . . ." Isherwood's disillusion with his adoptive country is evident throughout the review, but in a larger sense the *Chronicles* themes resonated with his own Modernist view (borne of his years in Berlin and his long exile in America) that there are no traditional homelands and values to save us anymore.[2] His praise of Bradbury's creative originality is unequivocal right to the conclusion: "In work such as this, the sheer lift and power of a truly original imagination exhilarates you, almost in spite of yourself. . . . His is a very great and unusual talent."

But 1951 would prove to be a more challenging year in terms of critical acceptance. *The Illustrated Man* received very few major market reviews beyond the expected endorsement by Don Fabun in the *San Francisco Chronicle*. "Time, Space and Literature," Fletcher Pratt's long survey in the July 28th issue of the *Saturday Review of Literature* contained only a partial paragraph on *The Illustrated Man*, but Pratt's observations advanced two undeniable realities of the times. First, Pratt noted that "of all science fiction writers, he probably commands the widest public"—words that underscored the growing debate over Bradbury's unique brand of science fiction. There was little debate, however, about Pratt's second point; he felt that the best stories in the collection were "memorable not only for the ideas they embody but also for their legitimate human values." The observation was apt, for *The Illustrated Man* showcased Bradbury's broadening quest to humanize the machines that increasingly seemed to control both the present and the future. But Pratt was best known as a science fiction writer, and his article was clearly intended to show mainstream readers what was going on in an exciting but still clearly marginalized field of writing.

In June the Bantam paperback edition of *The Martian Chronicles* brought a new wave of advertising to support the six-figure first printing, but it also brought trouble: one of the junior editors had apparently fabricated a Bradbury quotation to close the publisher's editorial note, framed by the anonymous assertion that "Bradbury doesn't care for science": "I don't like what science is doing to the world. I think science is a good thing to escape from." Bradbury was able to get the entire closing section of this note removed from the second printing, and Bantam editors were careful to steer readers and critics in a completely different direction with the paperback edition of *The Illustrated Man*: "He is not, as he has often been misquoted, against science, but rather against the mis-use of science by fools." The damage was done, however; perhaps 200,000 copies of the first paperback *Chronicles* printing continued to circulate for years. This gaffe, along with editorial comments introduced to subsequent editions and reissues of the *Chronicles* throughout the 1950s, would continue to confuse critics and readers for decades.[3]

British editions of both *The Martian Chronicles* (metaphorically cloaked as *The Silver Locusts*) and *The Illustrated Man* reached print about sixteen months after their American counterparts, and would generally draw good reviews. By and large, English reviewers praised Bradbury's ability to subordinate science to fantasy throughout the *Chronicles*. In *Punch*, B. A. Young noted how "scientific fact is for him only the raw material for fantasy, to be moulded as suits him best, and his real interest is in the aesthetic and moral questions involved when the inhabitants of one planet invade another." Here, as with Isherwood's *Tomorrow* review, Bradbury's condemnation of American commercialism was well-received, but Young went on to capture what clearly fascinated most British reviewers about Bradbury's breakthrough book: "By firmly subordinating probability to poetry Mr. Bradbury has created a world of curious beauty, glowing with sympathy and shot through with humour, which the lapidary quality of his writing presents to us in all its strange colours."

In his completely new review for the *London Observer*, Isherwood declared that Bradbury was "very little of a scientist and very much of a philosopher-poet." His closing genre-breaking verdict also helped to insure that Bradbury's book, under either of its titles, would find success in the mainstream markets: "The philosophic-prophetic fiction is the true legacy of Wells, and is as significant as anything that is being written today." *The Illustrated Man* also received excellent reviews throughout the British Isles, but there was more than a hint that the superficial cohesion supplied by the prologue-epilogue device of storytelling tattoos did not fully compensate for the unevenness of some of the individual tales. This time the influential critic Angus Wilson provided the *Observer* review, and although he praised Bradbury's achievement as a "romantic moralist," he felt (along with other reviewers) that the recurring theme of antirealist, antimaterialist caution was overworked. The removal of four stories from the British edition may have had an undetected impact on reviewers, since two of his better science fantasies ("The Rocket Man" and "The Fire Balloons") were omitted. Nevertheless, Wilson was drawn to Bradbury's curiously haunting imagery, and credited Bradbury with bridging the gap between "the outer darkness of the science-fiction magazines, which the literary world prefers to ignore, and the more traditional type of imaginative fiction."

Bradbury now had two books in print with major American and British trade houses, good reviews, and mass-market paperback contracts on both of them. But he had not yet achieved success with the novel form, and this was a primary source of worry throughout 1951. In Bradbury's mind, the critical success of the *Chronicles*, where his ability to weave a novelized story cycle out of distinct stories had been crucial, brought the next question into even sharper outline: would he be able to build a similar book-length success out of an expansion of "The Fireman" novella? He first voiced his intention to expand "The Fireman" to Congdon, and did so soon after his October 1950 sale of the novella to *Galaxy*. But he was reluctant to begin while the three-novella concept was circulating, and initially Congdon was not enthusiastic, either. Instead, he urged Bradbury to fashion a new novel out of two interrelated Mexican stories, "The Next in Line" and its unpublished prequel, "Interval in Sunlight." In his November 17th letter, Congdon opened an ongoing conversation that explicitly addressed what he described as Bradbury's "hesitancy about length."

Congdon gently urged him to pursue the conventional realism of the Mexican stories and develop them into a 60,000-word novel: "You proved to me that you could handle length in 'The Fire Man.' Writing about a more conventional experience, yet retaining the splendid quality of suspense and high drama you have, should make the Mexican novel come off." On January 12th Congdon suggested a very fundamental source of what he now described as Bradbury's anxiety about long fiction: "I've had people in the science-fiction field tell me they didn't think you'd ever write a novel, that you were too much of a short-story man in conception of plot. This is about as glib a comment as anyone can make about any writer, and I hold no part of it is true. I do think you have some kind of anxiety about not being able to handle a form you hold in too great a regard."

Congdon felt that Bradbury's lifelong worship of mainstream and genre classics blocked his ability to produce long fiction of his own. But Bradbury already had an antidote to this problem, for he was beginning to realize that the Great American Novel was an illusory goal. He saw, within his writing group and also among his other writing friends, that a single-minded attempt to pursue this goal was ultimately self-destructive. Instead, he would continue to rely on his unconscious to carry his characters through a plot of their own making, and at this point he felt most comfortable weaving related stories into larger fictional fabrics. At heart, however, Congdon's advice was grounded in common sense, and in closing the January 12th letter he echoed the admonition that Robert Bloch and Henry Kuttner had been urging on Bradbury for years: "Until you have actually finished something at forty to sixty thousand words, you can't know nor can anyone else that it isn't going to be good."

Bradbury continued to resist this advice, and rationalized by referring to the ever-present background fear that his Muse would abandon him. He had already expressed this to Derleth, just after the very successful launch of *The Martian Chronicles*: "I only hope that I can continue to go ahead and develop as the years pass, and not do what the typical American writer does, rise and fall like a rocket. The case of John Steinbeck has been a particularly discouraging one to me, and you can go on down the line with men like Dos Passos and Farrell and Hemingway. I don't know if it is a particular psychological aspect of the writers themselves, or the commercial gravity drawing them off center, or both." All but Farrell would rebound with critically successful work during the next few years, but Bradbury's short-term generalizations provided all the reasons he needed to justify his avoidance of the central challenge: "Anyway, I'm in no particular hurry to get my novels finished, they'll just tie themselves up in their own good time, I believe, I'm working on them right along."[4]

The submission deadline for the fall 1951 book season had already come and gone, and it was now crucial that Bradbury develop a viable book-length project to sustain his relationship with Doubleday. The trio of novellas was still on the table, but these lacked the thematic and structural continuities that Doubleday was looking for in his next book. Of the various novel-length concepts in his files, the Illinois novel was the most active. More Green Town stories were developing, and a number of these had now reached print as stand-alone magazine sales. Congdon had asked for an entirely new novel or play project during the spring of 1951, but he accepted Bradbury's decision to concentrate on the Green Town stories under the tentative title of *The Illinois Chronicles*. However, he was able to persuade Bradbury that another trip to New York would be the best way to break the logjam at Doubleday. The trip was scheduled for May, but Bradbury was reluctant to leave Maggie alone in the Clarkson Road house so soon after the April birth of Ramona, their second daughter. Fortunately a temporary but reliable housekeeper was soon found, and on May 1st, 1951 Bradbury set out by train on his third trip to New York in as many years.[5]

37 New York, 1951

Bradbury enjoyed the comforts of a larger roomette on his 1951 trip to New York; he wrote two new pages for "The Magical Kitchen" (one of the projected Illinois novel's chapter-stories) and coaxed his portable typewriter into producing a new page for a very short time-travel piece titled "The Dragon." Over the last few years these shorter bursts of writing had come more and more naturally to him, and proved to be the perfect daily creative interval during such weeks of travel. He had begun to write these very short pieces in 1949 to catch the interest of the *New Yorker*;[1] this strategy did not succeed, but several appeared in *Collier's* weekly short-short feature over the next few years. Others (such as "The Highway" and "Embroidery") reached print through smaller market publications, and helped to establish precedent for this kind of compressed storytelling in the Bradbury canon.

He also enjoyed the contrasting features of the passing countryside, noting in a letter to Maggie how much it reminded him of an earlier reading love: ". . . it has been eminently Tom Wolfish to see the little towns flash by, the small stations, the great plains, all of it. Wolfe really got it on paper. Nobody else will ever do what he did for this country." These comments represented a bit of a regression to his teenage literary judgments, but the impulse was forgivable; the year before Bradbury had published "Forever and the Earth," a science-fictional homage to Wolfe. It was perhaps too off-trail for the slicks and had ended up in the always-obliging *Planet Stories*. This story was nevertheless a significant creative marker, for it was the first of the many wish-fulfillment fantasies that Bradbury's imagination would concoct in order to save beloved writers from their various tragic fates.

By this time Bradbury felt that he could handle the unpredictability of the New York publishing world, but the trip would prove to be more personally stressful than any of his previous visits. His itinerary began well enough; on Tuesday May 5, 1951, he and Congdon managed to get a very favorable response on the three-novella collection concept from Walt Bradbury and other Doubleday editors. The next day, Bradbury had lunch with Eleanor Stierham of *Today's Woman*, one of the few major women's magazines that he had not appeared in. Stierham had always been a Bradbury fan, but in spite of concerted efforts by Bradbury and Congdon since 1947, she had not purchased any of his stories, and she never would. He had a more encouraging meeting with Van Woodward and his wife Deedee, who were collaborating on a musical version of "Mars Is Heaven!" Woodward had secured an option for stage rights and he hoped to bring his experience as a radio writer to the challenge of adapting science fiction for the musical stage.

On Thursday the 7th Bradbury and Congdon made some final adjustments to the Illinois novel proposal and pitched it to Walt Bradbury, who then began to read the core stories. On Friday he spoke on writing at Columbia University— probably his first university lecture outside of California. Martha Foley, perhaps his greatest supporter among New York literary editors, attended his Columbia presentation and was greatly impressed. Friday night was Bradbury's turn to be impressed—he joined *Mademoiselle*'s Rita Smith and his old friend Charlie Hornig and his wife for a first-run performance of *Darkness at Noon*. The Sidney Kingsley adaptation of Koestler's novel was in its fifth month, and was destined to win the Tony Award as Best Play for the 1950–51 Broadway season. This was, perhaps, the high point of the trip, and the experience renewed Bradbury's passion for what he considered one of the great novels of the previous decade.

He had managed to handle the daily stress by taking a hot shower and his usual afternoon nap each day, but the weekend included a full schedule and the beginning of a series of unpleasant encounters. On Saturday afternoon he was invited over to the Manhattan apartment of Sam Merwin Jr. and his wife for cocktails and dinner. Merwin would soon leave his editorial posts with *Thrilling Wonder Stories* and its companion pulp, *Startling Stories*, but during his tenure only Campbell's *Astounding* had a higher reputation within the genre. Bradbury's maturing postwar science fiction stories had played a large role in this success—between 1946 and 1950, Merwin published a total of nineteen Bradbury stories in the two magazines. But the afternoon and evening went poorly; Bradbury made the mistake of trying to keep up with the drinking of his hosts and their other guests, and he found their candid stories and intimate family histories unsettling. A late party at the apartment of *Galaxy* editor Horace Gold only added to his unease; several psychologists dominated the conversation, and their analytical banter completely unnerved him.

The next evening, Sunday the 10th, he and Martha Foley attended a party at Elliott Grennard's apartment. Although Grennard was one of the founding members of the Los Angeles writing group that had formed around Dolph Sharp and Bradbury a few years earlier, he had since returned to his musical roots in New York. Foley was glad to have two of her *Best American Short Stories* favorites under the same roof, but Bradbury found many of the other guests loud and intimidating. At ten-thirty he moved on to Harry Junkin's for still another party.

Junkin, producer of the *Manhattan* radio drama series, had adapted two Bradbury stories ("The Lake" and "The Wind") for NBC's *Radio City Playhouse* in late 1949 and greatly admired the dramatic qualities of Bradbury's short fiction. But to Bradbury, Junkin's admiration seemed to have a dark side that was more likely a manifestation of writer's anxiety combined with envy of Bradbury's originality.

On Monday he joined the Woodwards at a session of readings and song performances for their "Mars Is Heaven!" musical. Bradbury was only just beginning to see the complexities of Broadway stage production, and had no way of knowing that the project would never open. He remained guardedly optimistic about the musical, but was more hopeful about the two book projects. He had dinner with the Congdons that night and heard that Walt Bradbury had found the Illinois stories very impressive, even though they still lacked any unifying continuity. The novella collection suffered from the same lack of connectivity, and Bradbury would have to face the fact that he would head home without a firm commitment from Doubleday on either book.

The next day Congdon was able to arrange a meeting between Bradbury and Stuart Rose of the *Saturday Evening Post*, who came up from the Curtis Publishing Company offices in Philadelphia. The Post had published "The World the Children Made" the previous fall, and the June 23rd issue would carry "The Beast From 20,000 Fathoms." These stories, under their better-known titles of "The Veldt" and "The Fog Horn," would become two of Bradbury's best-known and most enduring fantasies. At the last minute he was able to meet Clifton Fadiman, who was now among the mainstream literary critics who had discovered his work. Bradbury was interviewed on Alma Dettinger's radio program, thanks to advance arrangements made by Doubleday, and managed to squeeze in an important interview with *New York Times* literary columnist Harvey Breit.

Bradbury left ahead of schedule on Wednesday May 17, missing his last meeting with Don Congdon. Clearly, the pressures of the trip had torn him in ways that a writer of his experience should have been able to repress. He had expressed his fears to Ed Hamilton and Leigh Brackett well before he arrived in New York: "It is distinctly unpleasant to talk with all the editors, agents, and authors who have just returned from their psycho-analyst's casting couch." He was, above all, appalled by what the industry did to those who lived in New York, and expressed his feelings with a typically explosive mix of metaphor and allusion: "Everybody is so damned unhappy. A bunch of Clowns bricked into a catacomb wall with several million bottles of Amontillado . . ."[2]

"A Flight of Ravens," Bradbury's highly autobiographical story of the final days of this visit, was written shortly after his return from New York. He offered a larger-than-life glimpse of the four editorial parties he attended, allowing a mix of comedy and expressionistic horror to exaggerate the personal encounters and, at the same time, to play fast and loose with the chronology. It was a purgative process, for the story allowed him to work out his growing dissatisfaction with the world of publishers and editors; it also set up the next logical step, the dethroning of the literary critics found at the narrative heart of "The Wonderful Death of Dudley Stone." But this proclamation of creative freedom was still several years off in the future, waiting for the more general acceptance and confidence he would earn during his overseas travels of 1953–54.

Bradbury had the good sense to place "A Flight of Ravens" in the *California Quarterly*, where none of the principals or their associates was likely to read it. He also took care to hold it out of his story collections until the 1964 publication of *The Machineries of Joy*, where a broader audience of writers and editors first encountered it. At least one writer took exception to the original publication of the tale, however; Fredric Brown, a good friend of Merwin's, recognized the characterization and felt that the revelations were improper as fiction, even if they were basically true. Bradbury explained to Brown that the characterization was meant to evoke compassion and pity rather than cruel laughter (Hank Kuttner smoothed the waters between his two friends, and assured Bradbury that Brown's alarm was short-lived).[3] For Bradbury, the need to distance himself from the problematic world of East Coast publishers and producers proved greater than the desire to shield these acquaintances from the risk of humiliation. Here too, as with other key autobiographical moments in his life, the fictionalization merged with the actual sequence of events. The power of suggestion, such a strong ally to his imagination, has subsequently merged truth and fiction in his many private and public retellings of these 1951 New York adventures.

But an even more important consequence of this trip is indisputable, and it centers on the tension he was beginning to feel as a writer destined to negotiate the sometimes harsh boundaries between popular and literary culture. A telling encounter occurred during the Sunday dinner party at Elliott Grennard's apartment, where certain international ballet dancers were present. During the war he had seen many of the touring troupes in Los Angeles, and he knew the prominent dancers by both reputation and performance. More recently he had followed the rise of the New York City Ballet and the groundbreaking original compositions choreographed by George Balanchine and Jerome Robbins. There were dancers that Bradbury wanted to see: Kaye, Eglovsky, Nicholas Magallanes, and prima ballerina Maria Tallchief—most of Balanchine's principal artists. To his great surprise, they were at the same party, and Bradbury was introduced to them. They were not familiar with his stories, but, as Bradbury recalled two decades later in the Congdon interviews, they attacked him for what they thought he represented:

Someone said, "You're writing what? This Buck Rogers—Flash Gordon stuff. You're a science fiction writer." Well, you know, it was embarrassing and I tried to keep my temper and be good-humored with them but they wouldn't have that; they just kept moving in on me. It was this kind of snobbism you see that I've had to put up with a good part of my life and keep my humor . . . I saw this everywhere I went, you know, people would look down their nose at me, what do you do for a living, well I write, well what kind, then you'd tell them and immediately they'd slough you off.

He had the strength of spirit to stand up to the bias, and he had done so to some degree ever since he had broken into the major magazines in the mid-1940s. But as time went by, his creative soul needed acceptance from some significant quarter of this high-culture world. That would come in the very near future, but during those stressful days in New York the encounter with Balanchine's dancers was perhaps the low point of the entire trip. Nevertheless, he admired their genius, and lamented the fact that he had no time to attend a performance. His love for the form never waivered, and although he had no training he soon wrote a brief stage treatment for ballet.[4] It was an ephemeral exercise, but it was an indication that he was restless to move into the performing arts as a writer. Bradbury would not pass through New York again for more than two years; he returned to Los Angeles exhausted, and with a growing dislike of the broader world of editors and critics.

38 Controversial Fictions

Almost immediately, the New York trip began to reap dividends. Doubleday soon agreed to a contract on *The Illinois Chronicles*, and Bradbury's first major-market interview, conducted during the last days of his New York trip by columnist Harvey Breit, was finally featured in the August 5, 1951, issue of the weekly *New York Times Book Review*. But the interview had occurred just after his Sunday night confrontation with the ballet dancers, and some of Bradbury's responses represent a somewhat harsh distancing from the object of their derision. His most critical comments came in response to Breit's query about the current status of writing in the field: "I'm afraid that as in any literary form there are only a few people who are trying to do something really good. In science fiction there are the space operas, a Western in space; you herd rockets instead of cattle. But there are some science fiction writers who are trying to think in human terms of real human problems. The form has a bad name because of the space operas. You say science fiction and people think of Buck Rogers and Flash Gordon."

This observation was an overreaction to his recent experience at Elliott Grennard's soireé, for his own apprentice work in the lower-tier science fiction pulps was itself closely akin to space opera. But subsequent comments in the interview denied even that history, and this was unfortunate for more than one reason—most of his own mentors, including Edmond Hamilton and Leigh Brackett, worked in and out of this subgenre, and his observations would also complicate his increasingly ambiguous relationship with writers and critics who believed that good science fiction depended on at least some interaction with the realities of technology and science. Bradbury never asked for the close association that the general reading public would establish between his name and the field of science fiction, but some of his *New York Times* interview comments could be far too easily taken out of context by those who felt otherwise.

The aftermath of his negotiations with Doubleday during the New York trip also proved to be problematic in some ways. Walt Bradbury continued to have reservations about the older science fiction material that had not been brought into *The Illustrated Man* collection, and he finally declined the three-novella proposal. Congdon still favored the concept because he was now actively representing Bradbury's TV and stage interests in New York for the Matson Agency and wanted to maintain visibility for all three of the novella properties. Congdon sometimes found himself out of the loop on film possibilities, however, for Bradbury had retained Ben Benjamin as his West Coast media agent. Benjamin had recently joined Ray Starke with the Famous Artists Agency, and this move increased studio interest in Bradbury's work.

Congdon advised caution, however, and tried to persuade Bradbury to avoid film and television options that would tie up stories for long periods of time. The motion picture industry was still coming to terms with the new world of television, and Congdon wanted to maximize Bradbury's media sales potential while avoiding long-term options that might never pan out. The majority of Bradbury's sales were going to the major market magazines now; his anthology sales were expanding, but the real exposure and income remained with the new stories. As Bradbury became more absorbed with the television and film opportunities, however, Congdon found himself with fewer new stories to circulate. He was even more concerned with Bradbury's growing tendency to hold stories back for revision, a process that often went on for months.

The situation was complicated by the fact that Bradbury was now trying to publish stories with themes that were politically charged, including creative forays into freedom of speech, freedom from fear (both foreign and domestic), and a topic that was only just beginning to gain momentum in America—the Civil Rights movement. These stories were, for the most part, not polemics, for Bradbury knew that thinly disguised rational arguments ran counter to everything he believed about the spontaneous nature of literary creativity. Fortunately, there was no need for him to strike a pose on these topics—all his life, he had known what it meant to live on the margins of the American experience, and his instinctive love of equality was sincere. In recounting his own mixed European ancestry for an undated high-school diary note, a teenaged Ray Bradbury offered these private thoughts as he closed: "That's the one thing I like about being an American. You have so many bloods and types mixed into you it is impossible to brag about one's racial credits, one just confusedly gives up and says 'Hell. I'm an American. Isn't that enough?' It seems to be to me. Doesn't it to you? Who cares where a man comes from? 'Where is he going?' is more important."

This is a fairly reliable commentary, penned for his eyes only, sometime in the late 1930s. During the 1920s Waukegan was not exempt from the racism of the times, and as a young boy he had seen the Klan march in Fourth of July parades through town (years later Bradbury satirized this memory in a short narrative sketch called "Halloween in July," but he never fully developed the story for sale). The racial biases of the times were all around him, but he had not bought into the ideology at all, and as he matured he managed to maintain the distance needed to write objectively about issues of race. Although these were not subjects that the mass-market magazines wanted to touch, his first circulating story of such childhood memories reached print with surprising ease. "The Big Black and White Game," his 1945 story of a baseball exhibition he had witnessed at one of Lake Delivan's summer resorts in 1932 may have succeeded because it was framed in a boy's perspective that was more reportorial than judgmental. The *American Mercury*, not yet moving toward the conservatism that would mark its final decades, was still eclectic enough to publish such a story at a time when the magazine was beginning to publish less and less fiction.

Bradbury's high-school and young-adult years on the West Coast had brought a whole new set of racial experiences. In multicultural Los Angeles he was sometimes caught between the larger forces of prejudice, but his years spent working and sometimes living in the downtown neighborhood around Figueroa and Temple reinforced his belief in racial equality. He saw a more sharply delineated form of segregation practiced at the nearby beaches, however; the Black population was relegated to a short section of beachfront between Santa Monica and Ocean Park. During his Sunday afternoon work sessions with Leigh Brackett, Bradbury would meet some of the Black athletes who came over to play volleyball on Santa Monica Beach, and was fascinated to learn that sunburn was even more serious for Blacks than for Whites.

Bradbury always took on a deep tan during his summers at the beach, and the underlying irony of his discovery about dark skin triggered his earliest stories of race. "Chrysalis," a very different story from the science fiction tale published under that title in 1946, was written between 1946 and 1947; the story centers on a White youth who strikes up a summer-long friendship on the beach with a young stranger from the "Negro beach." Neither boy pays much attention to the boundaries until the darkly tanned White youth is challenged at his concession stand—the attendant has mistaken him for his friend and will not serve him. The title metaphor is never stated, but it echoes the theme that Bradbury had begun to articulate a year earlier in his unpublished story "From Now On," where invisibility highlights the injustice of racial prejudice. In "Chrysalis," the tragedy of the Black youth's circumscribed future is the great unspoken core of the story. As Bradbury later recalled, it all began with his own discovery at the beach: "At the end of summer, I was peeling my own skin off. I was taking off my 'darkness,' and bringing out the 'white.' And of course, the Black person couldn't peel off his sunburn. That's how the story got written."

Bradbury soon extended his "what if" variations to imagine a white girl who has a similar experience, but whose skin develops a medical reaction to the sunburn that prolongs her dark pigmentation indefinitely. "Study in Bronze" brings home the trauma of prolonged role reversal with more power than "Chrysalis," but unfortunately only a few sections survive today. In the late 1940s, Bradbury wrote the darkest of these stories, "Transformation," which touches on all the capital crimes that can result from racial bigotry. The white man responsible for these crimes is completely and permanently darkened with tattoo ink, so that he may resemble those he has so terribly wronged. As he begins to lose his grasp on reality, the Tattooed Man's sole thought centers on how to break every mirror in his house. Only one of the stories in this group has a sentimental tone. "We'll Just Act Natural" is essentially a wish-fulfillment through which Bradbury hoped to make up for the fact that, due to their own poverty and lack of steady income, his family could not offer a new beginning in California to the maid who worked for his grandmother in Waukegan and who had often cared for him as a boy.

These stories, far more strident in tone than "The Big Black and White Game," were virtually unmarketable in the mainstream literary culture of the postwar years, and they remained largely unknown for more than a half-century. "From Now On," in which racial equality is only one of several humanistic themes, almost sold to Astounding before ending up among Bradbury's inactive files. "Chrysalis," "Transformation," and "Let's All Act Natural" never sold either, but on Donn Albright's recommendation Bradbury eventually included them in his story collection The Cat's Pajamas (2005). "Study in Bronze" finally appeared in lettered copies of the limited-edition Bradbury collection Masks (2008). It's remarkable, then, that three Bradbury stories on this theme actually reached print in the early 1950s, but this was not accomplished without a great deal of difficulty. For two of these stories, first publication came about only when Bradbury slipped them into his first two Doubleday books.

"Way in the Middle of the Air" describes how Blacks from the American South escape the de jure segregation of "separate but equal" by joining the mass migration to Mars. Although it centers on preparations to leave for Mars, this tale proved a perfect fit for the middle section of The Martian Chronicles. Bradbury hoped that his friends at Fantasy & Science Fiction might publish it in one of their first issues. Boucher and McComas both liked the story, but Bradbury sensed that they were afraid their publisher would veto the acquisition. For stories about race, publishing decisions were still made on the basis of fear rather than quality, and Bradbury's direct approach to the issue engendered even more editorial anxiety wherever the manuscript landed. The story was not serialized at all prior to the May 1950 release of The Martian Chronicles, but after many slick magazine rejections Congdon was finally able to place it in the July issue of the Chicago science fiction pulp Other Worlds.

"The Other Foot" had even more trouble reaching print. It is the natural sequel to "Way in the Middle of the Air," and evolved out of Bradbury's desire (both personal and editorial) to explain what happened to the Blacks who left for Mars. For his October 1949 submission of *The Martian Chronicles* typescript, he had prepared a short narrative bridge passage to explain why these people did not appear anywhere else in the saga. In this bridge, titled "The Wheel," the interplanetary journey is portrayed like a spiritual saga in miniature, an Old Testament–style journey to the Promised Land. In this brief interlude, the actual destination is really less important than the freedom that it stands for—the Black pioneers deviate from course and eventually end up on Venus. But this option was too facile and dismissive, and Bradbury soon realized it; "The Wheel" was deleted from the *Chronicles* before galleys were set, and Bradbury instead completed a full and logical sequel set on Mars. It was now too late to include "The Other Foot" in the *Chronicles*, so during the summer of 1950 Bradbury scheduled it for the projected February 1951 release of *The Illustrated Man* collection and, with Congdon, began to market the first serial rights.

But "The Other Foot" proved to be another tough sale, for Bradbury focused in on a thematic variation that was becoming increasingly problematic in the postwar world as more and more European colonies moved closer to becoming nation states. In this variation, only the Black communities had reached Mars before global tensions exploded into atomic warfare back home on Earth. When the final spaceship reaches Mars, the community is faced with taking on the last refugee from war-ravaged Earth—a White man. As Bradbury later reflected, "They have a choice: to behave the way the White people did originally, or to be good Christians and welcome them in."[1] Bradbury and Congdon couldn't negotiate a sale anywhere in America, including the pulp market. Instead, it was published in *New Story*, an English-language writing magazine published in Paris by David Burnett, son of *Story Magazine* editor Whit Burnett and Martha Foley, editor of the *Best American Short Stories* series for Houghton-Mifflin. It was now apparent that Bradbury would only be able to publish such stories in intellectual or avant-garde magazines, where circulation and readership did not necessarily reflect mainstream biases.

Bradbury had developed a very particular historical view in fashioning stories of race for science fiction. Predictably, his science fiction was more about the people than the technology they mastered, but he felt that certain foundational technologies had prepared the way. He has sometimes described his view of this history in public presentations as a three-stage progression:

The science-fictional environment in the twentieth century changed all of us in one way or another. We like to think we freed the slaves. We didn't. We passed laws. Laws are nothing—they're on paper. You've got to have some reality, you have to have pathways into the future. The first thing we had to build in the Civil War was railroads that helped win the war—the North won against the South partially because of railroads. Then, gradually, things like simple roads to the West, cinder paths, mudslides, nothing more. But then further on in the twentieth century, we began to build decent roads. And then the automobile was invented. So there was a science-fictional device.[2]

From Bradbury's point of view, the railroads, the highways, the automobile, and the promises of the radio and cinema led to the urban migrations of Black America during the first half of the twentieth century. The space age, as Bradbury envisioned it, would set the stage for the next logical move toward prosperity and a new start. This then, is the basis for the only two stories of race that he managed to publish prior to the Civil Rights era.

It was only natural that the anticipation of a coming postcolonial world order would lead Bradbury to the next, more universal level of stories about race. The course set by such documents as the Atlantic Charter and accelerated by the early years of the United Nations led to the very question posed by Bradbury's title metaphor: How would the emerging Third World deal with the economic and cultural vestiges of colonialism, now that the shoe was on the other foot? Given the often dehumanizing colonial history of the nineteenth and twentieth centuries, Bradbury chose to reflect on the very real possibility that retribution would play a significant role in coming changes; although the final resolution of "The Other Foot" was guardedly conciliatory, he once observed that "the title should have been 'The Other Shoe'—let the other shoe drop." To take it to that extreme possibility, Bradbury projected his own Mexican experiences into a Central American setting.

Bradbury's most recent Mexican story had offered a preview of things to come. "The Highway" was the shortest tale collected in *The Illustrated Man*. It had first appeared in the spring issue of *Copy*, Sid Stebel's promising but short-lived UCLA literary magazine, for it was too slight to place commercially. It centers on the point of view of a peasant tending his fields and watching the nearby highway as more and more Americans head home in their expensive cars, panicked by news that an atomic war has just devastated the entire northern hemisphere of the planet. One of the Americans screams, "It's the end of the world!" The peasant continues to tend his field in silence. In the evening, he returns to his small farmhouse and asks his wife, "What is this place they call, 'The World'?" The little story, barely more than a parable, set the stage for a new story that Bradbury began to circulate in 1951. He called it "And the Rock Cried Out," an allusion to a well-known spiritual: "I went to the Rock to hide my face | And the Rock Cried out, 'No Hiding Place, | There's no Hiding Place down here.'"

For this tale, Bradbury's "what if" began with his memory of the meat markets in the small villages, where one had to swat at the flies that blanketed the hanging carcasses. How would affluent Americans adjust to this kind of work, if their own way of life suddenly ended? "And the Rock Cried Out" is the story of an American husband and wife on an auto excursion deep in Central America when a nuclear war destroys their homeland. These tourists are no different than they were the day before, but there is a great change in the way that they are regarded. They have always been courteous travelers, but that doesn't matter now; they have no means, other than their shiny American car, and they must learn an entirely new lifestyle if they are to survive. They can no longer be guests in their favorite hotel; they must work in it. And there are others in the town who would just as soon exact an even greater price for the political and economic sins of America's past.

During the winter of 1951–52, an impasse between editors and publishing executives at Mademoiselle tied up the story for months.[3] Fiction editor Rita Smith couldn't push it through the front office for purchase approval because of the subject matter, and she unintentionally made matters worse by not explaining the situation to one of her favorite authors. "And the Rock Cried Out" was finally returned after six months, during which time Bradbury had made requested revisions on the assumption that the story would be purchased. This prompted him to seek compensation, which came in the form of a check for "travel expenses." Once again, one of Bradbury's best stories on the broader implications of race was sidestepped in ways that kept the debate out of the public eye.

Publishing stories of race was not the only midcentury challenge for Bradbury. It had also taken some time for him to sell any stories about censorship and creative freedom. "Pillar of Fire" and "Carnival of Madness" had sold only to pulps; "The Exiles" had made it into the slick-paper weekly Maclean's, but this was a Canadian magazine. "Bonfire" was given away to a fanzine in 1950. These stories all focused on the loss of our cultural past, but Bradbury chose a tangential subject to begin his deepest criticism of the overarching climate of fear that motivated all of these potential futures. "The Pedestrian" drew its inspiration from one of the few early pulp stories to have an abiding impact on his creativity—David H. Keller's "The Revolt of the Pedestrians" (1928).

Keller's dark psychological study of technology-driven genocide probably inspired Bradbury's anonymous 1938 high-school editorial about the hazards of being a pedestrian in an increasingly mechanized landscape. But real-world experiences provided the final creative spark. In 1940, Bradbury was questioned in Pershing Square by police during a late-night walk with Henry Hasse, and a similar incident with another friend occurred along Wilshire Boulevard sometime in 1949. Through these experiences he had come to see the pedestrian as a threshold or indicator species among urban dwellers—if the rights of the pedestrian were threatened, this would represent an early indicator that basic freedoms would soon be at risk.

He wrote "The Pedestrian" while the emotion of his latest run-in with the police was fresh in his mind, and in March 1950 he sent it on to Don Congdon for circulation. Collier's Knox Burger probably had the first shot at it, but Burger's recent acquisition of two more substantial Bradbury stories may have put him off. Mademoiselle's Rita Smith liked it, but she had no room for another think piece in any of the projected issues for that year.[4] It eventually became the first fiction piece purchased by Max Ascoli for The Reporter, a nice-looking slick with excellent artwork by Reg Massie. "The Pedestrian" was featured in the August 7, 1951, issue; Ascoli had founded the magazine just a few years earlier as a liberal weekly, and it quickly became what might best be described as a New Yorker of politics. This story proved to be the last stepping-stone to Bradbury's composition of "The Fireman": first, the terrifying inversion of freedoms he had experienced reading Koestler's Darkness at Noon; then, the denial of values that Bradbury had attempted in the unpublished novel, Where Ignorant Armies Clash by Night; and finally, the dreamlike reversal of standards in "The Pedestrian," where addiction to virtual realities such as television has made walking an abnormal activity. It took a relatively short creative leap to find Fireman Montag, not quite sure what he is looking for, taking late night walks down deserted streets.

Similar stories failed to reach print at all. "Bright Phoenix" emerged from a 1947 typescript with the allusive title of "Tiger, Tiger, Burning Bright." But this tale of a library under siege by increasingly totalitarian authorities was turned down by a number of magazine editors, including Kay Jackson at Harper's and Knox Burger at Collier's.[5] A decade after the McCarthy era, Bradbury slipped this story into the May 1963 Ray Bradbury special issue of the Magazine of Fantasy & Science Fiction. "Cricket on the Hearth," a story of electronic surveillance based on the experience of his writing group friend Sanora Babb and her husband, cinematographer James Wong Howe, also failed to reach print until it was pulled from Bradbury's inactive files at the suggestion of Donn Albright and published in the 2002 Bradbury collection, One More for the Road. Not all of these stories of race and censorship exhibit the care and development of a classic Bradbury tale; however, the reluctance of editors and publishers to print any of these stories during the early 1950s suppresses a significant aspect of Bradbury's evolution as a writer in postwar America.

New Worlds: Graphic and Television Adaptations

Martha Foley provided the only public literary recognition that Bradbury's more controversial stories achieved prior to *Fahrenheit 451*. By the end of the year she would select "The Other Foot" for the *Best American Short Stories 1952* annual. This was Bradbury's third selection, and it was one of the few science fiction stories to appear in the series to that point. Tony Boucher did not think it was as good as Bradbury's other five slick magazine stories that year; he felt that Foley selected it because it dealt with racial issues in a science fiction context, making it unique among stories in the major market magazines that she used as the basis for her anthology selections. Boucher felt that her focus on the so-called "snob market" magazines limited the value of her anthologies, but in reply Bradbury maintained that she "seems to exhibit none of the stigmata of the literary highbrow." Nevertheless he agreed in general with Boucher's assessment of the prize editors and extended the argument further to the bookstores, a market factor that he was finding more and more to blame in the marginalization of quality science fiction and fantasy: "I've made a steady try at getting booksellers in this community to sell s-f, but, better yet, read it."[1]

In spite of this criticism, bookstores still provided a favorite recreation for Bradbury. Now that there was a little more money coming in, he and Maggie were beginning to buy more books for their home library. His newer reading discoveries were more dramatic and increasingly international. Dick Donovan had led him to the works of Sean O'Casey, and during a span of months in 1951 and 1952, Bradbury bought a number of O'Casey titles. He was drawn to the autobiographies, and among the plays he favored the delightful comedy *A Pound on Demand* over the more influential early O'Casey plays of the 1916 rebellion and its aftermath. He would later compress his love of O'Casey into three aspects, "the language, the flow, the rhythm of his writing." This influence enriched Bradbury's 1953–54 sojourn in Ireland, and inspired his own series of short Irish plays in the years following. He stopped reading O'Casey during those years to prevent any unconscious borrowing, but O'Casey remained a Bradbury favorite nonetheless.[2]

Bradbury also began to read and acquire Luigi Pirandello's novels, stories, and plays during the early 1950s. Pirandello represented one of the relatively rare reading intersections with Maggie's love of continental literature, and they eventually purchased at least nine mostly secondhand editions in English. With his interest in Pirandello Bradbury had acquired still another masking influence, for all of Pirandello's best work depends on the drama of metaphorical and literal masks. He bought an English-language story collection by the French fantasy writer Marcel Aymé, who also wrote stories for children. A decade earlier Bradbury had read some of Jean Giono's contemporary French fantasy fables, but found Aymé far more interesting. Aymé's most famous story, "The Man Who Walked through Walls," had been translated for the January 1949 *Harper's* issue, and Bradbury's interest in his work began here.[3] Their approaches to fantasy were similar, and eventually Aymé, like Bradbury, reprinted some of his stories in the *Magazine of Fantasy and Science Fiction.* Aphorisms, more popular in the European literary traditions, also attracted him during this time. He had already read the aphorisms that structured Cyril Connolly's *The Unquiet Grave*; now he discovered those of the expatriate Spanish poet Juan Ramon Jiménez. Very soon, Bradbury would choose an early Jiménez aphorism as the epigraph of *Fahrenheit 451*: "If they give you ruled paper, write the other way."[4]

This expansion of his reading loves coincided with the opportunity to extend his rather limited interaction with the world of television and film. Perhaps the most significant event of 1951 for Bradbury was a dinner with John Huston, arranged by Ray Starke in early February.[5] Huston was always looking for screenwriters and was not afraid to take on new talent; he accepted Bradbury's gift of books and invited him to a preview of his latest film, *The Red Badge of Courage.* Over the next two and a half years he actually read Bradbury's work and answered his letters. Ray Starke knew Huston quite well, but even he had no idea whether this first meeting would lead anywhere. With Huston once again headed out of the country to film *The African Queen*, it was anyone's guess.

Another media opportunity soon followed, although it originated from a very different niche of popular culture. Given Bradbury's longtime friendships with editors (Julius Schwartz and Mort Weisinger) and writers (Otto Binder and Edmond Hamilton) involved with the National Periodical line of comics and its successor, DC Comics, it's hard to believe that graphic adaptations of his own stories didn't begin to surface until the early 1950s. When it came, the process began underground. By the beginning of 1952, he and Congdon were actively tracking down a number of possible "lifts" from various Bradbury stories, including Western Publishing's "The People Who Couldn't Exist!" ("Mars Is Heaven!"), *Spellbound Magazine*'s "The Last Tattoo" (Prologue-Epilogue of *The Illustrated Man*), and a Mort Ellard strip for Media Publications that resembled Bradbury's "Zero Hour." At times, Bradbury would prove to be too quick to assume that structural similarities equated to plagiarism, and, as his popularity continued to grow, this tendency would carry over into his interpretation of television shows as well. To be sure, some narrative comics and television productions of the 1950s and 1960s are generally regarded today as uncredited adaptations, but few of these were ever prosecuted. Given the relatively small fees involved with comic adaptations, these three cases proved to be too expensive to pursue in court, and the situation was made more complicated by the fact that in two of the cases, Bradbury's original magazine publishers would have to support any prosecution.[6]

These circumstances led Bradbury to develop a more proactive plan, and he didn't have long to wait before he had to use it. He soon discovered that William M. Gaines, who was rapidly turning EC Comics into a first-tier syndicate with four lines of horror and science fiction magazines, had apparently been impressed with the potential of Bradbury's stories; as Jerry Weist has observed, Gaines and his gifted artist-writer Al Feldstein studied all the pulps and no doubt found value in Bradbury's multiple-genre legacy. By the spring of 1952, Gaines and Feldstein had published horror strip stories that loosely resembled "The Handler" and "The Man Upstairs," as well as a closer horror-strip adaptation of "The Emissary" and a science fiction piece that combined Bradbury's "Kaleidoscope" and "The Rocket Man." On April 19th, Bradbury wrote a masterful letter complimenting them on their work, noting that he looked forward to receiving their $50.00 payment for the combined science fiction stories, and suggesting that they consider the full range of stories and story-chapters in his three books.[7]

The subtext was well received at the EC offices. By focusing only on the two stories that were obvious lifts, and approving of the quality of the EC strips by inviting a formal collaboration, Bradbury made it easy for Gaines and Feldstein to agree to terms. Although they never acknowledged Bradbury's influence on their earlier storyboards, they began a two-year, twenty-five–story series of Bradbury adaptations in the pages of their various comic lines. Bradbury wasted no time in revealing his ultimate goal—on April 28th, he proposed a slightly abridged adaptation of *The Martian Chronicles*, to be published as a stand-alone graphic novel titled *Rockets to Mars*: "I am vitally interested in seeing my book become a single comic-book issue because I believe it is the first step toward starting the younger readers on their way to reading my work later, in the Bantam or Doubleday editions. It has been my experience that reading magazines such as yours amply whets an appetite that grows by the year." Unfortunately, nothing ever came of this proposal, and within two years Frederic Wertham's notorious condemnation of the comic book culture, *Seduction of the Innocent*, cast a pall over the entire Bradbury-EC collaboration. He never bought into Wertham's arguments, but Bradbury's concern that these adaptations might diminish serious consideration of his work by the Hollywood studios overpowered his interest in nurturing young readers. He retired the EC graphic legacy for a decade, before arranging reprints in book form under the Ballantine mass-market titles *The Autumn People* (1965) and *Tomorrow Midnight* (1966).

Two other opportunities to extend the creative arc of *The Martian Chronicles* also failed to play out during this period. The Van Woodward "Mars Is Heaven!" musical, so carefully planned and negotiated throughout 1951, never won the necessary financial backing. In the spring of 1952, Alan Jay Lerner and Frederick Loewe approached Bradbury with a musical offer for the entire *Chronicles*. As collaborators they had already had success with the 1948 musical *Brigadoon*, but their great stage and film successes were still off in the future. Lerner was just coming off of a pair of 1951 screenwriting triumphs with *Royal Wedding* and *An American in Paris*, but in spite of his busy schedule he found the *Chronicles* worth considering for adaptation. Two dinner discussions with Loewe, Lerner, and Lerner's wife, actress Nancy Olson, failed to establish a working arrangement. Bradbury sensed that this was for the best—there were far more conventional properties and concepts waiting in the wings for the Lerner and Loewe team, and he felt that these would inevitably push the risky *Chronicles* project into the background.[8]

Bradbury nevertheless managed some degree of media success with a broader base of his science fiction stories. Bradbury's breakthrough into television came with the July 23, 1951 broadcast of "Zero Hour" on NBC's *Lights Out*, but CBS Television showed the strongest interest in Bradbury's work. Three science fiction adaptations by other writers aired on various CBS TV programs during the winter of 1951–52, culminating in Sidney Lumet's direction of "The Rocket" for *CBS Television Workshop*. Producer John Haggott asked for five more Bradbury science fiction stories to adapt in-house for the 1952 season of *Out There*. He was particularly interested in purchasing "The Fireman" and two *Martian Chronicles* stories, "The Earth Men" and "The Long Years."

But these negotiations were soon complicated by an unpleasant discovery—Congdon found that the Schwartz sales of many pulp stories during the early and mid-1940s had included all future rights. Congdon had run up against this problem a few years earlier in negotiating magazine reprints for Bradbury, and he now found that the same pulp houses also controlled all subsequent media options as well. This problem was bigger than the five science fiction stories that Haggott was purchasing, because Congdon was also trying to generate network television interest in Bradbury's detective and weird stories for such programs as *Danger* and *Suspense*. These stories introduced a whole new layer of pulp permissions—Alden Norton at Popular Publications was unwilling to let the detective stories go to television for less than 25 percent, and Dorothy MacIlwraith was asking 30 percent for television rights to the *Weird Tales* stories.

This discovery would soon complicate the negotiations with EC Comics as well, since most of the pulp houses considered graphic strips a form of serial reprint.[9] But the CBS situation was more urgent, and during March 1952 Bradbury wrote a strong letter to Al Norton at Popular, a house that he had always regarded as his best source of editorial support in the old days. He felt that the initial $25–$50 that the magazines had invested in these stories were being unfairly leveraged into a significant percentage on stories that Congdon was beginning to sell to television for upward of $600. But he had no legal ground to stand on, and apparently sent a less emotional version of the letter.

It soon became a moot point, for none of the detective or horror pulp properties were produced that season, or the next. Only "Summer Night," a *McCall's* story with even earlier roots as a *Suspense* radio play, aired on the CBS *Suspense* television series. During the spring and summer of 1952, freelance television writers Ann Noyes and Ellen Violette proposed serializing some of the detective and horror stories under the working title *Bradbury Showcase*. Unfortunately, this concept never sold, and Congdon would have to defer his plans to leverage a television series out of Bradbury's general suspense and fantasy story base.[10]

Bradbury still received a good return on his percentage of the five-story science fiction package, but once again he would have little luck with production—CBS canceled *Out There* before any more shows could be produced. Haggott subsequently tried to develop a new one-hour science fiction program on the strength of the Bradbury submissions and other stories by Robert Heinlein and Murray Leinster that had also been projected for the canceled second season of *Out There*. Although Haggott planned to launch the series with an adaptation of "The Fireman" novella, the hour-long series failed to materialize; for now, dreams of developing a network anchor for his science fiction stories would have to be deferred.[11]

40 The Wheel of Fortune

In early 1952 William F. Nolan, who was about to begin his own career as a genre author, published a booklet documenting Bradbury's creative output as projected through the end of the year. The Ray Bradbury Review included a comprehensive enumerative bibliography gathered over the three years that he had known Bradbury as a friend; the Review's final tally listed 170 individual stories in print, as well as more than 50 anthology appearances. The next year Nolan privately printed a supplemental Bradbury Index advancing the published story count to 190 and the reprint total (including both magazines and anthologies) to more than 350. Nolan also offered a detailed account of Bradbury's major works-in-progress as well as his media work, thus providing a valuable snapshot of the constantly increasing media projects that helped deflect Bradbury's very real anxiety about the longer works-in-progress that Nolan reported in the Review and the Index with both high hopes and great fanfare.

Other emerging writers were drawn to Bradbury, who provided inspiration and, for some of them, direct mentorship during the early 1950s. He had known Charles Beaumont the longest; as a teen, Beaumont had frequented Fowler's Bookstore and met Bradbury there around 1946. During the spring of 1951 Beaumont sent him two stories-in-progress to critique, and Bradbury was instantly captivated by the originality of his ideas and the sensual style of his prose. These were Bradburyesque tales that probed the boundaries of reality and fantasy with controlled but emotional impact, and Bradbury offered an immediate blessing: "I believe in you as I have never believed in anyone before who has sent me stories." Beaumont had an excellent sense for story structure, and his rich imagination led Bradbury to call him a "pomegranate writer," bursting with seed.[1] He would continue to critique Beaumont's story drafts for several more years as the younger writer moved from genre success to major market magazines and on to a career writing for television and film.

He carefully critiqued story drafts for both Beaumont and Nolan during these years, but his more distant relationships with other young writers were also influential. In 1950, Richard Matheson's love of Bradbury's social conscience, individualism, and "delicate sense of fantasy" prompted him to begin a correspondence. These letters allowed Matheson to discuss authorship rather than specific manuscripts and showed how Bradbury could tailor his engagement to the specific hopes and aspirations of the young writers he believed in. Within a few years he would offer similar encouragement to George Clayton Johnson. Together with Bill Nolan and Chad Oliver, these writers became close friends; by the end of the decade (and with Bradbury's encouragement), Beaumont, Johnson, and Matheson were writing for Rod Serling's *The Twilight Zone*. There were occasional collaborations as well, and over time Bradbury's young friends became known as the California group of authors.

In this way, Bradbury's writing influence radiated out from UCLA Bards alumni like Sid Stebel and Russ Burton on through the California group, and some of these writers (notably George Clayton Johnson) gravitated into Bradbury's original 1948 writing group during the 1950s. He also began to interact with professional writers' associations during these years; his friend Ken Crossen, creator of the Green Lama pulp and graphic fiction hero, introduced him to such organizations, an experience that paved the way for Bradbury's eventual involvement with the Science Fiction Writers of America and the Writers' Guild. He was beginning to interact easily with other established authors, and he was now a mentor for young authors who would figure prominently in the future development of the science fiction, fantasy, and horror genres. But he never forgot his own mentors, and in the early 1950s he tried to repay the blessings they had provided him a decade earlier.

Sadly, the cherished evenings of wine and literary conversation with Ed Hamilton and Leigh Brackett Hamilton were gone forever. In 1949 they moved out of the tiny Venice Beach bungalow and headed east for an extended stay in the western Pennsylvania and eastern Ohio borderlands where Hamilton had grown up and lived for much of his life. The next year they purchased a pioneer farmstead on the Ohio side of the border, and slowly began to transform this 132-year-old house into a modern home. It was close to Ed's aging family, and Leigh fell in love with the countryside; both of them feared that the opening rounds of the Korean Conflict would lead inevitably into a Third World War, and they felt safer living near the small self-sustained village of Kinsman. Bradbury shared these fears in the abstract, but his more immediate sense of impending loss centered on the realization that his best friends would never again live close by.

To some extent he was able to share his literary passions with Hank Kuttner and C. L. Moore, who now lived in Laguna. But the lives of these old friends were also in transition—they continued to write, often in collaboration, while they advanced through undergraduate programs and graduate work at USC. As his contact with the Kuttner-Moore writing entity lessened, he noted sadly to Hamilton and Brackett that "they become more like the chambered nautilus every day." There was now a different dynamic at play in all of these relationships, the result of Bradbury's rising prominence and multimedia success. By contrast, his friends neither needed nor wanted greater worlds to conquer. Hamilton's reputation was secure in the genre fields he had helped to establish, and he divided his efforts (like Alfred Bester and Otto Binder) between genre fiction and writing stories for the major comic lines. He was perhaps the most successful of the crossover authors, and the comics provided a significant income as Brackett turned away from screenwriting to create longer works of fiction.

His correspondence with Hamilton and Brackett remained warm and intimate, but during the early 1950s it also became more complicated. The sales and recognition that Bill Nolan was beginning to document for the general public led Bradbury to celebrate them in a more private manner with his older friends; they had been the first writers to believe in him, and it was only natural to show them how he was progressing. It also seemed perfectly natural to take on the role of encourager and facilitator. He soon convinced Kuttner to let Don Congdon represent him with the major New York publishers. He urged both Hamilton and Brackett to follow him into the pages of *Collier's*, where fiction editor Knox Burger hoped to serialize major new works of science fiction. Occasionally, his pitch became too enthusiastic: "I can't see why a Brackett-Hamilton collab, with the extra polish of a few weeks work that you could do on it, couldn't bring you about 10,000 dollars for just a little more effort than the usual thing you try for the pulps. . . . There's a lot of beautiful dough hanging around there. And it's worth the second or third draft going over a story sometimes needs."[2]

Strange words, indeed: Bradbury, now a mature writer, offering advice to his mentors while affecting the tone and diction of his apprentice years. Unfortunately, this particular mask could not hide the implied criticism of the genres and methods that his friends still practiced. Such passages reveal an underlying uneasiness, suggesting that Bradbury interpreted this new phase in the lives of his friends as a turning of the wheel of fortune; as his own fortunes rose, he became more and more determined to help the friends he perceived to be headed in the other direction. During 1951 he offered to read a new Brackett novel that several trade houses had rejected. Later that year, as CBS began to buy Bradbury's science fiction stories, he asked her to consider scripting them. He promised to find teleplay opportunities for them both, not yet realizing how much a small farm in Ohio had begun to change the lives of his friends.

Bradbury had the best of intentions, for they had helped him find his identity as a writer. In fact, their creativity still occasionally triggered his Muse. "The Beast from 20,000 Fathoms," Bradbury's recent *Saturday Evening Post* "Fog Horn" story, was inspired in part by a Brackett detective story with its description of the ruined

Venice Beach roller coaster as a vast prehistoric skeleton. "The Dwarf" would soon emerge from something Ed Hamilton had said about the mirror maze the last time they had all been at Ocean Park together.[3] Bradbury still had the creative wonderment of a child, and he could only lament the fact that maturity was beginning to lessen the excitement of the writer's craft: "Of course I'm still learning, but the older you get the slower the process becomes and you aren't learning obvious things and making tremendous strides all at once. Now the concentration is on detail and characterization and subtler things, which, in its own way, is fun, but not quite as exciting as having Kuttner or Brackett jump on me with both feet and put my ego through a ringer."[4]

41

Joe Mugnaini and
The Golden Apples of the Sun

Excitement did return to Bradbury's creative explorations, and the circumstances were purely serendipitous. It all began with his discovery of California artist Joseph Mugnaini, a product of Otis Art Institute who would have a long career teaching at Otis-Parsons and serving for a time as chair of the Drawing Department. He was also a prolific book illustrator, and by the early 1950s he had worked on a wide range of classics for Heritage Press, including *Bullfinch's Mythology* and *Ben Hur*. Otis emphasized fine arts over commercial art, and Mugnaini developed talent in a wide range of media, including pen-and-ink drawing, oil and watercolor painting, and lithography. He had served in the army through most of World War II, and many of his students at Otis were also former GIs. One of these veterans, Bill Crawford, recommended *The Martian Chronicles* to his instructor. Mugnaini read few books, unless he was assigned to illustrate them, and he didn't follow up on Crawford's suggestion. As it turned out, Mugnaini's art, and not Bradbury's stories, would forge the connection between the two men.

For all of his growing success as a book illustrator, Mugnaini was essentially a Fine Arts talent and his most creative pieces were often featured in gallery shows. In April of 1952 Ray and Maggie came upon a showing of Mugnaini's art in a Beverly Hills gallery, and Bradbury was instantly drawn to a pair of Mugnaini's fantasy compositions.[1] A lithograph based on a Mugnaini painting first caught his eye—it was "Modern Gothic," an eerie print of a large Victorian house in an urban setting. The original painting was in the next room of the gallery, and Bradbury soon realized that it was a study of the house on the southwest corner of Temple and Figueroa, diagonally across the intersection from Mrs. Beach's properties. He had spent many days and evenings during the war years in the shadow of this house, and now Mugnaini had given it a darkly fantastic life of its own. But "Modern Gothic" proved to be preamble to an even greater discovery within the exhibition—"The Caravan," depicting a carnival train full of faceless figures speeding over an abyss on a Romanesque stone arch bridge. A second glance revealed that the arch had long since collapsed behind and in front of the train, creating an impossible image of dark laughter. Bradbury immediately saw it as a grand metaphor for the long-deferred novel concept that had emerged from his story "The Black Ferris" under the working title of *The Dark Carnival*.

He had held this germinating concept out of his 1947 *Dark Carnival* story collection, and now this story-into-novel resurfaced as an active project in his mind as he studied Mugnaini's "Caravan." On his earnings, Bradbury could only put down money on the "Modern Gothic" lithograph and ask the gallery for Mugnaini's phone number. The next morning, a Sunday, he called Mugnaini and asked to meet him. Since Bradbury didn't drive, Mugnaini arranged for Bill Crawford to bring Bradbury to his home studio. Bradbury had come with the hope that Mugnaini might sell him the two paintings at half-price if they failed to sell at the gallery's commission-inflated figure. Mugnaini agreed and Bradbury, to his great astonishment, found himself with the paintings after the exhibition closed. It would be some time before he realized that Mugnaini had quietly pulled them out of the exhibition for him.

Bradbury was as reluctant to assign genres to Mugnaini's compositions as he was in discussing his own genre history. He knew that "Modern Gothic" might provide a useful way to enter Mugnaini's world, and that moods often dominated his work in all mediums. All he was sure about was that Mugnaini's paintings and line art had much in common with literary method, and his earliest surviving reflections carefully trace the parallels: "In some ways you might speak of him as a 'message' painter and as a symbolist, for there are innumerable symbols, carefully selected and utilized in his work. There is nothing haphazard or unintentional or unfathomable in his selection of those props or items which go to make the composition of each single production. His paintings are as logical as Poe's 'The Cask of Amontillado' or Henry James' 'Turn of the Screw.'"[2]

"Caravan" sparked their first collaboration, which they began to discuss sometime in the spring or early summer of 1952. Together, they planned a novel-in-pictures, an illustrated book with no narrative text whatsoever, based on *The Dark Carnival* novel concept that had emerged from his "Black Ferris" story of the mid-1940s. This experiment in form also drew on Bradbury's love of successful novels-in-pictures, including the burlesque humor of *He Done Her Wrong*, by cartoonist Milt Gross (the dust jacket proclaimed "The Great American Novel—and not a word of it!"). Bradbury was also fascinated by the far more somber working-class drama *Vertigo*, a novel in woodcuts by Lynd Ward. Both books extended through hundreds of wordless illustrations, lacking even page numbers, and suggested the kind of visual effect Bradbury was looking for. But a more immediate inspiration was also in play. Just before meeting Mugnaini, Bradbury had merged many of his carnival characters into a fully articulated treatment for ballet titled *Le Carnival Noir*. The picture-in-words of Bradbury's three-page unproduced treatment were intended for circulation; his marginal notes target Igor Stravinsky and the influential ballet set designer Eugene Berman, whose work he had seen in New York and on tour.

Mugnaini's painting refocused these older inspirations and brought Bradbury back on track with the original plot line of his *Dark Carnival* novel concept. He would later remark to his Hollywood agent Ben Benjamin that this collaboration marked the crucial shift in the evolution of the central metaphor.[3] The "Black Ferris" of the original story, which allows the carnival owner to become younger or older by changing the direction of rotation, was replaced by "the wondrous merry-go-round" that would stand at the center of *The Dark Carnival* as it evolved over the next decade into several unproduced screenplays and finally back into novel form as *Something Wicked This Way Comes*. Unfortunately, only a single page—a worksheet for the cover and title options—has been recovered, but this includes a Bradbury sketch of the circus train, based on Mugnaini's original "Caravan" oil.

He buried himself in his work, in the evolving collaborations with Mugnaini, in the various television, stage, and film negotiations, and he still imagined as many new stories as he had ever done during the 1940s. Many of these remained unfinished or unrevised, but the twenty-eight new stories he published in 1952 and 1953 were only a fraction of the material he was working up. He was spending longer hours in the detached garage of his Clarkson Road home, but it was a different garage from the powerhouse property on Venice Boulevard, and he was a very different writer. A new factor had come into play in his personal life; after the birth of Ramona, Maggie became somewhat distant for a time. He never really understood the cause—there was no talk, no discussion, but for much of 1952 he worked in the garage far into the night. By this time he had shaped the garage into a comfortable workplace; it had two bays, but Maggie had not yet learned to drive and it would be years yet before they owned a car, so there was plenty of room for a tool shop and a writing office. The previous owner had made interlocking bookshelves out of fruit crates, and Bradbury kept his working library of books and magazines in these shelves. He typed at a small wooden desk; there was a window to his left, and over time his daughters would paint pictures on it for their father.[4]

The Muse continued to visit the Clarkson Road garage with great regularity, but she vanished every time that Bradbury turned to the elusive task of weaving the Green Town stories into the full fabric of the Illinois novel. The subtle shift in his personal life may have had an impact, but it's not likely; the individual stories came spinning out with great regularity, and he wrote to Walt Bradbury about a running boy and his new tennis shoes, an inventor who builds a Happiness Machine, and a grandfather making dandelion wine. All three of these new stories entered the Illinois novel, but he could not bring these stories into a whole greater than the sum of the parts. Walt Bradbury and other Doubleday readers were already worried about the unevenness of the stories; many were good, but some were, to the eyes of his editors, "facile and sentimental."[5] Evening out the quality of the stories may have been the central challenge, but Bradbury still looked at it as a function of triggering his unconscious sources of memory and inspiration. In the spring of 1952, he offered Walt Bradbury this explanation:

> The book is going slowly because I won't fuss and fidget and push and monkey with it. I wait for the excitement. Not a passive waiting by any means; not neglect, at all. I read a hell of a lot of Robert Frost, I find he excites me and drives me back to my typewriter. I get the old motor warmed up with Frost anti-freeze and then conk along merrily on all eight. I've even, belatedly, found inspiration in some of Shakespeare's sonnets (which had been ruined for me in high school). The book is never out of my mind but, more important, it is never out of my subconscious. I wait for those good, fast, wonderful first drafts of material to come, Brad, and then I know I'm on track and headed for the truth.[6]

Walt Bradbury had asked for such a self-analysis a week earlier, probably at the suggestion of Congdon. If nothing else, Bradbury's response is consistent with the method he had used for at least a decade to write short fiction. But his words totally ignored the real problem: how to arc the best of these stories into a longer form of sustained fiction. He found himself unable to make any substantive progress in this direction through the rest of the spring, and tried another way to ease the pressure. In early June he asked Congdon and Walt Bradbury to support his intention to bring out another story collection first. His Doubleday editor agreed, since the fall book season was already lost, but only with the proviso that the collection be completed quickly. Although he had already passed on the three-novella science fiction collection, Walt Bradbury could understand the need to showcase newer and previously uncollected short stories.

The new collection would depart from the science fiction focus of his first two Doubleday titles. Bradbury's production of new stories was tending more and more toward fantasy, and The Illustrated Man had already featured what Bradbury considered to be the best of his older science fiction pulp stories. What remained uncollected from that period were most of his major market magazine tales of the mid- and late 1940s, including three of his first four award anthology stories. By June 10th he had a rough outline of contents and an as-yet unpublished title story, "The Golden Apples of the Sun." His renewed interest in poetry had led him back to Yeats and the closing couplet of "The Song of the Wandering Aengus" for this lyrical title, and the story itself would come to be considered an archetypal Bradbury space fantasy. It certainly could not be called science fantasy, for the concept is pure imagination: a spaceship crew, carefully cocooned in the ship's near–absolute zero atmospheric environment, must scoop a metaphorical golden apple from the surface of the sun in order to bring the secret of fusion energy back to Earth.

During August 1952 Bradbury sent Doubleday typescripts or tear sheets for twenty-four stories. The title story was not included because Bradbury was not yet satisfied with it. Of the submitted stories, Bradbury felt that his brief atomic war reverie "Embroidery" (too short and allusive) and "The Murderer" (too didactic, and too easily mistaken for an antitechnology sermon) were the weakest, but both of these passed muster with Walt Bradbury; instead, Doubleday editors seemed most uncomfortable with the controversial "And the Rock Cried Out," and it was dropped, along with "The Watchful Poker Chip" (a send-up of the avant-garde) and "A Scent of Sarsaparilla" (an anthology sale). The collection was weakened when *Esquire* could not bring out "The Playground" prior to the book's release date; since the *Esquire* payment had been substantial, "The Playground" was dropped for the teen-love satire "The Great Fire." In November, after ten revisions, Bradbury finally submitted "The Golden Apples of the Sun." The final twenty-two–story field included four of his early uncollected slick sales ("The Big Black and White Game," "Invisible Boy," "I See You Never," and "Power House"), one of his better crime pulp stories ("Touch and Go," which finally won Walt Bradbury's grudging approval as "The Fruit at the Bottom of the Bowl"), and two titles that Don Congdon called the Chinese stories ("The Flying Machine" and "The Golden Kite, the Silver Wind"). The second of these, along with Bradbury's "The Meadow," were built on themes of international cooperation that reflected the influence of Bradbury's friend and mentor, Norman Corwin.

This was a more eclectic range than Bradbury had ever attempted in a collection concept, and his initial intention was to compartmentalize the stories in fantasy, realism, and science fiction sections. He finally decided to blend the stories, however, and this proved an effective format for a collection that largely blurred the lines between genres anyway. There was no narrative frame, but Bradbury was able to link the stories together visually through cover art and interior illustrations drawn by Joe Mugnaini. Doubleday, however, was adamant in asserting that interior art must not drive up the cost of publication. The year before, when Bradbury suggested William Pene Du Bois as an illustrator for the Illinois novel, Walt Bradbury had made it clear that the artist would have to be compensated by the author or through a sizable portion of the author's royalty percentage. But Mugnaini was now reading Bradbury for the first time, and he found the stories "damned exciting," especially when compared to his recent work on *Ben Hur*, which he considered a boring romance of the Wild West, thinly veiled in Biblical and classical history. He was willing to illustrate the *Golden Apples* stories for virtually nothing, and Bradbury was able to purchase the interior line art outright. The challenge involved adapting a fine arts approach to the material limitations of a three-dollar novel. But Mugnaini already knew how to work with Doubleday's lightweight paper requirement, and prepared narrow-line pen-and-brush ink illustrations that would hold definition in this format.

The result added a new dimension to Bradbury's fiction. It could hardly be called collaboration, because Mugnaini worked quickly and had the compositions more or less established before Bradbury ever saw the preliminaries. But there was no need for Bradbury to get deeply involved with the art at all; he quickly came to see that Mugnaini naturally made his talent work for the stories above all other considerations. From Bradbury's perspective, the illustrations had to be suggestive rather than literal, and this was all Mugnaini needed to know. The story headpieces for the twenty-two selections contain many of the signature Mugnaini line-art characteristics, including intricate line work, dynamic figures, and what he considered one of the principal artifacts of human history: the architecture of the past. Above all, Mugnaini extended the subtle suggestiveness of his compositions into the very faces of the characters. A decade later, Bradbury described how important this was to his stories: "So, more often than not, Joe has been careful to turn the characters' faces away in the illustration, allowing the reader's imagination to fill in the details." Best of all, this quality came at no cost to the power of the artist's imagination.[7]

The more he worked with Joe Mugnaini, the more Bradbury was convinced that it was impossible to make comparisons beyond general historical allusions to the work of Berman, Dali, or El Greco. But he knew, beyond a doubt, that Mugnaini could add a new dimension of contemporary relevance to the *Golden Apples* stories. Even though he had finally rejected a realistic approach to modernity, Bradbury's reveries and his thematic yearning for traditional values had modernist elements similar to those evoked by Mugnaini's art; as the book neared completion, Bradbury felt that Mugnaini was destined to "paint many 'windows' for us to look through, in our lifetime, at his own peculiarly intense vision of life and living in this world, in this universe, in this century of modern man and the atom-bomb which poises so beautifully, as does much of Mugnaini's work, upon the brink of another Dark, another Gothic, age."[8] In many ways it was a shared destiny; their author-artist relationship continued, in a wide variety of media forms, for almost forty years.

Mugnaini would work on, largely with the Doubleday art and editorial staff, through the fall, and his quick turnaround on the late content modifications was instrumental in making the projected publication date of March 1953 a reality. Bradbury was also able to get the Doubleday science fiction colophon removed from the spine of the book, but as author he had to take on the expense of the Mugnaini illustration plates. Bradbury now held copyright for the illustrations, but he and Congdon continued to be concerned by Doubleday's unwillingness to plow any portion of the sizable paperback profits of their growing Bradbury catalog back into the production and marketing of new Bradbury titles. Walt Bradbury was sympathetic, but the problem was really a systemic one. Jason Epstein, who pioneered the trade paperback concept under Doubleday's Anchor Books imprint, later identified exactly what Ray Bradbury and Congdon were up against: "At Doubleday, the highly profitable book clubs—the Literary Guild was the largest—defined the company's culture, including that of the publishing division. Doubleday was run by direct-mail marketers who knew how to maximize book club margins but knew nothing about how books were actually conceived, gestated, and born."[9]

Congdon was very pleased with most of the major market reviews, which included Charles Lee's "Terrorizing, Tantalizing" in the *New York Times Book Review*. Lee was pleasantly surprised at the range of creativity and genre subjects and considered Bradbury to be at his "startling best." This entertaining survey of the *Golden Apples* stories couldn't quite hide the fact that Lee's review read more like a well-crafted liner note than true criticism. Congdon saw the increase in major reviews as a welcome result of the pressure he had applied to Doubleday and the genuine efforts of Walt Bradbury in support of his appeals. But there were also qualified and negative reviews, and these came from a surprising quarter—the genre editors and reviewers who had so admired Bradbury's first two Doubleday books. In his *San Francisco Chronicle* review, Don Fabun found some of the stories to be superb, especially "The Fog Horn." But his opinion of the overall collection was not at all positive: "Instead of a new direction, we find a retracing of steps, a stopping and picking up of relics that, in some cases, might more decently have been left buried."

Derleth's commentary in the Chicago *Tribune* was kinder, but Bradbury was appalled by his friend's dismissal of "The Fog Horn" as a potboiler. He was more concerned that Tony Boucher, whom he considered a discerning critic of his work, had also come down hard on *The Golden Apples of the Sun* in his New York *Herald Tribune* review. At the end of March Bradbury conceded to Boucher that he could accept much of the criticism of his philosophy and character development, because every story had been carefully developed to the best of his ability:

"I worked dreadfully hard on everything in it. Doubleday practically had to tear it out of my hands. Stories like 'The Golden Kite, the Silver Wind' went through seven or eight drafts. Ditto 'The Garbage Collector' and 'The Golden Apples' story itself." In his March 26, 1953, response, Boucher suggested that Bradbury shouldn't take the kind words of the "straight" fiction reviewers too seriously:

> To them there's a sort of discovery-surprise: My-isn't-this-good-for-a-pulp-writer! They haven't any idea how good you (or for that matter the best of other current & former pulp writers) can be.
>
> To my mind you're way past the discovery stage. I can't look on *Golden Apples* as a "find" in itself, but only in relation to the whole Bradbury corpus . . . in which light it seems something of a disappointment. [ellipsis Boucher's]

The Golden Apples of the Sun contained some remarkable new stories, and it more than hinted that the fabulous fantasies he was beginning to write, often punctuated with the trademark Bradbury twist of dark wonderment, would come to represent his best work of the 1950s. But this collection was also diluted to some degree by the sheer volume of his output—over little more than a decade he had published, as Bill Nolan had already documented, nearly 190 professional stories, many of which had radiated, often with authorial revisions, into scores of magazine reprints, anthologies, and his own story collections. Boucher, Congdon, and others who knew his work and believed in his talent, were waiting for him to cut away from the past and develop the sustained long fiction projects that he had so far been unable to produce.

42 Bantam and Ballantine

If Bradbury was still having trouble with the novel form, he was clearly maturing in other ways. As he settled back from work on the *Golden Apples* collection, he was gratified to see the Bantam mass-market paperback anthology *Timeless Stories for Today and Tomorrow* reach bookstores in time for the fall 1952 publishing season. This was his first achievement as a literary editor, and the introduction, penned more than a year earlier, reflected a more optimistic aspect of the myths he was developing to negotiate modernity as a writer. A new kind of storyteller's mask emerged as Bradbury matured into an editorial role, and it was based on an optimistic sense of wonder that was more and more frequently beginning to emerge from his fiction as well.

In a sense, the twenty-five authors that Bradbury carefully selected for this anthology were his "characters," and their stories offer clues to the larger view of fantasy that Bradbury was beginning to define for himself and for his public. To be sure, some of the selected stories contained characters not unlike Bradbury's darker subjects, strange people who wear masks to hide from the world, or who wear them to manipulate it. But the stories he selected also reflect the childhood impulse of wonderment that had really driven all of his own best stories for almost a decade—the need to understand and come to grips with the mysterious and terrifying real world, a world where we know all the "hows" but only a precious few "whys." He made this crystal clear in his introduction: "If this book achieves only one purpose, causes you to appreciate the stuff that holds you together, gives you an awareness of life that you may have lost somewhere between childhood and here, it will have done more than enough."

There was a psychology emerging that undercut the critics who felt that Bradbury simply wrote from a child's point of view. He was increasingly fascinated by the way that external nature, and our subjective perceptions of it, merge in what he referred to in his introduction as "the hidden theatre of the mind." The Illinois novel was clearly on his mind as he developed *Timeless Stories*, and he selected stories by other writers that, like his Green Town tales, explored the "margin of impossibility" that offers insights about where we are headed in life. In his introduction, he offered two universal and inextricably linked examples of such insights: "The First Day I Discovered I Was Really Alive," and "The First Day I

Finally Realized That Someday I Must Die." His own very personal versions of these milestones were already folded into the Illinois novel's working draft and would fully emerge in the prelude to that novel, *Dandelion Wine*, in 1957.

In this way *Timeless Stories* became his celebration of the fantasies and mysteries of life, a way of surviving in a world where "we live by approximations and shadows of reality." Every story centered on what Bradbury called "one small filament of the impossible": the momentary time-shifts of Christopher Isherwood's "I Am Waiting," the machine that hears all the voices of the tenement residents in Cheever's "The Enormous Radio," the animated scarecrow of Nigel Kneale's "Jeremy in the Wind," and the mannequin-ventriloquist of John Keir Cross's "The Glass Eye" are representative of that quality. Ironically, Bradbury selected many of these stories from magazines that he supposedly no longer read, even though his own stories had appeared in many of them. He selected six *New Yorker* stories, two from *Esquire*, and stories from a half-dozen other slicks. But he also harvested work from Isherwood's *Tomorrow* and Whit Burnett's *Story Magazine*.

Most of these selections played into a more fundamental Bradbury strategy—his long-standing goal of extending fantasy into the literary mainstream by including "authors who rarely write fantasy"—such figures as John Steinbeck, Walter Van Tilburg Clark, John Cheever, and E. B. White. Others, such as Roald Dahl and Shirley Jackson, already had reputations beyond genre fiction, and he was not afraid to include genre writers he knew personally. He secured a Henry Kuttner tale, and took the unusual step of including two stories by his friend Sidney Carroll, whom he was trying to save from the anonymity of a screenwriting career.

But above all, he wanted to define fantasy by guarding against the dangers that lurked just beyond its margins. To this end he opened the collection with Robert Coates's "The Hour after Westerly," an unsettling déjà vu narrative involving a traveling salesman and the small towns between Hartford and Providence: "Mr. Coates has given us a look at the mystery, he has not shown us the full face, and he goes away before the mystery becomes either intolerable or commonplace." Here was the Jamesian minimum of suggestion that he often attempted in his own work. The averted face of the mystery kept fantasy on course, neither intolerable nor laughable; it was a metaphor that Joe Mugnaini was beginning to parallel in his illustrations of Bradbury's story characters, and it provided the final piece of Bradbury's emerging definition of the form: "Good fantasy must be allowed to move casually upon the reader, in the air he breathes. It must be woven into the story so as to be, at times, almost unrecognizable." His newly crafted mask of author-editor also allowed him to take a more measured shot at realism than he had ever attempted before: "Fantasy enables us to look at life, sometimes, far more easily and recognizably, than the most real of realistic stories."

Bradbury would not always practice this kind of emotional restraint; at times sentiment would drown the wonderment, and at other times anger would turn a story into a tract, as Congdon had observed just a few months earlier in critiquing "Sun and Shadow." Unfortunately, it was a tendency that became more and more common in the years to come, as he spent more time adapting his work to other media and far less time writing new stories. But his editorship of *Timeless Stories for Today and Tomorrow* had forced him to articulate his sense of authorship in a way he had never done before. He was defining his views on fantasy, but he was also, finally, defining his philosophy as a writer: the world and the universe would always be great mysteries, but there is satisfaction in our small ability to make do, and occasionally to be "so keenly aware of living that we have felt a very real and deep gratitude for this chance to live." This conviction was becoming Bradbury's form of faith in an age of doubt.

The Bantam anthology represented a successful advancement of genre fiction, and it remained in print for decades. Bantam sold hundreds of thousands of copies, and as Bradbury became, whether he wished to or not, the name most commonly associated with fantasy and science fiction, Bantam coordinated the successive paperback cover illustrations of *Timeless Stories* with design elements common to all of their Bradbury titles. For many years, Bradbury's first anthology benefited from the perennial sales momentum generated by his growing number of Bantam paperbacks, and it remained in print for more than three decades. But *Timeless Stories* had an aesthetic momentum of its own; the range of selections extended the overlapping landscapes of fantasy and science fiction and ran parallel with the New Wave's impulse to extend the canon that Judy Merril and other anthologists were just beginning to set in motion.

Bradbury's successful effort to showcase the work of others came amidst his own continuing efforts to showcase his own work in book-length collections. In early August 1952, with Bantam's *Timeless Stories* nearing release and the stories for *The Golden Apples of the Sun* entering presswork at Doubleday, Congdon was finally able to find new interest for his old idea of a collection centered on Bradbury's three science fiction novellas. The catalyst was an August 7 dinner between Congdon and Stanley Kauffmann, who had recently followed Bantam founder Ian Ballantine into a new and unusual publishing venture. Ballantine Books was prepared to offer both hardbound and paperback editions under one roof, but the new house needed to attract authors who could bring in the sales needed to make this venture work.[1] They were prepared to offer Bradbury an advance as well as second-serial and anthology rights, free and clear; Ballantine would retain only a split of book-club rights.

It took the rest of the summer and fall of 1952, however, to hammer out the details of an actual Ballantine book contract for the novellas. In September Congdon began the sensitive process of securing Doubleday's acquiescence to the Ballantine negotiations. Bradbury still owed Doubleday the Illinois novel, but Congdon was now looking beyond that obligation. His objective was to generate competition for Bradbury among trade houses, and in particular to loosen up Doubleday's control of paperback royalties and other subsidiary rights. Fortunately, Congdon could depend on the goodwill of Walt Bradbury, and an accommodation was eventually reached. Brad had already declined the novella package a year earlier, and Congdon knew that he was not a great fan of "The Fireman" anyway—at least, not as it had originally been published. It looked like it would be up to Kauffmann and Ballantine to market the novellas and to deal with Bradbury's growing desire to expand "The Fireman" beyond the scope of the original contract offer.

During this time Bradbury was able to place two more stories with academic quarterlies. The acceptances meant far more than the small payments, and he was pleased to see "The Golden Kite, the Silver Wind" become his second story accepted for Cornell University's literary magazine Epoch. "The Tombling Day," an older story about the ambiguous borderlands between life and death, reached publication in the Autumn 1952 issue of Shenandoah, the literary review of Washington and Lee University. A month later Tom Carter, Shenandoah's editor, encountered W. H. Auden after a speaking engagement by the poet in Greensboro and handed him a copy of the Autumn issue. Auden immediately wanted to know how Carter had gotten a story from Bradbury, adding, "I think Bradbury is wonderful. He's the only one of those fellows I can stand."[2] Auden's awareness of Bradbury's work had almost certainly come by way of his close friend Christopher Isherwood, but the endorsement foregrounded Bradbury among "those fellows" of similar genre origins. When Carter relayed the compliment to Bradbury, the news added to the sense of self-confidence that Isherwood's circle was beginning to provide; nevertheless, he was still considered one of "those fellows" by his literary acquaintances, and also by the wider literary world of authors and critics.

43 Hollywood at Last

Before Bradbury could turn in earnest to his expansion of "The Fireman," new and largely unexpected opportunities were opening for him in Hollywood. During the summer and fall of 1952, he was able to establish his first writing credits in the motion picture industry. On one very basic level, his qualifications rested with his credentials as a moviegoer. Although his claim to have seen nearly every feature film made is not credible, during the studio era he probably did see every A-release and most of the B-productions as well, attending double-feature revivals or, during his newsstand days, bartering newspapers for first-run tickets. The proximity of the studios and the proliferation of affiliated and independent theaters in greater Los Angeles created many opportunities for a dedicated moviegoer, and Bradbury was able to attend more and more first-run films as his writing income increased. Having seen all the major films of an era is no qualification for screenwriting, but the experience has credibility in terms of the confidence that Bradbury gained from it: "If you digest hundreds of movies, especially the bad ones, you learn how not to do it. You can learn more from reading trash than from reading excellence, because excellent things are mysterious, and the bad things are quite obvious."

Bradbury was already beginning to forge some lasting connections in Hollywood, thanks in large part to his friendship with cinematographer James Wong Howe. Howe's wife, Sanora Babb, was a regular member of Bradbury's writing group, and Bradbury had quickly become close friends with both of them. Howe's distinguished career stretched back to silent pictures, and he soon introduced his young friend to some of the legendary directors he had worked with, including Fritz Lang and, a few years later, King Vidor.[1] Bradbury established lasting friendships with both directors, but studio heads were another matter entirely. His evolving dislike of film executives, first sparked by his 1946 run-in with the King Brothers, had been fueled by the way that Robert L. Lippert Sr. treated his friend Ray Harryhausen during a 1950 special effects audition for *Lost Continent*.

Bradbury expected Arthur Conan Doyle's *The Lost World*, but this was an improbable screen story of atomic rockets, dinosaurs, and a mysterious island. Lippert, originally a West Coast theater chain owner, had become a B-film producer known for his ability to turn out films on tight budgets and short shooting schedules. He had produced the somber science fiction film *Rocketship X-M*, which included a very dark and pessimistic view of first contact with a dying Martian civilization. Bradbury assisted Harryhausen as he showcased his dinosaur footage, but both men were appalled by Lippert's lack of courtesy and distance during the screening—he never shook hands or even approached them and only spoke to give terse commands.[2] In spite of Harryhausen's recent credit as an animation assistant on *Mighty Joe Young*, Lippert promptly rejected Harryhausen's approach and took the less expensive option of attaching fins to live lizards. A decade later, Bradbury took revenge with "The Prehistoric Producer" (subsequently titled "Tyrannosaurus Rex"), a story that satirically turned the tables and gave Harryhausen the last laugh.

In early 1951 Lippert made an offer to film "Mars Is Heaven!," but Bradbury passed.[3] In spite of its haunting Martian landscape, he had not liked *Rocketship X-M* at all, and the Harryhausen experience convinced him to give Lippert a wide berth. Nevertheless, more prominent producers were now interested in his work. That summer Twentieth-Century Fox executives showed strong interest in Bradbury's time travel tale "To the Future," featured in *Collier's* and subsequently collected in *The Illustrated Man* as "The Fox and the Forest"; as a prelude to negotiations they asked him to adapt "Hard-Luck Diggings," the first of Jack Vance's hasty "first draft" sales to *Startling Stories*. Bradbury's old bias against targeted pulp writing quickly resurfaced; he had trouble from the start and even tried inserting elements of his own pulp tale, "The Long Rain," to extend Vance's plot. After ten frustrating days the studio turned down his outline for the Vance story and eventually broke off negotiations for "The Fox and the Forest" as well.

By this time, though, *The Martian Chronicles* was beginning to generate major studio interest of its own. In 1952 John Houseman approached Bradbury about a *Chronicles* adaptation; Houseman and director Vincente Minnelli, fresh off their production of *The Beautiful and the Damned* for MGM, tried without success to get studio support.[4] But during the spring and summer of 1952, Bradbury's first screen credit evolved—together with Harryhausen's first solo animation credit—during preproduction work on *The Beast from 20,000 Fathoms*. Producer Hal Chester called him in to consult on the script, which included a brief dinosaur-and-lighthouse scene that Bradbury considered to be an uncredited adaptation of his June 1951 *Saturday Evening Post* story, "The Beast from 20,000 Fathoms." This story was one of his favorite children—it had been inspired by the sun-bleached skeletal wreckage of the old Venice Beach roller coaster (a Brackett metaphor) and by the late night echoes of a nearby foghorn during mist-filled nights. From these sights and sounds he had conceived a dinosaur, the last of its kind, drawn to a lighthouse by the foghorn that resembled the call of a long-lost mate.

It was never clear why Bradbury had been asked to read the screenplay, and Chester did not discuss the issue when Bradbury commented casually on the similarities between story and script. The producer may have wanted to test Bradbury's reactions to see whether a credit arrangement was necessary; he may have simply forgotten the scene's inspiration and, by chance, brought in a "script doctor" without connecting Bradbury with the source; or, given the brevity of the scene and its relative unimportance to the overall screen plot, there simply may have been no connection at all. The next day, however, Chester offered to buy the Bradbury story rights for $750, and Warner Brothers eventually billed the entire film as "Suggested by the Sensational *Saturday Evening Post* Story by Ray Bradbury."

The billing probably reflected Bradbury's rising name value rather than further compensation, and may have been included in the final agreement that Ben Benjamin negotiated with Chester's Mutual Pictures production company. This arrangement did not involve any work by Bradbury on the Moreheim-Freiberger script, so he would not have the pleasure of actually working on a film with Harryhausen. But Don Congdon was not pleased with the contract; although only one scene had been inspired by Bradbury's story, the entire film was now credited to him and Congdon was convinced that the property should have been sold for a far larger fee.[5] In general, Ben Benjamin kept Congdon informed on Hollywood transactions, but the options he executed for Bradbury over the next decade suggest that he never fully accepted Congdon's viewpoint that all media deals involving Bradbury's literary properties should be approved by the Matson Agency.

In spite of these restrictions, Ben Benjamin would soon secure something far more important—Bradbury's first studio writing experience.[6] During the late summer and early fall of 1952, Bradbury spent six highly productive weeks under contract at Universal Studios writing "a story for film" that director Jack Arnold and producer William Alland would soon turn into the 1953 Universal release, *It Came from Outer Space*. The contract provided an office as well as a $300 weekly paycheck; Bradbury worked in Bungalow 10, a two-office unit that he shared with fellow writer Sam Rolfe. He ate lunch now and again with Charles Beaumont, who worked in the music department, and sometimes he ate alone in a small-town back lot that reminded him of Waukegan. These weeks signaled the beginning of his entry into the life of Hollywood. He got to know writer and producer Sy Gomberg, who would introduce him to Gene Kelly and a number of actors who, over time, would all come to know his work and even work with him on various film and stage projects. But for now, he concentrated as much as possible on life in Bungalow 10. While Rolfe worked on a Western in his office, Bradbury prepared an original science fiction story concept. All four of his successive drafts survive, and demonstrate richly filmic qualities—including camera directions and fully developed dialog—that go well beyond the normal conventions of a screen treatment.

Alland provided Bradbury with a general topic that played to the flying saucer fever and cold war paranoia of the times: the invasion of Earth. This was code, of course, for a monster movie, but Bradbury was able to gain a significant degree of creative control by modifying the studio's premise: the spacecraft has been damaged, and the alien crew has only landed on Earth to effect repairs. In this way he was able to make the interactions more interesting than the usual invasion story—the aliens adopt what he would call "the face behind the mask, the assumed identity," to get the resources and the manpower to secretly make repairs to their ship, which has burrowed beneath an abandoned mine in the hills around the fictitious desert town of Sand Rock, Arizona.[7] Only John Putnam, a writer and amateur astronomer, and his fiancée Ellen Fields, suspect the alien presence and begin to investigate. These tactics allowed Bradbury the necessary creative breathing room, and he was able to develop a plot that helped define the scientist-protagonist concept that would be central to the better science fiction films that followed. But this plot also allowed him to explore a theme that he had brooded over since childhood: How do people deal with the fear of "otherness"?

To fully explore this theme Bradbury needed a powerful metaphor, and he began to write a variation on a new story that he had tried unsuccessfully to sell to Tony Boucher and Mick McComas for The Magazine of Fantasy & Science Fiction a few months earlier. This story, "A Matter of Taste," explores the alien point of view through a gentle species of giant arachnids that cannot understand the primal loathing expressed by the Earth crew that has just arrived on their planet. The arachnids are clearly the more advanced civilization, a poetic race that has chosen not to go out to the stars; in this decision they resemble, in temperament if not appearance, Bradbury's anthropomorphic Martians. These magnificent creatures adjust immediately to the strangeness of the humans, but the Earth crew can hardly eat or sleep and can only tolerate contact with their hosts after heavy sedation. The ship's captain has gone insane from the experience, and the primary contacts involve the arachnid narrator and the acting captain, who is clearly the ship's psychiatrist.

In "A Matter of Taste," Bradbury's aliens trigger a primal human fear and hatred, without even understanding what the Earthmen mean when they say the word "spider." The story remained unpublished for nearly fifty years, but Bradbury developed a variation on this dark view of human space exploration as he began work on It Came from Outer Space. For the film, the perspectives of "visitor" and "host" are reversed, and this time both cultures fear the loathsome shape of the other. The spider metaphor first seen in "A Matter of Taste" recurs in several of Putnam's analogies when he speaks of the aliens, and the shimmering, momentary lapses in the alien masquerade suggest to Ellen and Putnam the repellant forms of spider or lizard.

Bradbury was already a very visual writer, and it's not surprising that all four of his draft treatments went beyond the norm in terms of camera direction. Treatments are usually more suggestive than directive, but he also inserted precise descriptions of camera angles and shot composition. As both a story and a film, *It Came from Outer Space* depends on illusion and subtle distortion of image, and in many shots Bradbury also described the reflective or distorted images he wanted audiences to see and the sounds he wanted audiences to hear. These camera directions and sound cues bring Bradbury's themes to the forefront and highlight the eerie sense of otherness that became a hallmark of this film. At key moments, Bradbury turns the camera around to make the audience "see" what the aliens see as they move through the desert and as they assume the identities of isolated humans encountered near the crash site. The aliens are also presented through a recurring sound of faint harp strings or chimes lightly struck, signifying an alien presence on the ground or movement through the telephone lines as they observe, listen, and slowly gather what they need to repair their damaged star drive.

William Alland was impressed with Bradbury's final outline, but he hired Harry Essex, an experienced screenwriter, to restyle Bradbury's engaging present-tense story narrative into a more traditionally structured sequence of shots. As submitted, Bradbury's treatment still contained too many of the characteristics of narrative fiction—there were extended passages of dialog, and too many details of incident to present on screen. But he learned a great deal from the process and from the script compression and the minimal modifications that Essex would bring to the story itself. In October 1952, immediately after leaving the studio, Bradbury reflected on this experience through a series of unpublished notes. Although he would never fully embrace the process of narrative compression, Bradbury admitted the necessity for brevity in a characteristic string of metaphors: "The camera is an eye that sees everything quickly, instantaneously. It wants to get *on*. It does things with such economy as to be frightening. What takes several pages to describe in a story is over, done, and gone on the screen in a matter of seconds, and there you stand, center-stage, looking around for the prop just snatched out of your hands by a greedy camera."[8]

But the most striking comparison between Bradbury's hybrid treatment-screenplay and the Essex shooting script is the degree to which the darkness of Bradbury's overarching theme is significantly abbreviated in the film itself. John Putnam's extended use of the spider in his explanation of "otherness" to Sheriff

Warren is central to Bradbury's thematic view, but it was heavily cut by Essex; in its final form, the dialog is reduced from a carefully paced 200-word analogy to a rapid-fire exchange of 42 words that takes only twelve seconds to deliver. In Bradbury's original, the analogy ended with a full articulation of Putnam's point that is missing from the final script: "It all leads to the fact that space travel just won't work. We'll build rockets and go to far places, but when we *get* there and see the spider civilizations and the ant civilizations and the bird civilizations we won't understand them. They won't understand *us*."

The long-forgotten final draft of Bradbury's 1952 treatment-screenplay, available only in a 2001 private press limited edition, highlights one of the major ambiguities in Bradbury's fiction. Ray Bradbury, the writer who has always looked forward to the conquest of space, to the securing of immortality for mankind by spreading out to colonize the stars, was also profoundly ambivalent about our ability to react to the unknown and unknowable aspects of the cosmos. This was reflected in his largely marginalized dark science fiction tales of the late 1940s, and was further subdued when *It Came from Outer Space* was taken from his control in October 1952. In fact, this loss of intensity carries through to the very last words of dialog in the film. In Bradbury's final draft, Putnam is convinced that "they won't come back, ever. Now wasn't a good time for either of our races to meet. Maybe we were never meant to understand each other, our race and theirs." The Essex rewrite buys hope for the audience that Bradbury never intended: "But there'll be other nights, and other stars to watch. They'll be back."

As he worked on *It Came from Outer Space*, Bradbury was also developing a screen treatment for Universal involving a more earthly horror: the looming prospect of the hydrogen bomb, which was predicted to be far more powerful than the atomic weaponry so far produced. He imagined what would happen if the first test of the hydrogen bomb produced an unexpectedly large radius of total destruction, killing all of the scientific observers—except one man. In this way Bradbury provided a new "back story" for a screen treatment of his 1946 tale "Chrysalis," where mysterious laboratory radiations trigger an insectlike metamorphosis in one of the technicians.[9] Bradbury never finished the treatment, however; the successful first test of the hydrogen bomb was announced in early November, displacing his "back story" and effectively ending his negotiations with Universal for a second science fiction film.

Immediately after completing his screen treatment for *It Came From Outer Space*, Bradbury accepted another offer to write a film titled *Face of the Deep* for Twentieth-Century Fox. The adaptation was based on a Curt Siodmak science fiction story about deep ocean exploration, and during October 1952 Bradbury began work in another double-office arrangement with veteran screenwriter Buzz Bezzerides, a versatile novelist and proletarian poet who was writing *Beneath the Twelve-Mile Reef*. But Fox was entering a period of tough financial circumstances, and when studio head Sol Siegel returned from a hospital stay he read Bradbury's work-in-progress (about seventeen pages) and cancelled production of the film.[10] Bradbury had only been on the Twentieth-Century Fox lot for a few weeks, but it was long enough to remind him how much he had grown to dislike studio executives.

44 Political Controversy

The dark vision of space exploration at the core of Bradbury's extensive screen treatments for It Came from Outer Space reflected his concern with the sobering foreign and domestic challenges that America faced as the election of 1952 approached. For some time, he had been growing disenchanted with the Democratic Party. As he worked to sell his stories about race, he began to grow impatient with white liberal activists who were, from his perspective, avoiding any substantial advocacy of a real Civil Rights movement. And Bradbury was increasingly disturbed by the reluctance of liberals to stand up to Joe McCarthy.[1] Given the political climate of the day, and the ease with which any liberal could be labeled a Communist with significant consequences, it's easy to understand that reluctance. In fact, Bradbury was already targeted; as early as 1950, his lecture at Los Angeles City College was canceled by the English Department. He was certain that the underlying cause was his friendship with Norman Corwin, who had recently come under political scrutiny.

He soon passed this information on to Ed Hamilton and Leigh Brackett: "I'm verboten, and, of course, the fact that you get mail from me ruins your reputation, too."[2] But Bradbury was increasingly involved with writers' organizations, and he began to focus his natural activism on the rights of authorship. In June, the Science Fiction and Fantasy Writers of America emerged out of the annual Southwest Science Fiction Convention and Bradbury, the "Westercon" guest of honor for 1952, was elected president pro tem. In the fall, as he began to work under film studio contracts, he joined the Writers Guild of America.[3] His overlapping professions were easy targets of the ultraright, and as long as they could harness the very palpable fear of the people in the name of patriotism, Bradbury felt an instinctive urge to resist.

He decided to wait and see what the election would bring, and along with many of his Democratic friends he actively supported the Stevenson ticket. When Stevenson spoke at the Shriner Auditorium, Bradbury attended with his young writer-friends Sid Stebel, Russ Burton, and Harvey Edwards; but he was surprised to find that Stevenson avoided direct references to McCarthy, or to the bloody impasse in Korea. From his point of view, these were the most significant issues that the next president—Democrat or Republican—would have to face.

Just before the election, Bradbury listened to Eisenhower, in a radio address, pledge to go to Korea. He felt that Stevenson should have said that, and he quietly prepared to see the election go to the Republican Party. But it was the fear-induced campaign strategy of the Far Right that upset him the most. In the weeks leading up to the election, he had heard shouts of "Communist!" aimed at cars with Stevenson stickers. More than the usual number of anonymous letters and telephone calls seemed to target local and state Democratic candidates. From Bradbury's perspective, the unforgivable sin was the Far Right's insistence on denying the pride of citizenship to nearly half of the nation's electorate. The breaking point came when Hedda Hopper's Hollywood column quoted Gene Fowler's proclamation that, with a Republican Congress and, for the first time in twenty years, a Republican president, "It's great that Americans have finally won an election."[4]

Bradbury felt that it was imperative for moderate Republicans to maintain a distance from McCarthy, and two days after the election he arranged to place an open letter titled "To the Republican Party" in a large advertising block of the Hollywood trade magazine *Daily Variety*. It was both courageous and foolhardy, but it got right to the point by reversing the Republican campaign strategy that had declared the two-party system was under threat from the forces of the Left: "I remind you now that the two-party system exists and will continue to exist for the next four years. Every attempt that you make to identify the Republican Party as the *American* party I will resist. Every attempt that you make to identify the Democratic Party as the party of communism, as the 'left-wing' or 'subversive' party, I will attack with all my heart and soul." The six-paragraph letter focused on the need to eliminate fear as a means of governance, and asked that "in the name of all that is right and good and fair, let us send McCarthy and his friends back to Salem and the seventeenth century." His credibility rested on the strategy of speaking for "the more than 25,000,000 Americans who voted without fear and who voted Democratic . . . we will continue to be the other half of that wonderful two-party system you wailed so much about losing." His closing words were carefully measured, for the letter was intended as a mainstream appeal.

But few people close to him, other than Maggie and Don Congdon, supported his action. When he stopped into the Famous Artists agency offices, Ben Benjamin's response was blunt—he figured that Bradbury would never work in the film industry again. What neither Benjamin nor Bradbury could know was that less than a year later his next film offer would come from John Huston, one of Hollywood's great maverick producer-directors who, for the time being, preferred to work almost exclusively overseas. Furthermore, Bradbury had been openly critical of Stalinist Russia for years, and would always oppose dictatorships of any kind. He was a mixture of liberal and conservative, and enjoyed the political anonymity that authorship had, up to now, been able provide. He tried to apply only one restraint to his creativity, and that was Christopher Isherwood's advice to keep imagination equal to indignation. Imagination certainly provided cover, especially in his chosen field. In 1950, he had been able to reflect on the advantages of writing science fiction over other genres: "This is the last refuge for people who want to think at a time when thinking seems to be looked upon as something pink by too many exponents of McCarthyism in this country. I have yet to be called a communist, even though I have written stories against book-burning, excessive mechanization, police and thought control and fascism in high places. I imagine that no one has thought to call me a Communist because I have laid the stories in the future."[5]

What he hadn't accounted for was that the Far Left would call him something else entirely. His writing group was, given the times, politically polarized, and the left-leaning members like Wilma Shore, Sanora Babb, Ben Maddow, and even the more moderate Dolph Sharp could not understand how Bradbury could be against McCarthy and also be so openly hostile to the Soviet Union. Less than two months after the 1952 election, Bradbury was astonished to discover that the views of the others would affect the publication of one of his own new stories.

The controversy centered on his story "The Garbage Man," a spontaneous reaction to one of the most dehumanizing announcements that Bradbury would encounter during the early Cold War years. It came, literally, from his own back yard—the Los Angeles Times had published a statement by the mayor announcing that in the event of an atomic war, the bodies would be picked up by the city's garbage trucks: "I was so furious at the terrible irony of having the undignified thing—of having your body picked up as garbage—that I wrote the story. I was so mad, I was so upset. And of course I couldn't sell the story anywhere."[6] He immediately offered it to The California Quarterly, a literary magazine managed by a staff that included three members of his own writing group. They had published his story "A Flight of Ravens" a year earlier, but now refused "The Garbage Collector" out of hand.

Bradbury suddenly found himself caught in the bipolar complexities of post-war literary politics. He knew that conservative journals would not touch the story, but now he found that the editors of the liberal California Quarterly wouldn't accept it either—their editorial assumption was that Stalinist Russia would never start an atomic war. Bradbury was convinced that Russia would, but he was not a hard-liner by any means—his postelection open letter to the Republican party was evidence enough that he didn't buy into the fear tactics of the day; ironically, CQ's letter for "The Garbage Collector" even thanked Bradbury for his courageous stand. Given his well-documented moderate political views, his story should have been judged on aesthetic grounds. The hidden agenda revealed in the editorial board's vote infuriated him, and he never offered another selection to CQ. The story first appeared in his new collection, *The Golden Apples of the Sun*, in March 1953, but by now he had found a major market magazine that was interested in this kind of fiction. Carey McWilliams had already reprinted Bradbury's "To the Republican Party" in the *Nation*, and he eventually published "The Garbage Collector" as well. The CQ encounter did not affect the long-term relationships within the writing group, but it was yet another reminder of the literary repressions that were driving him to transform "The Fireman" into a full-length novel.

"To the Republican Party" was followed in print by two far more visionary critical commentaries, and together these three pieces signaled Bradbury's rise to prominence as a cultural commentator capable of ranging beyond the boundaries of his fiction. Four days after the national election, Bradbury delivered an address to the Los Angeles Chapter of Brandeis University's National Women's Committee. "No Man Is an Island" began as a commentary on the virtues of building "that particularly quiet fortress known in our society as a library." Building the university's library was a nationwide charge of the Brandeis committee, and Bradbury's cogent presentation was soon published and circulated as a pamphlet. But Bradbury centered his speech on the controversial climate of the times, applauding the courage and faith in mankind required to build a great private university library when public libraries at all levels were under siege from local authorities and special interest groups.

He cautioned these library-builders in a way that showed how much "The Fireman" remained in the forefront of his own mind: "books are dangerous, celebrities detest these handy memory courses which recollect their promises at midnight and their absentmindedness at dawn. They would rather life be lived and forgotten. How lovely, without books, when experience vanishes in thin air, in mouth-to-mouth mythology, and bedtime tales." But Bradbury went on to define the historical importance of books in a very fundamental way: "First, they can help us lay away those dreams which might hurt us, they can tell us that we are not so good as we think we are . . . the second thing books can give us are new and better dreams to replace the old bad ones . . . But the second cannot be done properly without the first. Without a knowledge of our lies, our deceits, our greed, through which runs a narrow vein of thoughtfulness and good, we would go on repeating the same mistakes in the same way."

For Bradbury, uncensored reading was the key to breaking historical cycles of intolerance: "Comprehension, identification, understanding, pity, mercy, love. To put your hand, freely, in a library, is to put out your blind hand and touch humanity." These were by no means original ideas, but he was taking a public position on books in a climate of fear that affected all aspects of publishing and reading in America. By moving on from simply proclaiming his childhood love of books to presenting an eloquently stated position that included the *defense* of books, Bradbury was laying the foundation for a new role as one of the nation's most recognized advocates for libraries and reading. Within a matter of weeks, he had offered public statements on why he wrote fantasy, why freedom from fear is essential in a democracy, and why he valued books. During the late winter of 1953, Bradbury carefully examined his motivation for writing science fiction, the genre with which he was still most closely identified.

Carey McWilliams of *The Nation*, America's premier liberal weekly, had solicited such a writer's essay shortly after reprinting Bradbury's letter "To the Republican Party" in a late November issue that was, in fact, dedicated to assessing the state of the country and the world in the aftermath of the Republican victory and the more recent announcement of America's development of the hydrogen bomb. McWilliams encouraged him to finish the piece by mid-April so that it could be featured in a special *Nation* issue on literature and books. In this new essay, his earlier allusions to "The Fireman" became explicit and extensive. Bradbury's "Day after Tomorrow: Why Science Fiction?" appeared in the May 2, 1953, issue with a long personal prologue devoted to describing the future he had envisioned as he wrote "The Fireman" three years earlier. There was a brief variation on the defiant references to McCarthy that he had first voiced in "To the Republican Party" and in his Brandeis address, but Bradbury was far more interested in his recent discovery that the radio earpieces he had described in his 1951 novella were beginning to appear, quite independently of his work, with pedestrians in the more affluent neighborhoods near his home: "I thought I had raced ahead of science, predicting the radio-induced semi-catatonic. In the long haul, science pulled abreast, tipped its hat, and fed me the dust."

"The Fireman" was now much on his mind, and the earpiece example provided a context for stating his love of writing science fiction: "There is great serious fun for the writer in asking himself, when does an invention stop being a reasonable escape mechanism—for we must all evade the world and its crushing responsibilities at times—and start being a paranoically dangerous device? How much of any one such invention is food for one person, fine for this man, fatal to the next?" For Bradbury, as for many of his peers, the problem of good and evil added an irresistible element of fascination: "Before us today we see the aluminum and steel and uranium chess pieces which the interested science-fiction writer can hope to move about, trying to guess how man will play out the game." But for Bradbury, it was far less about hard science and far more about "the fiction of ideas, the fiction where philosophy can be tinkered with, torn apart, and put back together again, it is the fiction of sociology and psychology and history compounded and squared by time."

He was becoming an effective apologist for the field, which he felt provided the most relevant themes and most imaginative concepts of any genre. But his own precarious status in the field—as portrayed by critics, fellow science fiction authors, and not a few fans—added to his natural aversion to genre labels, which surfaced in the final pages of his essay: "Certainly I have often wished that a new name might be applied to this field, since the old name has grown shopworn in the service of bug-eyed monsters and half-naked space women. But there seems to be no way to avoid that, and new writers coming into the field will have to carry the burden of the old label until someone provides a better one, in this land where everything must *absolutely* have a label" (emphasis Bradbury's).

The cultural criticism that had now spilled over from his fiction into published speeches, letters, and articles also motivated his expansion of "The Fireman" into a more fully developed characterization of McCarthyism that would also expose Modernity's more subtle signs of cultural decay. The original work had been largely apolitical in the sense that Bradbury had tried to navigate between the extreme political ideologies of both Left and Right, and as he prepared to expand "The Fireman" he indicated, in his *Nation* essay, that his cautionary views had not shifted. His main concern remained centered on the question of how to prevent a nightmare vision of the future from becoming "part of a past history our children will read. . . . Consider the similarity of two books—Koestler's *Darkness at Noon*, laid in our recent past, and George Orwell's 1984, set in our immediate future. And here *we* are, poised between the two, between a dreadful reality and an unformed terror, trying to make such decisions as will avoid the tyranny of the very far right and the tyranny of the very far left, the two of which can often be seen coalescing into a tyranny pure and simple, with no qualifying adjective in front of it at all."

This observation, made just as Bradbury was beginning to transform his novella into *Fahrenheit 451*, may explain why it would sell so well in both America and the Soviet Union in the decades to come. "No Man Is an Island" and "Day after Tomorrow" reveal very clearly that the themes he had pursued in "The Fireman" had finally returned to the center of his creative consciousness as Congdon and Kauffmann worked to finalize a contract for the three-novella collection. For a time, however, the political fires of the times led Bradbury to withdraw "The Fireman" from the collection to develop it into a stand-alone novel.

This interlude prompted Congdon to let Kauffmann work from a full list of Bradbury's older uncollected stories, and by early December 1952 the original three-novella focus had changed to a story collection. Only "The Creatures That Time Forgot," which Kauffmann favored over "Pillar of Fire," remained from the initial proposal. But Bradbury was still uncertain about how far he would be able to extend the story line of "The Fireman," and he soon decided that the fairly short novel he had in mind might best work as an anchor for the new Ballantine collection. By mid-January 1953, the contract was finalized with "Creatures" replaced by "The Fireman," to be expanded with a new title as yet undetermined.

45 | *Fahrenheit 451*

Bradbury already knew he wanted a title that would allude to the temperature at which book paper burns. This was an objective correlative of sorts for the cultural inversion at the center of the original novella, but the major university science departments in Los Angeles were unable to provide even an approximation of the combustion threshold for him. As early as January 18 he had a working title—*Fahrenheit 270*—and he began to work with Joe Mugnaini on cover illustrations. It's not clear when Mugnaini made his earliest watercolor preliminaries, but three have survived with the block-letter title *Fahrenheit 204*, and an even earlier pencil sketch is titled *Fahrenheit 205*. On January 22, Bradbury phoned the Los Angeles Fire Department and learned that the self-ignition threshold for book paper is 451 degrees Fahrenheit.

During the early months of the new year, Mugnaini made a verbal commitment to provide interior illustrations for the *Fahrenheit* stories as well as the cover work. He and Bradbury also continued to plan the textless carnival picture-book, which had now grown in concept to a 150-frame sequence of line cuts or watercolors. But Bradbury was also part of an effort by benefactors of the Pacific Art Foundation to fund an extended research trip to Milan and Florence for Mugnaini. The campaign proved successful, and Mugnaini left in mid-March 1953 for an extended stay in northern Italy. On the way, he stopped in New York and London to work with Bradbury's publishers. Bradbury had not been able to meet Ballantine's original March 15 deadline for *Fahrenheit*, but he did manage to send his publisher the stories that were under consideration for the *Fahrenheit* collection. These stories followed Mugnaini on to Europe, where he still planned to complete line cuts for each one.

Ballantine was impressed with the "burning man" cover concept, which was patterned on an earlier illustration of Don Quixote that Bradbury had seen in Mugnaini's studio; Bradbury had also seen a newsprint-clad illustration of Diogenes in the studio, which led to the now-famous newsprint pattern in the burning man's armor.[1] While in London Mugnaini met with Rupert Hart-Davis to discuss the dust jacket and interior line art for the forthcoming British edition of *Golden Apples*. Hart-Davis also saw Mugnaini's interior sketches for *Fahrenheit*, and wrote to Bradbury for permission to substitute the short novel-in-progress for some of the *Golden Apples* stories. Bradbury was at first willing, because he had worked with Hart-Davis to modify contents of his earlier British editions in ways that suited both author and publisher. But Congdon knew that merging two distinct collections in this way would cause great confusion with Bradbury's Continental publishers and reduce his earning potential overseas, and he soon persuaded Bradbury to decline the Hart-Davis request.

Meanwhile, in February Don Congdon was able to secure Doubleday's reluctant agreement not to interfere with Ballantine's *Fahrenheit* collection. But Walt Bradbury's acquiescence came with a reminder that reworking older material could threaten his friend's steady rise from genre to mainstream popularity. In his letter of March 31, 1953, Walt Bradbury reiterated the advice he had given directly during a recent West Coast visit: "I mentioned that the climb to the kind of recognition you should have is a slow process and that each successful publication cumulatively enhances the critical reception of the next. . . . [T]he important thing is your career, your development, your future as a writer. If you chose any course which jeopardizes this development and this future remember you can't go back again."

It was now clear that Doubleday had no further interest in Bradbury's uncollected older genre fiction, so Congdon wasted no time in approaching Ballantine about a paperback edition of *Dark Carnival* as well. It turned out that Derleth's agent, Oscar Friend, was independently probing Ballantine for interest, but it soon became clear that the same Arkham House contract that tied Bradbury to Derleth would require Derleth to pay Bradbury a steep 10 percent royalty on the new edition. No paperback house could meet this percentage, and in the end Derleth agreed to release the *Dark Carnival* rights to Bradbury for $200 and a buyout of the remaining hardbound stock.

Again, Walt Bradbury was willing to waive the Doubleday option on Ray Bradbury's next book-length work, but not before sending another direct caution to his friend: "I have attempted to dissuade you from turning back—turning back to worry about what you did yesterday and the day before, to re-evaluate it, [to] re-work it, to re-publish it with corrections, to look over your shoulder instead of looking ahead. . . . [I]t would be a detour in your mind even if it were not a compromise of your time."[2] The Doubleday position was clear: only Ray Bradbury himself could lift his reputation out of the old genre associations, and that could only happen by finishing the Illinois novel that promised so much and yet had so far failed to coalesce. As long as Ballantine's *Fahrenheit* collection was largely done and ready for submission, and as long as Ballantine's new *Dark Carnival* edition remained a distant prospect, Walt Bradbury could compromise with Congdon in an effort to minimize distractions from the Illinois novel.

In reality, however, the Illinois novel would continue to be deferred as Ray Bradbury hit a creative block with the *Fahrenheit* expansion. He was unable to meet Ballantine's adjusted April 15 deadline, and the new June 15 date put Ballantine up against tight deadlines with his designers and his Houghton-Mifflin publishing partners. Fortunately, Ballantine's editors were able to work effectively with Mugnaini during the interim. An ulcer and other complications led him to return early from Italy, but not before he had worked up illustrations for the shortened list of *Fahrenheit* stories and finished most of the research for his other Pacific Foundation–related projects. By now the idea for a large collection of older published stories had exploded, and Bradbury was working with a short list of eight as yet unpublished stories. The revised concept of new stories appealed to Ballantine, and he was especially taken by "And the Rock Cried Out" and "The Playground," two stories that had been through the revision mill a number of times and had finally, thanks to Congdon, found American magazine publishers who could get them out before Ballantine's October release date.

Most of these eight stories had been written for some time, but Bradbury was reluctant to release them until they were, in his mind, perfect. While Bradbury was deadlocked with *Fahrenheit*, Congdon focused on the *Bradbury Showcase* concept that was still at play with CBS Television.[3] By now Ann Noyes and Ellen Violette had worked up a number of adaptations, and Bradbury had critiqued at least one of the scripts. He and Congdon were impressed with the writing, and they were also encouraged by the fact that CBS was willing to give Noyes a degree of artistic control as assistant producer. Plans were made for a twenty-six–episode series of Bradbury tales, to begin with Kinescope productions of one pilot to secure sponsorship. CBS wanted the popular *Collier's* time-travel story "To the Future" as the pilot episode, but Congdon and Bradbury were reluctant to tie up such a property if the series failed to pan out.

Plans went ahead for a pilot of the old pulp story "The Visitor" instead, and for most of 1953 it looked like a *Bradbury Showcase* would finally reach production—the producers even wanted thirty-second voice-over introductions by Bradbury for each episode. But before the year was out, negotiations would reach an impasse over the CBS requirement that Bradbury attempt no further series for two years after cancellation. Congdon always advised against such limitations, especially now that Bradbury was in such media demand, and the series never materialized. It would take more than thirty years, and the evolution of cable networks, for Bradbury to bring a very similar concept to television—the award-winning *Ray Bradbury Theater*.

Congdon handled most of these media negotiations as Bradbury tried to break his creative impasse on *Fahrenheit*. More than 200 known pages of discards moving forward from "The Fireman" toward *Fahrenheit* suggest that Bradbury probably began work in earnest during the spring of 1953, but these pages also support Bradbury's well-known claim that much of the transformation occurred during early June, when he returned to the pay-typewriting machines in the basement of the UCLA library for another nine-day stint of work that mirrored his 1951 creation of the original novella. On June 15th he was still not finished, but he sent Congdon and Ballantine ribbon copy for the first 126 pages.[4] This won a reprieve until July 7, but Bradbury worked around this deadline by sending on periodic typescript installments for Congdon, Kauffmann, and Ballantine to review in turn. By the end of July it was apparent that the size of *Fahrenheit*, now reaching 50,000 words, meant that the complement of eight flanking stories would have to give way to two volume-closing stories, "The Playground" and the remarkable "And the Rock Cried Out." This configuration kept the volume manageable and honored the unofficial agreement with Doubleday not to publish a freestanding novel. All three of his New York readers were impressed by the nearly seamless way the novella had doubled in size over a few short weeks, but there were still rough spots and very little time available to revise them. Ballantine had galleys set, and on August 5 Kauffmann arrived in Los Angeles to work through corrections and final revisions in person with Bradbury.

They worked together in Kauffmann's hotel room for several days on the galleys. Weeks earlier, Kauffmann had suggested a few adjustments to the sequencing of minor scenes when he reviewed the first typescript installment. But he made very few suggestions during the galley work; his main job was to keep Bradbury on task and to offer editorial comments only when needed. At this late stage of revision, Bradbury apparently cut two of Montag's reveries from "Burning Bright," the final section of the novel. The first of these was a flashback linking the firelight of the Book People to his earlier memories of literary conversations Montag had overheard between Clarisse and her uncle before their disappearance. The second was a snow reverie following the atomic destruction of the city he had so recently left behind, a reverie that threatened, like the blast itself, to create a sensory overload. In the end, however, Bradbury felt that these scenes were expendable—other reveries remaining in the novel were perhaps more important to Montag's emerging sense of enduring cultural values.[5]

In later years, Kauffmann recalled little anxiety about the novel's controversial subject matter during the prepublication days. But Joe Mugnaini remembered one evening when Kauffmann expressed significant worry over publishing *Fahrenheit* while paranoia still had a strong hold on public opinion. School board decisions to ban controversial literature were a constant reminder of the times, and campaigns by Dr. Wertham and Mothers of America still prompted public burnings of comic books and even pulp magazines. During dinner with the Bradburys and the Mugnainis, Kauffmann asked Bradbury if it was indeed the right time for this book.[6] This question may have simply been a final editorial vetting, to be sure that Bradbury still had the determination he had shown in his "Letter to the Republican Party" and his subsequent statements on books and authorship. Bradbury offered strong assurances over dinner, and plans went ahead for the October release. Kauffmann dropped the corrected galleys off at the Chicago printing plant on his way back to New York, thus assuring that the book was back on schedule.

Ballantine shared the excitement that Congdon and Kauffmann felt about the book, and he sincerely wanted *Fahrenheit* to transcend genre labels. Although he was in the process of establishing a strong line of science fiction that already included Arthur C. Clarke and Henry Kuttner, he also agreed with Bradbury's desire to shape a broader literary reputation for his newest author. Ballantine's connections meant that promotion would be intense, and he sent out a large number of hardbound copies to a very wide range of major review outlets. Bradbury had initially found the hardbound design and execution quality uneven in the first few Ballantine titles, but the good working relationship established with Joe Mugnaini had reassured Bradbury very early in the process. As he monitored the presswork and marketing in New York, Congdon became convinced that the book would certainly take off in the fall; a year earlier he had doubted that the original novella could bear much revision without the addition or expansion of subplots and more direct thematic development. In June, when the Muse had finally returned, Bradbury found that the best way to enlarge the thematic implications was to concentrate on expanding Fireman Montag's interactions with his three major dialog partners—the young Clarisse McClellan, the secretive Professor Faber, and Fire Chief Leahy, the towering figure who represented Montag's potential future.

In revision Leahy became Beatty, and in this form Montag's nemesis brings out a far richer description of the way the world became a mindless consumer society incapable of saving itself from looming nuclear annihilation. And during the transformation of the text, Bradbury's "seashell" radio earpieces provided a new plot element—Professor Faber's two-way communicating earpiece, which keeps Montag and his new mentor in contact during the crucial stages when Montag begins to think things out for himself. Beatty senses what he terms a new cleverness in Montag, and holds him in check by relating a "dream"—an imaginary debate masking a one-sided and very persuasive attack on the dangers of book-learned wisdom. Through the secret earpiece, Faber's small-voice counterpoint urges Montag to stand up to this debate, which represents the greatest enemy of all: "But remember that the Captain belongs to the most dangerous enemy to truth and freedom, the solid moving cattle of the majority." As Faber observes, it's now up to Montag to decide for himself "which way to jump, or to fall." This was all new text that greatly enhanced the drama of the story and allowed Bradbury to raise the intensity to match the rising political tensions of the times.

In late July, just as he was finishing the final pages of his typescript, Bradbury confessed to Congdon that the central roadblock had been an inability to be sure that he understood Montag well enough to provide him with motivation equal to the ideas he had given him. It was this kind of structural integrity and consistency of character development that Bradbury wanted to achieve, because this was how he measured the literary quality of his own work. Congdon understood the process and offered some distanced observations intended to diminish the anxiety. Congdon's view was that the "intellectual elite" expected little from dramatic or passionate writing, and the magazines that catered to such a readership would always be likely to avoid the highly imaginative writer. This seemed to intensify Bradbury's fear that he could not convey ideas with the same degree of quality and insight as he could convey emotion. Congdon was convinced that this fear was behind Bradbury's returning reluctance to submit a story until it seemed perfect; it was also the primary obstacle to Bradbury's advancement into sustained long fiction beyond the fallback alternative of weaving previously published material into book-length forms.

46 The Last Night of the World

In the end, *Fahrenheit 451* illustrates how the ideas in Bradbury's science fiction, often dark and occasionally hopeful, had become cautionary. His goal had become one of protecting mankind from the future, not predicting it. For Bradbury, the future danger was not technology, but the humans who will control it; in creating Fire Chief Beatty, who mastered literature and philosophy long before he commanded the men who burn it, Bradbury approached the same Juvenalian dilemma that Aldous Huxley had considered two decades earlier, in writing *Brave New World*: "Quis custodiet ipsos custodes?"—who watches the watchers? Eventually Bradbury would come to call *Fahrenheit 451* a sociological study rather than conventional science fiction. In the novel, meaningful existence becomes a function of time and memory; in the secret encampment of Book People where Montag eventually finds sanctuary, books have become literal characters in their own right, surviving through the process of rote memorization until a time when these precious words can reach print again. The countdown toward that time begins with the nuclear war that destroys the city Montag has so recently escaped.

The nuclear exchange that flattens Montag's city has no scientific or technological foundation. It is a consequence of lost wisdom, of the inability to learn from the past or even to know the past. But it also signals a new beginning, and for Bradbury, scientific realities play no role in this vision. There's no sense of widespread collateral damage, or of the endgame promised by the inevitable nuclear fallout, or the climactic disaster that a later generation of scientists would call nuclear winter. Instead, Bradbury has Montag and the other Book People begin to move out of the forest and back toward the center of destruction, bringing comfort for the injured and hope, "when we reach the city," that those with a fundamental love of the planet and humanity will now inherit the Earth.

Bradbury's closing nuclear theater in *Fahrenheit* is as fantastic as his vision of the spaceship crew commissioned to bring back the golden apples of the sun. But even at a time when many of the lasting effects of nuclear warfare were just beginning to be discussed outside of scientific circles, Bradbury undoubtedly understood the potential for total destruction—at least as well as any lay reader did at the time. If the censorship and the loss of values at the heart of this novel had its precursors in a range of Bradbury's short stories and unpublished novels of the period, the nuclear war that closes both "The Fireman" and *Fahrenheit 451* ran parallel to a number of midcentury Bradbury stories. The last four tales gathered into *The Martian Chronicles*—"The Silent Towns," "The Long Years," "There Will Come Soft Rains," and "The Million Year Picnic"—describe how Earth's descent into nuclear Armageddon terminates the first pioneering wave of interplanetary colonization. Only "The Million Year Picnic" offers any hope that mankind will eventually gain a foothold in the stars. Other unchronicled Martian tales, such as "Holiday," where Martian children see the nuclear fires of Earth in the night sky and cheer the destruction of their colonial oppressors, and "Payment in Full," with its brutal murder of a Martian by astronauts marooned when Earth explodes in nuclear warfare, offer variations on the same nightmare. The forlorn lovers of "Bonfire," the three weird sisters incinerated in the atomic fires of "Embroidery," and the beautiful family of "The Last Night of the World" also reflect the postwar concerns that had slowly merged with the abiding fears of childhood that are never far from the surface in Bradbury's fiction.

Nearly all of these were written with an awareness of a new global metaphor that, since 1947, had graced every cover of the *Bulletin of Atomic Scientists*—the Doomsday Clock. It made no difference that this was an academic journal; every time that the editorial board moved the minute hand closer to midnight, the news was widely broadcast. Bradbury had taken up "The Fireman" and transformed it into *Fahrenheit 451* between two events that, taken together, ticked the clock and terrified the world: the development of the hydrogen bomb, a thermonuclear device that dwarfed the first generation of atomic weaponry—first by the Americans, in October 1952, and then, quite unexpectedly, by the Soviet Union in July 1953.

As Bradbury completed the final pages of *Fahrenheit*, the Doomsday Clock was advanced to two minutes before midnight. It had never been that close to warning of imminent global destruction; never, during the rest of the twentieth century, would it move that close again. For Bradbury, these revelations offered a postscript to his own vision of the final minutes before midnight, captured just three years earlier as he completed "The Last Night of the World." Every adult on Earth has the same dream: no bombs, no explosions, just "the closing of the book," as midnight moves across the planet, from nation to nation. Bradbury's metaphor of the final sleep, so obvious and yet so terribly sad, had replaced his teenage nightmare of the dogs of war with one of the most universal moments of self-reflection he would achieve as a fantasy writer.

In spite of the darkness of the world around him, Bradbury was beginning to develop his settled view on issues of faith. Although he remained uncomfortable with cosmic beginnings and endings, his "Powerhouse" metaphor offered a view of the universe that squared with the ambiguities of life and death that so often obsessed him: "for every light that was put out, another could come on . . . what seemed like death was simply a ceasing of power at one small point, while light and life were reapplied in another room a few miles distant." A faint echo of the Creator remained in Mankind, and Bradbury felt a growing certainty that it was up to mankind to survive on this planet, and to take this driving force of creativity to the stars.

Eventually, he would find validation for this viewpoint in Nikos Kazantzakis's *The Saviors of God*; for now, though, he simply felt that organized religion could not inspire this destiny, unless the holy fathers could accept the implications of life on other worlds.[1] Even his beloved books and libraries were only tools in the hands of enlightened mankind. "No Man Is an Island" ends with the briefest but clearest statement of this fundamental relationship that he would offer during the early decades of his career: "Books are fairly new things in the history of man. I do not for an instant claim they are the cure-all or that they can save us. Man, after all, is his own salvation."

In his own fiction, the short prose poems, or pensées, embedded in some of his best stories of the period come closest to capturing his sense of life and death. He wrote these intuitively, and for years he didn't know what he was doing—he didn't even know the term pensée, and he didn't read the form's master, Saint-John Perse, until years later. But from the mid-1940s through the early 1950s, his own fiction was flavored with occasional prose poems, prompted only by what he would later define as an "ability to describe sensually, with the eye, with the ear, with the tongue, with the nose."[2] Four of the best of these embedded passages reached print between 1951 and 1953, although most were written a year or two earlier. They include "A Scent of Sarsaparilla," where the attic smells and images of long-ago days transport a lonely man back through time for a second chance at life, and "A Sound of Thunder," with its tyrannosaurus rex charging toward the time travelers like a samurai warrior, the armored scales gleaming like golden coins, the coins sheltering prehistoric fleas and lice. Late in life, Bradbury would come to regard Fireman Montag's first ominous encounter with the Mechanical Hound, a scene created during his final phase of revisions toward *Fahrenheit 451*, as a prose poem.[3] But the self-contained passage he has always most closely identified with this literary tradition is the old light-keeper's fable from "The Fog Horn":

One day many years ago a man walked along and stood in the sound of the ocean on a cold sunless shore and said, "We need a voice to call across the water, to warn ships; I'll make one. I'll make a voice like all of time and all of the fog that ever was; I'll make a voice that is like an empty bed beside you all night long, and like an empty house when you open the door, and like trees in autumn with no leaves. A sound like the birds flying south, crying, and a sound like November wind and the sea on the hard, cold shore. I'll make a sound that's so alone that no one can miss it, that whoever hears it will weep in their souls, and hearths will seem warmer, and being inside will seem better to all who hear it in the distant towns. I'll make me a sound and an apparatus and they'll call it a Fog Horn and whoever hears it will know the sadness of eternity and the briefness of life."

And it was this prose poem of the fog horn that called John Huston back to him. In January 1953 he had sent Huston an advance copy of *The Golden Apples of the Sun*, which opened with this story under its original title as "The Fog Horn." Suddenly, in late August 1953, Huston asked to see him at his hotel; he was in town briefly to settle the financial arrangements for his next film, a new version of Melville's cinematically challenging novel *Moby Dick*, scheduled to be written and shot in Europe. The prose poem of the lighthouse that Huston had read in *Golden Apples* had convinced him that Bradbury manifested the qualities he needed to adapt Melville's work, and he was not put off when Bradbury confessed that he had never read his own bookshelf copy of the novel. There was not really enough time to think of all the challenges that might face a relatively inexperienced screenwriter working on location with a source text he had never studied before, but Huston liked to gamble with new talent and insisted that Bradbury had the originality and freshness that he was looking for. Bradbury knew only one thing for sure—given his outspoken history in the film industry, another chance like this might not come along again for some time. The pay was more than he had ever earned as a writer, and nearly twice what he had earned during his brief stint at Universal. Within two weeks, he arranged to bring his family to Europe for the better part of a year, and departed Los Angeles on September 12. For now, Doubleday's Illinois novel would have to be deferred—yet again. He would even have to leave America before Ballantine's release of *Fahrenheit 451*, and many months would pass before he was able to learn how his newest book was beginning to change his literary and cultural reputation.

★ ★ ★

By the time of Bradbury's departure for Europe, all of his strengths as a creative writer were firmly established—as were his shortcomings. There were still times in his work when the emotional fires of initial creativity remained unleavened by careful revision or refinement of idea. Occasionally, his stories were thinly veiled polemics lacking fictional refinements. And he was still unable to fashion a novel-length work without a heavy reliance on the shorter fictions that he wrote so well; as a consequence, he continued to refashion older published stories into new book concepts that distracted him from the difficulties he was having with the Illinois novel. But for the most part, Bradbury was able to turn his limitations to good effect, and this was largely due to the way he developed the characters that welled up from his storehouse of observations. California journalist Gene Beley identified Bradbury with a general observation on creativity made by the British novelist John Fowles:

> Narcissism, or pygmalionism, is the essential vice a writer must have. Characters (and even situations) are like children or lovers, they need constant caressing, concern, listening to, watching, admiring. All these occupations become tiring for the active partner—the writer—and only something akin to love can provide the energy. I've heard people say, "I want to write a book." But wanting to write a book, however ardently, is not enough. Even to say, "I want to be possessed by my own creations," is not enough; all natural or born writers are possessed, and in the old magical sense, by their own imaginations long before they even begin to think of writing.[4]

Bradbury's central strategy in releasing his unconscious has always been to believe, at least while he's writing, that his characters possess him. In this way thousands of story ideas welled up during the first dozen years of his writing career, and he was able to subsequently craft scores of these ideas into effective and uniquely styled fictions. He was able to win over many editors, and with the support of his first two agents he sold many stories on the power of his style and imagination even when these stories did not always fit the perceived preferences of a magazine's reader base. Even in rejecting his work, many editors expressed great enthusiasm for stories they knew their readers (or publishers) could not abide. Bradbury established a fan base among editors just as he did among Hollywood actors and producers, but he often found himself at odds with the executives of both worlds. The New York trips he made between 1946 and 1951 had introduced his exciting personality and abilities as a storyteller to a wide range of publishing figures, and extended Don Congdon's ability to market his work at a time when publishing and media entertainment were in an uncertain period of change and, in the case of radio and the genre pulps, in the early stages of decline.

Bradbury had emerged as a writer who never really fit the genres he was assigned to. His horror and weird tales helped bring the genre out of castles, manor houses, and forests and into the modern city and suburbs; his detective stories were wildly unpredictable; his science fiction stories were tales of mankind that used science and outer space as a backdrop. His use of asides, descriptive prose poems, and stream of consciousness reveries were key components of his style, and at their best these became hallmarks of a master storyteller. Nevertheless, so many of his stories from the first decades of his life remained unpublished for years, and even more remain unrevised or unfinished bursts of creativity. Hundreds of story narratives end at the bottom of the first typed page, or in the middle of the second. In terms of the short story, which would remain his most natural form of fiction, these were the most spontaneous and fruitful years of his career. Things were about to change in his life, and after his return from Europe many opportunities in television, film, and stage would slow his ability to produce fully developed short stories. More and more, he would produce shorter, anecdotal stories as he wrestled with the larger challenges of media adaptation and, finally, novel-length works of fiction that fully transcended their story origins.

Between 1942 and 1953, he had become a master at exploring his own child-hood terrors, but his work also came to manifest adult ambivalence concerning life and death and identity. He worked the same basic themes through an incredibly rich range of story ideas, moving from one genre to another without stopping to write the traditional kind of stories that each genre demanded. But his style was that of a first-tier writer, and his gift for fantasy fed into all of his best fiction. He was just beginning to overcome his sense of inadequacy as a writer through the assurances of major literary figures. Isherwood's blessing had radiated into the approval of Huxley, the encouragement of Heard, and the distant acknowledgment of W. H. Auden. Congdon knew how important this acceptance was to Bradbury, and noted, as Bradbury neared completion of *Fahrenheit*, "since your stories have given great pleasure and satisfaction to people who can be considered members of the intellectual elite, I do not see why you should ever be concerned with the malcontents. The great thing, which is pure, distilled Bradbury, is the skill with which you dramatize an idea and entertain the reader while he is absorbing it. The more you deepen your own understanding and experience with ideas, the more effective you will become."

He was also learning to write about writing, and eventually he would teach others through lectures and occasionally through more personal relationships. But in fashioning his final masks as an oral storyteller and as a very popular media interview subject, he began to draw the facts of his life into the world of his fictions. His accounts of his life always reflect inner truth, and for the most part even the most incredibly Dickensian coincidences of his life are basically accurate as accounted, for there has been a lot of great good fortune in his professional career. But the known correspondence of his life, his private notes, and even the surviving drafts of his manuscripts show how, occasionally, Bradbury could not resist the temptation of playing the storyteller with details of his own life. But these documents also show that he is absolutely true to his public convictions, and his desire to be true to his Muse, to write for himself with little regard for outside pressures, has been a constant hallmark of his writing career.

The first dozen years of that career would still be significant today, even without the remarkable half-century of success that followed. Bradbury's expansion of "The Fireman" into *Fahrenheit 451*, along with Ian Ballantine's multilevel marketing strategy, propelled this novel far beyond its original status as a science fiction novella—the next spring, it would win Bradbury a major prize from the American Academy of Arts and Letters. His fiction had now appeared in five annual award anthologies, and he found himself more and more singled out by the public and the media as the most broadly recognized name in the field of science fiction. Within the field itself, the debate continued as to whether or not Bradbury was a science fiction writer, or indeed whether or not he had ever written science fiction at all. But there was little debate over the fact that he had now fully emerged as a masterful stylist who could work comfortably across the themes of science fiction, fantasy, horror, and detective fiction. He was not interested in following the formula or traditions of any one genre, and he continued to go his own way with little regard for the marketing wisdom that editors, publishers, critics, or even his trusted literary agent might suggest.

Nevertheless, his subjects appealed to an ever-widening readership that came to him for genre fiction but often came away with a far broader reading experience. His metaphor-rich prose, his often startling ideas and situations, and his universal themes had extended the traditional boundaries of all the genres he touched. His Bantam paperbacks were reaching school children, and many of his early stories would soon begin to appear in an impressive range of textbooks. The darkness of his themes put off some educators, but the thematic ambivalence and metaphorical richness of his stories created an interpretive challenge that is always valued in the classroom. In an early assessment of Bradbury's career, Damon Knight pointed out the fundamental significance of his themes: "Bradbury's strength lies in the fact that he writes about the things that are really important to us—not the things we pretend we are interested in—science, marriage, sports, politics, crime—but the fundamental prerational fears and longings and desires: the rage at being born; the will to be loved; the longing to communicate; the hatred of parents and siblings, the fear of things that are not the self."[5]

But Knight also observed that Bradbury's movement into pure fantasy in the early 1950s was beginning to lose the tension, the striking underlayment of neurosis, and the chilling midnight feel of his earlier work. Critics were always looking for sentiment to wash over and destroy the edginess and originality of his prose, and it's unclear how this tendency might have progressed if Bradbury's work had not been interrupted by the great career-changing dislocations of 1953–54. Was his subconscious wellspring of experience running dry? The vast number of undeveloped story ideas and unfinished opening pages from this period suggests otherwise, but there's no denying that in spite of his talent and drive, there was a larger world that he had as yet never experienced. In spite of occasional adventures and hardships common to many who grew to maturity during the Great Depression, the first thirty-three years of his life had been relatively uneventful.

Bradbury was still living a largely self-taught life of creativity, with little acceptance from or understanding of the wider cultural fabric that existed beyond the mediating filters of books, motion pictures, the dramatic stage, or a few New York editorial offices. He was only just beginning to feel the personal acceptance of a larger literary world, but this still didn't extend much beyond Norman Corwin's friendship and Gerald Heard's cottage tea parlor. On the eve of his departure for Europe, Bradbury had not yet finished his first reading of *Moby Dick*, and he was not even sure where Huston would set up camp for the preproduction work. This script, largely written under Huston's dominating presence in Ireland, would prove to be the most stressful writing experience of his life, but in the end it opened many doors in Hollywood, and provided the means to discover—all at once—the classical, medieval, and Renaissance heritage of the Western World under the subtle tutelage of Bernard Berenson. It all depended on the success or failure of the very uncertain creative venture he was about to begin with the unpredictable John Huston. For decades, this encounter would spread through his writing like a circle in the water, changing everything in its wake.

Notes

Unless otherwise indicated in individual note citations, Bradbury's unpublished papers are located in the following repositories: The Albright Collection contains the manuscripts of published and unpublished works, diary notes, and letters to Ray Bradbury; the State Historical Society of Wisconsin (Madison) holds his letters to August Derleth; the Rare Book and Manuscript Library of Columbia University's Butler Library is the depository for Bradbury's letters to his agent, Don Congdon, and to *Ellery Queen's* Frederic Dannay; the Jack Williamson Library at Eastern New Mexico University holds Bradbury's letters to Williamson, Edmond Hamilton, and Leigh Brackett; Syracuse University's Bird Library holds Bradbury's letters to Frederik Pohl and the editors of the *Magazine of Fantasy & Science Fiction*; the Lilly Library at Indiana University (Bloomington) contains Bradbury's F&SF letters addressed specifically to Anthony Boucher. A few passages from chapters 15, 34, and 35 were rewritten and condensed from my portions of Eller and Touponce, *Ray Bradbury: The Life of Fiction* (2004). Portions of chapter 43 were rewritten and expanded from an essay in Ray Bradbury's *It Came from Outer Space* (2001). These passages are all identified in individual notes. Unless otherwise noted, all interviews with Bradbury were conducted in Los Angeles.

Chapter 1. From the Nursery to the Library

1 Bradbury, interview with Donn Albright, Oct. 2000.
2 Bradbury typescript, Oct. 26, 1957. The NEA distributed the essay for newspaper syndication during the inaugural National Library Week, Mar. 16–22, 1958.
3 Bradbury, "The Brother," unpublished, c. 1950.
4 Bradbury, Congdon interviews, 1969 (Albright Collection), I.19.
5 Bradbury, draft introduction for *In Memoriam: Clark Ashton Smith*, composed Apr. 7, 1957; published Baltimore, Md., Mirage/Anthem, 1963. He has always been careful to distance himself from Smith's work by calling this introduction a favor for Smith's widow.
6 Bradbury to Hamilton, undated, c. 1949.
7 Bradbury to Derleth, May 18, 1950.
8 Bradbury, interview with the author, Mar. 17, 2010.
9 Bradbury, interview with the author, Oct. 13, 2006.
10 Bradbury to Rhymer, Dec. 1, 1949; Bradbury to Koenig, May 3, 1961 (carbons, Albright Collection).

Chapter 2. L.A. High and the Science Fiction League

1 Bradbury, interview with the author, Oct. 20, 2007.
2 Ibid.

3　These include "The Monster Maker" (1944), "Final Victim" (1946), and "Asleep in Armageddon" (1948), all written in 1942–43. Bradbury's reading of Lowell's *Mars as the Abode of Life* is known from a copy of this book, now owned by publisher and bookseller Craig Graham, that reads: "This book inspired me, age 10!"

4　Bradbury, interview with the author, Oct. 7, 2006.

5　Bradbury, diary notes; Bradbury, interview with the author, Palm Springs, Oct. 1998.

6　Bradbury, unpublished note on the Jan. 6, 1938 LASFL meeting.

7　Johnson to Bradbury, July 19 and Sept. 7 [1962], Jan. 20 [1963], and Oct. 29 [1964].

8　Bradbury, Congdon interviews, 1-B.55–56 and 2.1; Bradbury, interview with the author, Oct. 20, 2008.

Chapter 3. Hannes Bok and the Lorelei

1　Bradbury, interview with the author, April 4, 2009.

2　Bradbury, interviews with the author, Oct. 20, 2007, Oct. 20, 2008, and Apr. 4, 2009. Bradbury, introduction to the expanded edition of *Dark Carnival* (Springfield, Penn.: Gauntlet, 2001), xvi.

3　Lin Carter, "The Gate of Khoire," introduction to *Beyond the Golden Stair*, by Hannes Bok (New York: Ballantine, 1970), vii–x; Emil Petaja, *And Flights of Angels: The Life and Legend of Hannes Bok* (San Francisco: Bokanalia Memorial Foundation, 1969); Bradbury, foreword to *A Hannes Bok Treasury* (Philadelphia: Underwood-Miller, 1993).

4　Laurence S. Cutler and Judy Goffman Cutler, *Maxfield Parrish and the American Imagists* (Edison, N.J.: The Wellfleet Press, 2004), 78.

5　Bradbury, interview with the author, Oct. 2002.

6　Bradbury, "The Butterfly Maker, an Interview with Amy Jones," *VC* [Ventura County] *Life & Style* (Spring 2006): 13. When asked to speak at memorial services, he would often read the closing passages from his Green Town story "Goodbye, Grandma" (1958), which offers what he considers the best variation on his master dream metaphor for Eternity: "That story is so beautiful, because when she dies, she rolls over and takes up the dream she has in Eternity. She's not dying, she's going back to Eternity—she's not dead, she's continuing." Bradbury, interview with the author, Manhattan Beach, Oct. 20, 2008.

Chapter 4. NYCon 1939

1　Bok to Bradbury, postmarked May 12 and June 14, 1939.

2　Bradbury, diary notes.

3　Bradbury, preface to the collected edition of *Futuria Fantasia* (Los Angeles: Vagabond Books, 2007), [xi]; Bradbury, interview with the author, Oct. 2008.

4　Jack Williamson, *Wonder's Child* (New York: Bluejay Books, 1984), 116; Frederik Pohl, "Jack," *Locus* 57:6 (Dec. 2006): 82–83.

5　Bradbury to Hasse, [c. Oct.], Oct. 15, and Nov. 6, 1939 (photocopies, Albright Collection); Bradbury, interview with the author, Oct. 2009; *Futuria Fantasia* (Los Angeles: Vagabond Books, 2007), [xiii].

6　Michael Ashley, *The Time Machines* (Liverpool, U.K.: Liverpool UP, 2000), 106–23, 140.

7 Bradbury's trip notes.

8 Ibid.; Bradbury, "As I Remember," editor's column in *Futuria Fantasia* 3 (Winter 1940), 19.

Chapter 5. *Futuria Fantasia*

1 Bradbury's NYCon trip notes end with the Tuesday-Wednesday [Aug. 1–2] Technocracy entry.

2 "An Introduction to Science," *Technocracy Study Course* (New York: Technocracy, Inc., 1934), 9. Bradbury still has two copies of the 5th printing (Jan. 1939). William E. Atkin's *Technocracy and the American Dream* (Berkeley: Univ. of California Press, 1977) is the best single reference for the intellectual history of Technocracy, but it lacks sufficient coverage of the sociological aspects that motivated Bradbury. I relied more directly on Dr. John D. Jones's background readings for the Engineering Science curricula at Simon Fraser University, British Columbia, Canada, online at www.ensc.sfu.ca/~jones/ensc100.

3 Hasse to Bradbury [postscript], Oct. 6, 1939.

4 Bradbury to Hasse, Nov. 6, 1939 (photocopy, Albright Collection).

5 Knight to Bradbury, June 14, [1940].

Chapter 6. *From the Fanzines to the Prozines*

1 Bradbury, interviews with the author, Oct. 12, 2006, and Oct. 23, 2010; UCLA Oral History Interview (1962): 88–90.

2 Bradbury, interviews with the author, Oct. 12, 2006; Oct. 18, 2008; Mar. 13, 14, 2010. Bradbury's diary notes, July 1940.

3 Bradbury to Pohl, [Aug. 1939], [Jan. 1940]; Pohl to Bradbury, Aug. 19, 1939.

4 Two undated [c. 1940] letters to Pohl; Pohl to Bradbury, Apr. 7, 1941.

5 Bradbury, "Author's Note," *Forever and the Earth: Radio Dramatization*; Sam Weller, *The Bradbury Chronicles: The Life of Ray Bradbury* (New York: Morrow, 2005) 91–92; Bradbury library survey (Eller), Oct. 2005.

6 Bradbury to Williamson, Apr. 23, 1941.

Chapter 7. Early Disappointments: The Science Fiction Pulps

1 Schwartz to Bradbury, Sept. 2, 1942.

2 Bradbury, Congdon interviews, II.20.

3 The surviving typescript for "City of Intangibles" is dated, in Hasse's hand, July 5, 1941, but it was typed by Bradbury and sent on to Hasse on Aug. 6, 1942.

4 Bradbury to Bond, Feb. 15, 1949 (Christopher Bond).

5 Bradbury, "Wells: His Crystal Ball Was Crystal Clear," a review of *The H. G. Wells Scrapbook*, *Los Angeles Times Book Review* (July 1, 1979): 7, and Arthur C. Clarke, Introduction to *The Invisible Man* (New York: Modern Library, 2002).

Chapter 8. Living in Two Worlds

1 Bradbury, interview with the author, Oct. 24, 2007.

2 Bradbury to Jim McKimmey, Oct. 24, 1963, White (Boucher) papers, Lilly Library.

3   The most comprehensive study of the riots and the events leading up to them remains Eduardo Obregón Pagán's *Murder at the Sleepy Lagoon: Zoot Suits, Race, and Riot in Wartime L. A.* (Chapel Hill: Univ. of North Carolina Press, 2003). Pagán cites Mauricio Mazón's *The Zoot Suit Riots* (1984) as the primary study of the underlying psychology of the unrest.

4   Bradbury to Hasse, Aug. 6, 1942 (photocopy, Albright Collection); Bradbury interview with the author, Oct. 2004.

Chapter 9. Reading about Writing

1   Bradbury, interview with the author, Oct. 10, 2005. His further comments on Egri and Elwood are also from this interview.

2   Bradbury, "The Mixture as Before" (1996), a draft introduction for an unpublished anthology of Maugham's stories.

3   W. Somerset Maugham, *The Summing Up* (New York: The Literary Guild, 1938), 82–83.

4   Dorothea Brande, *Becoming a Writer* (New York: Harcourt Brace, 1934), 36, 38; William F. Touponce, *Ray Bradbury and the Poetics of Reverie* (revised edition; San Bernardino: Borgo, 1998).

5   Brande, 70–71.

6   Bradbury, interview with the author, Oct. 10, 2005. His recollection is that he read Brande in 1939, Egri in 1942, and Maren Elwood's *Characters Make Your Story* in 1943.

7   Bradbury to Kuttner (draft; Albright Collection), Dec. 25, 1944.

Chapter 10. Early Mentors: Hamilton, Williamson, and Brackett

1   Bradbury, interview with the author, Mar. 2002.

2   Bradbury, author interviews, Mar. 2002 and Oct. 2005; Bradbury, interview (Albright), Jan. 2005; Bradbury, "Henry Kuttner: A Neglected Master," introduction to *The Best of Henry Kuttner* (Garden City, N.Y.: Doubleday, 1974); Weller, 103.

3   Bradbury, "Author, Author," *Fanscient* Winter (Jan.–Mar.) 1949.

4   Brackett to Bradbury, undated (postmarked May 10, 1944); Bradbury, interview with the author, Oct. 2004.

5   Kuttner to Bradbury, Nov. 23, 1942, and Bradbury to Kuttner, Dec. 25, 1944 (draft; Albright Collection).

6   Bradbury, interview with Albright (for the author), Mar. 2003; Arthur Jean Cox, "Introduction: A Man for All Magazines," in *The Work of Ross Rocklynne: An Annotated Bibliography and Guide*, by Doug Menville (San Bernardino, Calif.: Borgo Press, 1989).

7   Bradbury, interview with the author, Oct. 2004 and Oct. 2007; Williamson, *Wonder's Child*, 127. Bradbury's Nov. 6, 1940, diary note documents Williamson's *Darker than You Think* as a reading highlight.

8   Williamson, *Wonder's Child*, 129.

9   Bradbury, interview with the author, Oct. 2004.

10 Williamson, *Wonder's Child*, 123.

11 Brackett to Joel Frieman, May 27, 1969 (Lilly Bradbury MS. III); John L. Carr, *Leigh Brackett: American Writer* (Polk City, Iowa: Chris Drumm, 1986): 30–49.

12 Bradbury, interview with the author, Oct. 2004.

13 Bradbury to Hamilton and Brackett, Mar. 22, 1951.

14 Michael Moorcock, "Queen of the Martian Mysteries," introduction to *Martian Quest: The Early Brackett* (Royal Oak, Mich.: Haffner Press, 2002), xiv–xvii.

15 Bradbury to Hamilton and Brackett, [Nov. 1951].

Chapter 11. "Chrysalis": Bradbury and Henry Kuttner

1 Bradbury to Congdon, Feb. 7, 1958.

2 Bradbury, "Henry Kuttner: A Neglected Master," introduction to *The Best of Henry Kuttner*, viii; Bradbury, "Kuttner Recalled," in *Etchings & Odysseys 3* (Madison, Wis.: The Strange Co., 1984): 7.

3 Michael Ashley, *The Time Machines*, 170.

4 Kuttner to Bradbury, Oct. 21, 1942.

5 Kuttner to Bradbury, [Oct.] 23, [1942].

6 Kuttner to Bradbury, Nov. 23, 1942.

7 Kuttner to Bradbury, ibid.

8 Bradbury interview with the author, Mar. 13, 2002.

Chapter 12. A New World of Reading

1 Bradbury, interview with the author, Mar. 14, 2002.

2 Bradbury to Derleth, Sept. 21, 1944; Bradbury, "How I Wrote My Book" unpublished manuscript, Oct. 17, 1950: 1.

3 Bradbury, interview with the author, Oct. 10, 2005.

4 These recollections of Lewton and Woolrich are from Bradbury, interview with the author, Oct. 25, 2007, and Oct. 18, 2008.

5 Bradbury to William F. Nolan, Oct. 31, 1950.

6 Bradbury, "John Collier Probes the Darker Regions," *Los Angeles Times* (Dec. 10, 1972): 17; Introduction, *Fancies and Goodnights* (New York: New York Review of Books, 2003), vii–xi.

Chapter 13. An Emerging Sense of Critical Judgment

1 Bradbury, interview with the author, Oct. 24, 2008.

2 Bradbury to Derleth, Jan. 29, 1945.

3 Bradbury, "A Few Notes on *The Martian Chronicles*," in *Rhodomagnetic Digest* 1:6 (May 1950) contains his earliest published reference to his 1944 reading of Jean Giono's work. His comparison of Giono to Aymé is from Bradbury, interview with the author, Oct. 18, 2008.

4 Frederic Prokosch, *The Asiatics* (New York: The Readers Club, 1941) second edition, 359.

5 Bradbury, interview with Donn Albright, (for the author) Oct. 2003.

Chapter 14. On the Shoulders of Giants

1 Bradbury, notation on the fragment typescript of *Where Ignorant Armies Clash by Night*.

2 Bradbury to Hamilton, Oct. 7, 1943.

3　Bradbury, interview with Nard Kordell, Mar. 2007 (raybradbury.com).

4　Bradbury, interview with the author, Oct. 13, 2005: "The relationship of the fire chief and Montag, in many ways, is reflected in the communist leader and the dissident." Bradbury recalls that he saw the Broadway production of *Darkness at Noon* during his May 1950 trip to New York; however, only his June 1951 trip overlapped with the play's Broadway run.

5　Bradbury, interview with the author, Oct. 8, 2006. At first, Bradbury had reservations about the prose quality of *The Fountainhead*, or at least intimated as much in an unlocated letter to Kuttner, who noted in reply: "No use having a sound theme if you make it ridiculous in the writing. All the characters in *Fountainhead* were Ayn Rand—did you notice?" Kuttner to Bradbury, Oct. 13, 1945.

Chapter 15. The Road to Autumn's House
1　Bradbury to Hasse, Jan. 30, 1940; Bradbury to Derleth, June 15, 1946.

2　Bradbury to Derleth, June 7 and 15, 1946.

3　Kuttner to Bradbury, July 8, 1944.

4　Schwartz to Bradbury, Mar. 25, 1944.

Chapter 16. Exploring the Human Mind
1　Sigmund Freud, *Psychopathology of Everyday Life*, in *The Basic Writings of Sigmund Freud* (New York: Random House, 1938, The Modern Library Edition), 177.

2　Karen Horney, *The Neurotic Personality of Our Time* (New York: Norton, 1937), 94–95.

3　Bradbury, "What Can a Writer Say?" in *Weird Tales*, Jan. 1945 (Mar. 1945, Canada): 4, 48.

4　Bradbury, interview with the author, Oct. 2008. Melanie Klein's *The Psycho-Analysis of Children* (London: Hogarth Press, 1932) is the most representative volume of her theory of child development.

5　William F. Touponce, "Reverie in the Utopian Novel," chapter 6 in *Ray Bradbury and the Poetics of Reverie* (1984; revised 1998), and Jonathan Eller and William F. Touponce, *Ray Bradbury: The Life of Fiction*, (Kent, Ohio: Kent State Univ. Press, 2004), chapter 3. I'm also grateful to Bill Touponce for discussing fundamental distinctions between Freud and Jung in the context of Bradbury's fiction.

6　Kuttner to Bradbury, July 8, 1944.

7　Bradbury, interviews with the author, Oct. 2, 2004, and Oct. 8, 2006.

8　Bradbury, interview with the author, Oct. 2, 2004.

Chapter 17. Exploring the Human Condition
1　Sterling North, "Strictly Personal." *Saturday Review of Literature*, 27:49 (Dec. 2, 1944): 20–21.

2　In his June 11, 1948, letter to August Derleth, Bradbury confessed to having only read and owned various Wells novels, G. Edward Pendray's *The Earth Tube*, and the Balmer-Wylie collaboration *When Worlds Collide*. Bradbury's reading of Wylie's *Generation of Vipers* is inferred from Julius Schwartz to Bradbury, Apr. 1, 1944.

3   These three passages are quoted from Philip Wylie, *Generation of Vipers* (New York: Farrar & Rinehart, 1942), 44, 86, 35, respectively.

Chapter 18. With the Blessings of His Mentors
1   Brackett's single-page, handwritten cover note survives, but it is undated; her earlier postcard (postmarked Aug. 31) and her studio schedule together provide the basis for dating the hand-off to Bradbury.
2   Schwartz to Bradbury, Feb. 24, 1945, acknowledges receipt of the completed novella. Bradbury's working log indicates that he finished "Lorelei of the Red Mist" in February 1945.
3   Leigh Brackett, "Introduction," in *Best of Planet Stories #1* (New York: Ballantine, 1975), 7.

Chapter 19. New Stories and New Opportunities
1   Bradbury, interview with the author and Donn Albright, Mar. 2002.
2   Schwartz to Bradbury, Mar. 3 and 10, 1945.
3   Kuttner to Bradbury, June 15, 1943; Bradbury to Hamilton, Oct. 7, 1943; Schwartz to Bradbury, Dec. 25, 1944; Bradbury, interview with the author, Oct. 23, 2010.
4   Kuttner to Bradbury, Dec. 21, 1944; Schwartz to Bradbury, Feb. 4, 1945.
5   Bradbury, interview with the author, Oct. 20, 2007. Bradbury has long maintained that the sales all occurred within a week of his Aug. 22 birthday, but his own sales log dates the *Collier's* sale to Aug. 25, the *Mademoiselle* sale to Sept. 1, and the *Charm* sale to Sept. 24, 1945. Surviving acceptance letters are dated Aug. 24 (*Mademoiselle*) and Sept. 21 (*Charm*).
6   Bradbury to William F. Nolan, Aug. 23, 1951.

Chapter 20. Life and Death in Mexico
1   Bradbury, "*Dark Carnival* Revisited," introduction to the expanded edition of *Dark Carnival* (Springfield, Penn.: Gauntlet, 2001), xviii.
2   Bradbury, interview with Donn Albright (for the author), Mar. 2008; Bradbury, interview with the author, Oct. 18, 2008.
3   Bradbury, "Introduction: Alive and Kicking and Writing," in *The Cat's Pajamas* (New York: Morrow, 2004).
4   Bradbury, interview with the author, Oct. 20, 2007.
5   Ibid.
6   Bradbury, interview with the author and Donn Albright, Mar. 2002.

Chapter 21. Transitions: Bradbury and Don Congdon
1   Friend's offer is dated July 30, 1945; Spier's letter, on CBS Pacific Network letterhead, is dated Jan. 8, 1945; Rex Stout's offer was made through his coeditor, Louis Greenfield, on Oct. 5, 1945.
2   Chambrun to Bradbury, Nov. 1 and Dec. 10, 1945. Bradbury wrote of Leland Hayward's offer in a Nov. 3 letter posted to his parents from Patzcuaro. Burnett's inquiry is dated Nov. 30, 1945; Strauss to Bradbury, Mar. 28, Apr. 11, 1946.

3   Bradbury maintains that the first contact was an unsolicited letter from Congdon forwarded to Mexico. However, the surviving letters (and a dated note typed on the cover page of "The Smiling People" typescript) confirm that at least three letters passed between them *before* Bradbury left for Mexico.

4   Angoff's April 15 telegram to Bradbury survives in Bradbury's papers; the text is quoted in Weller, 133. Martha Foley's recollection of these events is recorded in the editor's introduction to her posthumous memoir, *The Story of "Story" Magazine* (New York: Norton, 1980), 21–22.

5   Schwartz to Bradbury, May 11, 1946; Bradbury to Derleth, May 4, 1946.

Chapter 22. The Power of Love

1   Bradbury, interview with the author, Oct. 12, 2006. Bradbury's surviving copy of *The Castle* is dated (in his hand) April 1946.

Chapter 23. From Arkham to New York

1   Jonathan Eller and William F. Touponce, *Ray Bradbury: The Life of Fiction* (Kent, Ohio: Kent State Univ., 2004), 60; Bradbury, interview with the author, Oct. 7, 2006.

2   Eller and Touponce, 61–62, 62n; Bradbury to Derleth, June 15, 1946.

3   Kuttner to Bradbury, Dec. 2, 1944, and Sept. 13, 1945.

4   Kuttner to Bradbury, Sept. 13, 1945.

5   Bradbury to Derleth, July 10, Oct. 30, 1946; Bloch to Bradbury, undated [c. Aug. 1946]; Bradbury to his Aunt Edna Hutchinson, Sept. 2, 1946; Marguerite McClure to Bradbury (en route), Sept. 6, 1946; and notes made in Bradbury's surviving address book of that period.

6   "I've asked E. Hoffmann Price to forward The Strange Island of Dr. Nork to you." Bloch to Bradbury, undated [July–Aug. 1946].

7   MacCammond to Bradbury, Sept. 10, 1946; Bradbury to Derleth, Oct. 30, 1946.

8   Bradbury to Derleth, Oct. 30, 1946. In an April 17, 1946, letter, Jack Snow had strongly recommended that Bradbury read the latest McCullers novel, *The Member of the Wedding*: "It should be of great interest to you, as it comes so very close to your own child psychology."

9   Bradbury, interview with the author, Oct. 18, 2008.

10 Bradbury, interview with the author, Oct. 11, 2005. Jay Nergeboren's introduction to Martha Foley's *The Story of "Story" Magazine* (New York: Norton, 1980) attributes the forged letter to a vengeful girlfriend (21–22).

11 Snow to Bradbury, Aug. 29 and Nov. 4, 1946. His earlier attempts to generate NBC's interest in the Johnny Choir stories are related in Snow to Bradbury, Aug. 10, Sept. 6, and Nov. 10, 1944.

12 Marguerite McClure to Bradbury (en route), Sept. 8, 9, and 15, 1946.

Chapter 24. Obsessed with Perfection

1   Bradbury, interview with the author, Oct. 20, 2007.

2   Maurice King to Bradbury, Aug. 13, 1946.

3   Bradbury, interview with the author, Oct. 2007.

4   Snow to Bradbury, May 23, June 7 and 18, Aug. 29, and Nov. 4, 1946.

Chapter 25. *Dark Carnival*

1   A detailed textual history of Bradbury's *Dark Carnival* revisions appears, along with an account of the evolving Bradbury-Derleth relationship, in Jonathan Eller and William F. Touponce, *Ray Bradbury: The Life of Fiction* (Kent, Ohio: Kent State Univ., 2004), 52–71.

2   Bradbury to Dannay, Mar. 12, 1947 (Columbia).

3   Bradbury, interview with the author, Oct. 2004.

4   Ivan Foxwell to Bradbury, July 5, 1948.

5   Damon Knight, "When I Was in Knee-Pants: Ray Bradbury," from *In Search of Wonder* (Chicago: Advent, 1956), 108–13. Originally from Knight's review of *The Illustrated Man* in his "Readin' and Writin'" column, *Science Fiction Quarterly* 1.2 (Feb. 1953), 82.

6   "Brian W. Aldiss" and "J. G. Ballard," in Charles Platt, *Dream Makers* (New York: Ungar, 1980, 1987) 80, 92. Ballard, interview with Werner Fuchs and Sascha Mamczak, "A Conversation with J. G. Ballard," *Ballardian* (online) May 17, 2008 (www.ballardian .com); originally published in *Das Science Fiction Jahr 2007* (Munich: Heyne, 2007).

Chapter 26. Lifetime Partnerships

1   Bradbury to Derleth, May 12, June 23, and Aug. 27, 1947; Brackett to Bradbury, [summer 1947].

2   Bradbury to Derleth, May 12 and 21, July 2, 1947; Congdon to Bradbury, undated [June 1947].

3   Bradbury to Derleth, Sept. 24, 1947.

4   Bradbury to Boucher, Jan. 10, 1952 (Lilly Library); Jonathan Eller and William F. Touponce, *Ray Bradbury: The Life of Fiction* (Kent, Ohio: Kent State Univ., 2004), 90.

5   Bradbury to Derleth, Sept. 24, 1947.

6   Bradbury, interview with the author, Oct. 18, 2008; interview with Donn Albright, Apr. 1, 2003; Weller, 149.

7   Ray Bradbury, "Leigh Brackett and Edmond Hamilton: My Great Loves, My Great Teachers, My Great Friends," *Readercon 10 Souvenir Book* (1998; rpt. in Leigh Brackett, *Lorelei of the Red Mist: Planetary Romances*. Royal Oak, Mich.: Haffner Press, 2007), ix–xi.

Chapter 27. The Illinois Novel

1   Christopher Morley, *Thunder on the Left* (Garden City, N.Y.: Doubleday Page, 1925), 9. Further references appear parenthetically in the text.

Chapter 28. Bradbury and Modernity

1   Jonathan Eller and William F. Touponce, *Ray Bradbury: The Life of Fiction* (Kent, Ohio: Kent State Univ., 2004), 24–30 *(Masks)* and 199–201 *(Where Ignorant Armies Clash by Night)*. *Ignorant Armies* appears in Ray Bradbury, *Match to Flame* (Colorado Springs: Gauntlet, 2006), and the *Masks* manuscripts subsequently appeared as the title piece in Bradbury's *Masks*

collection (Gauntlet, 2008). Portions of my comments on these two unfinished novels are revised from my essays and bridging commentaries in the two Gauntlet editions.

2 During the summer of 1947 he registered and mailed two brief but separate typescript samples to himself in order to establish proof of authorship. On one of these pages, he noted that *The Masks* was "conceived in the year 1946, in April . . . an original psychological novel."

3 Touponce, introduction to Ray Bradbury's story collection *Masks* (Gauntlet, 2008), 11–14. Bradbury's responses to Modernism are also discussed in the introduction (largely laid out by Touponce) in Eller and Touponce, *The Life of Fiction* (2004). The general concept of Modernism in the arts is drawn from Martin Jay's "From Modernism to Postmodernism," chapter 10 of the *Oxford Illustrated History of Modern Europe*, edited by T. C. W. Blanning (New York: Oxford, 1996), 255–78.

4 One page of Bradbury's typescript contains a note identifying the edition of "Dover Beach" that he used as his source text—Louis Untermeyer's *Treasury of Great Poems*, (New York: Simon & Schuster, 1942).

5 Robert Heinlein, introduction to *The Best from Startling Stories*, ed. Sam Mines (New York: Holt, 1953), x.

6 Ray Bradbury, interview with the author, Oct. 2002.

7 Martha Foley, "Foreword," *The Best American Short Stories 1948* (Cambridge, Mass.: Houghton Mifflin, 1948), ix.

8 The single-page refashioned ending for *Masks* bears this tantalizing two-line note in the top margin: "suggested ending for this book: THE MASKS. | page 250:" No other pages are known.

Chapter 29. Modernist Alternatives

1 Ashley, *The Time Machines*, 190; Malcolm J. Edwards, "Thrilling Wonder Stories," in Clute and Nicholls, eds., *Encyclopedia of Science Fiction* (London, U.K.: Orbit, 1993), 1222–23.

2 Bradbury to Congdon, Apr. 18, 1955.

3 Jonathan Eller and William F. Touponce, *Ray Bradbury: The Life of Fiction* (Kent, Ohio: Kent State Univ., 2004), 11–50; David Mogen, *Ray Bradbury* (Boston: Twayne Publishers, 1986), chapters 4–6, 8.

Chapter 30. Finding His Own Way

1 Olmsted to Bradbury, Sept. 8, 1947; Snow to Bradbury, May 26, 1947.

2 Schaffner to Bradbury, May 9, 1947; MacCammond to Bradbury, Jan. 29, Feb. 4 and 18, and May 7, 1947.

3 Leiber to Bradbury, Feb. 1, [1948]. Leiber also felt that Bradbury's early enthusiasm for a wide range of visual and verbal humor sometimes interfered with the quality of his weird tales: "To sum up, it may be that your quick, sharp feeling for joke and irony may at times lead you astray in certain realistic tales which start off by suggesting a much larger world than can be explained by an ironic or humorous twist at the end (as a humorous story *can* be finished off)."

4 Bradbury to Derleth, Sept. 12, 1947.
5 Sturgeon to Bradbury, Mar. 5, 1948.
6 Congdon to Bradbury, Feb. 28, 1947.
7 Congdon to Bradbury, Sept. 6, 1946, and Apr. 10, 1947.

Chapter 31. The Anthology Game

1 Bradbury, interview with the author, Oct. 12, 2006.
2 Sturgeon's reaction to the final submitted introduction survives in a letter of Mar. 18, 1948: "It's just *fine*, Ray. It *is* good Bradbury, the kind I had hoped for from the start; the kind of bubblable stuff that I tried so hard to describe in my last letter to you. I'm not touching a thing in it."
3 Derleth to Bradbury, June 9, 1948; Bradbury to Derleth, June 11, 1948. Bradbury's file card with the final author list for *Curiouser and Curiouser* is dated Mar. 29, 1949.
4 Bradbury to Congdon, draft, Dec. 30, 1948; Derleth to Bradbury, Jan. 3, 1949.

Chapter 32. Paradise Postponed

1 John Troy Sternwood, "Ray Bradbury: An Appraisal," in *Spearhead* (Aug. 1948): 17–18; Bradbury, interview with R. Walton Williams, "The Market Is Not the Story," *Writers' Markets & Methods*, Mar. 1948 (rptd. *Shangri-LA* 8 (Conference Edition, Sept.–Oct. 1948): 10–13.
2 Helen King (for William Morrow, Inc.), Feb. 6 and May 13, 1948; Charles Addams to Bradbury, Feb. 16, 1948; Derleth to Bradbury, Apr. 7 and June 9, 1948; Congdon to Bradbury, May 25, 1948; Bradbury to Derleth, June 7, 1948.
3 Bradbury to Derleth, Oct. 15, 1948.
4 Two draft content lists of the 1948–49 *Illustrated Man* collection concept survive in the Albright Collection; the title page of the formal submission of stories also survives, dated Dec. 8, 1948, along with a listing of twenty-two stories updated on Mar. 29, 1949, just before the Farrar-Straus rejection. Seven of these stories were Martian tales, both sold and unsold.

Chapter 33. Broadening Horizons

1 Bradbury, "Report on Stories With Don—June—1949."
2 Stebel, interview with the author, Santa Monica, Apr. 4, 2009.
3 Bradbury, interview with the author, Oct. 20, 2008.
4 Bradbury to Hamilton and Bradbury to Williamson, both Aug. 3, 1949.
5 Bradbury, transcript of questionnaire answers provided on tape for Dean Robert G. Franke, University of Arkansas, Little Rock, February 1982; courtesy of Deb Dewick and the Albright Collection.
6 Bradbury, "The Watching and the Waiting" (unpublished; composed 1958).
7 A thinly veiled critique of Algren's *The Man with the Golden Arm* appears in his typescript essay "How I Wrote My Book," a presentation on *The Martian Chronicles* dated Oct. 17, 1950.

8 Derleth dated July 4, 1949.

9 Sturgeon had expressed his warning more than a year earlier: "Ray, these people are, whether they recognize it or not, motivated by a strange and even force which looks like a monumental trowel, which travels ponderously back and forth over the unset concrete of humanity, driving down any peak or height to the level of the rest of the mass" (Sturgeon to Bradbury, Mar. 5, 1948).

10 Bradbury to Hamilton and Brackett, June 8, 1949.

11 Bradbury to Congdon, Apr. 16, 1958. Bradbury's note card file lists the titles he brought to New York, including a two-act dramatic version of "Way in the Middle of the Air."

12 Bradbury to Derleth, July 4, 1949.

13 Bradbury, interview with the author, Oct. 22, 2008 and Oct. 24, 2010; Weller, 159.

14 Congdon to Bradbury, Oct. 7, 1949. Congdon used the lesson of the June trip to bring home the point he had been making for months in his earlier letters: "From talking to you while you were in New York, I could see that the endless number of stories you have in your head and which excite you and drive you are jammed up against a very high ideal of yours for literary perfection. Not for a second do I think you should sacrifice your own sense of artistic perfection, but as I hope you saw clearly last June the magazines and most of the book publishers put very little appreciation on this count *when it comes to the difference between acceptance and rejection*. Consequently on the majority of stories and projects you do, I think you should strive to free yourself of the perfectionistic reins you hold on yourself, let the stories get away from you more easily" [emphasis Congdon's].

Chapter 34. The Miracle Year: Winter and Spring

1 Bradbury to Frederic Dannay, July 22, 1948.

2 Bradbury to Derleth, May 18, 1950; Bradbury to Hamilton and Brackett, June 8, 1950.

3 The original is preserved in the Albright Collection.

4 Bradbury's Feb. 18, 1952 letter to Tony Boucher offers the usually unspoken part of the *Chronicles* creative arc: "In 1944, I laid the plan for that book, did some of the early sketches and stories, put them in my file, forgot them. Then I went on with other Martian stories, unconsciously following a pattern. On occasion I revived interest in the *Chronicles en toto*." This reference to the *Chronicles en toto* would explain the occasional appearance of *The Martian Chronicles* in his working papers as a possible story collection title, and probably not as a novelized concept, prior to the New York trip of June 1949.

5 Bradbury to Congdon, July 29, 1960.

Chapter 35. The Miracle Year: Summer and Fall

1 Peter Parker, *Isherwood: A Life Revealed* (New York: Random House, 2004), 516, 534.

2 Bradbury, interview with the author, Oct. 23, 2010; Jonathan Eller and William F. Touponce, *Ray Bradbury: The Life of Fiction* (Kent, Ohio: Kent State Univ., 2004), 123–24; Weller, 164–65, 172–75. Bradbury's bookstore meeting with Isherwood happened not late in the spring (Weller), but on or about July 8, 1950 (Bradbury to Walt Bradbury, July 22, 1950).

3   Bradbury to Hamilton and Brackett, Mar. 30, 1951.

4   Heard to Bradbury, Nov. 4 and 13, 1950.

5   Lewis to Boucher, Feb. 5, 1953; Lewis to Joy Davidman, Dec. 22, 1953 (Wheaton College).

6   Eller and Touponce, *The Life of Fiction*, 124–25.

7   R. Bradbury to W. Bradbury, July 16, 1950 (Lilly); W. Bradbury to R. Bradbury, Sept. 6, 1950.

8   He was able to remove "The Concrete Mixer," but Hart-Davis removed "The Exiles" and "The Rocket Man." Bradbury reluctantly retained "The Visitor" and "No Particular Night or Morning" to maintain the size of the collection.

9   Bradbury to Boucher and McComas, undated (postmarked Sept. 23, 1950).

10 Circulation history and *Galaxy* negotiations draw on Bradbury to Boucher and McComas, undated (postmarked Sept. 21, 1950), Congdon to Bradbury, Sept. 21, Oct. 4 and 20, 1950, and Horace Gold to Bradbury, Oct. 30, 1950.

11 Congdon to Bradbury, Sept. 21, Oct. 20, Nov. 3 and 7, 1950.

12 Congdon to Bradbury, Oct. 20, Nov. 3 and 17, 1950, and Jan. 12, 1951.

13 Bradbury to Derleth, May 18, 1950.

Chapter 36. Critical Praise, Private Worries

1   A. S. Burack *(The Writer)* to Bradbury, Sept. 27, 1950, shows a strong determination to secure a Bradbury essay, but Burack's desire to limit the scope to genre-based techniques apparently led Bradbury to decline.

2   In developing this observation, I'm grateful to Professor William F. Touponce for long discussions on Isherwood and Modernism.

3   Bradbury noted that Bantam's removal of the *Chronicles* editorial passage happened "after I had written them a letter blasting their hides off for conjuring up a 'quote' like that" (quoted back to Bradbury in Oscar Shaftel to Bradbury, July 2, 1953). See Jonathan Eller and William F. Touponce, *Ray Bradbury: The Life of Fiction* (Kent, Ohio: Kent State Univ., 2004), 127–29.

4   Bradbury to Derleth, May 28, 1950.

5   R. Bradbury to Maggie Bradbury, May 3, May 4 [misdated June 4], May 6, and [May 12], 1951.

Chapter 37. New York, 1951

1   Congdon to Bradbury, May 25, 1994.

2   Bradbury to Hamilton and Brackett, Mar. 30, 1951.

3   Frederic Brown to Bradbury, Dec. 2, 1952; Kuttner to Bradbury, Dec. 15, 1952.

4   Congdon interviews (1969; Albright Collection), 2.83.

Chapter 38. Controversial Fictions

1   Bradbury, interview by Donn Albright (for the author), Mar. 31, 2003.

2   Bradbury, interview with the author, Oct. 2, 2004.

3 Bradbury, interview with the author, Mar. 14, 2002; Congdon to Bradbury, Dec. 1951; Bradbury to William F. Nolan, Mar. 4, 1952.

4 *Mademoiselle* (Margarita Smith) to the Harold Matson Agency (Don Congdon), Sept. 13 and Dec. 28, 1950.

5 Congdon to Bradbury, Jan. 2, 1951.

Chapter 39. New Worlds

1 Bradbury to Boucher, Feb. 18, 1952.

2 Bradbury, interview with the author, Oct. 10, 2005; Bradbury to Congdon, Dec. 24, 1958.

3 Bradbury to Tony Boucher, Aug. 21, 1950.

4 The now-famous aphorism first appeared in the Nov. 20, 1920, issue of the Madrid magazine *Spain* as "Si te dan papel rayado, escribe de través. Sería travesura." A literal translation is: "If they give you ruled paper, write across. It would be mischief" (courtesy of Rocío Bejarano Alvarez, Centro de Estudios Juanramonianos, and Lisa King, Indiana University School of Medicine). It's not clear how Bradbury's translation evolved.

5 Bradbury has always insisted that the dinner occurred on St. Valentine's night 1951, but most of the preview performances of *The Red Badge of Courage* occurred before that date. Given the range of previews reported by various Huston biographers (Nolan, Grobel, and Madsen), Bradbury's sense of the chronology may be accurate.

6 Congdon to Bradbury, Jan. 7, Feb. 26, Mar. 19, 1952.

7 Extensive excerpts from the Bradbury-Gaines correspondence appears with commentary in Jerry Weist's *Bradbury: An Illustrated Life* (New York: Morrow, 2002), 89–110. A complete photocopy set is in the Albright Collection.

8 Bradbury, interview with the author, Oct. 20, 2008.

9 Congdon to Bradbury, Mar. 26, May 29, June 4 and 26, July 2 and 10, 1952.

10 The *Bradbury Showcase* proposal is found in Congdon to Bradbury, May 29, 1952.

11 Congdon to Bradbury, Dec. 15, 1951, Jan. 25, Mar. 14 and 19, 1952.

Chapter 40. The Wheel of Fortune

1 Bradbury to Beaumont, Mar. 27, 1951 (Bradbury photocopy); Bradbury, Foreword to Beaumont's *The Magic Man* (Greenwich, Conn.: Gold Medal, 1965); Bradbury, interview with the author, Mar. 13, 2010.

2 Bradbury to Hamilton and Brackett, Mar. 7, 1950.

3 Bradbury to Hamilton and Brackett, June 25, 1951, Aug. 23, 1953.

4 Bradbury to Hamilton and Brackett, June 25, 1951.

Chapter 41. Joe Mugnaini and *The Golden Apples of the Sun*

1 Bradbury and Mugnaini memories differ to some degree; see Weller, 188fn.

2 Bradbury, "Joe Mugnaini," an unpublished promotional essay, Jan. 18, 1953: 6.

3 Bradbury to Ben Benjamin, cc, undated (c. Nov.–Dec. 1960).

4 Bradbury, interview with the author, Oct. 24, 2007.

5 W. Bradbury to R. Bradbury, July 12, 1951: "Facile sentimentality is the one thing you have to be very careful to avoid in this book; it must be warm but not corny, nostalgic but not maudlin."

6 R. Bradbury to W. Bradbury, Mar. 13, 1952 (carbon; Albright Collection).

7 Bradbury is quoted in Janice Lovoos, "Joseph Mugnaini: A Spirited Draughtsman," *American Artist*, Mar. 1963: 22–27.

8 Bradbury, "Joe Mugnaini," 8.

9 Jason Epstein, *Book Business: Publishing Past Present and Future* (New York: Norton, 2001), 39–40.

Chapter 42. Bantam and Ballantine

1 Congdon to Bradbury, Aug. 8, 1952.

2 Tom Carter (Washington and Lee University) to Bradbury, Dec. 20, 1952.

Chapter 43. Hollywood at Last

1 Bradbury, interviews with the author, Apr. 4 and 7, 2009.

2 Bradbury, interview with the author, Oct. 21, 2002.

3 Bradbury to Hamilton and Brackett, Mar. 30, 1951, [Nov. 1951].

4 Bradbury, interview with Lawrence French, Walt Disney Studios, 1983 (www.wellesnet .com).

5 Congdon to Bradbury, Aug. 29, 1952; Bradbury, interview with the author, Palm Springs, Oct. 12, 1998; UCLA Oral History interview (1962): 103–6; Weller, 189–90.

6 Bradbury's Universal Studio experience is condensed and revised from my essay, "Bradbury's Web of Fear," in *It Came from Outer Space* (Colorado Springs: Gauntlet, 2004): 27–41.

7 Bradbury, "A Few Notes on Film Writing," Oct. 1952, 5 (unpublished).

8 Ibid., 2.

9 An eight-page opening for Bradbury's *Chrysalis* screen treatment, dated Aug. 1952, survives in the Albright Collection.

10 Eller, introductory note to *Face of the Deep*, included in lettered issue of Bradbury's *It Came from Outer Space* (Gauntlet, 2002); Fox Studio (Mathilde Moser) to Bradbury, Sept. 8, 1953.

Chapter 44. Political Controversy

1 Bradbury, interviews with the author, Palm Springs, Oct. 12, 1998 and Los Angeles, Oct. 19, 2008; Sid Stebel, interview with the author, Santa Monica, Apr. 4, 2009.

2 Bradbury to Hamilton and Brackett, Mar. 30, 1951.

3 William F. Nolan, *Bradbury Companion* (Detroit: Gale, 1975), 59.

4 Bradbury's account of the demonizing of the Democratic Party is summarized in "Mr. Bradbury Talks Back," the editorial header to the *Nation's* Nov. 29, 1952 reprinting of Bradbury's "To the Republican Party."

5 Bradbury, "How I Wrote My Book," Oct. 17, 1950.

6 Bradbury, interview with Donn Albright (for the author), Mar. 31, 2003.

Chapter 45. *Fahrenheit 451*

1 Mugnaini estate historian Ryan Leasher made the connection between Mugnaini's 1950 newspaper-clad Diogenes illustration and the 1953 *Fahrenheit 451* cover art (Leasher to Touponce, Dec. 12, 2008 email exchange). Touponce has noted that Bradbury's choice of Quixote as a model for the jacket art forms a significant literary bridge to the Cervantes chapter where Quixote's library is burned by his persecutors.

2 W. Bradbury to R. Bradbury, May 6, 1953.

3 The *Bradbury Showcase* negotiations played out in Congdon to Bradbury, Jan. 8, Mar. 10, Apr. 1, May 25, June 3, July 8 and 29, Aug.6, Nov. 6 and 20, and Dec. 17, 1953.

4 The history of final composition and presswork revision is preserved in Ballantine to Bradbury, June 18 and 30, July 24 (telegram), 1953; Kauffmann to Bradbury, July 9 and 12, 1953; and Bradbury, interview with the author, Oct. 2004.

5 Jonathan Eller and William F. Touponce, *Ray Bradbury: The Life of Fiction* (Kent, Ohio: Kent State Univ., 2004), 195–96.

6 Joe Mugnaini, interview with Gene Beley, Altadena, Calif., Sept. 6, 1982.

Chapter 46. The Last Night of the World

1 Breit, Harvey, "A Talk with Mr. Bradbury," *New York Times Book Review*, Aug. 5, 1951.

2 Bradbury, interview with the author, Mar. 14, 2002.

3 Bradbury, interviews with the author, Mar. 14, 2002 and Oct. 20, 2008. "The Fog Horn" (published in the *Saturday Evening Post* as "The Beast From 20,000 Fathoms) was written in the spring of 1949; "A Sound of Thunder" and "A Scent of Sarsaparilla" probably date from the Winter-Spring of 1951.

4 John Fowles, "Notes on an Unfinished Novel," in *Afterwords*, ed. Thomas McCormack (New York: Harper & Row, 1969), 137. Gene Beley, email with the author, 2008.

5 Damon Knight, "When I Was in Knee-Pants: Ray Bradbury," from *In Search of Wonder*, 109. Originally from Knight's review of *The Illustrated Man* in *Science Fiction Quarterly* 1.2 (Feb. 1953) 81.

Index

with, 259–60; and Bradbury's rights, 276; *Dark Carnival*, 276, 290; *Fahrenheit 451*, 275, 276, 277, 284

Balmer, Edwin, *When Worlds Collide*, 107

Baltadonis, John, *Science Fiction Collector*, editor of, 30

Bantam, Ballantine: and Bradbury's works, 287; and "The Creatures That Time Forgot," 216; founder of, 217; and *The Illustrated Man*, 223; and *The Martian Chronicles*, 214, 215, 223; Merril, house editor of, 217; *Timeless Stories for Today and Tomorrow*, Bradbury's anthology, 216–17, 221, 257, 259

Bards, 199, 246

Barrows, George: *Circle*, cover illustrator for, 135; *Dark Carnival*, his cover for, 135–36

Battle for Siberia, The, 55, 56

Beach, Grant, 121, 122–23, 124, 126; Bradbury's mail, 129; Bradbury's typewriter, 125, 132; ceramics studio, 83; critiques Bradbury, 118; his mother's tenement 53, 54, 55, 120; Mexico, 104–5, 119, 167; and Nielson, 103

Beaumont, Charles, 263; Bradbury correspondence with, 245–46; his writing, Bradbury critiqued, 245; *Twilight Zone*, writer for, 246

Beley, Gene, 285

Benjamin, Ben, 251; and Congdon, 263; and Famous Artists Agency, 233; represents Bradbury, 233, 263; "To the Republican Party," reaction to, 269

Berenson, Bernard, 109, 288

Bergson, Henri: *Creative Evolution*, 202; *Time and Free Will*, 114–15

Berrara, Eddie, and *Imagination!* 26

Best American Short Stories 1948: "The Cape," 187; "I See You Never," 186, 194; "The Lilacs," 187; "Reconciliation," 187;

"The Tragedy in Jancie Brierman's Life," 187

Best American Short Stories of 1952, 240; "The Other Foot," 240

Beyond Time and Space (ed. Derleth): "Colossus" (Wandrei), 13; "Fessenden's Worlds" (Hamilton), 13; "The Revolt of the Pedestrians" (Keller), 13;

Bezzerides, Buzz, *Beneath the Twelve-Mile Reef*, screenplay for, 267

Binder, Otto (Eando), 31; WorldCon, 30

Blake, William, "Piper," 85, 86

Blixen, Karen (pseud. Isak Dinesen), 78

Bloch, Robert, Bradbury, 1; and Bradbury's anthology outline, 41; Bradbury visits, 137; correspondence with, 188; his writing, 153, 182–83; suggestions for Bradbury, 183, 225

Bok, Hans (Hannes): Bradbury, friendship with, 21, 22, 143–44; Bradbury shops drawings for, 28, 30–31; and fairy tales, 22; and *Futuria Fantasia*, 33, 37, 38, 40; his artwork, 42, 142–43; his artwork, Bradbury, correspondence with, 188; his career and Bradbury, 32; his cover art, 143; Hugo Award, 32; "Lorelei," his art inspiration for, 22–23, 38; and Parrish, Maxfield, 22, 143; and romantic aesthetic, 21; and *Weird Tales*, 30–31, 32; his writing method, 142–43, 145, 153

Bond, Nelson, his *Blue Book* series, 115; Bradbury reads, 75; science fiction, his humor in, 47; WorldCon, 30

Boucher, Anthony, 207, 240, 255, 300; and *Magazine of Fantasy & Science Fiction*, 207, 212, 264; *The Martian Chronicles*, and proofs of, 208; review of, 221

Brackett, Leigh, 99, 229, 268, 295; *Astounding Science Fiction*, stories in, 67; *The Big Sleep*, her screenplay for, 65, 69, 82, 110, 169; Bradbury, correspondence with, 247; Bradbury, friendship with, 68, 246–47; Bradbury reads, 75, 169; Bradbury's mentor, 67, 68–69, 73, 86, 110; "Child of the Green Light," 69; "The Demons of Darkside," 69; Hamilton, her husband, 69; "Interplanetary Reporter," 69; and Kuttner, 67; "Lorelei of the Red Mist" (with Bradbury), 69, 110–11; and the Mañana Literary Society, 43; and Moorcock, 68–69; *No Good from a Corpse*, 169; and *Planet Stories*, 68; recommended reading for Bradbury, 64, 65; and the Science Fiction League (LA chapter), 67; and screenwriting, 68, 110, 263–264; and "The Scythe," 94; "The Sorcerer of Rhiannon," 69; "The Stellar Legion," 69; suggestions for Bradbury, 180; and *The Vampire's Ghost*, 116; "A World is Born," 69

Bradbury, Esther Moberg (Bradbury's mother), 10, 14, 157

Bradbury, Leo(nard Sr) (Bradbury's father), 10, 13–14

Bradbury, Leonard Jr "Skip," (Bradbury's brother), 10, 53; his relationship with his brother, 157–58

Bradbury, Marguerite "Maggie" (Mc-Clure): Bradbury, engagement to, 134; Bradbury, relationship with, 131–32; Bradbury's wife, 65; her career, 159; her love of reading, 131–32; mentioned, 140

Bradbury, Ray: and acting, 40; and adaptation, 11; alcohol, discusses affects of, 102; anecdotes of, 5–6, 9–10, 14; anxiety, 1, 100; art, his appreciation for, 83; authorship, sense of, 14, 259; his birth, memories of, 9; California, life in, 14; and childhood, 100, 384; and the cinema, 14, 55, 170, 233, 241, 261; diary entries, 20, 24, 233; and, education 11–12, 108; Europe, visits,

284; fairy tales, 22; and faith, 105–6, 282–83; and family dynamics, 10; and fanzine contributions, 27–28; the future, 281; and genre pulps, 3; genre reading, 13; *Herald and Express*, sold, 21; and Hollywood, 16; homosexuality, discusses, 102; interviews, 2, 4, 20; and intuition, 2; and libraries, 14; his line-art drawings, 18; and literary labels, 60; literature, feelings on, 2; Los Angeles High School, 16, 71; manuscripts, 6; Mars, interest in, 17; McClure, Marguerite, his wife, 65; and Mexico, 3, 104–5, 118; *Moby Dick*, screenplay of, 4, 101, 284, 285; and Modernist novel-length fiction, 4; and music for films, 56; a neo-Romantic, 86; his notes, 17, 28, 29; perfection, 1, 4; and the performing arts, 40; plagiarize his work, people, 241, 242; as a prose stylist, 4; and psychology, 99, 100, 101, 108, 202; and race, 112, 233–35, 236–37; reading, passion for, 14; religious experiences, 24; and religious faith, 23–24, 282–83; romantic aesthetic, 21; his science fiction cautionary, 281; as a short-story writer, 3, 4, 10; and society, 67; space, beginning interest in, 17; and space travel, 17; and story drafts, 1; Technocracy, disillusioned by, 38–39; and Technocracy Inc., 34; and the Technocracy movement, 33, 34, 53; and time travel, 17; truth, seeker of, 3; his vision, 12, 53, 82–83; visits, New York City, 29–31, 137, 203–04, 208, 227–29; visits Chicago, 137–38; and Waukegan, 138, 160, 177, 233; Waukegan's Central School, 11; West, his move out, 14

—(Books), *Dandelion Wine* (Green town stories), 15, 127; and "The Magical Kitchen," 227; and "At Midnight, in the

Month of June," 178; and *Farewell Summer*, 148; and "Green Wine for Dreaming," 164; and "The Tarot Witch," 164; and "The Whole Town is Sleeping" (vt "Summer Night"), 164, 177, 178; *Dark Carnival*, 3–4, 29, 76, 91, 127, 129–30, 133, 135–36, 140, 145, 193–94, 249–50, 290; *Death is a Lonely Business*, 54, 96, 199; *Fahrenheit 451*, and "The Fireman," 4, 90,169, 206, 215–16, 221, 224, 239, 243, 260, 261, 271, 272, 273, 274, 277, 282, 287; 275; and "The Playground," 277, 278; and public opinion, 278; and revisions for, 279; and a sociological study, 281; and temperature paper burns at, 275; mentioned, 4, 66, 89, 90, 92, 101, 106, 168, 169, 206, 241, 273; *Farewell Summer*, 127, 161; *The Golden Apples of the Sun*, 255, 257, 259, 271, 275–76; and "The Playground," 253; *A Graveyard for Lunatics*, 199; *The Halloween Tree*, 119, 120, 123, 167; *The Illustrated Man*, and "The City" (vt "Purpose"), 208; and "The Concrete Mixer," 214, 301; and "The Fire Balloons," 213, 215, 224; and framing used for, 221; and "The Highway," 199, 227, 237; and "The Illustrated Man, 180, 208; and "The Long Rain," 208, 262; and "No Particular Night or Morning," 208, 214; and "The Other Foot," 112, 236, 237, 240; and "The Playground," 215; and reception for, 222; and reviews for, 223–24; and "The Rocket Man," 224, 242, 301; mentioned, 72, 134, 174, 195–96, 198, 206, 208, 241, 252, 299; *Let's All Kill Constance!* 199; *The Machineries of Joy*, 230; *Masks*, 166–68; 166–67, 170, 182, 235, 298; *The Martian Chronicles*, and "And the Moon Be Still As Bright," 156, 174, 175; and "The Earth Men," 156, 174, 243; and "The Long Years," 156,

174, 243, 282; and "Mars is Heaven!" 156, 174; and "The Martian," 174; and "The Million Year Picnic," 96, 155, 156; and "The Off-Season," 174, 175; and proofs of, 208; and reviews of, 214, 221–22; and "The Silent Towns," 139; and *The Silver Locusts*, 207; and "There Will Come Soft Rains," 206; and "The Third Expedition," 174; and typescript for, 206, 236; and "Usher II," 213, 215; and "The Wheel," 236; and "Ylla," 174; mentioned, 4, 32, 72, 73, 96, 106, 112, 134, 156, 166, 205, 300, 301; *A Medicine for Melancholy*, 61; *The October Country*, 105, 148; *One More for the Road*, 239; *S Is for Space*, 72; *Something Wicked This Way Comes*, 11, 15, 88, 96, 138, 148, 160, 162–64, 167, 173, 251; *Summer Morning, Summer Night*, 127, 195, 243; *Where Ignorant Armies Clash by Night*, 66, 168–70, 172, 182, 215, 293;

—(Editor): *Curiouser and Curiouser*, 190; development as an, 36, 37, 40; early attempts at, 26; and the future, 34, 35; *Futuria Fantasia* (FuFa), 23, 34, 35, 40; *Timeless Stories for Today and Tomorrow*, 216–17, 221, 257

—(Nonfiction): "Author, Author," 64, 292; "Author's Note," 42, 291; "As I Remember," 31, 291; "Day after Tomorrow: Why Science Fiction?," 272, 273; "Dark Carnival Revisited," 119, 295; "A Few Notes on *The Martian Chronicles*," 84, 293; "Henry Kuttner: A Neglected Master," 64, 292, 293; "How I Wrote My Book," 270, 303; "Introduction: Alive and Kicking and Writing," 119, 295; "John Collier Probes the Darker Regions," 80, 293; "Leigh Brackett and Edmond Hamilton: My Great Loves, My Great Teachers, My Great Friends," 159, 297; "Mexicali Mirage," 105; "Monday

Night In Green Town," 10–11; "Report on Stories With Don-June-1949," 198, 299; "To the Republican Party," 269, 303; "Wells: His Crystal Ball Was Crystal Clear," 48, 291; What Can a Writer Say," 100, 294

—(Poetry): "god in small letters," 57; in *Imagination!* 18; Los Angeles poetry annual, 20; "My Typewriter Wife," 58; "Satan's Mistress," 37; unpublished, 57

—(Radio): "Bang! You're Dead!" 140; "The Ducker," 140; "Killer, Come Back to Me!"115, 129; "The Meadow," 141, 168, 195, 253; mentioned, 14–15; "The Miracles of Jamie," 179; "The Night," 179; "One Timeless Spring," 179; "Powerhouse," 179; "Riabouchinska," 137, 160; "To the Future," 277; "The Visitor," 277

—(Stories): and adapting, 115; "All Summer in a Day," 148; "A Matter of Taste," 263–64; "And the Rock Cried Out," 237–38, 253, 277, 278; "And Watch the Fountains," 71, "Asleep in Armageddon," 69, 174, 290; "The Beast from 20,000 Fathoms" (vt "The Fog Horn"), 229, 247, 255, 262, 283–84, 304; "The Big Black and White Game," 113, 116, 117, 129, 131, 139, 141, 171, 179, 185, 234, 235, 253; "The Black Ferris," 136, 155, 249, 250, 251; "A Blade of Grass," 174; "The Blue Bottle (vt "Death Wish"), 174; "The Bonfire," 238, 282; "The Candle," 46, 47, 93; "The Candy Skull," 123; "Carnival of Madness," 238 (vt Usher II); "Chrysalis" (1946), 72, 73, 96, 107, 111, 114, 155, 266, 303; "Chrysalis" (2004), 234, 235; "The Cistern," 138, 141, 179; "The City" (vt "Purpose"), 174; "The Coffin," 155; "The Creatures That Time Forgot" (vt "Frost and Fire"), 69, 114, 115, 155, 204, 208, 216, 274; "Cricket on the Hearth," 239; "The Crowd," 29, 96,100, 181; "Death Warmed Over," 2; "Death Wish" (vt "The Blue Bottle"), 174; "Defense Mech," 69; "Don't Get Technatal," 34; "Doodad," 47, 71, 111; "The Dragon," 227; "The Ducker," 100; "The Dwarf," 248; "Eat, Drink, and Be Wary," 46, 71; "El Dia De Muerte," 154; "Embroidery," 227, 253, 282; "The Emissary," 57, 242; "The Exiles" (vt "The Mad Wizards of Mars"), 189, 198, 207, 238, 301; "Fever Dream," 155; "The Fight of the Good Ship Clarissa," 37; "Final Victim," 45, 47, 290; "A Flight of Ravens," 229–30, 270; "The Flying Machine," 253; "Forever and the Earth," 227; "Frost and Fire" (vt "The Creatures That Time Forgot"), 69, 115; "Gabriel's Horn," 45; "The Garbage Collector," 256, 270–71; "The Golden Apples of the Sun," 252–53, 256; "The Golden Kite, the Silver Wind," 253, 256, 260; "The Great Fire," 253; "The Handler," 199, 242; "Hail and Farewell," 148; "Holiday," 174, 282; "Hollerbochen Comes Back," 27; "Hollerbochen's Dilemma," 18, 27; "[The] Homecoming," 127, 138–39, 153, 179, 193; "Interim," 154; "Interval in Sunlight," 87, 176–77; "The Invisible Boy," 96, 117, 121, 126, 127, 129, 133, 253; "I See You Never," 54, 160, 185, 253; "It's Not the Heat, It's the Hu-," 43; "The Jar," 9, 126; "Kaleidoscope," 242; "King of the Gray Spaces," 57, 113, 155; "The Lake," 56, 78, 96, 113, 116, 126, 131, 142; "The Last Night of the World," 203, 282; "The Last, the Very Last," 164; "Lazarus Come Forth," 69; "The Lonely One," 41; "The Long Night," 55, 94; "Lorelei of the Red Mist" (with Brackett), 69, 110–11; "The

Corpse Are U," 96; writer's narrative, 23–24; "A Young Writer I Know" (lecture), 200

—(Working titles): "The Baby," 164; *The Blue Remembered Hills,* 164; "The Children's Hour, 148; *A Child's Garden of Terror,* 135, 148; "The Dark Carnival," 136; "Eight-Day World," 69, 114; *The Illinois Chronicles,* working title, 224–26, 228, 232, 251–52, 257, 277, 284, 285; *The Winds of Time,* 164

—writing, art of, 63, 143; author, nature of, 59, 259; and characterization, 63; and conscious and unconscious mind, 63; and his creative unconscious, 61; and creativity, 23, 24, 57; and criticism, 59; development of, 19, 68, 19; editorial, 41; and ethics, 92; fantasy, 81, 149, 258–59; first major period, 3; and generating ideas for, 74; graphic adaptations of, 241–43; and his grammar and usage, 29; guest lecturer of, 199–200; and the human experience, 99; and his humor, 41, 43, 47; and imagination, 34, 48; imitation of others, 16; and inner realism, 177; and literary reading, 59, 64, 74; and memory, 24, 56–57, 62; and metaphor, 37, 53, 58, 75, 88; and Modernists themes, 166, 170, 171, 176, 179, 254; and morals in, 92; narrative, 24, 149; and his narrative voice, 28–29, 53, 56, 110; and novel-length, 224–25, 385; and observation, 24, 48; and openness, 11; and perfection, 142, 145; and personal style, 3, 25; and polemics, 285; and the powerhouse, 132–33, 158, 176, 282; prewriting strategies, 48; process of, 62, 63; and recognition for, 103; his regimen for, 48, 53, 55; and reverie, 60, 62, 149; reviews of, 18; revision, process of, 1, 384–85; his rights to, 243; and his science fiction, 68; and slanting, 42, 60,

90, 94; his style, 47, 48, 75; and typing, 14, 57–58; and the unhappy ending, 170–71; and viewpoint, 72, 73; and vocabulary, 29; writing about, 63, 286

Bradbury, Sam(uel) (Bradbury's brother), 10

Bradbury, Walter: Bradbury, friendship with, 214; on Bradbury's Martian stories, 204, 209; and Bradbury's rights over his works, 276; Bradbury's three-novella collection, 227, 232, 274; and Doubleday, 204, 216; and the *Golden Apples* stories, 255; and *The Illinois Chronicles,* 228, 229, 251–52; and "The Illustrated Man," 208, 213–14; *The Illustrated Man,* 232; mentioned, 260

Bradbury Index (Nolan), 245

Brande, Dorothea: *Becoming a Writer,* 23, 48, 61, 292; influences Bradbury, 48, 63; and prose writing, 64; and reverie, 62, 254; and the unconscious, 62, 95

Brandeis University's National Women's Committee (Los Angeles Chapter), "No Man Is an Island," 271, 272, 273

Breit, Harvey: interviews Bradbury, 229, 232; *New York Times,* literary columnist for, 229

Brickell, Hirschell, and "Homecoming," 139, 153, 185–87

Bronowski, Jacob, *Face of Violence,* 202

Brooks, Richard, *The Brick Foxhole,* 102

Buchanan, Montgomery, 144; *Weird Tales,* associate editor for, 93, 140

Burnett, Whit, 127; *Story Magazine,* editor of, 117, 127; *The Story Press,* 127

Burroughs, Edgar Rice: Bradbury's imitation of, 16; influences Bradbury, 42, 86; John Carter of Mars character, 12, 14; and "lost race" novels, 21; *Tarzan of the Apes,* 12; *The Warlord of Mars,* 14

Burton, Russ, 246, 268; and *Copy,* 199; "Why We Care," 199

"The Man Wizards of Mars," 198; "Ylla," 198

Maddow, Ben, 187, 270; *The Asphalt Jungle*, cowriter on script for, 188; *Intruder in the Dust*, 187–88; "The Lilacs," 187

Mademoiselle: and Capote, 128; "The Cistern," 138, 141; Davis, fiction editor of, 128, 141, 195; "Homecoming," 128; "Invisible Boy," 117, 121, 126, 127, 129, 195; Smith, assistant fiction of, 128, 141, 179, 181, 228, 238; "Ylla," 156, 181–82

'Madge. See *Imagination!*

Madle, Robert, *Fantascience Digest*, editor of, 30

Magazine of Fantasy & Science Fiction: and Aymé, 241; and Boucher, 207, 212; "The Exiles," 207; and McComas, 207; "Tiger, Tiger, Burning Bright," 239

Mañana Literary Society, 43, 66

Mann, Thomas: *Death in Venice*, 84; *Mario and the Magician*, 84

Margulies, Leo, WorldCon, 30

Marvel Science Stories, and Erisman, 31

Matheson, Richard, 245; *Twilight Zone*, writer for, 246

Maugham, W[illiam] Somerset, 59–61, 176, 212; and entropic process, 60; and narrative, 87, 88; and naturalism, 60; *The Painted Veil*, 87, 88; praises Bradbury, 61; and reverie, 60–61, 62; *The Summing Up*, 59, 60, 87, 292; his writing, morals in, 88

McCalls: "Summer Night," 243; "The Whole Town's Sleeping," 177

McComas, J. Francis, 207–8; and *Magazine of Fantasy & Science*, 207, 264; *The Martian Chronicles*, review of, 221

McCoy, Esther, 187

McCullers, Carson, 138

McIlwraith, Dorothy, *Weird Tales*, editor of, 93

McWilliams, Carey, 271, 272

Merril, Judith: Bantam, 259; house editor for, 217; *Shot in the Dark*, 217

Merritt, Abe, 14; and *American Weekly*, 31; and "lost race" novels, 21

Merwin, Sam Jr, 230; *The Martian Chronicles*, review of, 221; and *Thrilling Wonder Stories*, 155, 175–76, 228

Metropolis, 30

Mexico, 3, 104–5, 118, 119, 176; and the art work of, Orosco, Siqueiros, and Rivera, 121; Church of the Blessed Virgin, 121; Emperor Maximilian's Palace, 120; Guanajuato, mummies of, 122, 123–24, 138, 177; "Mexicali Mirage," 105; Mexico City, 120; poverty in, 121, 124; and racial bias, 121; Tarascan Indian Culture, 122; "That Old Dog Lying in the Dust," 105; Vera Cruz, 120; Zimapan, 119, 120, 124

Meynel, Alice, 65

Mikros, "Hollerbochen Comes Back," 27

Minnelli, Vincente, *The Beast from 20,000 Fathoms*, film adaptation, 262

Moby Dick, screenplay, and Bradbury, 4, 101, 284, 288

Mogen, David, 206

Mollé Mystery Theatre: "Killer, Come Back to Me!" 115–16, 129; Telford, director of, 115–16

Moorcock, Michael, 68–69, 293

Moore, C[atherine] L[ucille] "Kat," 73, 75, 246; and *Astounding Science Fiction*, 71; and Bradbury's anthology outline, 41; Kuttner, her husband, 47, 70, 101

Morley, Christopher, 88; *Thunder on the Left*, 87–88, 160–61, 162, 164, 297

Morris, Edita, 78

Moskowitz, Sam, 30

Mugnaini, Joseph: artist, 249; Bradbury, collaboration with, 250–56, 279; Bradbury on, 249, 254, 258; on Bradbury's works, 254; "The Caravan," 249, 250; and *Dark Carnival*, 249, 250, 251; *Fahren-*

Poe, Edgar Allen, 42, 86, 222; *Tales of Mystery*, 201

Pohl, Fred: *Astounding*, editor of, 42; a Futurian, 30, 42; *The Martian Chronicles*, review of, 221; represents Bradbury, 41–42; *Super Science*, editor of, 42

politics, 4, 106, 233–34, 270; and cultural criticism, 273; and Eisenhower, 269; and libraries, 271–72; and McCarthy, 268, 269; and "No Man Is an Island," 271, 272, 273, 283; and political parties, 269; and Stevenson, 268–69

Pope, Alexander, 60

Popular Publications, 42; and *Dime Mystery*, 94; *New Detective*, 94; Norton, editorial director of, 95; *Weird Tales*, 93

Porter, Katherine Anne, 64, 76, 78; *Flowering Judas*, 76, 140; *The Learning Tower*, 76

Pratt, Fletcher, 203, 222–23; *The Martian Chronicles*, review of, 222

Priestly, J[ohn] B[oynton], 212

Prokosch, Frederic, 42, 85; *The Asiatics*, 84–85, 293; and fatalism, 85; his dark ages, 85; Modernist, 86; and nihilism, 85; *The Seven Who Fled*, 84, 86

Prozine(s), 31, 41–43

Quinn, Seabury, 41

Radio City Playhouse (NBC), 207; and "The Lake," 229; "The Wind," 229

Rand, Ayn, *The Fountainhead*, 88–89, 90, 92, 113, 294

Ray Bradbury: The Life of Fiction (Eller and Touponce), 136, 296–301

Ray Bradbury Review, The (Nolon), 245

Reporter, The, "The Pedestrian," 239

Rhodomagnetic Digest, 208, 209, 293

Rhymer, Paul, *Vic and Sade*, 15, 115

Rocklynne, Ross, 31; "The Best Ways to Get Around," 37; "Into the Darkness" series, 65–66; "Promotion to Satellite," critiqued, 65; "The Wind," critiqued, 65, 66; WorldCon, 30

Rolfe, Sam, 263

Rose, Stuart, *Saturday Evening Post*, editor of, 206, 229

Rothman, Milton, 30

Roundup: The Stories of Ring Lardner, 76

Rousseau, Jean-Jacques, 84

Rue Morgue No. 1, and "The Watchers," 126, 140

Rupert, Corad, and WorldCon, 29

Russell, Bertrand, *A History of Western Philosophy*, 114

Rylands, George, *William Shakespeare: The Ages of Man*, 76–77

San Francisco Chronicle: and Fabun's review of Bradbury, 221; *The Golden Apples of the Sun*, Fabun's review of, 255; "Time, Space and Literature" (Fabun), 222

Saturday Evening Post, 41; "The Beast From 20,000 Fathoms" (vt "The Fog Horn), 229, 247, 262; "The Long Years," 156; Rose, editor of, 206, 229; "The World the Children Made" (vt The Veldt), 206, 229

Saturday Review of Literature, 76, 77, 222; Cousins, editor of, 77

Schaffner, John, and *Good Housekeeping*, 180

Schmitt, Gladys, "All Souls'," 78

Schorer, Mark, 171

Schwartz, Julius "Julie," 29, 44, 77; and Bradbury's, 243; Bradbury's agent, 31, 42, 126, 142; and Bradbury's works, 47, 56, 71, 95, 116, 163; critiqued Bradbury, 65; and DC comics, 139; and fanzines, 26

Schweitzer, Darrell, 147

Science Fiction, Hornig, founder of, 29

Van Druten, John, 211
Van Vogt, A[lfred] E[lton], 101; and *Astounding Science Fiction*, 47, 71; *The Weapon Makers*, 71; "The Weapon Shop," 71
Vidor, King, 261
Vincent, Harl, WorldCon, 30

Wagner, Rob, and *Script*, 43
Wakeman, Frederic, *The Hucksters*, 141
Waller, Fred, 29, 30
Wandrei, Donald, "Colossus," 13;
Weinbaum, Stanley, "Martian Odyssey," 37
Weird Tales, 40–41, 70, 94, 140; "The Black Ferris," 155; and Bradbury's works for, 75, 90, 91, 93, 148, 196; "Bride of the Lightning," 13; Buchanan, associated editor of, 93, 140; "The Candle," 46, 47, 93; "Child of the Winds," 13; "Fever Dream," 155; McIlwraith, editor of, 93; "The Night," 160; and "The Pendulum," 37; "The Smiling People," 126, 296; "The Wind," 13; Wright, editor of, 30, 37, 93
Weisinger, Mort, 26; *Startling Stories*, 31; *Thrilling Wonder Stories*, editor of, 31, 47; WorldCon, 30
Weller, Sam, 291–92, 296–97, 300, 302–3
Welles, Orson, 182; and *Invasion From Mars*, 207
Wellman, Manly Wade, WorldCon, 30
Wells, H[erbert] G[eorge], 42, 48, 62, 67, 101, 212; *Invisible Man*, 48, 67, 107; and science fiction, 48; *The Shape of Things to Come*, 35; *Things to Come*, movie adaptation, 35
Welty, Eudora, 64, 76, 78; *The Curtain of Green*, 64, 76; *Golden Apple*, 201; *A Wide Net*, 76
Werfel, Franz, 77; *The Song of Bernadette*, 105
Wertham, Frederic: and comic book culture, 242; *Dark Legend*, 202; *Seduction of the Innocent*, 202, 242; *Show of Violence*, 202
West, Jessamyn, "The Illumination," 78
White, E[lwyn] B[rooks], 258; *One Man's Meat*, 77
Whittier, John Greenleaf, *Poems*, 201
Wilder, Thornton, *The Cabala*, 88
William Morrow, and *Dark Carnival*, 193–94
Williamson, Jack, 13, 44, 67, 107; and *Amazing*, 66; and *Astounding Science Fiction*, 47, 71; and "Black Symphony," 67; *Darker than You Think*, 66, 148; a Futurian, 30; *The Humanoids*, 201–2; and the Mañana Literary Society, 43, 66; WorldCon, 30
Wilson, Angus, 212; *The Illustrated Man*, review of, 224
Windsor, Kathleen, *Forever Amber*, 77
Wodehouse, P[elham] G[renville], 16
Wolfe, Thomas, 65; *Angel*, 42; *The Face of the Nation*, 76; and "Forever and the Earth," 227; *Look Homeward*, 42; *Of Time and the River*, 42; *The Web and the Rock*, 42
Wollheim, Donald A.: *Avon Fantasy Reader*, 153; *Cosmic Stories*, founder of, 42; a Futurian, 30, 42; and "Homecoming," 153; and "The Man Upstairs," 153; *Stirring Science Stories*, founder of, 42
Wonder Stories: becomes *Thrilling Wonder Stories*, 29; "The City of Singing Flame," 12; Hornig, editor of, 29; "The Master of the Asteroid" (Smith), 12; and the Science Fiction League, 18
Wood, Valentine, 12
Woodford, Jack, 21; *Trial and Error*, 16, 21, 143
Woodward, Van, "Mars is Heaven!" and a musical version of, 228, 229, 243
Woolrich, Cornell: *Black Alibi*, 79; "Dime a Dance," 79; *Rendezvous in Black*, 79

WorldCon, 28, 41; and First Fandom, 30; and Futurians, 30

World Fair (1939), 29–30

World War II: Bradbury's fears of, 23; and Bradbury's writing, 3, 47, 53, 55, 57; and ethics, 105–6; and religion, 105; and Technocracy, 34

Wright, Farnsworth, 30–31; *Weird Tales*, editor of, 30, 37, 93

Wright, Frank Lloyd, 109

Writers Guild of America, 246, 268

Writer's Markets & Methods, "The Market Is Not the Story," 192

Wylie, Philip, 107–8; *Generation of Vipers*, 101, 107, 109, 294, 295; *Gladiator*, 107; *The Murderer Invisible*, 107; *The Savage Gentlemen*, 107

Yerke, Bruce, "The Revolt of the Scientists," 34

Young & Rubicam, *Mollé Mystery Theatre*, 115–16

JONATHAN R. ELLER is a professor of English at Indiana
University in Indianapolis, the senior textual editor of the Institute
for American Thought, and the cofounder of the Center for
Ray Bradbury Studies at IUPUI. He is the coauthor of *Ray Bradbury:
The Life of Fiction* and the textual editor of *The Collected Stories of
Ray Bradbury, Volume 1: 1938–1943*.

The University of Illinois Press
is a founding member of the
Association of American University Presses.

_____

Designed by Rich Hendel
Composed in 10.2/14 Quadraat
with Aller display
by Jim Proefrock
at the University of Illinois Press
Manufactured by Thomson-Shore, Inc.

University of Illinois Press
1325 South Oak Street
Champaign, IL 61820-6903
www.press.uillinois.edu

5/2/12 4X 4/1/12